Praise for

WAR OF THE WHALES

A *New York Times* Bestseller
Winner of the PEN/E. O. Wilson Literary Science Writing Award

"Horwitz's dogged reporting . . . combined with crisp, cinematic writing, produces a powerful narrative. . . . He has written a book that is instructive and passionate and deserving a wide audience."
—PEN/E. O. Wilson Literary Science Writing Award Citation

"Intimate and urgent storytelling. . . . Horwitz's years of research and observation lend genuine drama to this save-the-whales tale." —*Chicago Tribune*

"A strong and valuable narrative. . . . As *War of the Whales* makes convincingly clear, the connection between naval sonar and deadly mass strandings of whales is scientifically undeniable."
—*The Washington Post*, one of the 50 Notable Books of 2014

"Engrossing. . . . A fascinating, colorful, deeply researched chronicle. . . . A ripping real-life yarn well told." —*Tampa Bay Times*

"*War of the Whales* offers a vivid portrait of unexpected intersections between humans and marine mammals. I, for one, will never again think about whales and marine mammal researchers and Navy maneuvers in the ways I did before reading Horwitz's book." —*Minneapolis Star Tribune*

"In this gripping detective tale, science writer Horwitz recreates a day-by-day account of the quest to find the reasons for the mass strandings. . . . Riveting." —*Publishers Weekly*

"The story is so artfully constructed that you are drawn in and forget that you are not reading a novel. . . . [A] story that is fascinating even if you have no interest in whales or navy sonar. . . . This masterfully crafted book is guaranteed to bring the issues to a larger audience." —*Seattle Post-Intelligencer*

"Joshua Horwitz has come up with an outstanding book about whales, the environment, and the clash between whales and the US Navy. Deeply researched over six years, this well-paced and exciting book is both an education in whale and acoustic science and in how environmental issues grow from relative obscurity to become front-page news. War of the Whales is also one of the best books I've read that shows how environmentalists and scientists actually work, and how they often can work in tandem to address important issues that would otherwise be ignored by political decision-makers. . . . Horwitz makes it interesting and involving—the tension in the book never lets up."

—*Earth Island Journal*

"For those looking for the perfect nonfiction beach read, you couldn't do better than *War of the Whales*, Joshua Horwitz's recounting of an attorney and marine biologist who take on the Navy and the fatal harm they are causing the ocean's mammals." —*CBS Watch!*

"A riveting and groundbreaking new book. . . . It reads like the best investigative journalism, with cinematic scenes of strandings and dramatic David-and-Goliath courtroom dramas." —*The Huffington Post*

"As riveting and as involved as a good novel with a lengthy cast of characters."
—*The Journal of Supreme Court History*

WAR OF THE WHALES

A True Story

JOSHUA HORWITZ

SIMON & SCHUSTER PAPERBACKS

New York London Toronto Sydney New Delhi

Simon & Schuster Paperbacks
An Imprint of Simon & Schuster, Inc.
1230 Avenue of the Americas
New York, NY 10020

First Simon & Schuster trade paperback edition July 2015

SIMON & SCHUSTER PAPERBACKS and colophon are
registered trademarks of Simon & Schuster, Inc.

For information about special discounts for bulk purchases,
please contact Simon & Schuster Special Sales
at 1-866-506-1949 or business@simonandschuster.com.

The Simon & Schuster Speakers Bureau can bring authors to your live event.
For more information or to book an event contact the Simon & Schuster Speakers Bureau
at 1-866-248-3049 or visit our website at www.simonspeakers.com.

Interior design by Joy O'Meara
Jacket design by Jackie Seow
Jacket photograph © Frans Lanting/National Geographic Creative
Inside cover maps by Paula Robbins of Mapping Specialists

Manufactured in the United States of America

Printed on Domtar EarthChoice® trade book paper
with up to 30 percent post-consumer recycled content.

1   3   5   7   9   10   8   6   4   2

Library of Congress Cataloging-in-Publication Data is available.

ISBN 978-1-4516-4501-9
ISBN 978-1-4516-4502-6 (pbk)
ISBN 978-1-4516-4503-3 (ebook)

For Kenny and Stephen, foxhole buddies forever
and
To Ericka, who dazzled from day one

CONTENTS

PART THREE: THE RELUCTANT WHISTLE-BLOWER

PART FOUR: WHALES V. NAVY

CAST OF CHARACTERS *

THE MARINE MAMMAL SCIENTISTS

Ken Balcomb Beaked whale and killer-whale researcher in the Bahamas and San Juan Islands, Washington, respectively.

Diane Claridge Dolphin and beaked whale researcher; wife and research partner of Ken Balcomb.

Darlene Ketten Whale and human hearing expert; forensic pathologist, Harvard Medical School and Woods Hole Oceanographic Institution.

Roger Payne First cetologist to decode and promote humpback whale song and conservation.

Chris Clark Director, Bioacoustics Research Program, Cornell University Lab of Ornithology; protégé of Roger Payne.

Hal Whitehead Beaked whale and sperm whale researcher; professor, Department of Biology, Dalhousie University, Nova Scotia, Canada.

Lindy Weilgart Whale researcher; Hal Whitehead's wife and research partner.

Peter Tyack Dolphin and whale behavioral researcher, Woods Hole Oceanographic Institution.

Jim Mead Curator of marine mammals, Smithsonian Institution, Washington, DC.

John Lilly Neuroscientist who studied and popularized dolphin communication.

---

* The job titles and descriptors in the Cast of Characters refer to their positions at the time they were participants in the narrative.

THE ENVIRONMENTAL ACTIVISTS

Joel Reynolds   Senior attorney, director of Los Angeles office of Natural Resources Defense Council (NRDC); founder and director, Marine Mammal Protection Project.

Michael Jasny   Policy advocate, NRDC. Later, director, Marine Mammal Protection Project.

Andrew Wetzler   Staff attorney, NRDC.

Naomi Rose   Director of marine mammal programs, Humane Society of the United States.

Ben White   Animal rights activist, Animal Welfare Institute.

THE UNIFORMED NAVY

Admiral Richard Pittenger   Director of Antisubmarine Warfare for the Chief of Naval Operations; Oceanographer of the Navy; later Vice President for Marine Operations, Woods Hole Oceanographic Institution.

Admiral Paul Gaffney II   Chief of Naval Research, Office of Naval Research.

Commander Robin Pirie   Former submarine commander; Undersecretary of Navy.

Admiral Robert Natter   Commander, US Atlantic Fleet.

Admiral William Fallon   Commander, US Second Fleet.

Admiral Larry Baucom   Head of N-45, Navy Office of Environmental Readiness.

Admiral Peter Daly   Aide to Chief of Naval Operations Admiral Mike Mullen.

THE CIVILIAN NAVY

Bob Gisiner   Manager, Marine Bioacoustics Program, Office of Naval Research, Washington, DC.

Frank Stone   Head civilian at N-45, Navy Office of Environmental Readiness.

Sam Ridgway   Veterinarian; head of Navy Marine Mammal Research Program, San Diego.

Richard Danzig   Secretary of the Navy during Clinton administration.

Steven Honigman   General Counsel of the Navy during Clinton administration.

NATIONAL MARINE FISHERIES SERVICE (FISHERIES)

Roger Gentry Head of acoustic research, Office of Protected Resources.

Teri Rowles Director, Marine Mammal Health and Stranding Response Program, Washington, DC.

Ruth Ewing Veterinarian at Southeast Fisheries Science Center; a first responder to the Bahamas strandings.

THE WHALES

Beaked Whales of Great Bahama Canyon

More than 20 species of beaked whales dwell in deep-water canyons and coastal shelves around the world. They are the deepest-diving air-breathing creatures in the ocean and are rarely seen on the surface.

Pacific Gray Whales of Baja, Mexico

These "friendly" baleen whales (whales that filter feed through brushlike baleen, in lieu of teeth) migrate farther than any other mammal: 6,000 miles from Baja, where they give birth in winter, to their summer feeding grounds in the Bering Sea, above the Arctic Circle.

Orcas (also known as *Killer Whales*) of Puget Sound, Washington

The largest of the dolphin family, killer whales are the top predator in the ocean, preying on salmon, sea lions, other whales, and even great white sharks. The Puget Sound resident community feeds on Chinook salmon.

Dolphins of California and Florida

Highly social, easily trained, and among the smallest cetaceans, various species of dolphins were the first marine mammals to be captured, displayed, studied, and trained—both in marine parks and in the Navy Marine Mammal Program.

A NOTE ABOUT ACRONYMS

US Navy and government agencies are fond of using acronyms to denote programs, weapons systems, and departments. To spare readers the struggle of decoding this alphabet soup, I have tried to avoid acronyms in general, and in certain cases have substituted contractions, specifically:

National Marine Fisheries Service (NMFS) is referred to as "Fisheries."
Acoustic Thermometry of Ocean Climate (ATOC) is shortened to "Acoustic Thermometry."
Littoral Warfare Advanced Development (LWAD) is shortened to "Littoral Warfare."

In a few instances, where the long form is cumbersome, I have employed the commonly used acronym after the first use:

ONR for Office of Naval Research
AUTEC for Atlantic Undersea Test and Evaluation Center
NRDC for Natural Resources Defense Council
LFA sonar for Low Frequency Active sonar

PROLOGUE

Perhaps the war of the whales was inevitable. Perhaps the two most successful hunters on the planet were destined to collide. Humans had dominated life on land for 150 centuries, while whales had held dominion over the world's oceans for 40 million years.

Following the mass extinction of dinosaurs and enormous seafaring reptiles, the cetacean ancestors of whales and dolphins abandoned life on land and returned to the oceans that first spawned them. It proved to be a hugely successful reverse migration. Diversifying into dozens of species, whales dominated marine habitats throughout the world's waterways. Hunting alone or in small family groupings, in pods of a dozen or herds a thousand strong, whales owed their success to a weapon that set them apart from every other marine predator: biosonar, using beams of sound to hunt and navigate in the dark ocean depths.

Small wonder, then, that whales ruled the oceans for tens of millions of years—until another highly social, intelligent, and adaptive terrestrial mammal dipped its toes into the water.

Homo sapiens arrived at the 11th hour of animal evolution, a mere 160,000 years ago. Compared to cetaceans, humans evolved rapidly, adapting to the rigors of life on Earth through a deft combination of social cooperation, cunning, and organized aggression. Five thousand years ago, humans began stalking the largest animals on the planet—first from canoes, then under sail, and eventually aboard floating factory ships that slaughtered and processed whale populations from the South Pacific to the Arctic Ocean.

As they rose to top predator on land and at sea, humans turned their technological zeal to weapons of war, spurring an arms race without end. In the twentieth century, submarine weaponry evolved from primitive torpedoes to intercontinental ballistic missiles armed with nuclear warheads. Like their cetacean counterparts, submariners lived and died by their ability to navigate and hunt acoustically in the black depths of the oceans.

In the early hours of March 15, 2000, the paths of the world's most powerful navy and the ocean's most mysterious species of whales were about to converge. Though on the calm surface of the Great Bahama Canyon, nothing hinted at anything amiss. It was just another morning in paradise, the day the whales came ashore.

PART ONE
STRANDED

I have met with a story which, although authenticated by undoubted evidence, looks very like a fable.

—*Pliny the Younger,* Letters *(on hearing reports of a boy riding on the back of a dolphin in the first century AD)*

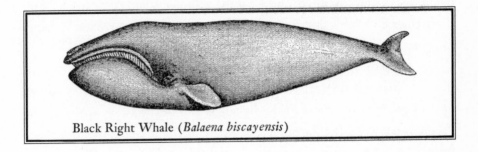

Black Right Whale (*Balaena biscayensis*)

I

The Day the Whales Came Ashore

DAY 1: MARCH 15, 2000, 7:45 A.M.
Sandy Point, Abaco Island, the Bahamas

Powered by his second cup of coffee, Ken Balcomb was motoring through his orientation speech for the Earthwatch Institute volunteers who had flown in the night before. The workday started early at Sandy Point, and Balcomb was eager to finish his spiel and head out onto the water before the sun got high and hot.

"Take as many pictures as you like," he told them, "but leave the marine life in the ocean. Conches in the Bahamas are listed as a threatened species, so you can't take their shells home as souvenirs."

After a breakfast of sliced papaya and peanut butter sandwiches, a dozen volunteers sprawled across the worn couches of the modest beachfront house that Balcomb rented with his wife and research partner, Diane Claridge. Here, on the underpopulated southwestern tip of Abaco, far from the posh resorts on the tiny Out Islands elsewhere in the Bahamas, the only tourist activity was bonefishing in the clear, bright shallows of the continental shelf. What the tourists rarely glimpsed, and what the volunteers had come to see, were the reclusive Cuvier's and Blainville's beaked whales of the Great Bahama Canyon.

For the past 15 years, the Earthwatch volunteer program had provided the sole financial support for the decadelong photo-identification survey of the beaked whales here in the Bahamas and of the killer whales in the Pacific Northwest. The Earthlings, as Ken and Diane called them, traveled from across the United States and around the world to assist their survey and to catch a fleeting glance of the deepest-diving creatures in the ocean: the beaked whales that lived inside the underwater canyon offshore from Sandy Point. For the most part, they were altruistic tourists, from teenagers to golden-agers, looking for a useful vacation from the winter doldrums up north. At Sandy Point, they could learn a little about whales, lend a hand in a righteous eco-science project, and enjoy the Bahamian sunshine.

Occasionally, one of the volunteers got hooked on the research and never went home. While still a teenager in landlocked Missouri, Dave Ellifrit had seen Balcomb's photos of killer whales in a magazine. That summer, he showed up at Smugglers Cove on San Juan Island, off the coast of Washington, to help with the annual survey. Ellifrit was immediately at home with the open-boat work, despite the pale complexion that came with his bright red hair. Fifteen years later, he was still working for room and board as a year-round researcher—at Smugglers Cove in the summer and at Sandy Point in the winter. Balcomb and Claridge had more or less adopted the young man, mentoring him in whale research and helping pay his way through an environmental science program at Evergreen State College in Washington.

While Balcomb finished briefing the Earthlings on the details of photo identification and log entries, Ellifrit was on the beach readying the motorboats for the day's survey. "Don't be disappointed if you don't see any beaked whales your first day out," Balcomb explained to the volunteers. "They range all over the canyon and surface only about once an hour, rarely in the same place twice. So unless you get lucky, you won't be grabbing any photos at first."

Balcomb explained the differences between the Cuvier's and Blainville's beaked whales that he and Claridge had catalogued over the past decade. Some of the more studious Earthlings took notes. Others were busy applying an extra layer of sunblock, which was fine with Balcomb. He didn't want to spend his evening nursing sunburned volunteers.

Balcomb had the weather-beaten look of someone who'd spent most of his six decades on the water, and about ten minutes focused on his wardrobe. Every morning, he pulled on whatever free promotional T-shirt he'd fished out of the pile in his closet and stepped into a nondescript pair of sun-bleached shorts and the flip-flops he'd stepped out of the night before. He wore his hair shaggy or cropped short, depending on how recently Diane had taken the shears to him, topped off by whatever baseball cap the last group of Earthlings had left behind. Balcomb's face was mostly covered by a thick salt-and-pepper beard, and his bright, constantly watchful eyes had the reverse-raccoon look that comes from wearing sunglasses 12 months a year.

Even standing in the living room, he kept his legs planted in the wide stance of a man accustomed to life on boats, flexed just enough to absorb any unexpected pitch or roll. "There are only a few dozen whales in the whole canyon, and some weeks we only see a handful of them," he continued. "But there's lots of other marine life out there if you keep your eyes peeled."

A college-aged young woman raised her hand. "What do we do about the sharks?"

"The sharks are nothing to worry about unless there's blood in the water," Balcomb said with a smile. "So any of you women . . ." Claridge winced in anticipation of an off-color punch line she'd heard too many times. Balcomb liked to tease his beautiful Bahamian wife about her British reserve, and he couldn't resist trying to bring a blush to her pale, almost Nordic face. ". . . if it's your time of month, you might want to stay in the boat, because—"

The screen door banged open. Everyone looked up to see Dave Ellifrit, out of breath and wide eyed. When his eyes found Balcomb's, he said, almost matter-of-factly, "There's a whale on the beach."

Claridge grabbed the camcorder off the kitchen counter and raced out the door. Balcomb jogged down the beach behind her, slowing to a walk as he reached the water's edge.

The whale lay helpless in three feet of water, its spindle-shaped body lodged in the sand, while its tail fluke splashed listlessly in the shallows.

Balcomb couldn't believe how close to the house the animal had stranded:

less than 100 feet up the beach. It was a Cuvier's—and it was alive. A live Cuvier's beaked whale! How was that possible? His mind raced to fix on a reference point. The last beaked whale to strand alive in these waters had come ashore decades ago, back in the early 1950s, on the north side of the island.

Balcomb had been chasing after various species of beaked whales for most of his life.* As a teenaged beachcomber in California, he'd thought of beaked whales as emissaries from the distant past: modern dinosaurs that jealously guarded the secrets of their evolutionary journey from the Eocene Age. He'd walked countless miles of coastline in search of bone fragments, hoping to piece together small skeletal sections, waded knee-deep through piles of discarded organs outside whaling stations on four continents, searching for some anatomical prize tucked away inside—a tusk or a vertebra or, the rarest of treasures, a skull. In his twenties, he'd begun photographing beaked whales during whale survey expeditions in the Pacific. For a dozen winters, he'd sailed a tall ship along the Atlantic Seaboard, charting whale migrations and searching for beaked whales from Newfoundland to the Dominican Republic.

For the past ten seasons, he and Claridge had staked out a "species hot spot" in the Great Bahama Canyon, waiting with loaded cameras in small boats to photograph and videotape, classify and catalogue the resident community of Cuvier's and Blainville's beaked whales. But until the morning of March 15, 2000, he had never touched a live beaked whale. And now, right at his feet, lay a living, breathing specimen. For a hardcore bone-hunting beachcomber like Balcomb, this was an embarrassment of riches. An intact beaked whale that could provide a window into its functional anatomy, and a complete skeleton!

Balcomb was a realist. He knew that most whales that strand alive don't survive. By the time a whale comes ashore, too much has already gone wrong. Stranding is simply too severe a trauma for most whales to sustain. If he pushed this one back out to sea in such shaky condition, the sharks would likely tear it to pieces before it traversed the two-mile gauntlet of shallows and reached the safety of the canyon depths. He considered the possibility of

---

* More than 25 percent of the 78 whale species are beaked whales, though only a few species of beaked whales have been well studied.

ushering the whale alongside a boat to the nearby lagoon. If it died, he could harvest the organs, fix them in formaldehyde, and ship the skeleton up to Jim Mead, the marine mammal curator at the Smithsonian Institution. Even Mead had never collected a complete Cuvier's skeleton.

Balcomb crouched down in the water beside the whale. It was about 16 feet long; average for an immature male Cuvier's. He could tell its sex and approximate age from the distinctive pair of slightly protruding lower tusks that are visible only in males. Balcomb leaned in close to get a whiff of his breath. It smelled fine, not putrid like a sick whale's would be. And he wasn't wasted away by ear parasites, a common affliction of stranded whales.

The whale certainly looked healthy. His eyes weren't dilated, and he didn't show any outward signs of a ship collision that would have caused a concussion or brain damage. The whale's right eye gazed steadily back at him, signaling—what? Confusion? Fear? How the hell could he tell? He was a whale researcher, not a mind reader. He'd never made close eye contact with a beaked whale before. Had anyone?

"What in the world are you doing here?" Balcomb asked aloud. He laid a hand gently on the whale's back. Its skin was as soft and smooth as an inner tube. It still felt cool to the touch, not overheated or dehydrated. That would change in a hurry if they couldn't get him off the beach. Balcomb noted the position of the sun, already well above the horizon line and climbing. He rocked the whale to one side and examined the fresh scratches along its belly, probably from the nearby coral reef. Just a thin strand of blood hanging in the water. Nothing life threatening, so long as the sharks didn't pick up the scent.

That's when he saw the rake marks across the whale's flank and the cookie-cutter scars on his dorsal fin. For a decade, their team had been photo-identifying the local beaked whales by their unique scarring patterns. Torso scrapes were from the jagged canyon walls or else souvenir tooth rakes from sparring matches among bulls during mating season. The distinctive scar pattern on the dorsal fins came from encounters with small cookie-cutter sharks that feed on their prey by gouging tiny round plugs, as if cut out with a cookie cutter.

Balcomb recognized the pattern from a photo he'd shot two weeks earlier. "Look at this," he said to Ellifrit, who stood watch for sharks in the shallows.

Ellifrit crouched down next to Balcomb. "Zc-34, right?" he said. "We ID'd him off of South Point. Last month."

"That's what I think. Yeah, definitely." Balcomb and Claridge assigned their research subjects alphanumeric identifiers, according to their species and social rank in the pod. Zc stood for the Cuvier's scientific name: *Ziphius cavirostris.* They weren't interested in giving them cute and cuddly names, as if they were house pets. Balcomb and Claridge were serious scientists, not whale huggers.

But now that Balcomb had recognized the animal and remembered the afternoon when they'd patiently tracked him through three dives and ascents before finally grabbing a clear-enough photo to make a positive ID . . . now it was impossible to see him as just a skeleton surrounded by organs and blubber. Balcomb snapped out of his fantasy of collecting a complete beaked whale specimen and began working to dislodge Zc-34 from the beach.

He scanned the water's surface for sharks. No problems on that front. *Yet.* The Earthlings stood around in a loose semicircle on the beach, looking as disoriented as the whale. Ten minutes earlier they'd been sipping coffee and wondering if they'd applied enough sunscreen for the day's outing. They didn't understand what was happening, and no one was stopping to explain it to them. Balcomb couldn't make sense of it himself. All he knew was that this whale was in the wrong place, going in the wrong direction, and if he didn't get him back to deep water in a hurry, he would die here on the beach.

"Get out of the water, before some shark shows up," Balcomb said to Ellifrit. "And keep the Earthwatchers on the beach. I'm going to try to dig this guy out of here." He reached underneath the whale's belly and scooped out handfuls of wet sand and shells. If he cut his hands on coral or shells, it would only bring the sharks in faster. So he worked slowly, handful by handful, to excavate a trench beneath the whale. Claridge, who routinely videotaped everything of documentary significance in their survey, stood just outside the water's edge and kept recording.

After ten minutes of digging, Balcomb had created enough space beneath the whale's belly to rock him slightly from side to side. It was exhausting work, like dislodging a car from a deep snowbank. Even at age 60, Balcomb still had strong legs and muscular arms, but each time he heaved his body against the whale, he barely budged. Finally, a small wave washed in, buoying the whale and allowing Balcomb to pivot his body to face out toward deeper water. He steadied the whale upright in the water and then slowly withdrew his arms to make sure the animal could keep himself level. He pushed-walked the whale into chest-deep water and then gave him a strong shove in the direction of the canyon.

The Earthlings cheered from the shore. The whale fluked once or twice toward the open water—only to make a wide left turn and head back to shore. The Earthlings groaned. Claridge handed the camera to Ellifrit to continue recording while she joined Balcomb in the water. Together they tried in vain to block the whale's path back to the beach as his belly lodged in the sand once more. Something was desperately wrong with this whale's compass, Balcomb concluded. Either that, or something back in the canyon had totally freaked him out.

For the next half hour, they kept pushing the whale back out to deeper water, only to watch him circle back to shore and try to strand. Claridge had always been the strongest swimmer on their team, often trolling in the water behind their survey boat to videotape the whales underwater. Now, with Balcomb blocking the path back to the beach, Claridge swam out alongside the whale until they were 200 feet from shore, in 15 feet of water. Finally, the whale dove and disappeared from sight.[1]

They were still watching to make sure he didn't circle back to the beach when a local fisherman motored by in a small skiff. "Ken!" he shouted. "There's a whale stranded down at Rocky Point!"

That was a mile south. Claridge stayed behind to keep an eye out for the Cuvier's, while Balcomb and Ellifrit divided the Earthlings between one of the motorboats and the back of the red pickup. Balcomb jumped into the cab and sped down the beach.

Balcomb could see the stranded animal as they approached Rocky Point. It was perched on a coral shelf that was completely exposed in the low tide. As he approached on foot, he could tell it was another Cuvier's. Another adolescent male. He'd probably beached there an hour or so earlier and stranded as the tide receded. This one was bleeding badly from the jagged coral cuts, and sharks were already circling offshore from the reef. Two tiger sharks, at first glance, plus a bull shark, and a few smaller nurse sharks. The seven-foot tigers and the bull could be fierce when there was blood in the water. The smaller nurse sharks would hang back till the big guys were done, and then swoop in to pick at whatever was left.

Balcomb figured he could manage the sharks, at least while the whale was on dry land. The bigger problem would be keeping the whale hydrated and protected from the sun for the next few hours until the tide came back in and they could float him out to deeper water. Even on a cloudy day, a stranded whale quickly becomes overheated and sunburned, and then dies of dehydration. On this spring morning in the Bahamas, there was barely a cloud in the sky.

As warm-blooded mammals, whales evolved an elegant system of internal heat regulation to maintain a 98-degree body temperature when swimming below the Arctic ice pack or hunting in the 40-degree waters of the ocean depths. Below a thick layer of insulating blubber, their closely packed circulatory system allows the warm blood in their arteries to heat the cold blood in adjacent veins—a biological example of "countercurrent exchange" that has been mimicked in many industrial systems. But the most pressing biological challenge for whales isn't staying warm, it's how to dump enough heat through their skin, mouth, and tongue to maintain a constant body temperature below 100 degrees. When a whale strands in the tropical sun, it overheats and dies within hours.

Balcomb dispatched the Earthlings to scavenge as many sheets, towels, and buckets as they could find from the brightly colored houses scattered along the beach. Ten minutes later, they had the Cuvier's wrapped from fluke to blowhole, with a bucket brigade keeping the fabric soaked in seawater. Four of the Earthlings held a sheet overhead as a canopy to shield the whale from the midmorning sun.

Balcomb heard the radio crackling from the pickup. It was Claridge, reporting that yet another beaked whale, a Blainville's, had stranded back up the coast, northeast of their house. Balcomb left Ellifrit in charge of the Earthlings contingent and climbed into the pickup.

"Something is going on," Balcomb thought as he barreled back toward Sandy Point. "Something big."

He called a neighbor on the radio and asked him to paddle two kayaks out to Sandy Point. By the time he arrived, three of his neighbors had dislodged the Blainville's from the beach and were standing beside him in the shallows. Balcomb and Claridge waded out to photograph the whale and scrape DNA skin samples for later identification. When the kayakers arrived, they helped guide the animal back out to deep water. Balcomb asked the kayakers to meet them back at Rocky Point as soon as they could paddle out there. As they drove past their house, Balcomb and Claridge ran in to grab a blue poly tarp from the garage.

By the time they returned to Rocky Point, the tide had moved back in—and so had the sharks. A lemon shark and what looked liked two tigers had joined the fray. To judge by the position of the sun, Balcomb figured it was close to high noon. A cluster of young Bahamian schoolgirls dressed in starched blue and white uniforms had stopped on their way home for lunch to watch.

The whale was still alive, though his breathing seemed to Balcomb to be heavy and forced. Meanwhile, the Earthwatch volunteers were beginning to fray around the edges. They had come to the Bahamas to photograph whales, not to stand by helplessly and watch them die of dehydration or be devoured by sharks. Two college-aged volunteers were kneeling by the whale's head, trying to soothe him with gentle strokes and murmurs. Another one, a middle-aged woman from Cincinnati, swatted flies away from an angry scrape on his tail fluke. She was sobbing quietly to herself but wiped away her tears when Claridge approached with the tarp. The sight of dorsal fins circling in the water just offshore wasn't helping morale.

Balcomb threw Claridge a look that she recognized as "You're the den mother here. I'm the guy who keeps the boats running." But she had more pressing business to tend to. She crouched low to examine the coral cuts on the whale's belly, which were starting to congeal and clot. A promising sign, unless it meant he was dehydrating. At least his eyes were still clear. She collected a skin-scrape sample and peeled back a towel to study the scarring on his flank. "Zc-12," she said as Balcomb photographed the dorsal fin from both sides.

The kayaks arrived, and Balcomb motioned to them to stop offshore on the far side of the shark swirl. Now Claridge took charge of the Earthlings. "Who knows how to shoot video?" she called. One of the younger women raised her hand. "Okay, get the camera from the truck and run tape, with time-code stamp. And stay out of the water when you're shooting. You four, lose that canopy and help me with this tarp. The rest of you gather some pieces of driftwood up there," she said, pointing toward a nearby house. "Something you can swing like a bat."

Claridge peeled back the wet towels and sheets with the tenderness of a mother removing a child's Band-Aid. She examined the animal for other wounds, but found none. Then she unrolled the large blue tarp. She and Balcomb and Ellifrit drew the edge of the tarp underneath the whale's head. As the Earthlings rocked the whale from side to side, they worked the tarp up under his trunk.

Ellifrit handed out driftwood clubs to three of the bravest-looking souls and hefted one himself. "Beat the water in front of the whale as we move him out," Balcomb directed them. "Dave will show you how. Fan out in a semicircle. The sharks aren't interested in you, unless your feet are bleeding, so check them now for cuts, and watch out for the coral."

Ellifrit led the three Earthlings out into the water, thrashing the surface as hard as they could and shouting as they went. Claridge and Balcomb, alongside four more Earthlings, grabbed hold of the blue tarp.

"Now lift and drag," Claridge commanded. "Just a few feet at a time." The tarp made a nasty tearing sound against the coral. "I said *lift!*"

In a moment, they were off the ledge and half hauling, half floating the whale through the shallows. The kayakers beat their paddles in the water to disrupt the sharks, which scattered, then quickly regrouped. The sharks maintained a constant distance, circling and darting in feints toward the whale, but eventually giving way in front of the V formation of wildly thrashing beaters. The kayaks fell in beside the tarp bearers, creating a floating barrier between the sharks and the whale.

When they pulled the tarp out from under the whale, he listed slowly to the left. Balcomb and Claridge propped him up on opposite sides, as if he were a drunken sailor.

"What do you think?" she asked.

"Seems kind of wobbly," he said. "But he's not bleeding. Anyway, we're out of time."

"Right. Let's give him a go, then."

They eased him ahead into open water. The whale hung in the water, not moving forward, but not listing to the side, either. Ellifrit ran over and gave him a final shove from behind. "Get outahere!"

The whale moved his fluke weakly up and down, ducked his head, and dove. Balcomb held his breath as he watched him fluking away in the direction of the canyon. It occurred to him that he'd never seen a beaked whale swim in the shallows, until today. Was that a normal fluking action? Was he actually heading back to the canyon, or was he simply swimming away from the commotion of sharks and humans?

He waited and watched. Nothing. Nothing was good.

Claridge tugged at his T-shirt. "Let's get out of the water," she said.

They didn't talk on the short drive back to the house. It was past 1:00 p.m., and Claridge was fielding calls on the truck's VHF radio. Reports were still coming in of other strandings on nearby cays. Two whales, probably minkes, had stranded alive near Royal Island, 25 miles to the southeast. A beaked whale mother and calf had come ashore two hours ago on a small cay near Grand Bahama, 60 miles northwest of their house. The calf was already dead. It was unprecedented—and unexplainable.

Balcomb knew it was time to make a call.

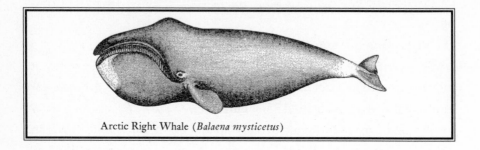

Arctic Right Whale (*Balaena mysticetus*)

2

Castaways

DAY 1: MARCH 15, 2000, 1:30 P.M.
Sandy Point, Abaco Island, the Bahamas

Back in the house at Sandy Point, Balcomb rifled his desk drawers for Bob Gisiner's business card. He distinctly remembered Gisiner handing him his Office of Naval Research card at the Society for Marine Mammalogy conference in Maui, Hawaii, back in December. Balcomb had thrown it into some drawer along with all the other cards he collected that week. Now where was it?

Balcomb wasn't used to reaching out for help. He always fixed his own cars and boats when they broke. Money was chronically tight, but he managed to keep his boats gassed up and in the water. A couple of wealthy donors had helped along the way with the gift of a survey boat and a down payment loan on his house, which doubled as the research headquarters back in Smugglers Cove, Washington. Otherwise he was proudly, stubbornly self-sufficient, and over the years, he'd managed to scrape together what he needed to continue his research.

But now he needed help, and he knew it. The elation he'd first felt on seeing and touching a live Cuvier's had given way to dismay at the multiple strandings, then to anxiety that something catastrophic had befallen the whales they'd been studying for the past decade. What could have happened out there to send them streaming out of the canyon and into the dangerous shallows? He tried to clear his head of exhaustion and confusion, so he could sort it out. Something extraordinary had happened in the canyon that morning. Of that much he was certain.

He'd heard that Disney Cruise Line had been dynamiting offshore of Castaway Cay as part of a new pier construction. But that was 15 miles from Sandy Point. An undersea earthquake, or some other seismic event, could produce intense pressure waves that could drive whales ashore. But that would have also created unusually high surf, and he hadn't seen the kind of driftwood or debris that would have washed ashore after a tidal storm.

His thoughts kept circling back to the US Navy, which maintained an underwater testing range 100 miles to the southeast, off Andros Island. If the Navy had something going on anywhere near Abaco, Bob Gisiner would know about it. Or he could call someone who would know. In the meantime, Gisiner had the resources to jump-start an investigation here on the ground. There was no way Balcomb and his team could manage forensics on a multispecies mass stranding. He didn't have the manpower or the labs. And he sure didn't have the money.

Gisiner had been Balcomb's graduate school classmate at the University of California, Santa Cruz, back in the early 1970s. In those days, UC Santa Cruz was the leading—really, the only—university offering a marine mammal program. Marine mammalogy had barely been named, much less codified, and the prior generation of pioneering researchers had emerged from disciplines as disparate as neurology, marine biology veterinary medicine, zoology and ichthyology. The graduate program was tiny, and the students who collaborated on field research along the California coast worked at such close quarters that no one had any secrets. By the end of the semester, they knew one another the way a submariner knows his bunkmate: by smell. That first generation of university-trained marine mammal scientists remained a tight-knit, mostly male fraternity for decades afterward, even if they were conducting research on opposite ends of the globe and only crossed paths at annual conferences.

Balcomb and Gisiner hadn't been close friends at Santa Cruz. Gisiner studied seals and sea lions—the "pinniped" branch of the marine mammal family tree—while Balcomb was focused exclusively on whales. With his droopy mustache and wizened eyes, Gisiner had eventually come to resemble his research subjects, in much the way some dog owners seem to morph into their pet's particular breed. Gisiner was smart, like everyone else in the PhD program. But he'd also been ambitious and shrewd in a way that made him stand out among the laid-back California students of the day.

After grad school, Balcomb's and Gisiner's careers went in opposite directions. Balcomb left Santa Cruz for Japan, where he studied the local Baird's beaked whales. Then he moved to the San Juan Islands in the Pacific Northwest to begin a photo census of the resident killer-whale population that he continued every summer for decades. Throughout the 1980s and 1990s he subsisted on donations from local donors and grants from small foundations, plus the trickle of money he netted from hosting the Earthwatch program. Balcomb didn't publish very often in the peer-reviewed journals, and when he did, he was always happy to give first-author credit to his collaborators. His highest-profile publication had been the Baird's beaked whale chapter in the *Handbook of Marine Mammals*. Balcomb was proud to be included among the PhDs and career academic contributors to that multivolume textbook. But unlike most of his classmates from Santa Cruz, Balcomb never established any institutional affiliation. And because he didn't complete his PhD coursework, the plum jobs inside academia, the National Marine Fisheries Service, and the Office of Naval Research remained out of Balcomb's reach. Not that he could ever have navigated the institutional politics that seemed like Gisiner's natural habitat. Truth be told, Balcomb couldn't bear to be indoors for long, much less work at a desk or sit in meetings.

Gisiner had always been more of an organization man. With so few university-based marine mammal programs nationwide, he didn't see much of a future in academics. So he went to work for the Navy as a civilian researcher—first training pigeons to locate downed pilots in the Pacific Ocean, and then working with seals in Hawaii and with pilot whales and dolphins at the Navy's marine mammal training and research center in San Diego. Gisiner's big promotion came in the midnineties when he was transferred to Washington, DC, to run the marine mammal division at the Office of Naval Research (ONR).

ONR is the Navy's great hall of academe. When most people think of the Navy, they conjure images of battleships, aircraft carriers, and submarines. But the combat arm of the Navy—the operating fleet of ships, submarines, and planes—is simply one branch of a massive organizational tree whose roots traverse the uniform and civilian worlds. One of the biggest civilian-staffed branches of the Navy is the Office of Naval Research, a billion-dollar agency spread over naval labs and academic research centers across the country and around the globe.

The Navy took pride in having been the first of the armed services to establish a world-class research program. By the time World War II ended, it had become clear that knowledge of the oceans was the key to dominating the high seas. US naval strategists understood that the Soviet Union would soon be vying for control of the borderless oceans, and that antisubmarine warfare would become the most critical battle space of the Cold War. To compete in the underwater arena, they embarked on an intensive campaign to recruit the best and brightest marine scientists to the Cold War effort. In 1946 President Harry Truman established ONR to coordinate the nation's investment in underwater research. Flush with Navy money, small oceanographic institutes such as the Scripps Institution of Oceanography in La Jolla, California, and the Woods Hole Oceanographic Institution in Massachusetts metamorphosed from sleepy academic centers into well-funded research labs.

During the second half of the twentieth century, ONR became the world's leading funder of oceanographic research, as well as a college catalogue of other scientific disciplines including meteorology, medicine, aeronautics, communications, logistics, engineering, satellite surveillance, nuclear propulsion, ballistics, hydrodynamics, sonar, acoustics, and marine mammal biology—the last being Gisiner's niche. The Navy had been active in marine mammal research for decades, but during Gisiner's tenure ONR's budget in this area tripled. By 2000, he had become the funding czar for marine mammal researchers from the Arctic to the Antarctic, and every latitude in between.

Somehow Balcomb never found himself downstream from any of ONR's grants. Not even in the past few years, when ONR felt obliged to fund beaked whale research following a 1996 mass stranding of beaked whales in Greece during NATO naval exercises. When they ran into each other at the recent marine mammal conference in Hawaii, Gisiner gave Balcomb his card, and they agreed to stay in closer touch.

Balcomb finally found the card paper-clipped inside the conference program guide. When Gisiner picked up after the first ring, Balcomb didn't pause for pleasantries. "Bob, this is Ken Balcomb. On Abaco Island. I'm standing in the middle of a mass stranding down here. Two, probably three or more species."

For a moment, there was silence on the other end. "Tell me what you know," said Gisiner.

"Three beaked whales stranded live this morning within a two-mile stretch here on the southwest end of Abaco. Two Cuvier's, one Blainville's. We've got calls coming in from other islands. Sounds like a pair of minke whales also came ashore."

"How many animals are involved?"

"A dozen or more, spread across at least three islands."

"What's the outlook for specimens?" Gisiner asked.

"So far everything's stranded live, and we pushed three back out to sea this morning. But those came ashore right on top of us. There are bound to be some specimens on the outer islands. I'll collect whatever I can."

Gisiner said he'd get on the horn to Fisheries and pull together an investigative team. "I want to get Darlene Ketten down there in a hurry," he said. "I don't know where she is now, but we'll track her down."

When he heard Ketten's name, Balcomb knew that he had Gisiner's attention. Though an academic and a civilian, Ketten was the US Navy's top-gun whale pathologist, the go-to forensics expert for any "unusual mortality event" (UME) that Fisheries or the Navy needed to investigate. Her specialty was hearing, in both whales and humans. She had joint appointments at Harvard Medical School and Woods Hole Oceanographic Institution, though she spent much of her time flying around the world to investigate unexplained strandings. After the Greek stranding in '96, Gisiner had dispatched her from Woods Hole to join the NATO scientific investigation—which reached no definitive finding of cause in 1998. She'd been on-site at most of the atypical whale strandings since.

"Ketten would be great," said Balcomb. "I'll make sure she has what she needs on the ground. And I'll collect all the ear bones I can find."

"Better to take the whole head," Gisiner advised. "Darlene's going to want them whole. Get as many heads as you can, as fast as you can, and keep them on ice."

It was time for Balcomb to talk to Gisiner about money. Never his strong suit. "I'm going to need a plane to survey the outer islands. And we'll need to get more boats in the water to check the coastlines and ferry the heads back to our field station." After some back-and-forth, Gisiner agreed to cover up to $5,000 in expenses. If costs ran higher, Gisiner said, he'd find more funds.

Before he rang off, Balcomb had to ask the question that had been weighing on his mind all day: "Bob, does the fleet have something going on down here?"

Gisiner said he didn't know but promised to find out.

"One other thing." Balcomb paused to figure out how to say it right. "Make sure they save the tapes. From AUTEC. Those tapes will tell the tale."

There was silence on the other end. Balcomb wondered if he'd overstepped the line with Gisiner. AUTEC was the Atlantic Undersea Test and Evaluation Center, one of the Navy's most classified, tightly controlled testing ranges for simulated warfare. Even though it was located just over the horizon offshore from Andros Island, most Bahamians had no notion of what went on there. Even Claridge, who grew up in Nassau, had only a vague idea.[1]

Gisiner said he'd call over there and see what he could find out. But AUTEC was run out of the Naval Undersea Warfare Center, he reminded Balcomb, which wasn't fond of sharing data.

"They used to keep the tapes for thirty days," Balcomb said. "I don't know what their protocol is these days."

"Stay focused on the whales, Ken, and let me know what you're able to collect on the ground. In the meantime, I'll track down Darlene and get her in motion."

Balcomb emerged from his office to find the Earthlings spread out across the living room. Some were resting, while others were tending to coral cuts on their feet and hands. It was midafternoon, but no one had eaten lunch.

The phone rang in the kitchen, where Claridge was slapping together some peanut butter sandwiches. Someone reported that a dolphin had stranded alive but in bad shape on Powell Cay, a barrier island just east of Abaco. They hoped that Claridge, who was known throughout the islands as the resident dolphin expert, would come try to save it. She grabbed a sandwich and a bottle of water, and headed off in the truck toward the Powell Cay ferry.

Moments later, the phone rang again. It was someone at Castaway Cay, Disney's private Out Island 15 miles offshore from Abaco, reporting that a "huge, funny-looking dolphin" had swum into its mangrove lagoon. It was swimming in circles, and the guests were starting to freak out. Could Balcomb help them get it out of there?

Balcomb suspected it was a beaked whale, which locals often mistook for dolphins, even though beaked whales are significantly larger than dolphins, with rounder bodies and long snouts. He and Ellifrit identified half a dozen Earthlings who could still walk and were game for another rescue operation. They grabbed the blue tarp from the truck and headed out in the motorboat for Castaway Cay.

Before the Disney Company bought Gorda Cay in 1996 and rechristened it Castaway Cay, the three-mile-long island had seen service as a way station for drug runners and as a set for the movie *Splash*. Disney spent $25 million transforming the cay into a private port of call for Disney cruise ships in the Bahamas. The island theme park, where Captain Hook, Peter Pan, and the Lost Boys roamed about in full costume, featured castaway shacks serving piña coladas in coconut shells and a snorkeling lagoon housing two sunken "submarines" retired from the 20,000 Leagues Under the Sea ride at the Walt Disney World Magic Kingdom. The island's three beaches had been built atop a coral shelf, using 35,000 truckloads of sand dredged from the ocean floor.

By the time Balcomb's boat arrived at Castaway Cay, the snorkelers had exited the lagoon and were standing on the beach taking pictures of the "funny-looking dolphin" that lolled near the surface. Balcomb identified it as a dense-beaked Blainville's whale. He waded into the lagoon and moved quietly toward the animal. Ordinarily, beaked whales are the most skittish of creatures, almost impossible to approach without spooking. This one submitted uncomplainingly to Balcomb's examination. Like the other stranded whales Balcomb had seen that day, it showed no outward signs of trauma.

Luckily, it wasn't bleeding. Balcomb could just imagine the melee that would ensue on Castaway Cay if a shiver of tiger sharks suddenly entered the lagoon.

In a few minutes, they had secured the tarp beneath the whale and were leading him out to sea. Buoys painted as Mickey, Minnie, and Goofy stood sentinel at the mouth of the lagoon. It was sunset, and daiquiris were being served on the deck of the *Disney Wonder*, which lay at anchor nearby. The cruise passengers clustered at the railings, pointing at the whale and taking pictures of the rescue. A few people rested their daiquiris on the rail and clapped.

Two Castaway employees approached on Jet Skis and offered to escort the whale to deeper water. Spouting water from their tails, the two Jet Skiers steered the dazed and confused Blainville's toward the setting sun and its canyon home.

Forty miles to the northeast, Claridge stepped off the ferry in Powell Cay to find the beached dolphin in dire condition. It was an Atlantic spotted dolphin, one of 12 species of oceanic dolphins found in the Bahamas. Highly social and usually found in groups of 20 or more, these fast swimmers are ubiquitous in the islands, bow riding speedboats and executing aerial acrobatics wherever they congregate. But this full-grown female lay in the shallows close to death, listless and barely moving. The tourists who had found her on the beach that morning, and had kept her hydrated and shaded all day, were distraught.

A veterinarian named Alan Bater had arrived from Grand Bahama just ahead of Claridge. Bater was in charge of keeping the captive dolphins alive at "the Dolphin Experience" tourist attraction in the capital city of Freeport. He'd brought a stomach pump with him in hopes of giving the dolphin some nourishment. But after 20 minutes of feeding, she wasn't showing any signs of revival. They decided to ferry her by boat to Bater's clinic and treat her there.

On the ride back, Claridge cradled the animal in her arms. The dolphin was five feet long and almost as large as her caregiver. Halfway back across the channel, the dolphin began to convulse, and moments later she died. Her body grew cold, but Claridge kept rocking her in her arms.

Claridge didn't cry. It wasn't her style. But she felt overwhelmed by helplessness and confusion. She'd grown up in these waters, and dolphins were her first love. They were so wild and free. Their beauty took her breath away. She often felt they were too charming for their own good. Since the early 1990s, the tourist trade had turned these fabulous creatures into circus performers. Worse, they'd been prostituted to tourists who could purchase dolphin "experiences" by the hour. Throughout the Bahamas, "dolphin swim" offerings in captive settings had become a must-have attraction for cruise ships and fly-in tourists.

Dolphin tourism had become big business. The going price for a wild-caught dolphin had risen to $40,000, and worth it at the price. At $100 an "experience," dolphins could earn back their investor's money in two years. After that, they were pure profit machines. No one asked where the animals were captured, or how. Since the Bahamas banned dolphin capture in 1995, a black market pipeline had emerged from both the Solomon Islands and Taiji, Japan. As long as the tourists were happy and kept swiping their credit cards, local authorities turned a blind eye. Back in 1994, when dolphins began dying at various dolphin swim venues, local activists made as much noise as they could in the press. Eventually dolphin tourism was debated in Parliament, and the government briefly shut down a facility on Abaco, but not in Freeport or Nassau.

So now one more dolphin had died—for what? The dolphins and beaked whales of the Bahamas had been Claridge's life and her work for the past ten years. Then overnight, everything had been turned upside down.

They were still traveling back with the dead dolphin when Bater's cell phone rang. Two whales had stranded and died on the beach outside Freeport in Grand Bahama. Bater decided to call a veterinarian he knew at the Southeast Fisheries Science Center, in Miami. Shouting over the outboard motor noise, he briefed her on the mass stranding and suggested she get some folks over to the Bahamas to help sort it out.

When they came ashore, Claridge declined Bater's assistance and tried to fireman-carry the dolphin across the parking lot. But it was too heavy, and she finally let him help her hoist the body onto a bed of sponge pads in the back of the red pickup truck. Then she bought three 50-pound bags of ice from the fish store at the dock, and one by one gently poured them over the corpse.

Balcomb was waiting for her at the house, eager to learn how things had gone. "We need to find a place to store the body," was all she could manage, gesturing to the back of the truck.

He could see that she was hurting, but they both understood what they had to do. "Maybe Les can help us out," he said. "Let's drive down to Nancy's."

Nancy's Restaurant was a popular eating and drinking spot in Sandy Point. The owner, Les Adderly, was a black Bahamian lobster fisherman whose daughter cooked and served conch fritters on the deck overlooking the channel. Les was happy to clear the bait out of one of his oversized freezer chests to make room for the dolphin. They could leave it there as long as they needed to, he told them. They placed the dolphin in the chest and closed the lid tight.

When they got back to the house, the Earthlings were full of questions that Balcomb and Claridge couldn't answer. They didn't know how many animals had stranded, how many had been pushed back out to sea, or how many of those had found their way back to the safety of the underwater canyon. And they had no idea why so many whales had stranded across so many islands. All they knew was that they had witnessed the largest multispecies whale stranding ever recorded.

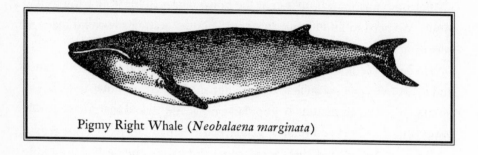

Pigmy Right Whale (*Neobalaena marginata*)

3

Taking Heads

The sound of the small plane droned in Balcomb's head like an alarm that wouldn't shut off. Finally, it jerked him awake.

His arms and legs ached. He stank. He needed a shower. And a younger body. He needed a strong cup of coffee that he knew he didn't have time to brew because he had to get up in that plane before the sun rose above the horizon.

Yesterday had been a sprint to rescue the whales from the beach. Any other whales that had stranded would be dead and rotting by now. Today would be a race to collect whatever fresh specimens he could find before the sun and the sharks had their way with them. If he didn't get their heads on ice by midday, their brains would be cooked to jelly—useless as forensic evidence.

Balcomb knew it was going to be another mad day, following a long night of preparation. After they'd finished logging all the stranding reports that had come in, he and Claridge had stayed up past midnight poring over a nautical chart of Great Bahama Canyon. They marked the locations of all the reported strandings across 150 miles of shoreline: five along the west coast of Abaco Island, six on the south shore of Grand Bahama, and three along the smaller cays in between. Then they circled the X-marks of the eight whales that they and others had pushed back into the channel. They figured that some of the rescued whales might come back ashore in the night, and that others might have stranded unseen on remote beaches.

Balcomb broke down their search and retrieval area into a grid of ten-by-ten-mile squares. Their plan was for Claridge, Ellifrit, and the Earthlings to survey the Abaco coastline in their inflatable research boat while Balcomb searched the shores of the small Out Islands from the air. Balcomb's last call of the night had been to a pilot friend, Bill Anspach, who agreed to pick him up at dawn.

After nudging Claridge awake and getting only a groan of farewell, Balcomb forced himself out of bed. He lumbered past a cluster of Earthlings who had crashed on the living room sofas and gathered up the camera gear, binoculars, and notepad he'd piled by the door the night before. Anspach and his plane were waiting on the dirt strip, just a stone's throw from the house.

As soon as the single-engine plane lifted off and veered toward the sunrise, Balcomb felt the anguish of the past 24 hours drop away. He loved flying, particularly that first rush of pulling away from earthbound gravity, when everything receded into miniature below. For a moment, at least, the pall of stranded whales gave way to the excitement of the scavenger hunt. Balcomb was a lifelong beachcomber and whalebone hunter, and he couldn't suppress his excitement at the treasure trove of specimens that lay in wait.

Balcomb never savored the Bahamas more than from the cockpit of a small plane. Flying just a few hundred feet above Providence Channel, it was easy to see what made the Bahamas such a magnet for scuba divers and marine biologists. The waters are the most transparent in the world, with visibility of more than 200 feet. The 30 low-lying islands and hundreds of smaller cays of the Bahamas were once underwater coral reefs that became dry land when the sea level dropped following the last ice age, 20,000 years ago. Ringed by pink and white sand beaches, the islands barely peek above sea level. From the air, you could see where the pale turquoise of the shallows shifted quickly to the royal blue depths of Great Bahama Canyon.

Canyons on land are created by the steady erosive force of rivers. Underwater, it's the ceaseless gyre of the ocean currents that carve their signature into the seabed. The Bahamas were once joined in a contiguous landmass with Florida and Cuba. Over the course of 150 million years, the Atlantic and Gulf Streams ground away at the limestone ocean floor, creating a 3-mile-deep, 140-mile-long underwater canyon separating the Bahamas from the mainland. The Great Bahama Canyon is the largest, deepest gorge in the world, on land or at sea—twice as wide and three times as deep as Arizona's Grand Canyon.

Beaked whales have lived in Great Bahama Canyon for 40 million years, ever since they migrated from the shark-infested reefs guarding the Atlantic side of the islands. In the canyon, they found a feeding ground rich with hard-shelled nautiloids that fed on microorganisms near the surface. Before they learned to hunt with sound, beaked whales foraged visually, alongside other whales and fish. To escape predators, their hard-shelled prey descended to the dark depths during sunlight hours, returning to the upper layers at night to feed in the relative safety of darkness.

The upper 600 feet of the ocean is called the sunlight zone, where plants dependent on photosynthesis and the marine life that feed on them live. Below 600 feet lies the twilight zone where almost no light penetrates, even in the transparent waters of the Bahamas. To follow their prey into the twilight zone, and even deeper into the lightless midnight zone below 2,500 feet, beaked whales had to learn to hunt in total darkness—which required echolocating with sound.

Not all whales echolocate. Echolocation, or "biosonar," was an adaptation that emerged relatively early in cetacean evolution. The fossil record of whales reveals a radical metamorphosis from furry, hoofed land-dweller to sleek marine mammal. Forelegs gave way to fins, hind legs and hair disappeared, tails transformed into flukes, and nostrils receded high onto the head to become blowholes suitable for breathing air at the ocean's surface. The oceans offered whales a buoyant and spacious home with few predators and abundant food.

Some whales became filter feeders, trapping tiny krill in the baleen brushes of their mouths. Released from the weight constraints of terrestrial gravity, these "baleen" whales evolved into the largest animals ever to roam the world. A 100-foot-long, 150-ton blue whale could consume up to 8,000 pounds of krill in a day.

Other whales, hunting in packs, used their teeth to seize their prey. These "toothed" whales—including dolphins,* orcas, beaked whales, sperm whales, and others—developed the ability to hunt and navigate in the dark using sound, the same way that bats do. Though bats and toothed whales have evolved different specialized anatomy for the task, the principle is the same: they emit high-frequency sound pulses and listen for the echo. The distance between their two ears—which act as separate receivers—allows echolocators to triangulate the precise distance, direction, and dimensions of an object.[1] Other animals navigate with biosonar. Shrews have been shown to echolocate underground, and blind humans can learn to echolocate by tapping a cane— or simply by making clicking sounds with their mouths—and then listening for the echo from nearby objects.

During their first 10 million years in the Great Bahama Canyon, beaked whales developed primitive biosonar. By bouncing sound clicks off their prey's hard shell, day or night, beaked whales easily outcompeted the other predators in the canyon who could only hunt by daylight. Their ability to hunt squid at increasing depth drove the beaked whales' ascent to the top of the canyon's food chain.

When the hard-shelled nautiloids evolved to abandon their shells to avoid biosonar detection, beaked whales refined their biosonar to echolocate the *internal* structures of the soft-bodied squid—which then developed survival countermeasures including camouflage, shape-shifting, and ink-cloud diversions. Millennium by millennium, the beaked whales improved their sonar to defeat these escape mechanisms and chase the squid deeper into the canyon. This evolutionary pursuit-and-escape minuet between squid and beaked whales continued for thousands of generations, until the whales could hunt squid at depths of a mile or more—deeper than any other predator. [2]

To hunt at such extreme depths, beaked whales made several physical and metabolic adaptations, allowing them to dive quickly with a minimum of drag, to tolerate the cold temperatures and crushing hydrostatic pressure at

---

* Dolphins are small whales whose neurology, physiology, and biosonar resemble other "toothed" whales.

depth, and most importantly, to regulate their breathing to enable deep foraging dives that could last an hour or longer. Other deep-diving cetaceans, such
as sperm whales in pursuit of giant squid, have made similar adaptations. But
none dive as deep, and surface as briefly, as the beaked whales of the Great
Bahama Canyon.

Beaked whales routinely dive deeper than 5,000 feet and remain underwater for more than an hour; the deepest dive ever recorded by an air-breathing mammal was a Cuvier's beaked whale that descended 9,816 feet in a dive
that lasted 137 minutes.[3] Humans can dive only to a few hundred feet without
risking decompression sickness, or "the bends."[4] By comparison, a WWII
German U-boat reached its crush depth at 860 to 920 feet. Even the deepest-
diving of modern military submarines can't dive as deep as a beaked whale.[5]

The plane flew due north over dozens of tiny cays offshore of Abaco, many
of them unnamed and uninhabited patches of sand and scrub barely poking
out of the water. From the co-pilot seat, Balcomb scanned each of the cay's
shoreline through binoculars. For the first hour aloft, he didn't spot anything.

Just then, as they flew over Water Cay, off the southern bight of Abaco,
Balcomb spotted something on the beach. He motioned to Anspach, who
took the plane into a steep circle dive and made a low pass over the island.
Balcomb videotaped the dark spindle-shaped carcass lying at an angle in the
sand, while Anspach noted its GPS position.

As they were taking a second low pass over the beach, a call came in
from Claridge over the plane's VHF radio. She'd found a Blainville's behind
Cross Harbor. "The sharks must have chased it into the lagoon yesterday," she
said, her voice crackling. "It probably stranded when the tide went out this
morning. I can still see the grooves in the sand where it tried to work itself
free." Despite the static, Balcomb could hear her excitement at finding such
a well-preserved specimen. "I'd say it's only been dead a few hours. Couldn't
be fresher."

Five minutes later, they flew over the lagoon, and Balcomb could see
Claridge, Ellifrit, and several Earthlings hovered over the whale's body.
Anspach set the plane down nearby and Balcomb hustled over to join them.

Just as Claridge had reported, the whale was newly dead. No bad smell or decomposition. Tissue was fresh and firm to the touch. And the carcass was in pristine condition. Not a shark bite on it.

He wanted to get the whale up on dry land where he could take the head and necropsy the organs. The head would tell them if there was damage to the ears and brain, but he hoped that the other organs might also hold clues to what had driven the whale ashore.

The tide was just starting to come back in, so it would be an hour or more before there would be enough water in the lagoon to float the body to shore. Balcomb hated the idea of leaving it exposed to the elements for even a minute longer. The whale was a juvenile, only about 11 feet long. But it still weighed more than 1,500 pounds, and they couldn't budge it off the sandy bottom of the lagoon. After some rocking and rolling, they managed to get a tarp underneath the whale's belly, tie a rope around its tail fluke, and tow it out of the lagoon and up onto the beach.

It's shockingly easy to cut off the head of a Blainville's whale. All you need is the right kind of knife, a strong stomach, and a detailed knowledge of beaked whale anatomy. Balcomb had all three.

He'd procured the knife, a 16-inch blade with a weathered oak handle, during a research trip to Norway a decade earlier. Scandinavians had been using long-handled flensing knives to carve the blubber off of whales for 1,000 years, but this was a specialty blade designed to cut up large fish and seals. Balcomb called it his "O.J.," as in Simpson—much to Claridge's chagrin—and he always kept it honed to a razor's edge, just in case something interesting washed up on the beach.

Knowing how to decapitate a beaked whale was a hard-won bit of arcana, something he'd picked up during four decades of roaming the globe in search of *Cetacea: Ziphiidae*. He'd studied every textbook on whale anatomy, picked through the cutting room floors of whaling stations from California to Japan to Iceland in search of skeletons. While on Midway Island in his late-twenties, he dissected his first beaked whale, a Cuvier's that had washed ashore dead on a coral shelf in the very middle of the Pacific Ocean. While living in Japan he'd frequented a family-run whaling station that still hunted the largest beaked whales in the world—the 40-foot Baird's beaked whales—in the waters outside Tokyo Bay. After the workers were done with their butchering, Balcomb was free to study and sketch the skeleton and internal anatomy. Though the Baird's whales are twice the size of Cuvier's, all beaked whales are deep divers that share the same basic anatomy and physiology.

Cutting off a beaked whale's head can take an hour if you don't know your way around its distinctive anatomy. Balcomb figured he could get it done in just under ten minutes. The tricky part is figuring out where the whale's head ends and its trunk begins. All mammals, from giraffes to moles, have seven vertebrae in their necks. But over the course of its evolution, the beaked whale's cervical vertebrae have fused into a bony mass, creating the appearance of a no-necked creature. Balcomb knew the precise spot to cut in—a foot behind the blowhole, halfway between the eye and the flipper—and how to feel his way with the blade through the blubber and muscle all the way down to the bone. A 16th inch too far back, and the knife can't sever the cervicals. A 16th inch too far forward, and the blade bangs up against the cranial vault.

The crevice between the skull and the first cervical vertebra is curved, so he had to work the blade at an angle until he found the precise seam, and then pivot it back and forth like a clam knife until the spinal cord gave way. It was quick work to slice through the cranial nerves and the network of arteries that feed oxygenated blood to the brain. As the blood poured out of the whale's neck, Balcomb was grateful that at low tide the lagoon was too shallow to attract sharks.

Balcomb worked deep inside the carcass, more by touch than by sight. He pushed the blade through the soft tissue of the esophagus, and then past the cartilage and other connective tissue of the larynx and the windpipe. There was only a half foot of muscle and blubber below the throat. Deftly avoiding the hyoid bone collar at the base of the throat, Balcomb completed his cut, and the head hinged away from the carcass like a stout felled tree.

"Bravo," Claridge said softly as she lowered the video camera from her shoulder and stooped to admire the specimen. Balcomb was pleased by what a clean cut he'd made, and by how well articulated and intact the vascular structures had remained. For a bone hunter like Balcomb, a beaked whale skull is the rarest of trophies. If it hadn't been a vital piece of forensic evidence, he'd have buried the head deep in the sand and let the underground beetles and sand flies pick the cranium clean over the next few weeks. Then he'd place the treasure on the high shelf at the beach house, alongside the other two *Ziphius cavirostris* (beaked whale) skulls he'd collected in four decades of beachcombing.

A beaked whale's head tells the entire tale of its remarkable evolution. Its cranium is almost twice as thick as a dolphin's, the better to withstand extreme water pressure at depth. Its dense, beaked rostrum is both a powerful weapon against mate-competing males and a potent defense against sharks. The beaked whale's sound-emitting powers originate in its nasal cavities, which transmit both communication sounds and sonar clicks. Its concave forehead cradles an acoustic lens, or melon, that focuses sound into different beam forms. Its long jawbone conducts return echoes and incoming communications from other whales to the three small ear bones common to all mammals, which are nested well back in its head. Elaborately convoluted, with an enormous auditory cortex, the beaked whale's brain is a masterpiece of signal processing. It can conduct multiple conversations simultaneously, as well as translate biosonar echoes into exquisitely detailed, three-dimensional maps.

As far as Balcomb was concerned, the beaked whales of Great Bahama Canyon were the niftiest piece of biotechnology ever engineered. Ever since he was a kid, he had taken things apart so he could study their design, then put them back together. He was a connoisseur of well-made machines: cars, boats, planes. To hear his wives tell it, Balcomb was an incurable tightwad who never wanted to spend a dime on clothes or restaurants or home improvement. But back at Smugglers Cove, he kept a half dozen mint-condition classic and vintage cars parked in makeshift garages on the grounds around his house.

Spattered with sweat and sand and bits of flesh, Balcomb knelt in the sand and stared at the decapitated Blainville's. All that magnificent engineering, he thought, couldn't save this whale from whatever the hell had happened in the canyon.

While two Earthlings videotaped and took photographs, Balcomb, Claridge, and Ellifrit went to work collecting tissue specimens. They took samples of the blubber, lungs, heart, kidney, and intestines. A beaked whale's liver, the size of a large shoulder bag, is usually the first organ to rot. But

Balcomb was reassured to find that this one was still firm and fresh. They washed each specimen with acetone, wrapping several slices in aluminum foil and fixing others in formalin.

Though he was normally laconic, Balcomb gave the Earthlings a running anatomy tutorial on the Blainville's beaked whale he was dissecting. He explained that a Blainville's is smaller than a Cuvier's, and that it's also called a dense-beaked whale, because its beaked rostrum is the densest bone found in any animal. He showed them the specialized lipids in the blubber and the vascular plumbing in the fin, flukes, and flippers that keep a whale from overheating in the warm surface waters. He explained the overbuilt *retia mirabilia*, or "wonderful network" of veins and arteries that engorge during deep dives to conserve core body heat and allow the gradual reabsorption of respiratory gas in the blood on ascent. He opened up each of the beaked whale's 13 stomachs, designed for efficient food storage and digestion during long dives, and carefully catalogued the half-digested squid he found there. Balcomb divided the specimens into two batches—one for US Fisheries, and one as backup in case the Fisheries' specimens went missing.

When they were finally done, they loaded the head into the back of the pickup and raced to Nancy's. There was room inside Les' freezer to nestle the Blainville's head atop the dolphin. Balcomb would have loved to grab a beer on Les' back porch, but he needed to get back aloft and continue the aerial search, and there was less than an hour of sunlight left.

The sun was setting behind the plane as Anspach headed east toward Tilloo Cay. The bay was empty of fishing boats now. A lone catamaran tacked into the late-day wind. To look down on this postcard panorama, it was hard to imagine that just a day earlier something had gone horribly wrong inside the canyon.

"What's that, coming around the point?" Anspach shouted over the engine noise. He motioned to a ship emerging from behind a small cay, about a mile to the south. "A trawler?"

Balcomb swung his binoculars around to the pilot-side window. It was too big for a fishing trawler. To judge by its length and blue-gray color, it was military.

"Let's take a closer look," said Balcomb. "But not too close."

Anspach banked the plane to the left and circled, giving the vessel a wide berth. Once he got a side view, it was easy for Balcomb to ID the ship. It was a destroyer, with US Navy markings. Through the viewfinder of his video camera, he could clearly make out the antiaircraft guns mounted on its foredeck. He checked the plane's instrument panel to confirm that they were safely outside the warship's no-fly radius.

"Don't go any closer," Balcomb said to Anspach, as he shot stills through his longest lens.[6]

There was nothing subtle about a modern naval destroyer, Balcomb mused as he peered at the rows of guided-missile batteries and antisubmarine rocket launchers. Its name pretty much said it all. He knew that destroyers rarely sailed alone, that they usually ran escort for a full battle group. So, where were the other ships? A more urgent question pressed against his brain, and his heart: What was a US Navy destroyer doing in Great Bahama Canyon?

Balcomb didn't share any of these questions with his friend. In the 25 years since he'd worked undercover for the Navy, Balcomb had never spoken to anyone about the details of his military service. If you were involved in classified work, you didn't talk about it to civilians. Period. Those were the rules of his security clearance, and he'd always remained faithful to his oath of secrecy. Even inside his marriages—including his marriage to Diane.

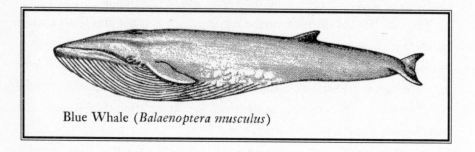

Blue Whale (*Balaenoptera musculus*)

4

The Loneliness of the Long-Distance Beachcomber

1943
Albuquerque, New Mexico

There had always been a lot of military in Ken Balcomb's family. Just not much family.

His first memory, at age three, was of hugging a soldier good-bye and pressing his face into the jacket of his uniform. The soldier who knelt in front of him was leaving for Marine Corps officer training school before shipping out to fight the Japanese in the South Pacific. Ken cried and held the soldier tight. Then the soldier began to cry, too.

Ken's father survived the war, but he never returned to his wife and son in New Mexico. Instead, he married a Wave he'd met during training and started a new family with her in Colorado. He never wrote to Ken; never called on his birthday. Growing up, Ken's only memento of his father was a framed studio photo of a handsome, well-groomed man in a suit and tie. Everyone called him "Blue" because of his piercing blue eyes. But the photo was black and white, so Ken could only guess if his father's eyes were the same shade of blue that stared back at him from the mirror.

Ken's mother, Barbara, refused to mention Blue by name. So Ken had to mine nuggets of information about his father from his grandfather and uncles. Blue and Barbara had met at the University of New Mexico where she was studying music. Blue was restless in college, and when Ken was born shortly after he married Barbara, he dropped out of school and took a job as a pipefitter laying gas lines. As soon as the war broke out, Blue enlisted in the Marines. Barbara was furious at him for leaving her alone with an infant, since he was eligible for a family exemption from the draft.

Once it became clear that Blue wasn't coming home, Barbara moved on to her next husband. And the next, and the next. Whether they were warm to him or indifferent, Ken reached out to each of his stepfathers as they passed by, as if he were floating down a river and grasping at exposed tree roots along the banks.

First there was Robert Garrett, a debonair pilot from nearby Kirkland Air Force Base. He and Barbara would take Ken to the officers' club with them, and give him a bag of nickels to play the slot machines, while they drank and danced the night away. They divorced a few years later, shortly after Barbara gave birth to Ken's half brothers, Howie and Rick.

When Ken was ten, Barbara married Cal Nelson, who moved the family to Sacramento, California. Cal had been a big game hunter, and their house was filled with exotic stuffed trophy heads. Cal took Ken duck hunting and taught him how to lead the bird and judge the trajectory of the buckshot. Cal and Barbara opened a dance hall/saloon they called the 1199 Club because it was 11 miles outside of Sacramento on Route 99. Barbara played the piano, Cal tended bar, and Ken and his half brothers got all the free hamburgers they could eat back in the kitchen. But Cal turned out to be more interested in drinking than in bartending. Barbara divorced her third husband the month the club closed, and Cal was dead a year later from cirrhosis of the liver.

Once Barbara became a single mother, freelancing as a piano player at Parisi's Cocktail Lounge and the Palomino Club out on Route 50, Ken barely saw her at all. By the time he came home from school, she'd be pulling on a cocktail dress and heading off to work. She wouldn't return until well past midnight, and she'd still be sleeping when Ken and his younger half brothers got themselves up and off to school.

There was no confusing Barbara with the other mothers of Sacramento.

She was an attractive, slim brunette with dark eyes who always seemed to have a lit cigarette in her hand. To Ken, she was beautiful and glamorous, aloof, and hard to please. She didn't go in much for hugs and kisses, and she insisted that her sons call her Barbara, never Mom. "Laissez-faire" was how she described her mothering style.

When Ken was a teenager, Barbara met her last husband while playing piano at Parisi's. A colonel from nearby McClellan Air Force Base, he was a no-nonsense authoritarian who insisted that Ken wouldn't amount to anything unless he served in the military. The colonel reserved all his paternal pride for his own son, a Navy test pilot. Six months after the colonel married Barbara, his son's F-8 Crusader jet crashed into flames during a training mission. After that, the colonel turned dark and violent. He drank and hit Ken's mother and glowered at the boys.

That's when the family pretty much split apart—like billiard balls after the break, is how Ken remembered it. Ashamed that he couldn't protect his mother from the colonel, Ken threw himself into any physical work or sports that would bulk up his spindly frame. He found summer work driving a tractor in the hops fields 12 hours a day, and fixing any farm machinery that broke down. In the fall, he loaded 150-pound bales of hops onto trucks and drove them to a warehouse in West Sacramento where he stacked them four high. It was hard, sweaty work, but it made him stronger. He dabbled at boxing and martial arts, but he found his niche on the track team. Long-distance running suited his solitary temperament. By 10th grade, he'd become the star runner on his high school cross-country team and a competitive miler statewide.

His true salvation was being alone in the outdoors. Ken lost himself—and found himself—in the wild country outside of Sacramento. He'd wade across the American River with his .22 rifle held overhead, shoot rabbits on the river islands, skin and dress them, and bring them home to eat with his brothers. He'd stay out past dark searching the river's edge for animal bones and snakeskins to study. Ken befriended some shepherds in the foothills of the Sierra Nevadas near Sacramento, and sometimes they'd let him bring home a sickly baby sheep to bottle-feed back to health. As a shy, bookish adolescent, he devoured stories about wild animals and wild places, especially anything by Jack London or Joseph Conrad.

One day when he was 15, Ken hitchhiked to Point Reyes, which was popu-
lated only by a few cattle ranches back in the 1950s. It was the first time he'd
ever seen the ocean—or the beach. He returned home that day laden with
treasure: shells and beach glass, a piece of weathered driftwood, and a single
bone. He had no idea what animal it had come from, but the possibilities set
his imagination on fire.

As soon as he got his driver's license and a car that summer, he took off
for Point Reyes at every opportunity. He'd walk the shoreline alone for hours,
combing the beach for whatever had washed ashore in an ocean storm. By
age 16, he was already searching for beaked whale bones. They were mythical creatures to him, like dinosaurs, known only by their fossil remains.
The precious relics he recovered over the years—a gray whale's vertebrae, a
sperm whale's tooth, and, later, the complete skeleton of a Blainville's beaked
whale—were Ken's bridge to the world of prehistoric cetaceans. As he scoured
the beach, with only his dog for company, Ken tried to imagine the first close
encounters between a stranded whale and the Chumash Indians who had
settled on the California shoreline 13,000 years earlier. What must it have
felt like to wander down to the beach one morning, maybe to fish or dig for
clams, and find something amazing: a leviathan lying helpless on dry land.

During summertime visits with his grandfather in Albuquerque, Ken
would gather fragments of information about Blue's life apart from him. He
learned that after the war, Blue had finished college and gone to law school.
He had three more kids with his second wife and became a very successful
water rights attorney in Glenwood Springs, Colorado, even winning a landmark case he argued in front of the US Supreme Court. When Ken turned 17
and told his grandfather he wanted to go see Blue, he agreed to drive him out
to the Rockies for a visit.

There were no hugs and tears this time, just a man-to-man handshake at
the door to Blue's big house in the hills outside of Glenwood Springs—a much
grander home, Ken couldn't help but notice, than his mother's modest ranch
house. Blue had a rigid, military bearing that made Ken straighten his posture
to meet his gaze. As they stood with their hands clasped, Ken could feel his
father's steel blue eyes searching his, appraising what kind of man the boy he'd
left behind had become.

As soon as they entered the house, Blue grew tense. His wife was clearly unhappy about Ken's visit, so the Balcomb men spent most of the week outdoors, building a stone wall to run along the curved driveway to the house. Ken and Blue hauled granite rocks from the field behind the house, while Ken's grandfather—a civilian engineer and road builder by profession— chiseled the stones into shape and cemented them into place along the wall. It was hard physical labor, the kind Ken liked. He was happy showing off his hard-earned muscles and exerting himself in silence alongside his father.

When it was time to say good-bye, Blue didn't suggest another visit or promise to stay in touch. On the long drive home to Sacramento, Ken became convinced that he hadn't measured up in his father's eyes.

Five years later, Ken was a senior at UC Berkeley and had been accepted to Berkeley Law School for the following fall. Though he'd been a serious student throughout high school and college, his heart wasn't really in a law career. Still, Blue was the closest thing he had to a father or a role model, and Ken continued to crave his approval, even if they hadn't spoken since his visit to Colorado.

Ken had become a father himself by the age of 20. The summer after his sophomore year, when he was filling up his prized '34 Ford at the Texaco station in Sacramento, a girl pulled up in a Chevy convertible and started to flirt with him. Anne liked that he was a good listener with kind eyes and a gentle manner. And he had a preppy look that told her he was heading places, and she liked that too. They started dating, and when Anne soon became pregnant, Ken married her before returning with her to school that fall—which is what you did in 1961 if you were a stand-up guy.

Then, in the spring of his senior year of college, Ken took a fish and wildlife management course, and it turned his life around. While studying the skull of a West African lion (*Panthera leo senegalensis*), he was transported back to his first teenaged encounters with whale bones on the beaches of Point Reyes. Suddenly the idea of spending his adult life indoors—in law libraries and conference rooms and courtrooms—horrified him. He wasn't sure how it would translate into a career yet, but he knew that what he wanted, even more than his father's approval, was to work outdoors studying animals in the wild.

He announced to Anne that he'd decided to follow his passion and enroll in the University of California at Davis' graduate zoology program, instead of law school. The next fall Ken moved his young family—including their infant son, Kelley—into a mobile home in a trailer park not far from UC Davis.

Like so many cetologists of his generation, Ken found his way into whale research by accident. As a grad student, he was in charge of collecting fresh horse lungs for an emphysema study funded by the National Institutes of Health (NIH). Twice a week he'd drive from Davis to a horse slaughterhouse in south Oakland, retrieve whatever fresh lungs he could find, ice them down, and drive the specimens back to the lab. Returning from one of these trips, Ken saw a sign for the Richmond whaling station just north of Oakland, and took a detour to investigate.

In 1963 Richmond was home to the last two whaling outfits in the United States: Del Monte Fishing Company and the Golden Gate Fishing Company. Most of the world's whaling fleet had followed the remaining whale populations to South America and Antarctica, where they were hunted and processed at sea aboard huge factory ships. But Del Monte and Golden Gate still hunted whales off the California coast, hauling about 200 whales a year—mostly fin, humpback, and sperm whales—into the Richmond processing plant.

Each of their five boats would set out through the Golden Gate on 100-mile-long day trips, searching the waters from Bodega Bay down to Monterey. Their gunners fired deck-mounted cannons with explosive harpoons into the whales, reeled in their catch with three-quarter-inch steel cables, lashed them to the side of the boat, and pumped them full of air to keep them from sinking. With one or two whales tied to their gunwales, they'd head back home to Richmond.

When Ken passed by the whaling station that first evening with his collection of horse lungs, the crews were untying the whale carcasses from the boats and hauling them up the rampway into the processing building. He had smelled the cookers from a mile away. The 40-man Richmond crews could reduce a humpback whale to oil, bone meal, and pet food in an hour and a half. They flensed off the meat in long strips and sold it to Kal Kan dog food in Southern California for 10 cents a pound. They ground the bones into meal for sale to chicken farms. The blubber was cooked down into oil and sold as an additive to margarine, cosmetics, and motor oil.

Watching the whales' deconstruction gave Ken an idea: Why not conduct a parallel comparative anatomy study using whale lungs as the animal model? His professor endorsed the concept. So several times a week, Ken would stop by the Richmond station and sort through the mountains of oversized organs that Del Monte and Golden Gate discarded as garbage every day. Wading among the maggots that undulated in the ripe tissue and the indescribable aroma of half-rotted offal, Ken would search for an intact lung. It was during one of these gruesome scavenger hunts that Ken discovered his first beaked whale specimen—a rare Baird's beaked whale head, almost six feet long. It was about to be hauled off with the rest of the refuse when Ken grabbed it with both hands and rolled it off the pile. He was so excited to finally hold a beaked whale head in his hands that he barely minded the stench or the maggots swarming out of its eye sockets.

A week later, Ken heard that a research team had chartered one of Golden Gate's whaling ships, the *Lynnann*, for a two-week whale-tagging expedition in the Santa Barbara Islands. When Ken discovered that the expedition was being led by the premier American and Japanese cetologists of the day, Dale Rice and Masaharu Nishiwaki, he begged the *Lynnann*'s captain for a job. Any job. When the captain said he needed a dishwasher, Ken pounced.

Whale tagging dated back to the 1920s when researchers aboard the British vessel *Discovery* set sail for the Southern Ocean to conduct the first scientific survey of whale migrations. The original *Discovery* "tags" were foot-long stainless-steel cylinders engraved with date, the sponsor's address, and—in the 1920s—the promise of a cash reward to any whaler who found one while flensing or cooking the whale's blubber and mailed it back to the researchers in London. Comparing the location of the tagging to the location of its recovery, the researchers could then plot the migration path of the whale.

Forty years later, Rice and Nishiwaki decided to use the same tags and tagging method. But it was harder than they had anticipated. You had to stand on the deck of a fast-moving boat giving chase to a whale that surfaced for just a few seconds to breathe. In that instant, you had to fire the tag from a 12-gauge shotgun and hit the whale. If the tag lodged in the tissue below the blubber layer, you had a successful "mark." But fired from a distance of 100 to 300 feet, most of the tags missed their target altogether or else hit the dorsal fin and bounced into the ocean.

Ken turned out to be the only person on board who could handle a shot-gun well enough to actually make a mark. After a couple of shots, he figured out that the tags were heavy, so you had to aim high to compensate for gravity. And you had to lead the moving target, just as his stepfather Cal had taught him to do while duck hunting. Before dinner of the first day's tagging, Ken was promoted from dishwasher to marksman/dishwasher. By the end of their two-week tour, he'd successfully tagged almost 200 whales.

Those two weeks aboard the *Lynnann* were bliss. After years as a loner adrift in his own world, Ken had finally found a peer group and a mission. It was his first time at sea, and he loved everything about it: the boat, the whales, the shotguns, and especially the company of two world-renowned cetologists who knew the answers to all his questions about whales.

During that tagging trip, Ken began photographing whales. He'd been taking nature photos ever since high school, and shortly before the tagging trip Ken had seen a spectacular photo-spread of humpback whales in *Life* magazine.[1] At the time, almost no one had photographed whales in the wild. Fortunately for Ken, the same keen eyes and quick reflexes that made him a good whale tagger enabled him to capture photographs of whales from the deck of the *Lynnann*.

By the end the trip, Rice offered Ken the job of expedition leader on an-other tagging trip over the summer. When Ken returned home, triumphant, Anne wasn't there to celebrate. She'd taken their one-year-old son, Kelley, and moved back with her parents in Sacramento. Ken begged her to come home, but she refused. She knew that Ken was doing what he'd always wanted, but it wasn't what she'd signed up for. She missed the clean-cut kid with the winning smile she'd met at the gas station. The one who was heading to law school, not the one who hung out in whale processing plants, who went to sea for weeks at a time and came home smelling like a fishmonger.

Ken was crushed that his young family was breaking apart. A month later, when Anne began seeing a medical student across campus, Ken couldn't han-dle it. He dropped out of grad school and took a volunteer job with Dale Rice tagging whales. After a series of trips marking gray whales in Baja, Rice offered him a full-time job working for the US Fish and Wildlife Service. So Ken moved to Berkeley and worked at the Richmond whaling station collect-ing specimens. Day after day he searched for Discovery tags in the piles of offal and in the cookers, verified the length and legality of the catch, and took samples of their blubber, earwax, stomach contents, and gonads.

His divorce papers arrived that spring. Two months later, he heard from the draft board. Now that he was neither married nor a student, Ken was reclassified as 1-A eligible. It was the summer of 1965, and troop levels in Vietnam were escalating rapidly. Dale Rice suggested a "deferred occupation" that might keep the draft board at bay. The Smithsonian was directing a contract job for the US Army, banding birds in the Pacific, based out of Honolulu. All things considered, the middle of the Pacific Ocean sounded to Ken like a pretty good destination.[2]

Ken spent a year at sea, moving from dot to dot in the central Pacific and the Hawaiian island chain. From there, he progressed to a seemingly endless string of central and South Pacific atolls. Every few days, he would disembark from the mother ship aboard an inflatable boat packed with a tent, food, and water, and thousands of aluminum leg bands. He'd find landfall, set up camp, sleep all day, and work all night banding birds that nested on the ground along the shore.

It was classic stoop labor, like planting rice in a paddy. Insects feasted on his arms and legs. Coral sliced his feet and ankles. It was the kind of work that only a masochist, or a man in flight from his mainland life, could tolerate. If it felt a bit like working on a chain gang, that suited Ken too. He felt guilty for making a mess of his family life and for being an absentee father, as Blue had been.

Then, in August 1966, when his ship was crossing the equator precisely at the international date line, a message came over the ship's Teletype from Dale Rice: "Sorry, Ken, the draft board rejected your deferral. Report for immediate induction at first US landfall."

When he returned to Berkeley, Ken crashed with his half brothers, Howie and Rick. In the year Ken had been at sea, the Bay Area had become the epicenter of the antiwar movement. Flower power was in full blossom. Rick had joined the US Navy reserves in college, and Howie, also 1-A eligible, was moving to Canada to escape the draft. But Ken didn't want to run away to Canada. He wasn't antiwar or antimilitary. Rather than waiting to be drafted into the infantry—which seemed to him like a death trap—Ken decided to apply to the same Naval Aviation Corps that the colonel's son had served in before his fatal crash. Despite the colonel's scorn and abuse, Ken still wanted his stepfather to think he'd amounted to something.

Ken showed up for basic training in Pensacola, Florida, with long, raggedy hair and a beard, looking like an island castaway crossed with a Berkeley hippy. They gave him the standard issue high-and-tight crew cut, then sent him through the *Top Gun* indoc routine: break you down and build you back up to fit the mold. By the seventh day of indoc, he was ready to quit. Then he started to notice that he was doing better than his classmates, who were mostly three or four years younger. The push-up and sit-up drills were nothing compared to what he'd endured during his year of bird banding. And he could still clock the fastest mile in his squadron.

In flight training, Ken learned aviation and aeronautics and how to shine his shoes. He grew to appreciate the Navy's merit system. You learned your shit and did your job, and you got recognition. After 12 weeks, he graduated first in his class.

Every Navy flyboy worth his salt had to get himself a blonde and a Corvette after being commissioned an officer. Ken had no quarrel with that directive. As a connoisseur of vintage cars, he passed on the Corvette and bought himself a '57 Mercedes Gullwing. He never loved a car like he loved that one. Blondes were even easier to come by. It seemed that every girl from New Orleans to Tallahassee would show up in Pensacola on the weekends to try to snag a flyboy. Julie Byrd was from Mobile, Alabama. She followed Ken to advanced flight training in Corpus Christi, Texas, and they got married in Norfolk, Virginia, where he was assigned to the air group at the naval base. Julie didn't want kids, which suited Ken just fine. She was a go-along-get-along kind of girl, a useful quality in a Navy wife.

After he completed advanced flight school in the top 1 percent of his class and got his "wings," Ken submitted his "dream sheet" for his first assignment. He wasn't keen to pilot bombing runs over Vietnam. His first choice was to fly research aircraft, either as a hurricane hunter or to supply expeditions in Antarctica. His second choice was fixed-wing antisubmarine surveillance.

So what assignment did he draw? Airborne Warning and Control System, or AWACS, what he considered the most boring flight job in the sky! You take off from a carrier and fly racetrack ovals while the guys back in air traffic control look for bogies on your radar screens. He'd flown AWACS for a week during flight training, and it bored him to death. He couldn't believe it. He'd finished at the top of his class, and he'd drawn AWACS duty?

Ken applied for an assignment change. He begged for a research job—any kind of research. So they assigned him to oceanographic research and sent him to Fleet Sonar School in Key West, Florida. For a Navy flight officer, sonar was a total dead end. It wasn't even a flight assignment. He figured it was retaliation for refusing AWACS. But at least it would get him back to sea, or at least seaside.

What Oceanographic Officer Ken Balcomb didn't realize was that naval sound surveillance would offer him a privileged porthole into the hidden world of whales.

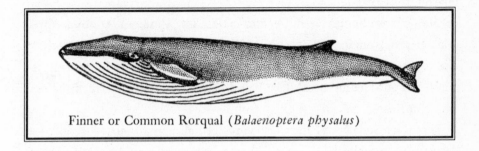

Finner or Common Rorqual (*Balaenoptera physalus*)

5

In the Silent Service

As Balcomb soon discovered, everything about Navy sonar was cloaked in secrecy. Classes at Fleet Sonar School were held inside a windowless cinderblock building shuttered behind a large green security door—perhaps to prepare the student for the bunkerlike sonar stations where they'd be working. The curriculum was a rigorous course load of acoustics, physics, sonar, and antisubmarine warfare history and tactics. Less than half the class passed. Balcomb loved it. The math and physics of underwater acoustics came easily to him. Learning the secret science of sound in the ocean made him feel like the sorcerer's apprentice.

The best-kept military secret of the Cold War was the Sound Surveillance System, called SOSUS for short, that Balcomb was being trained to operate in the Pacific. SOSUS was a radical innovation in antisubmarine warfare that enabled the US Navy to maintain a crucial tactical advantage over the Soviets for 25 years.

• • •

At the end of the nineteenth century, US Navy strategist Admiral Alfred Mahan proclaimed, "Whoever rules the waves, rules the world." Early in the twentieth century, the submarine quickly emerged as the preeminent naval weapon, trumping surface-based battleships that had ruled the seas for centuries.

The Germans became the world's most lethal submariners. During World War II, "wolf packs" of German U-boats sank more than 3,000 Allied ships and were neutralized only late in the war when the Allies finally cracked the code of their radio transmissions. After the fall of Berlin in May 1945, Soviet and American naval commanders scrambled for the spoils of war. They seized German U-boats—as well as the German engineers who designed them—in hopes of gaining an edge in the next generation of submarine development.

Just before the war ended, the Germans had launched the fastest, most stealthy submarine ever built. The Soviets adopted the German quiet-diesel designs and moved aggressively to produce an armada of snorkeling submarines that could stay submerged for days, making them almost impossible to detect by visual or radar surveillance.[1] By the early fifties, Soviet production lines were cranking out these vessels by the dozens each year. Due to the budgetary politics of peacetime, the US Navy knew that it couldn't match Stalin's resolve to produce submarines at a wartime pace. Over the course of the Cold War, the Soviets built almost four times as many submarines as the Americans.[2] The US Navy resolved to overcome its numerical disadvantage by excelling at acoustic warfare.

The traditional way to locate a submarine with sound was *active sonar*. First invented in 1912 in response to the *Titanic* disaster, the "echo-ranger" that enabled ships to locate submerged icebergs was soon repurposed to track the deadly U-boats unleashed by Germany in the first months of World War I. Active sonar locates submarines the same way bats and toothed whales use echolocation to hunt their prey—by sending out a sound signal and calculating the time and trajectory of the echo to fix the location of the target.

But WWII-era active sonar had a serious limitation: it could only detect submerged submarines at short ranges of a mile or less. During the Cold War, America needed to track a vast Soviet fleet of submarines across wide ocean basins.

Throughout the 1950s, both the United States and the Soviets raced to transform their submarines from fearsome stealth vessels into truly apocalyptic weapons of mass destruction. In 1955 the Soviets deployed the first submarine capable of launching nuclear-armed, ballistic missiles. The Americans soon followed suit. By the end of the decade, both navies had equipped their nuclear-armed subs with nuclear-powered turbines that enabled them to stay submerged for months. Unlike land and air-based ballistic missile systems, submarines were invisible and ever-moving missile silos that could hide and launch from anywhere in the world's oceans—even under the Arctic ice cap.

Faced with the threat of intercontinental ballistic missiles launched from thousands of miles away, the question driving US antisubmarine strategy became: How can we detect and track Soviet submarines *across whole ocean basins*?

The answer was simple in concept and wildly ambitious in scope. If—as hypothesized by one of its physicists—the Navy could discover and exploit a hidden whispering chamber that extended throughout the deep ocean, then it could wiretap the world's oceans and track the movements of every submarine in the Soviet fleet. SOSUS marked the beginning of a bold new era in sound surveillance: *passive sonar*. Instead of sending out an active sound signal and hoping to hear an echo, SOSUS' passive sonar simply listened—intently and silently—for whatever sound a submarine or its propeller made as it moved through the water.

It all began in the spring of 1944, while the Allies were still battling German U-boats in the North Atlantic. A geophysicist working at Woods Hole Oceanographic Institution, Maurice Ewing, and his graduate student J. Lamar Worzel, sailed aboard the research vessel USS *Saluda* to the Bahamian island of Eleuthera. Their mission was to discover a hidden sound pipeline that Ewing was convinced lay deep beneath the ocean surface.

Ewing theorized that low-frequency sound waves, which were known to travel farther with less absorption in water than higher-frequency waves, could be transmitted across great distances in the deep ocean. He deduced that several thousand feet below the ocean surface, the intense pressure and cold temperature combine to create a distinct layer of water—a whispering chamber of sorts—that traps and focuses sound. Any sound that descended into what Ewing called the "deep sound channel" would travel horizontally for hundreds or even thousands of miles without diffusion or distortion, as if inside a sound pipeline.

Ewing's hypothesis was based on the first principle of underwater sound that Balcomb learned in Fleet Sonar School: "Sound is lazy." Meaning, sound waves always refract toward the slowest sound layer in the water column. Since sound accelerates in warmer water, it refracts away from the heated surface layer toward the slower, colder water below. Eventually, at approximately 3,000 feet, the increasing pressure at depth compresses and speeds the sound up again, refracting it upward toward the slower, lower-pressure water near the surface. Ewing hypothesized that the deep sound channel would attract and trap "lazy" sound waves into this deep ocean layer, and then transmit the sound signal horizontally through this sound channel, more or less indefinitely.

To test this theory, Ewing directed his escort vessel, the destroyer USS *Buckley*, to drop four-pound bombs timed to detonate 3,000 feet below the surface—explosives being the high-decibel, low-frequency sound source of choice for Ewing and his generation of acoustic experimenters. Detonating explosives at deep-sea pressures of 8,000 pounds per square inch was considered impossible by most physicists. But Worzel, the inventive engineer in their partnership, packed the explosives into automobile inner tubes and jury-rigged a detonator using paper caps from toy pistols.

Ewing suspended an underwater microphone, called a hydrophone, over the bow of the *Saluda* to a depth of 3,000 feet. After each detonation, the *Buckley* moved ten miles farther into the Atlantic and detonated another bomb. When the *Buckley* ran out of bombs, 900 miles out to sea, Ewing could still hear the explosions clearly from the *Saluda*, with almost no signal loss! He happily set sail for Woods Hole to announce that his hypothesis of a deep sound channel was now fact.[3]

To measure the outer limits of sound propagation in the deep sound channel, Ewing asked a favor of a colleague who was flying to Dakar, West Africa, aboard a military transport plane. Ewing gave his colleague a suitcase full of time-delayed hand grenades and asked him to drop one from the plane every hour during the Atlantic crossing. (As it happened, the only way to drop bombs from a transport plane was by flushing them down the toilet.) When the last grenade was flushed into the sky and detonated, as intended, in the deep ocean just off the coast of Africa, Ewing could hear the explosion from aboard the *Saluda*, 6,000 miles to the west in the Bahamas. He'd proven that the deep sound channel could transmit sound across an entire ocean basin, even across the underwater mid-Atlantic mountain range. (In 1960 Ewing replicated this experiment across *two* oceans by dropping depth charges off Perth, Australia, and recording the explosion four hours later and 12,000 miles to the west in Bermuda.)

Ewing's ambition was to use the deep sound channel (which he renamed the sound fixing and ranging, or SOFAR, channel) to triangulate the location of a downed pilot in the open ocean.[4] Ewing's pilot rescue system was successfully built and deployed briefly in the Pacific after the war, but the game-changing impact of the deep sound channel was on long-range submarine detection.

In 1949 Ewing and Worzel set up the first demonstration SOSUS listening station, a deep-water hydrophone five miles offshore from Bermuda. Connected to the shore by 25,000 feet of armored cable, their hydrophone could detect and track a snorkeling diesel sub at 500 miles.

Beginning in 1951, the Office of Naval Research recruited both academic and private sector partners to construct the initial SOSUS network throughout the Caribbean, code-named Project Caesar. Woods Hole researchers surveyed the ocean bottom and selected the optimal locations to anchor the hydrophone arrays, while American Telephone and Telegraph (AT&T) lay telephone cable connecting the hydrophones to the shore-based Navy listening stations.

In 1954 the Navy launched Project Jezebel to wiretap the entire Eastern Seaboard. The Massachusetts Institute of Technology, Columbia University, and Bell Labs installed SOSUS arrays of 40 high-fidelity hydrophones—each 1,000 feet wide—across the deep sea floor and connected by cable to shore-based listening stations in Cape Hatteras, Delaware, Nantucket, Newfoundland, Nova Scotia, and Iceland.

SOSUS was fully operational in the Atlantic by 1955, and in 1960 it tracked the first US submarine armed with a nuclear missile, the *George Washington*, as it made its maiden voyage across the Atlantic. Two years later, during the Cuban Missile Crisis, SOSUS picked up four Soviet Foxtrot submarines as they passed through the United Kingdom–Iceland gap and tracked them to within 100 miles of the coast of Florida, where two US destroyers forced the subs to the surface.

In the 1960s, the Navy expanded the SOSUS network to the Pacific, building listening stations that stretched from Alaska and Vancouver Island to Washington, Oregon, and California, with forward stations in Hawaii and Midway Island.

By the end of the 1960s, when Ken Balcomb was assigned as Oceanographic Officer to his first SOSUS station in the Pacific Northwest, the Navy had installed a multi-ocean burglar alarm system manned by 2,200 personnel and connected by 30,000 miles of telephone cable to centralized control stations in Norfolk and Pearl Harbor. With trip wires at every conceivable choke point heading in and out of the Pacific and Atlantic, the US Navy could track every Soviet submarine at sea, from nuclear-powered, nuclear-armed "boomers" to diesel-engine attack subs. Most remarkable of all, the Navy had managed to keep this massive construction and installation project a secret.

1969
Pacific Beach SOSUS Station, Olympic Peninsula, Washington

The Pacific Beach SOSUS station was housed inside a windowless concrete bunker at a secured coastal base. Hydrophone feeds from across the North Pacific were broadcast from speakers in the main listening room, which was the size of a large basketball gymnasium. A hundred men stood beside row upon row of sound-analyzer consoles where a hot stylus burned black and gray images onto rolls of heat-sensitive paper.[5]

The first thing that hit Balcomb when he came through the cipher-locked double doors to begin his shift each morning was the smell of ozone and burning carbon. No matter how much air-conditioning and filtering were deployed, a haze of fine carbon dust still hung in the air, glinting in the bright fluorescent lights.

The low-frequency sound analyzer that generated the audiograms of the Soviet submarines was the brainchild of Bell Laboratories. Based on the human voiceprints Bell had developed for its telephone business, the sound analyzer created a visual graph of the low-frequency signals transmitted from SOSUS hydrophones anchored hundreds of miles offshore. The sound sources, such as engine noise from Soviet submarines, originated thousands of miles farther offshore, transmitted to the hydrophones via the deep sound channel.

Lieutenant Balcomb managed the station's sonar technicians and worked with neighboring SOSUS stations to track the Soviet fleet across the wide Pacific basin. He assessed the incoming audiograms and audiotapes in search of a target. It was more art than science, relying on interpretive skills he honed over thousands of hours of analysis.

Balcomb's task was to identify the sound signature of Soviet submarines based on the low-frequency noise and vibration from their turbines. The Soviets' Delta-class submarines were nicknamed boomers because they were 500 feet long and armed with nuclear ballistic missiles. With their nuclear-powered steam turbines, the Deltas could stay submerged for months at a time, rendering them invisible to radar, aircraft, and satellites. But their turbines were much noisier than American boomers, making them relatively easy to track through the deep sound channel using SOSUS hydrophones. The diesel-powered "hunter-killer" attack subs were less than half the size of boomers, and armed with torpedoes rather than missiles. They were quieter and harder to track acoustically, except when charging their batteries.[6]

There were a host of other, more subtle sounds emanating from submarines that SOSUS operators like Balcomb became expert at detecting: noise from propeller shafts, gears, pumps, electric motors, hull vibration—even the sound of water flowing past the submarine hull. Taken together, these sounds comprised an acoustic signature as individual as a human fingerprint. SOSUS operators were constantly compiling and updating a database of sound signatures for Soviet submarines—not just by class and type, but for individual submarines within each class. As successive generations of Soviet subs gradually became quieter, the US Navy continually improved its signal processing software to maintain its acoustic advantage.

SOSUS signal processing in the late sixties was crude compared to the supercomputers deployed in the seventies and eighties. But they were good enough—with the help of protractors, slide rules, and Balcomb's HP-65 hand calculator—to fix a sub's position within a few miles. Close enough for Pacific Command to dispatch a plane from a carrier deck or a Navy airfield to sprinkle the area with short- to medium-range sonobuoys. These floating minitransmitters deployed both active and passive sonar to get a better fix on the sub's location and bearing.

Once the target was positively located and identified, it was simply a matter of "delousing" the pest. If it was a boomer carrying ballistic missiles, Pacific Command would assign a US hunter-killer sub to tail it—ideally, without being detected. If the boomer were ever to flush its missile chambers and begin its launch sequence, the hunter-killer sub would be in position to take it out before its missiles launched.

Of course, the Soviets assumed their boomers were being tailed, as did their American counterparts. And boomers were well aware of their vulnerability to the smaller, torpedo-armed attack subs. It was all a part of the elaborate cat-and-mouse game that the two antagonists played in deadly earnest throughout the Cold War. But the Soviet sub commanders *didn't* know that the deck was stacked against them—by SOSUS. Within days or even hours of leaving their home port in Vladivostok, they were tagged, sorted, and tracked for the duration of their tour.[7]

The biggest challenge, from Balcomb's end of the acoustic telescope, was sorting out the submarine sound signatures from the clutter of other sound signals in the deep sound channel.

Back in 1953, Jacques-Yves Cousteau wrote a bestselling book, *The Silent World*, which he then made into an Academy Award–winning documentary.[8] The underwater photography of the previously opaque oceans certainly *appeared* eerily quiet. But as soon as SOSUS operators began listening in on the deep sound channel, they discovered that the oceans are anything but silent.

The sound channel funneled a symphony of low-frequency sound waves: from seismic activity such as oil exploration, undersea earthquakes, and volcano eruptions; surface weather patterns including lightning strikes, thunderstorms, and typhoons; as well as the everyday drone of commercial shipping and recreational boating.

The most perplexing sound signals came from "biologicals," which was the Navy's label for any sound it couldn't identify as man-made or weather related. The croaks, hisses, moans, groans, clicks, snaps, crackles, and pops heard through the sound channel were presumed to emanate from marine life, but when SOSUS first went on line in the 1950s, no one could tell which animals were making which sounds—some of which sounded like submarine noise. To decode the biological cacophony in the sound channel, the Office of Naval Research turned to a marine biologist–engineer team at Woods Hole Oceanographic Institution: William Schevill and Bill Watkins.

Schevill had worked for the Navy in antisubmarine acoustics during the war. In peacetime he became curator of the Museum of Comparative Zoology at Harvard University, where he taught in the biology department. Bill Watkins knew nothing about marine mammals when he came to Woods Hole to help Schevill compile the Navy's catalogue of underwater biological sounds in the 1950s. But he was already an accomplished linguist, having learned 30 African languages growing up in French Guinea, West Africa, where his missionary father translated the King James Bible into local dialects.

Watkins and Schevill began their project with a blank slate. The personal journals of mariners and whalers had described the moaning of large baleen whales they heard through the hulls of their ships. But no one had ever figured out how to listen to specific marine life underwater and identify the source. Watkins and Schevill decided to record from small boats for optimal maneuverability and to keep a low acoustic profile in the water. Watkins invented compact underwater microphones using a novel combination of salt crystals and refined castor oil. Then he built customized "suitcase amplifiers" out of solid-state transistors, and adapted a tape recorder from a hand-crank phonograph drive.

Schevill's challenge was how to match the sounds that Watkins recorded to their biological source. His zoology museum at Harvard consisted mostly of scavenged bones and skeletons. Schevill couldn't visually identify most of the marine mammals or other marine life in the ocean. So he devised a brutally efficient deductive process for classifying bioacoustic sounds: when Watkins' hydrophones picked up a biological sound, they'd maneuver their small boat close enough to confirm the source. Then they'd capture and kill the animal, skin it down to its bones, and ship the skeleton back to the zoology museum. When the collected specimen matched a skeleton at the museum, they would fill in the name of the species alongside the recording log.

They followed the same protocol with fish and shellfish, some of which turned out to be surprisingly vocal. They recorded and identified choruses of fish and colonies of snapping shrimp. Some fish produce sound by rubbing their skeletal parts together, in the same fashion as a cricket rubs its wings. Others use powerful "sonic muscles" in their bladder to make noise, a process called drumming. Snapping shrimp produce a loud popping sound by crushing air bubbles between their claws, like kids popping bubble wrap.

Their decades-long acoustic safari took Schevill and Watkins across the globe, from the South Pacific to Japan, from the South Atlantic to the Arctic Circle. They even received clearance to use SOSUS surveillance stations to extend their census. At the first demonstration SOSUS station in Bermuda, they recorded the melodious moaning of humpback whales as they migrated past. Watkins and Schevill would continue their collaboration for 40 years, compiling a database of 20,000 calls from more than 70 marine mammal species. In 1962 they published a phonograph recording, "Whales and Porpoise Voices," featuring the first underwater recordings of 18 species of marine mammals. But they weren't able to publish their research, which all remained classified. For decades, the only end-users of their extensive database of bioacoustic recordings and data were SOSUS officers like Balcomb.[9]

For Balcomb, the Watkins-Schevill catalogue of biological sound signatures was a seminal part of his education as a whale researcher. What made the biggest impression on Balcomb, when he listened to their recordings and listened live through the SOSUS hydrophones, were the low-frequency calls of the solo journeyers among the great whales: the blue whale, the sei, and the fin whale. These were the species that foraged and migrated alone along 1,000-mile trajectories across whole hemispheres. Like every other animal on earth, they had to communicate with others of their species, if only to mate. It was clear that millions of years before Ewing was detonating bombs in the deep sound channel, the ocean's biggest whales had discovered and deployed the same sonic bandwidth to communicate across whole ocean basins. He had no idea *what* they were saying in their encrypted code of moans and groans. But they were clearly engaged in conversation across the sound channel's party line.[10]

Balcomb accepted the cloak of secrecy surrounding SOSUS as part of his job description. The submarine arm of the Navy was known as "the Silent Service" because of the extreme secrecy it demanded of all submariners. So it made sense to him that antisubmarine warfare would also operate in a black box. The code of silence bound him closer to his fellow sonar operators, but it created a lot of blank spaces in his marriage to his second wife, Julie.

Balcomb's closest companion in those years was his long-haired Australian sheepdog, Wizerella. On weekends, they would walk the beach in search of specimens, with Wizerella running up ahead of him to root out anything that stank. Over the course of his tour at Pacific Beach, they beachcombed all 300 miles of the Washington coastline. In 1970 he found a Cuvier's beaked whale that had stranded about three months earlier, to guess from the state of the carcass that was lodged under a layer of driftwood logs. Even Wizerella was disgusted by the stench—*after* she had rolled around in its rotted remains. The head measured six feet in diameter, and it was a Herculean task getting it off the beach. That skull remained Balcomb's proudest trophy for years.

By 1972, his five-year commitment to the Navy was up. So, apparently, was his marriage. Julie wanted to return to Key West. Balcomb wanted to study marine biology in grad school in Santa Cruz. They agreed that their marriage had run its course. If nobody's feelings got hurt, it was probably because there weren't deep feelings involved on either side. Balcomb sold his only worldly asset, his Mercedes Gullwing, for $9,000 to pay for the divorce. Truth be told, it was harder for him to part with that car than with Julie.

At the age of 30, Balcomb was no longer a brokenhearted boy in flight from a busted home. A seasoned Cold War veteran, he was ready to embark on his research career. He had to admit that his stepfather had been right. Military service had made a man of him.

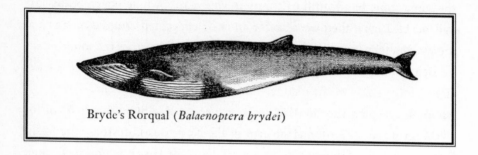

Bryde's Rorqual (*Balaenoptera brydei*)

6

The Stranding Goes Viral

Decades after he left the Navy, Balcomb was still a sharp observer of warships. Sitting at his cluttered desk back at the beach house, Balcomb scanned the videotape he'd shot of the destroyer from the seaplane that afternoon. He squinted into the camcorder's playback screen and hit the freeze-frame button when the destroyer's bow came into view.

"I can't make out the hull number," he mumbled to himself. Then, to Ellifrit, who was shut inside the darkroom next door, he shouted, "What's holding things up in there?"

Balcomb was normally patient with his young assistant. But stumbling onto the destroyer in the canyon had rattled him. If he could identify the ship, he reasoned, maybe he could piece together what the Navy was up to. He wanted to know what was going on—and he didn't want to know. The Navy was the closest thing he'd had to family, and it still stirred up feelings of attachment. He didn't get all misty eyed about it, but it was a bloodline that ran deep.

Ellifrit emerged from the darkroom with a handful of wet enlargements and tacked them onto the corkboard behind the desktop computer. "We'll see if you did any better with the stills," he said.

Balcomb could barely make out the destroyer's hull number on the enlargements. "DD-970," he read aloud, typing the hull number into the search panel on the *Jane's Naval Weapons Systems* website, the go-to database of all things military. "It's the USS *Caron*—a Spruance-class destroyer. What's a Spru-can doing down here?"

Ellifrit peered over Balcomb's shoulder as he scrolled through the catalogue of the *Caron's* standard armaments: Mark 29 missile batteries, ASROC antisubmarine rocket launcher, Tomahawk cruise missiles, Phalanx anti-aircraft guns, Aegis air and surface radar.

"Those choppers parked on the back deck," said Balcomb, "are Sikorsky Seahawks—antisubmarine warfare birds." Balcomb scanned down to "Sensors and Surveillance" and found the sonar transmitter: AN/SQS-53, aka 53-Charlie. "State-of-the-art in hull-mounted active sonar," he explained. "Search, detection, and tracking, all tied into ship-based computerized processing."

"Meaning?"

"Meaning someone's playing war games in Great Bahama Canyon."

Balcomb wanted the room to himself, so he told Dave to get himself some dinner. If the Navy had a carrier group in the Bahamas, Balcomb figured that Gisiner would be working late. He was.

"Gisiner, here."

"Bob, this is Ken. Good news. We found a great specimen today. A Blainville's, fresh enough to eat. And I spotted another one from the air that I'm going to collect in the morning."

"Good. You have the Blainville's on ice?"

Balcomb explained that the head was in a deep freeze, and that a complete set of organ sections was securely fixed in formalin. Everything would keep until the Bahamians cleared them for transport to the States.

Gisiner updated him on the team he'd been pulling together from the Southeast Regional Office of Fisheries, from the Smithsonian, and from Woods Hole. He'd tracked down Darlene Ketten in California.

"Ketten will be arriving in Freeport on the red-eye the morning after next," Gisiner told him. "Can you meet her flight?"

"No problem," replied Balcomb, searching for a graceful segue to the subject foremost in his mind. As usual, he opted for the direct approach. "What are you hearing from the fleet?" he asked.

"Nothing yet. ONR has a research ship on the ocean side of the islands, working with sonobuoys. But no word from the fleet about anything going on in the area."

"I saw something interesting when I was up in the search plane today." Balcomb waited a moment for Gisiner to respond. He didn't. "A destroyer. One of ours."

"Are you sure?"

"I've got a photo of the hull number. I can fax it to you. You know . . . a destroyer never sails solo away from port. It runs escort for a carrier group."

"You're way above my pay grade," said Gisiner with a dry laugh. "I'm just a humble scientist."

Gisiner knew Balcomb had done a couple of Navy tours, one before and one after grad school. Fresh off his first tour, with his crew cut and yessir-ing the professors, Balcomb stuck out like G.I. Joe among the long-haired grad students back in the early 1970s. But he'd remained vague about the details of his Navy assignments, which made him something of a mystery man and a source of rumors. Now Gisiner was the one inside the Navy, and Balcomb was on the outside trying to peer in.

The Office of Naval Research was staffed largely by civilian scientists who briefed the fleet on anything science related, including marine biology. And as head of the marine mammal division, Gisiner would be ONR's point person on any internal investigation of an atypical mass stranding.

Balcomb thought Gisiner knew more than he was willing to share. "You'd think the fleet would know if it had a carrier group in the Bahamas," Balcomb said, "and what it was doing here."

"I'm focused on getting the best people on the ground for you," said Gisiner. "So why don't you stay focused on collecting specimens?"

"And don't forget about the tapes from AUTEC, okay?" Balcomb added. "We need to find out what's on them."

Balcomb was about to say more. But Gisiner clearly wanted the conversation to be over. So it was.

After he got off the phone with Gisiner, Ken joined Diane on the beach-side deck of the house. It was their favorite spot, and tonight it felt like a safe port in the storm of the past two days. But even sitting there with her, watching the half-moon rise over the Abaco pine forest, his mind was stuck on the destroyer. If the *Caron* had been operating in the channel three nights ago would anyone on board have seen the moonlight glint off the whales' dorsal fins when they surfaced? Probably not. The Navy liked to conduct nighttime exercises to test the crew's ability to operate in the dark, both above and below the water. But they could only see what they were looking for, and a destroyer wouldn't be hunting for whales.

"It's a good thing we had the Earthlings over at Cross Harbor today," said Diane, "or we'd never have gotten that Blainville's onto dry land. And they were great sports about cleaning up the beach when we were done."

Ken nodded his agreement but didn't say anything. After a pause, he explained that he had to get up and out early the next morning to retrieve the whale from Water Cay that he'd spotted from the plane. He planned to take Dave with him in one of the boats, if she could stay behind and cover the Earthlings. He told her about Ketten coming into Grand Bahama, and his plan to fly over and meet her there. But he didn't mention the destroyer. Not yet. He wanted to figure out what the Navy was up to first. Right now all he had were questions.

Diane knew he had served in the Navy. But that was a storyline out of his distant past, long before they'd met. She would have been in kindergarten when he entered flight school. To a schoolgirl in the Bahamas, Vietnam and the Cold War were a distant galaxy. He'd never told her what he did in the Navy, and she'd never asked any probing questions. For a quarter century, he'd been able to keep his undercover work for the Navy under wraps and out of sight. Until the USS *Caron* showed up in the canyon.

Six months after his divorce from Julie, Ken met his future third wife, Camille, at UC Santa Cruz. They were both studying marine biology, she as an undergraduate and he as a graduate student. After serving as a naval officer with 100 men under his command, Ken found it hard to be back in school as a student. He was 30 years old, and most of the other grad students were still in their early twenties. After two restless semesters, he heard from a

Navy buddy about an assignment working undercover in Japan, and decided to reenlist.

Officially, there were no American military advisors on Japanese naval bases, so Balcomb's mission was sensitive. He worked in Top Secret Special Category, tutoring the Japanese navy at Yokosuka on how to use the latest generation of American listening equipment to track Soviet submarines heading out of Vladivostok. Balcomb's "cover" was posing as a bearded American biologist doing field research—which, in fact, he was, on his own time, touring Japanese whaling stations in search of Baird's beaked whale specimens for his PhD thesis. A year into his tour, Camille joined him in Japan, where they were married. She fit in perfectly as Balcomb's wife and fellow researcher, since she was studying the dolphin drive fishery in Taiji for her master's thesis.

Ken's second Navy tour ended in 1975, and he and Camille resettled in Puget Sound. When he launched his orca survey that first summer back, Camille proved to be a stalwart research partner. But then the *Regina Maris* appeared on the horizon, and his marriage was soon on the rocks.

The *Regina Maris* was a floating dream of a boat, a tall ship straight out of an Errol Flynn swashbuckler: a three-masted, 144-foot barkentine driven by 16 canvas sails and a square-rigged foremast. George Nichols, Jr., a retired medical researcher from Harvard and a great-grandson of J. P. Morgan, had retrofitted the *Regina* as the flagship of his newly launched Ocean Research and Education Society. The *Regina's* mission was to track and study Atlantic humpback whales while instructing college students in marine biology. Nichols hired Ken as his chief scientist and paid him $1 a day. From Ken's point of view, it was a great deal. He'd saved up $10,000 from his Navy tours, and the *Regina* provided him free room and board and the chance to survey whales from the deck of the most fabulous ship under sail on any sea.

Camille was less enchanted by life aboard the *Regina*. The wooden deck boards leaked when it rained, and she soon grew weary of sleeping in dank, mildewed sheets. During their maiden voyage in the North Atlantic, the *Regina* sailed headlong into a winter hurricane and almost sank. When they finally made port, Camille jumped ship, and their marriage.

After the exit of the third Mrs. Balcomb, Ken wasn't exactly bereft of female companionship. The first generation of whale researchers in the fifties and sixties were almost all men. But by the late 1970s, there were more women than men studying marine biology. Every winter, another crew of mostly female grad students would board the *Regina Maris* at Gloucester, Massachusetts, for a Semester at Sea program. Ken taught them marine mammal biology and oceanography, currents and tides, and all things cetacean.

Ken enjoyed the seasonal ebb and flow of "boat girls." It was the 1970s, after all, and he'd come of age a decade before the sexual revolution and had spent the late 1960s in the all-male Navy. But for Ken, the main attraction of life on the *Regina* were the whales. For 12 winters aboard the *Regina*, he tracked the humpback whale migration from the coast of Newfoundland to the Silver Banks of the Dominican Republic, working with researchers at the College of the Atlantic to compile a photo catalogue of humpbacks in the North Atlantic. The highlight of the *Regina*'s winter tour was the Caribbean leg, where the beaked whales lived. From Bermuda to the Bahamas to the Silver Banks, he could count on six or seven sightings of various species—which for beaked whales was a lot of sightings.

By the time Diane sailed into his life, Ken was 41 years old with three failed marriages in his wake. A loner since childhood, Ken had never shown much aptitude for the shared decision making and compromises that come with marriage. He'd always enjoyed the company of women, but until he met Diane, his only true romance had been with the sea and with the whales.

The first thing Ken noticed about Diane when she came aboard the *Regina* was her Bahamian accent. A second-generation islander of British and Canadian extraction, Diane grew up in Nassau, went away to boarding school in Canada, and then returned to the islands because she couldn't imagine living anywhere else. After spending her teenaged summers working aboard chartered catamarans and renting ski boats to vacationers off Nassau, Diane knew she didn't want to babysit tourists all her life. While studying marine biology as an undergraduate in Florida, the best career path she could envision was training dolphins to perform in marine parks. But when she met Ken aboard the *Regina*, a wide world opened up to her. In Ken she saw a marine biologist whose field station was as boundless as the seas. There wasn't anything in the ocean he couldn't name and explain. And he was totally comfortable on the water, even in the middle of a storm. That, to Diane, seemed like the ultimate freedom.

Ken was almost 20 years older than Diane. But when they met, he felt like a teenager again. He was swept away by this Caribbean island girl who seemed altogether at home tracking humpbacks through the Arctic ice north of Labrador. Whenever he went above deck, he found Diane—who'd grown up wearing a bathing suit and flip-flops year-round—wrapped in an over-sized down parka, laughing into the headwinds like a beautiful bowsprit sculpture. She knew how to sail, how to tie knots, how to spot barely visible whales surfacing in the dark gray ocean. He was convinced that she must be part mermaid.

When Diane returned to school at the Florida Institute of Technology, Ken's life aboard the *Regina* faded to black and white. He courted her from afar with letters he illustrated with drawings and photos of whales he'd sighted from the deck of the *Regina*. After her months at sea, Diane felt trapped inside the lecture halls and labs. She could barely breathe. And the men who flirted with her in class—the ones she used to date and sail with—now seemed like clueless boys.

The week after she graduated with a degree in environmental science in the spring of 1989, Diane showed up at Smugglers Cove to volunteer on Ken's orca survey. By the end of the summer, Diane and Ken were deeply in love and plotting their next move together.

Diane wanted to take him home with her for Christmas in the Bahamas, but Ken was leery of meeting her parents. What would they think of their daughter showing up with a middle-aged American trailing three scuttled marriages, an itinerant whale-chaser with no fixed address and no visible means of support? To his shock and delight, they embraced him as one of the family. So did Diane's five siblings.

That winter, after Ken resigned from the *Regina Maris*, he and Diane toured the Bahamas in an inflatable Zodiac, camping on the beach or sleeping in the boat. They interviewed fishermen about local marine mammals and distributed sighting report flyers across the smaller cays. When they heard reports of "weird-looking dolphins with horns growing out of their heads," Ken figured they must be referring to the stalked barnacles on Blainville's beaked whales. Diane was well schooled in the local marine wildlife.

She knew all about the dolphins and the sailfish and every creature on the reef. But she'd never seen or even heard of beaked whales in the Bahamas. The afternoon they had a three-hour encounter near Abaco with a group of Blainville's whales that circled their boat, they knew they had found their research home.

Beaked whales aren't the most charismatic of marine mammals. They're not nearly as sleek and beautiful as the black-on-white orcas. They can't compete with the spectacle of a breaching humpback or a spyhopping gray whale. In truth, beaked whales do look a lot like "weird-looking dolphins," on the rare occasions when they show themselves. But for marine mammal researchers in 1990, beaked whales were a virtual tabula rasa. Other than the large Baird's species of the North Pacific, beaked whales were too small and elusive to interest whalers, so no one had ever bothered researching their behavior. The academic study of beaked whales was essentially a "dead" science, based on skeletal remains reconstructed by museum-based paleontologists and a few obsessive beachcombers such as Balcomb. Only one population of Atlantic beaked whales had ever been studied systematically—the northern bottlenose whales of Nova Scotia.[1] No one had ever surveyed the beaked whales in the Bahamas.

Ken and Diane launched the Bahamas Marine Mammal Survey in 1991. Even for most field researchers, it would have been tedious work: waiting and watching the water's surface for hours at a time, holding camera and field notes at the ready for a fleeting glimpse of a dorsal fin or fluke. But for Ken and Diane, it was a custom fit. They shared the requisite combination of patience, keen observational skills, and a bottomless appreciation for the exquisite ecology of the Bahamas. And they never tired of each other's quiet company on the water. It's not an accident that so many marine mammal field researchers are husband-wife teams, and often childless. Ken and Diane became a hand-in-glove research couple, and the beaked whales became the object of their passionate, tireless attention. Over time, Ken and Diane learned subtle ways to enter the whales' domain without scaring them off. By trailing along behind the boat with a mask and snorkel, Diane could spot the whales as they prepared to surface. Meanwhile, Ken built customized underwater microphones to gather audio cues of the whales' movements.

In 1994 Ken proposed to Diane. They were married that summer on the

beach in Snug Harbor on San Juan Island, and again for good measure in the
Bahamas that fall.

By the winter of 2000, ten years into their survey, Ken and Diane had catalogued and studied the entire population of marine mammals in the northern
Bahamas, including 150 Blainville's, Cuvier's, and Gervais' beaked whales in
residence. It was always a scramble to find enough funding to keep the boats
on the water and film in their cameras. During the lean times, they ran bird-
watching expeditions and eco-tours to pay the bills. Ken had finally found
his true love and an equal partner in his life's work. For the first time, he felt
at home and at peace.

DAY 3: MARCH 17, 2000

Early the next morning, Balcomb and Ellifrit set off on the 65-mile trip to
Water Cay in one of their inflatable boats, hoping that the carcass Balcomb
had spotted from the air would still be salvageable. Three hours later, they
anchored the boat 20 feet from shore and waded through the shallows to
the beach. What was left of the whale was lying just out of the water on
the sand.

It didn't look like a very promising specimen. Sharks had ravaged the
Cuvier's, taking all of its tail and large chunks of its trunk and head meat.
Balcomb took some measurements and calculated that it would have been a
four-ton whale before the sharks hit it. While taking a skin sample for DNA,
he realized they'd caught a lucky break.

"It's totally exsanguinated," he said to Ellifrit. "Thanks to the sharks." Ordinarily, the blood in the whale's tissue and blubber becomes rancid as soon
as the carcass is exposed to air. But because of the shark attack, this whale had
completely bled out before it died, leaving its tissue and organs remarkably
fresh. Best of all, its braincase was still intact!

With the sun approaching its apex, Balcomb was in a hurry to get the
head off the carcass and into a freezer. When he made his first cut, some fluid
seeped out of the whale and trickled down to the water. Within minutes, two
tiger sharks had appeared offshore. Balcomb did his best to ignore them while
Ellifrit stood guard in case a more aggressive bull shark showed up.

Ten minutes later, the head fell away from the trunk. "Okay, we've got it," Balcomb said. "Let's get this into the boat."

Only then did it dawn on them that the tide had receded. The boat, which weighed about 2,500 pounds with its engine, would run aground if they tried to bring it closer to shore in the shallow water. Then they'd be stuck until the next tide, and the head would be exposed to the elements for another five hours. They had no choice but to muscle the head through the shallows—which were now aswarm with sharks—and lift it into the boat.

The head weighed close to 300 pounds, and was so slippery with slime that they could barely grab hold of it. After a few practice lifts, they hoisted it to hip height and waded into the water. Floating the head out to the boat would have been relatively easy. But lowering the oozing specimen below the waterline wasn't an option. Not if they hoped to get it past the sharks. Balcomb eyeballed the distance to the inflatable—only about 15 feet, now that the tide had receded—and made a quick count of the half dozen sharks swirling in the shallows. While he tried to calculate their odds, the head grew heavier in their arms. There was nothing to do but make a go for it. If things got out of control, he figured they could always chuck the head and run back to shore.

After exchanging a curt nod, they let loose a wild war cry and thrashed through the water toward the boat. They managed to keep the head above the water, but two of the sharks darted in to grab at bits of flesh that splattered into the shallows.

"On two!" Balcomb shouted as they drew close to the boat. "One . . ." They didn't wait for two. With a heave, they rolled the head above the gunwale and into the boat. Then they dove in after it.

They both looked down instinctively to confirm that their feet and legs were intact. All clear. But Balcomb knew they weren't out of danger yet. Once—during a walrus count off Round Island, Alaska—he'd been inside another inflatable boat that was reduced to flaps by an angry bull walrus when it attacked the boat and punctured all the forward tubes. He shivered at the thought of what would happen if the sharks started to bite into this one. Rolling to his knees, he lowered the engine into the water and yanked it to life.

The boat roared away from shore, pointing dead ahead for Les Adderly's bait freezer.

10:00 P.M.
Sandy Point

Balcomb had to fly to Grand Bahama in the morning to meet Ketten's flight, and he desperately needed some shut-eye. But first he wanted to check online to see if anything had been posted about the stranding.

Traditionally, cetacean field researchers were scattered as far and wide as the animals they studied, tracking belugas and bowheads in the Arctic, river dolphins in the Amazon and Southeast Asia, right whales on the Atlantic Coast, grays on the Pacific Seaboard, vaquita porpoises in the Sea of Cortez, and humpbacks migrating toward both poles in search of krill. Other researchers were based in academic labs on every continent. At one- or two-year intervals, those who could afford to travel would meet at international conferences to share their research and whale tales. Otherwise they toiled in far-flung isolation, communicating mostly through articles published in academic journals.

The internet changed all that.

In 1993 the University of Victoria in Canada established the first international Listserv for researchers and wildlife managers working with marine mammals. Overnight, decades of pent-up conversation bubbled over online. The marine mammal Listserv, known as MARMAM, became the town square for posting research data, conferences and speaker announcements, grant queries, job notices, rumors, and gossip. Heated debates broke out from time to time, but, for the most part, MARMAM was a forum for informed conversation among hundreds, and then thousands, of researchers, bureaucrats, and animal protection activists around the globe.

On the night of March 17, Balcomb logged on to MARMAM to find that neither the Bahamian nor US Fisheries departments had posted anything about the stranding. No scientists anywhere had. Balcomb stared at the screen. He pulled the prints of the USS *Caron* out of his desk drawer. He stared at photos of the Blainville's, its severed head matted with flies. Then he started to type.

Post to: MARMAM Newsgroup

"Just the facts, ma'am," Balcomb intoned quietly. "No need to editorialize." He continued typing.

From: Ken Balcomb, Bahamas Marine Mammal Survey, Abaco, Bahamas
Subject: Whale Strandings in the Bahamas Islands
Date: 17 March 2000

> The following is a summary of whale and dolphin stranding events in the northern Bahama Islands during March 15, 2000. We were directly involved in assisting with rescue or necropsy during nine of these events and can document them in some detail.

He methodically detailed the location and time and species of each of the reported strandings based on the logs they had compiled over the past three days. Then he added a final paragraph:

> It is worth noting that we have been gathering reports of marine mammal strandings, and have been conducting field studies of living marine mammals in the Bahama Islands since 1991; the stranding rate of cetaceans is typically on the order of one or two reported per year in the entire island chain. Beaked whale strandings are particularly rare.

When he was finished, Balcomb reread his entry twice. He took a breath and exhaled. Then he clicked the Submit Post button.

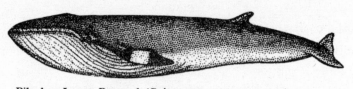

Piked or Lesser Rorqual (*Balaenoptera acutorostrata*)

7

"Unusual Mortality Event"

A whale on a beach has always been a mystery that cried out for explanation. Ancient coastal dwellers from the South Pacific to the Bering Sea interpreted strandings as a bounty of food and other blessings sent to them by their gods. In the fourth century BC, Aristotle remarked on the conundrum of beached whales in his *Historia Animalium*: "It is not known for what reason they run themselves aground on dry land; at all events it is said that they do so at times, and for no obvious reason."

Millennia later, at the end of the twentieth century, marine scientists were still pondering the question Why do whales strand? And why do they sometimes strand en masse?

Many theories had been advanced, none of them definitive. Since toothed whales and dolphins are particularly prone to stranding, researchers looked to possible sources of biosonar navigational errors. One hypothesis suggested that echolocating whales have trouble discerning gently sloping coastlines, which would explain mass-stranding hot spots such as Ocean Beach in Tasmania and Western Australia's Geographe Bay.

Baleen whales—such as humpbacks, grays, fins, and blues—follow long migration paths and are believed to navigate by magnetically tracking iron deposits in the earth's crust. Some researchers speculate that when earthquakes rearrange the tectonic plates in the ocean floor, misaligned veins of iron ore can misdirect migrating whales into shore.

Whales that hunt close to shore are the most likely to run aground—though paradoxically, killer whales that hunt sea lions in the shallows rarely do. The strong social bonds of certain species, such as pilot whales, have led some scientists to embrace a "follow me" theory of mass strandings: pods that hunt close together, often following a lead animal, might strand when the leader is caught in a strong onshore current.

One fact is not in dispute: whales and dolphins have been stranding for as long as they've lived in the oceans. Most of them die at sea, either from old age or disease, and then wash ashore with the tide. Occasionally they strand alive, usually alone, sometimes in groups. For the vast majority of whales that strand alive, the beach is their final destination.

When Congress passed the 1972 Marine Mammal Protection Act, it assigned Fisheries the task of enforcing its provisions and determining if any laws, civil or criminal, had been violated. Any marine mammal that stranded on US shores or nearby coastlines immediately became the property of Fisheries for investigative purposes. But Congress never properly funded its marine mammal mission, and Fisheries was none too eager to embrace it—especially when fishing and marine mammal interests conflicted. Until the 1970s, the agency's central focus had been managing the country's fishing stocks for the benefit of American fishing interests. When dolphins became ensnared in tuna fishermen's nets, or when orcas competed with fishermen for Chinook salmon, it was Fisheries' job to untangle the legal and commercial threads. In the minds of many Fisheries administrators, whales would always be "fish out of water" at their agency.

But the same public that had pressed Congress to pass the Marine Mammal Protection Act was passionate about saving whales and other marine mammals. Volunteer stranding response groups quickly sprang up along

American coastlines to alert Fisheries of stranded animals. By the late 1990s, Fisheries was coordinating over 100 local groups of volunteers inside its National Stranding Response Network.

Most citizens volunteered in hopes of rescuing stranded whales from the beach. In reality, relatively few marine mammals strand alive, and most that do end up dying on the beach. In 1999 approximately 1,500 marine mammals—including whales, dolphins, porpoises, seals, sea lions, and manatees—beached on US shorelines. All but 200 of them had already died at sea, mostly from disease or old age. Of the 200 that stranded alive, some were euthanized on the beach by Fisheries officials. Most of the others soon died of exposure to the elements, or suffocated when their bodies collapsed under their own weight, or drowned when the high tide washed over their blowholes. Only five marine mammals that stranded alive that year were actually rescued from the beach and returned to the ocean.

In the case of most strandings, Fisheries' primary job was to safely dispose of the bodies. A dead whale was an ideal environment for anaerobic microorganisms and can quickly become a biohazard. Beyond containing the immediate health risks associated with active bacteria, Fisheries faced the engineering task of removing gigantic carcasses from the beach. It costs tens of thousands of dollars in manpower and heavy equipment to dismember, remove, and dispose of a single large whale.

Beyond beach cleanup, it was also Fisheries' responsibility to sort out the whys and wherefores of any "unusual mortality event," or UME, as defined by the Marine Mammal Protection Act: "a stranding that is unexpected; involves a significant die-off of any marine mammal population; and demands immediate response."

In response to a stranding it designated as "unusual," Fisheries would dispatch one of a small roster of marine mammal pathologists to the scene to investigate, perform a necropsy on-site, and recover evidence for laboratory analysis. Fisheries investigations sometimes became crime scenes whose evidence trails led to prosecutions. If, for instance, a hunter or a hooligan had used a harbor porpoise for target practice, a pathologist with the right training and equipment could compile a complete ballistics profile.

As human development increasingly encroached on marine habitats, more whales and dolphins turned up dead or dying on beaches. Many drowned after becoming entangled in fishing nets and floating plastic refuse. Fatalities from collisions with commercial ships and recreational boats increased year by year. And runoff from agriculture fertilizer created toxic, sometimes lethal, algae blooms that passed up the food chain, from zooplankton, to fish, and, finally, to whales and other marine mammals.

Despite the rise in marine mammal deaths from human activity, Fisheries had designated relatively few strandings as "unusual mortality events." From 1991, when the UME investigative program was initiated, until the Bahamas stranding in 2000, fewer than 20 events had been so classified, and most of those involved seals and dolphins. To date, Fisheries had resisted classifying any whale deaths connected to naval exercises as unusual. While the investigative pathologists were civilians working at academic research labs like Woods Hole Oceanographic Institution, those same labs and researchers were usually funded by the Office of Naval Research. The potential for conflicts of interest was ubiquitous.

The first suggestion of a possible link between naval exercises and mass whale strandings emerged in 1991 when two European researchers wrote a letter to the correspondence section of the journal *Nature* titled "Whales and the Military."[1] The authors noted that three recent mass strandings of whales in the Canary Islands in 1985, 1988, and 1989 coincided with nearby NATO naval exercises. It was such a small and speculative item—more a curiosity than a finding—that few cetologists took notice.

It wasn't until the Greek stranding in May 1996 that the wider community of marine mammal scientists seriously considered a connection between mass strandings and naval sonar exercises. On May 11, NATO naval forces began antisubmarine training exercises at the edge of the three-mile-deep Hellenic Trench in the Ionian Sea. On May 12, a dozen Cuvier's beaked whales stranded on nearby beaches. Because it was peak tourist season and many of the strandings occurred on resort beaches, local officials quickly buried most of the dead whales.

Several days later, Dr. Alexandros Frantzis, a Greek veterinarian from the Pelagos Cetacean Research Institute, exhumed and examined 11 of the whales, 9 of which were immature males. He supervised limited necropsies of the partially decayed animals. But as Frantzis explained in a paper he subsequently published in the journal *Nature*, "No ears were collected, no entire organs or histological samples were conserved because of problems related to permits, lack of facilities and means, and lack of relevant knowledge and trained specialists. In photos taken at the time, four of the whales were bleeding from the eyes."[2]

Because the stranding happened in plain sight of tourists, and because of Frantzis' independent inquiry, NATO was forced to investigate. Experts were assembled from around the world, including an ONR delegation selected by Gisiner and led by Darlene Ketten from Woods Hole. The investigators examined the full range of possible causes such as underground earthquakes, magnetic anomalies, major pollution events, and conventional military exercises. All possible causes were eliminated—*except* for the midfrequency and Low Frequency Active sonar exercises NATO had conducted in close proximity to the strandings. However, the final NATO report found no conclusive evidence of a direct causal link between the exercises and the strandings. Stating that "the adverse effect of sonar on marine mammals has been poorly studied," the NATO investigators called for further research.[3]

Like other researchers around the world, Balcomb followed the accounts on MARMAM and in scientific journals. Over the next three years, two other "unusual" strandings were reported in the presence of NATO exercises—one in the Mediterranean Sea and one in the deep ocean trench along the Canary Islands. Two other strandings occurred on or near US naval bases in the Caribbean. But no independent researchers had been able to retrieve fresh-enough specimens to establish a conclusive causal link.

Coming just a few years after the Greek stranding, Balcomb's report of a mass stranding in the Bahamas set off alarm bells at Fisheries and Navy offices up and down the East Coast. Hours after Balcomb first called Gisiner at ONR, the regional stranding coordinator at the Southeast Fisheries Science Center in Miami heard about the stranded dolphin on Powell Cay and the whales that had stranded on Grand Bahama.

The Southeast office was the first-response center for any strandings in the Caribbean, including the half dozen US naval bases on the islands. Even though the stranding occurred in Bahamian waters, it was inside Fisheries' jurisdiction, which extended 200 miles offshore. The regional stranding coordinator in Miami knew that processing the paperwork to get an investigative team on the ground would likely crawl through the Bahamian bureaucracy on "island time"—and time was the most perishable element in any stranding investigation. A more daunting hurdle would be negotiating with the US Navy—*if* the stranding turned out to involve American naval assets or exercises.

In the past few years, the Navy had obstructed investigations by Fisheries' Southeast Regional Office of strandings on and around its bases. When a whale stranded in Puerto Rico, the Navy handed over the carcass to a local veterinarian. Darlene Ketten flew down from Woods Hole to examine the head, but the vet denied her access until the specimen had decayed for a week, and then he refused to let her take the head back to the States for CT scanning. A year later, when four beaked whales stranded in the US Virgin Islands during naval exercises, the US Navy rebuffed all efforts by the Southeast Office to investigate.

The mass stranding in the Bahamas was of a different order of magnitude. It wasn't just the number of animals involved, but also the number of different species and the extended geographical area. Fisheries didn't have the money or resources to properly investigate a mass stranding across five or six islands. At least the regional office didn't. So the Miami office was only too happy to pass the whole mess up to the chain to the national stranding coordinator at Fisheries headquarters: Teri Rowles. Then it would be headquarters' investigation to manage, and it would be Rowles' job to wrestle the bears in the navy blue suits.

DAY 3: MARCH 17, 2000
National Marine Fisheries Service Headquarters, Silver Spring, Maryland

By the time the Southeast office called Teri Rowles, she'd already heard about the Bahamian strandings from Bob Gisiner at ONR. Rowles and Gisiner had agreed that there needed to be an investigation, though they deferred discussion of whether to designate it an unusual mortality event. They both wanted Darlene Ketten to lead the investigative team, which would also include someone from the Southeast Fisheries office and someone from the Smithsonian Institution in Washington. Rowles would manage the logistics and paperwork, and Gisiner agreed to cover the up-front costs. Rowles promised to do her best to find money to reimburse ONR, but it was a little bit like a secretary offering to go dutch with her boss at an expense-account restaurant. Gisiner was used to picking up the tab for stranding investigations, because he could afford to—and because he wanted to stay involved on the Navy's behalf.

To an outside observer, Fisheries and ONR might seem like unlikely investigative partners. By statute, Fisheries was charged with enforcing the Navy's compliance with marine mammal protection laws. Whenever the Navy planned to conduct exercises that might "harm or harass" marine mammals—as defined under the Marine Mammal Protection Act—the Navy was supposed to apply for permits from Fisheries. And if the Navy was involved in a marine mammal injury or death, Fisheries was supposed to investigate the incident.

But in the real world, Fisheries didn't have the budget, personnel, or expertise to properly evaluate Navy permit applications, much less to conduct investigations of mass strandings. Fisheries employed many marine biology experts at its regional offices. But ONR funded almost all the best marine acousticians, pathologists, and whale and dolphin researchers, whether they were based inside ONR, at Navy labs, or at academic research institutes across the country and around the world. The mismatch between the size of ONR's and Fisheries' research staffs was reflected in the 30–1 disparity in their annual budgets—which in turn mirrored their political muscle on Capitol Hill.

The feeding chain within the Washington, DC, ecosystem was as clearly stratified as the Bahamian coral reef. The Pentagon occupied the top of the food chain on Capitol Hill, and the Navy boasted an $84 billion budget in 1999, with 700,000 active-duty and reserve sailors and Marines, as well as 200,000 civilian employees on its payroll. Four Navy colleges and a network of research and development labs added another $9 billion to its annual allocation from Congress. By comparison, Fisheries' entire budget was a paltry $550 million, with less than $25 million supporting its Office of Protected Resources and with only five staff people devoted to marine mammals.

Rowles was a realist. She and her colleagues in Fisheries leadership recognized that they didn't have the clout to challenge the veracity of the Navy's permit applications. A few of the more legally compliant divisions of the Navy had only recently "come in under the permitting tent," as Fisheries leadership delicately described the process. If Fisheries pushed too hard for fuller compliance, it feared that the Navy would either stop applying for permits or, worse, would go to Congress for a legislative exemption from the Marine Mammal Protection Act and other laws protecting endangered species.

When faced with a mass stranding investigation that promised to be expensive and complex, both scientifically and politically, Rowles was prepared to accept whatever assistance the Navy could provide.

DAY 4: MARCH 18, 2000
Navy Office of Environmental Readiness, Alexandria, Virginia

It was Rear Admiral Larry Baucom's first day on duty as the new flag officer at N-45, the Navy Office of Environmental Readiness. (Both ONR and N-45 were staffed largely by civilians, but both offices were traditionally headed by an admiral, or "flag officer"—so called because admirals are entitled to fly a flag, most often on the hood of their staff cars.) As a one-star admiral, Baucom's posting at N-45 was the soft landing before retirement from active duty, en route to a faculty position at a naval college or a more lucrative consulting job inside one of the dozens of military contractors that vied for the chance to hire newly retired admirals.

In the course of his 30-year career, Baucom had commanded a naval flight squadron, an amphibious warfare ship, and, most recently, the nuclear-powered aircraft carrier USS *Carl Vinson* in the Pacific Fleet. He knew every aspect of naval combat operations, from the air, on land, and at sea. He knew nothing about marine mammals. But he was about to get a crash course.

His principal tutor would be Frank Stone, N-45's head civilian and liaison with the fleet on the Navy's compliance with environmental laws, from waste discharge aboard ships to marine mammal protection. Stone was a civilian administrator who had served under a half dozen admirals at N-45, and would likely outlast a half dozen more. Regardless of which admiral was rotating through the leadership, N-45 remained Stone's fiefdom, a minor principality inside the sprawling bureaucracy of the US Navy. His job was to keep the fleet looking like a responsible environmental steward of the ocean environment—especially in peacetime when the Navy was lobbying hard on Capitol Hill to preserve its funding.

Environmental compliance was a tough sell to the fleet commanders, whose DNA seemed coiled around the twin missions of national defense and defending the status quo. They tended to ignore N-45 until circumstances compelled them to do otherwise. Stone's colleagues surmised that he had survived at the operational helm of N-45 by doing just enough to keep the Navy in putative compliance with whichever environmental laws were being enforced by Fisheries at the time, without pushing the admirals beyond the limits of their tolerance.

For most fleet exercises, the permitting application involved the Navy conducting an internal Environmental Assessment, a pro forma checklist executed inside the fleet or by an outside contractor. If, in the sole judgment of the Navy, the assessment resulted in a "Finding of No Significant Impact (FOSNI)"—which was uniformly its determination—Stone processed the paperwork and forwarded a copy to Fisheries. By statute, Fisheries was responsible for reviewing the Navy's Environmental Assessment and Finding of No Significant Impact. In fact, Fisheries had never challenged the fleet's internal assessments.

Recently, Stone's primary marine mammal focus had been the North Atlantic right whales. This highly endangered species had a troublesome tendency to migrate close to the shoreline, directly in the path of shipping and other sea traffic, including naval vessels. Every time a right whale died in a collision with a Navy ship, N-45 had to work with Fisheries on an investigation and a report—as well as manage the predictably negative press attention. It became a monumental headache, and for the past year, Stone had been working with ONR and Fleet Command to figure out how to reduce collisions.

Right whales had long been losers in their encounters with humans, going back to the Basque whalers of the eleventh century. Their name derived from their unfortunate distinction of being deemed the "right" whale to hunt because they fed at the surface along the coastline; and because they floated rather than sank after being killed, right whales could easily be towed ashore for flensing. They were large and slow moving—up to 60 feet long, weighing 80 tons—which made them easy targets for harpooners. The American whaling industry almost wiped out the North Atlantic right whales by the end of the eighteenth century. Despite being the first species protected by a worldwide whaling ban in 1937, and being declared an endangered and protected species in 1973, only a few hundred North Atlantic right whales survived into the twenty-first century.

Beaked whales had also been on Frank Stone's screen lately. Ever since the mass stranding in Greece in 1996, he and Bob Gisiner had become the Navy's point men on beaked whale research. At the Society for Marine Mammalogy's biennial meeting in Maui a few months earlier, two of Stone's assistants had passed out business cards to prospective beaked whale researchers who were interested in conducting population and distribution surveys. Balcomb showed them his recent survey data, but no one called him back.

Stone was one of the first people Gisiner called as soon as Balcomb alerted him to the mass stranding. Over the next 72 hours, Gisiner and Stone were in constant communication. While Gisiner worked with Teri Rowles to get the investigative team up and running, Stone was playing phone tag with the Atlantic Fleet admirals so that he could brief the new flag officer at N-45. He was also trying to track down any Environmental Assessments that had passed through his office in the past three months.

Stone knocked on Admiral Baucom's door at 0800 hours to introduce himself to his new boss. Baucom was reading the *Early Bird*, the composite file of news clippings assembled each morning by the Armed Forces Information Service. The Judge Advocate General, or JAG, attorney assigned to N-45 stood in front of Baucom's desk while the admiral read the clips from that day's newspapers from the Bahamas and Miami.

"This whale stranding in the Bahamas," said Baucom. "Is this something I need to be concerned about?"

Stone and the Judge Advocate exchanged a Do-you-want-to-tell-him-or-should-I? look. "Yes, sir," said Stone. "I'd say that's our number one focus right now."

"Any chance this will stay a local story?"

"No, sir, I doubt it," replied his attorney.

PART TWO

ACOUSTIC STORM

No sooner does man discover intelligence than he tries to involve it in his own stupidity.

—*Jacques-Yves Cousteau*

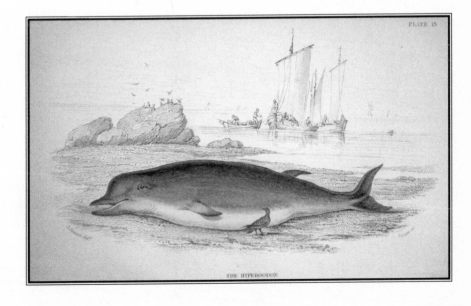

THE HYPEROODON

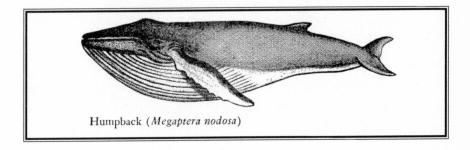

Humpback (*Megaptera nodosa*)

8

The Lone Rangers of the Environment

DAY 3: MARCH 17, 2000
Los Angeles, California

Overnight, Balcomb's posting on MARMAM pinballed throughout the whale research and conservation universe. One of the first to read it was Michael Jasny, the number two person inside the Marine Mammal Protection Project at the Natural Resources Defense Council (NRDC). An hour past midnight, he was still online trying to ferret out the details when he got a call from a marine biologist at a regional office of Fisheries who shared what he knew about the response team being dispatched to the Bahamas—including how closely the Office of Naval Research was collaborating with Fisheries on the investigation.

Ordinarily, Fisheries staff didn't fraternize with NRDC, whose attorneys kept tabs on regulatory agencies to make sure they were doing their job, and sued them when they weren't. But like many of his scientific colleagues at regional offices, the marine biologist worried that Fisheries leadership in Washington was more interested in protecting the interests of the Navy and commercial fishing than in saving whales. This wasn't the first time he'd placed an after-hours call to his friend at NRDC.

Ever since its founding in 1970, NRDC had occupied a special niche in the conservation community: helping to draft, and then enforce, environmental legislation. In the early 1970s, Congress passed a series of sweeping environmental laws and established the Environmental Protection Agency to enforce them. NRDC earned its watchdog reputation as "the shadow EPA" when it successfully sued the Environmental Protection Agency for failing to implement the Clean Air Act and the Clean Water Act. NRDC proved adept at playing the insider-outsider game of environmental policy making: it maintained close-enough ties inside Washington to advance its conservation agenda, then remained vigilant about making sure the laws were obeyed.

With seed funding from the Ford Foundation, NRDC began as a public interest law firm devoted exclusively to environmental defense. Staffed largely by idealistic young lawyers who'd recently graduated from Yale Law School, its board was drawn from Wall Street law firms and the ranks of science. John Adams, a former federal prosecutor for the US District Court for the Southern District of New York, became NRDC's first executive director and, for the next 40 years, the paterfamilias to generations of environmental lawyers. Adams cultivated an entrepreneurial culture that encouraged NRDC's senior attorneys to pursue any high-impact case they believed they could win. As he expressed his management philosophy, "I hire the smartest, most committed attorneys I can find. Then I let them go out and kick ass."

By the 1980s, NRDC was bypassing federal regulators and going after corporate polluters directly. In a novel application of the "citizen enforcement" provision of the Clean Water Act, NRDC successfully sued the Bethlehem Steel Corporation, on behalf of its mid-Atlantic members, for polluting the Chesapeake Bay. In the eighties and nineties, NRDC brought over 100 such cases against corporations, almost all of them successful.

By adopting a lone ranger model of dragging corporate polluters into court and deputizing its members as a posse, NRDC created a new paradigm for environmental enforcement that combined citizen activism and civil litigation. Along the way, NRDC managed to do for environmental law what

Bob Woodward and Carl Bernstein had done for investigative journalism: they made it sexy. As a group, lawyers were generally disdained by the public. But individual gunslinger attorneys who sued polluters on behalf of citizens became heroic figures in the environmental movement.

By the late 1980s, NRDC's legal eagles had emerged as the most formidable adversaries of corporate polluters and federal agencies that failed to prosecute them. And with more than 100,000 members, NRDC could mobilize public pressure in support of its lawsuits—and raise enough money through membership contributions to stay in court for as long as it took to prevail. When it sued Texaco to compel the company to clean up its pollution of the Delaware River, it took NRDC 20 years to win the case.

In 1990, when NRDC launched a Los Angeles office and was looking for a litigator who could stand up to polluters and developers, John Adams hired a young lawyer who'd been "kicking ass" in California for more than a decade. Although still in his thirties, Joel Reynolds had earned a reputation as a relentless environmental crusader—based in no small part on a legal battle he lost.

Riverside, California, where Joel Reynolds grew up in the fifties and sixties, was infamous for having the worst smog in America. In the summer months, a gray-brown haze obscured the views of the surrounding orange groves as the exhaust fumes from Los Angeles' newly built freeways blew east across the valley and lodged against the base of the San Bernardino Mountains. This inversion layer of smog could hang over Riverside for days at a stretch. By midday, it was difficult—and downright dangerous—to draw a full breath of air.

Despite the 100-degree heat and noxious air, Joel spent most summer afternoons on a public tennis court pounding balls against a wall or against anyone who would brave the smog. When he'd worn out his father or older brother, he'd go back to hitting against the wall. Reynolds was a natural athlete with a compulsive streak that helped him hone his talents in any sport he set his mind to. He could also be as competitive and tenacious as it took to prevail. He was typically the last boy standing on the tennis court, the baseball diamond, or the basketball court. In the winter, he would ski until after the last lift had closed. He liked to ski fast, arms flailing, straight down the mountain.

Joel's only athletic deficit was his poor depth perception. He'd been born with badly crossed eyes, a condition his mother attributed to an allergic reaction to strawberries she suffered while pregnant. Only one of his eyes could focus at a time. The other wandered, collecting unfocused information, unable to track or fuse with its mate. He was also seriously nearsighted. Joel's early childhood was a perpetual round of visits to eye doctors who prescribed ocular exercises that never seemed to help. By the age of five, he'd undergone three operations to reengineer his eye muscles into alignment, but they were only partially successful. He wore thick, clunky glasses through grade school, and his vision was never fully corrected until a follow-up surgery decades later.

Joel was a smart kid who understood that his lousy depth perception meant he'd never play sports professionally. But he was talented and adaptive enough to compete and win. And winning is what made it worth the effort. Tall, lanky, and graceful, he played with finesse or power as the situation required, and he didn't wilt under pressure. He enjoyed baseball and basketball, but tennis was the sport he competed in through high school. His tactic was simply to rally his opponent to death, patiently returning any shot across the net until he forced the other guy to make an error. It was an effective stratagem. With no formal instruction, he became the number one seed on his high school tennis team, winning the regional singles championship during his junior and senior years.

Identifying and then relentlessly exploiting his adversary's weakest point would be the hallmarks of Joel Reynolds' long-running legal battles, beginning with his first big case after graduating from Columbia Law School in 1978. After completing a federal court clerkship in New York, Reynolds turned down a job offer from a corporate firm where he'd worked the previous summer. Instead, he accepted a one-year fellowship with the Center for Law in the Public Interest in Los Angeles. It paid only $12,500, but it was the premier public interest firm in the country.

For four years, the Center had been fighting a rear guard action to keep the Diablo Canyon nuclear power plant, being constructed along the stunningly beautiful California coast at San Luis Obispo, from going on line. The other lawyers at the Center had come to view the case as a headache and a loser. When they offered Diablo Canyon to Reynolds, he jumped in with both feet.

By the time Reynolds entered the fray, Diablo Canyon's construction was 98 percent complete, and its owner, Pacific Gas & Electric Company (PG&E), was well on its way to getting license approvals from the Nuclear Regulatory Commission to start up its two nuclear reactors. In the 17 years since PG&E first bought the 750 acres of pristine coastline as the plant site, Diablo Canyon had become a flashpoint in the antinuclear movement. Demonstrations, lawsuits, and the belated discovery of a major earthquake fault running offshore of the plant had already cost PG&E a billion and a half dollars in overruns. The utility was determined to do whatever it took to get its reactors on line and generating electricity—and revenue.

The controversy had all the elements that fueled Reynolds' sense of outrage: an irreplaceable and spectacular natural environment under assault by a huge corporation in league with a captive federal regulatory agency. His local client, the San Luis Obispo Mothers for Peace,[1] was composed of scores of smart, determined women and their families who welcomed Reynolds warmly to their cause. Although he realized that the plant was a virtual fait accompli, Reynolds relished the chance to dive into a high-profile, high-impact case. It was 1980, just a year after the partial core meltdown at Pennsylvania's Three Mile Island nuclear plant. The showdown between the nuclear power industry and the antinuclear movement had come to a head at Diablo Canyon.

The only problem was that Reynolds had never actually practiced law. He'd recently passed the California bar, but he'd never filed a lawsuit or sought an injunction, much less attended a regulatory hearing. He knew nothing about nuclear energy, public utility law, or the Nuclear Regulatory Commission. Commuting to San Luis Obispo by motorcycle, he found himself living for weeks at a time in a strange town with no support staff or supervision, faced off against the country's second largest utility and its army of staff attorneys, outside counsel, consultants, and experts.

Reynolds' legal strategy for derailing the PG&E juggernaut was simple:

poke a stick into its spokes as many times and in as many ways as possible. If one stick broke, find a bigger stick. If that didn't work, roll a boulder onto the tracks. Whatever slowed down the utility's march toward an operating license increased the chances that public and judicial opinion would keep it from going on line—or at least make it safer if it did.

Reynolds' life became an adrenaline-fueled blur of work, stress, and elation, as he scrambled to put together a case and run it with no money, staff, or experience. He asked for advice wherever he could find it: about deposing experts, cross-examining witnesses, filing lawsuits, and arguing appeals, the physics of pressurized water reactors, quality assurance, nuclear risk assessment, emergency preparedness, and the differences between Westinghouse and Babcock & Wilcox reactor designs. And he had to learn it all inside a fishbowl, because the administrative trials were conducted in front of packed hearing rooms and covered daily by the Los Angeles Times and California news stations.

Reynolds found no shortage of safety violations to pursue, from design and construction problems to evacuation plans that ignored the possibility of an earthquake. He filed lawsuits challenging the loading of the radioactive fuel, testing of the plant, and then operation. In August 1984 the court of appeals in Washington, DC, blocked the operating license the Nuclear Regulatory Commission had issued to PG&E—an order Reynolds successfully defended in his first appearance before the US Supreme Court. But two years later, in a 5–4 decision written by Judge Robert Bork, the court of appeals upheld the Commission's issuance of a full-power license for Diablo Canyon.

Though he'd lost a long, hard-fought campaign, Reynolds had the satisfaction of knowing that by the time it finally went on line, Diablo Canyon was the most rigorously reviewed nuclear plant in the country. And PG&E was $5 billion over budget. Any utility that might consider building a nuclear power plant would worry that Joel Reynolds, or someone like him, would tie it and its profits up in court for a decade or more. For the next quarter century, no utility in America dared to try.

Regardless, the Diablo Canyon defeat would haunt Reynolds for as long as its twin containment domes loomed over his beloved California coastline. He resolved to carry the tough lessons of Diablo Canyon into future battles:

If you let yourself be outmanned and outgunned, you're likely to lose. Be skeptical of government regulators, since they're likely to become captive to the interests they're supposed to police. You can't win every fight—in fact, if you're always winning, you're not taking on tough-enough battles—but do everything you can to improve your odds of winning.

He moved on to win a string of legal victories, both before and after he joined NRDC in 1990. He sued cities and counties to clean up sewage discharges into Santa Monica Bay. He blocked construction of incinerators and prisons in low-income neighborhoods that opposed them. He secured lead screening for all poor children in California, and near his hometown of Riverside, he sued for cleanup of the Stringfellow Acid Pits, one of the largest toxic waste dumps in the country.

It wasn't until 1994 that Reynolds began butting heads with Fisheries—and with the US Navy—over threats to whales and other marine mammals along the California coast. For several years, he was the only person at NRDC working on whale issues. But he was determined not to fight solo against well-armed adversaries, as he had on Diablo Canyon.

When Reynolds found funding to staff up his marine mammal program, he recruited Michael Jasny to the fight. Or more precisely, Jasny enlisted. After graduating from Harvard Law School, Jasny had gone back to school to study his first love, English literature. Midway through his PhD program at UCLA, Jasny started hearing about the lawsuits that Reynolds was filing, and winning, across town. He couldn't resist stopping by NRDC's office to introduce himself and offer his services. Reynolds needed a young gun who could keep up with him intellectually, master both the legal and scientific complexities of marine mammal law, and write for judges and for the lay public with equal persuasion. Jasny filled the bill. And he was whip-smart enough to recruit and work with scientific experts in bioacoustics and marine mammalogy.

As a temperamental counterpoint to Jasny, Reynolds also hired Andrew Wetzler, an associate at the whitest of white-shoe law firms: Cravath, Swaine & Moore. Where Jasny was intense and passionate, Wetzler was relaxed and even-tempered. A religious studies major at Brown University before diving deep into environmental philosophy and then law school, he was as steadfast and as tireless as a Clydesdale. He clinched his job interview with Reynolds—an inveterate workhorse himself—when he remarked, "I haven't eaten at home in two years. I eat all my meals in the Cravath dining room."

After his late-night call from his friend at Fisheries, Jasny barely slept. An obsessive perfectionist and sweater of details, he soothed himself by working hard, and then harder. Early the next morning, he was parked outside a marine supply store in Marina del Rey, waiting for it to open. He bought its largest nautical map of the Bahamas, mounted it on foam board, and hung it on his office wall. By noon, the map was dotted with color-coded pushpins marking every beached whale by species and location and time of stranding. By day's end, he and Wetzler had also mapped every US naval installation within 500 miles of Abaco.

Jasny was ready to brief his boss. But first he had to track him down.

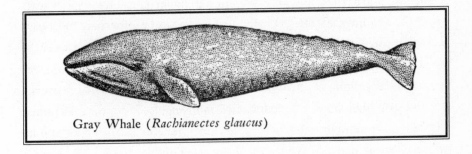

Gray Whale (*Rachianectes glaucus*)

9

Joel Reynolds Among the Friendlies

MARCH 17, 2000
Laguna San Ignacio, Baja Peninsula, Mexico

For the first time in years, Joel Reynolds was enjoying a few days off.

NRDC's five-year battle to save the last pristine nursery of the California gray whale from industrial development had recently come to a sudden, unexpected, and victorious ending. So while Ken Balcomb was cutting off beaked whale heads in the Bahamas, Reynolds was savoring the playful company of gray whale mothers and their calves.

Each winter, as they have for millennia, hundreds of pregnant gray whales migrate 6,000 miles from their feeding grounds in the Bering Sea of Alaska to the lagoons of central Baja to give birth. After two months of nursing and rearing their newborns in the sanctuary of the lagoons, the mothers lead their calves out into the Pacific Ocean for the return trip to Alaska—the longest annual mammal migration on the planet.

Balcomb had to wait his whole career to reach out and touch a live beaked whale. But the gray whales of Laguna San Ignacio had been inviting human contact for three decades.

Beginning in 1972, and continuing each winter since, the local whales broke the mold of mammal behavior. Just when most mothers are most protective of their young—soon after giving birth and before their calves are weaned—the mother whales of the lagoon initiated close encounters with humans. The enigmatic phenomenon of "friendly whales" baffled researchers and delighted the strictly controlled number of eco-tourists permitted inside the lagoon. No one could explain this paradoxical behavior among wild whales, which occurred nowhere else on earth.

Reynolds would never forget the first time he sat inside an idling motorboat and watched with excitement and alarm as a 30-ton, 40-foot gray whale and her calf approached. The mother whale was twice the size of the small boat, or *panga*, which she could easily have capsized or crushed with a wave of her fluke. Just as a collision seemed imminent, the whale deftly slalomed alongside the vessel and exhaled a misty whoosh of air through its blowhole. She raised her head just enough to lift one eye out of the water and stare up at Reynolds. When he extended his hand to touch the whale, the mother guided her two-ton calf forward to receive it. Then she sidled up alongside the boat and invited caresses herself. Eventually the whales disengaged and slid below the surface of the lagoon, leaving barely a ripple in their wake.

Over the course of the campaign to save Laguna San Ignacio, Reynolds had often deployed the power of these transformative encounters to tactical advantage with visiting politicians, scientists, journalists, and NRDC donors. Hardened businessmen were routinely reduced to childish glee, and serious scientists dissolved into wonderment and uncontrolled laughter. They all wanted a photo of themselves leaning over the edge of the *panga* to kiss the barnacled giants or to stroke the soft brush of baleen inside their open mouths.

For Reynolds, the whale lagoon was the perfect antidote to the smog, noise, and congestion of Los Angeles. The lagoon was only 700 miles south of LA, but to get there, he had to take a bus to Tijuana, Mexico, fly halfway down the Baja Peninsula in a prop plane, land on a dirt runway carved out of scrub desert, take a van from the airstrip to a boat launch at the far end of the lagoon, and travel by boat to a tent camp perched on the shore. The absence of human imprint was palpable. No electricity or phone lines. No plumbing, cars, cell phones, or internet connection. The nearest paved road lay 50 miles to the east. The entire lagoon was wrapped in silence, save for the rush of the wind and the audible whoosh of whales spouting. On moonless nights, the camp was as dark as a bat cave—except for the stars that hung so low and bright overhead he felt he could pluck them out of the sky. And, of course, he really could reach out and touch the whales.

After a day among the "friendlies," it was easy for Reynolds to forget that Laguna San Ignacio was the site of the most ruthless whale hunt in history. In the winter of 1857, American whaling captain Charles Melville Scammon heard from local fishermen about the unmapped Baja lagoons where California gray whales nursed their young in the calm, warm waters. Sandbars guarded the entrance of the lagoons against killer whales, the grays' only natural predators. As soon as Scammon figured out how to breach the sandbars at high tide and enter the whale nursery, the rest was easy. After anchoring his ship, the *Ocean Bird*, at the mouth of the 16-mile-long lagoon to bar any escape, Scammon lowered three whaleboats into the water. The boats moved into position between mother and calf, causing the mother to surface in defense—and bringing her within easy range of the harpooners.

Unlike their "friendly" descendants, the gray whale mothers were ferocious when attacked, lashing out at their tormentors with barnacled fins and flukes, and earning the nickname "devilfish" among the whalers who stalked them. As Scammon himself observed in his ship's log:

> When the parent animal is attacked, they show a power of resistance and tenacity of life that distinguish them from all other cetaceans. Many an expert whaleman suffered in his encounters with them, and many a one has paid the penalty with his life.

In the course of a morning's hunt, Scammon's harpooners could kill a dozen pregnant and nursing mothers, planting red flags in the floating carcasses to guide the *Ocean Bird* to the kill. Within hours, their blubber was flensed and cooked down to lamp oil. The flexible baleen was harvested from their mouths to feed the current fashion in corset stays and umbrella ribs. By day's end, Scammon observed, the waters of the lagoon had turned the very color of the claret he drank at dinner.

The whale calves were spared the harpoon. They didn't have enough blubber or baleen to merit hunting. But without mothers to nurse them, they starved to death within the week.

It took Scammon just five winter hunts to empty the Baja lagoons of whales. During the 1850s, 20,000 gray whales migrated past the California coastline each year. Twenty years later, only 2,000 made the passage. By then, Scammon had made his fortune and retired from whaling to become a gentleman naturalist. He authored the first comprehensive text on marine mammals of the Pacific Coast, in which he ruefully recorded—without a trace of irony—the passing of the gray whale:

> The large bays and lagoons, where these animals once congregated, brought forth and nurtured their young, are already nearly deserted. The mammoth bones of the California gray lie bleaching on the shores of those silvery waters, and are scattered among the broken coasts from Siberia to the Gulf of California; and ere long it may be questioned whether this mammal will not be numbered among the extinct species of the Pacific.

Left for dead, the California gray whale population rebounded at the end of the nineteenth century, only to face annihilation again with the advent of exploding harpoons and steam-powered whaling ships. By 1930, researchers estimated the survivors in the dozens. Other gray whale populations fared no better. North Atlantic grays were hunted to extinction by 1800, while only about 100 West Pacific gray whales survived off the coasts of Japan and Korea. In 1937, gray whales became the first protected species under the newly drafted International Agreement for the Regulation of Whaling.

Thanks to the ban on their hunting, California grays staged a dramatic comeback in the second half of the twentieth century. After they were protected as "threatened" under the US Endangered Species Act in 1973, their population swelled to an estimated 18,000. Laguna San Ignacio was once again home to nursing mothers and calves. Soon the whale lagoon became a magnet for whale researchers and a model of sustainable eco-tourism. In 1994, gray whales were the first federally protected species of whale to be delisted.

Then, just a month after the gray whales were removed from the endangered species list, the Mitsubishi Corporation, along with its Mexican government partner, announced plans to build the world's largest industrial saltworks on the shores of Laguna San Ignacio. Mitsubishi wanted to convert the natural salt flats bordering the lagoon into a 116-square-mile matrix of dikes and evaporation ponds. Diesel pumps operating 24 hours a day would siphon seawater out of the lagoon and into the ponds at a rate of 6,000 gallons a second—about 30 Olympic-sized swimming pools of water per minute. The seawater would then evaporate, leaving a stockpile of 7 million tons of crystalized industrial salt a year.

Mitsubishi's plan was to store billions of gallons a year of toxic by-products of the salt distillation process in retaining ponds that would discharge through a diffuser into the Bay of Whales to the west of the lagoon—unless the holding ponds leaked toxins directly into the lagoon, as they had at the Mitsubishi saltworks to the north, causing fish die-offs and major turtle kills. Mitsubishi and the government promised jobs, roads, schools, and a hospital in the neighboring town of Punta Abreojos.

There was only scattered opposition to the announced plan. Unlike America and Europe, Mexico had little in the way of a grassroots environmental movement. "Save the Whales!" had not yet entered the local lexicon. A group of artists and intellectuals led by poet Homero Aridjis in Mexico City organized to protest the development plan. Aridjis contacted Jacob Scherr, head of NRDC's international programs, and Reynolds, who ran its Marine Mammal Protection Project, to ask for help.

Reynolds never shied away from confrontations with big corporations and government agencies. But Mitsubishi was unlike any company he had ever gone up against. Mitsubishi wasn't simply a goliath of a multinational corporation. It was Godzilla.

Mitsubishi's corporate family tree had roots reaching back to the beginning of the twentieth century, when it first supplied warships and fighter aircraft to the Japanese Emperor. The Mitsubishi Trust had constructed and owned most of Japan's vast whaling fleet, and its whale oil production became an important source of hard currency for the government during the military buildup to World War II. After the war, with the active encouragement of American general Douglas MacArthur, Mitsubishi helped revive whaling and promoted whale meat as a protein source for the starving, conquered empire—enshrining whale meat as the ultimate comfort food in the hearts and souls of generations of Japanese. As late as the mid-1960s, Mitsubishi had lobbied the Mexican government to build a whaling station on the Baja coast, despite the gray whale's long-standing protected status. In the 1970s, Mitsubishi diversified into cars, steel, electronics, banking, mining, forestry, and consumer products, from Kirin beer to Nikon. By 1995, with 28 corporations and 160 subsidiaries, offices in 85 countries, and annual revenues two times Mexico's annual budget, the Mitsubishi Group had grown into the world's largest trading company.

Veterans of Mexican politics advised Reynolds and Scherr that the saltworks project was unstoppable. NRDC had run successful international campaigns in Canada to protect old-growth forests against industrialization. But Mexico's single-party government was widely viewed as a corrupt and business-friendly oligarchy unconstrained by federal environmental laws like those in the United States and Canada. Mexican conservation laws and agencies had little credibility and an anemic history of enforcement. And the only Mexican opponents—the kind of grassroots organization that NRDC needed to partner with on international campaigns—were a small group of writers and artists who lived 1,000 miles from the lagoon.

Finally, NRDC had no legal standing in Mexico. If the federal government wanted to enter into an agreement with a foreign corporation, there was nothing NRDC could do in court to challenge it. And since there were no American companies involved, it couldn't file suit in American courts.

Reynolds was a pragmatist who avoided quixotic crusades. He had racked up an impressive winning streak over the previous decade by picking his spots and doing his legal due diligence before committing to a case. Winning was how you built momentum, created leverage, and instilled fear in potential adversaries. The more cases you won, the more likely your next opponent would be to negotiate rather than go to court. In the high-stakes arena of environmental law, losing was more than a personal and professional disappointment. It meant that a highway got built across vital wetlands or an endangered species was shoved closer to the abyss. And losing a lawsuit risked setting a damaging legal precedent that could sabotage environmental actions for decades. Any way you calculated it—in time, money, resources, or credibility—losing was an unaffordable luxury. And this campaign had all the earmarks of a loser.

But then Reynolds traveled to the lagoon and spent a day with the whales. After that, he never considered walking away from the fight for Laguna San Ignacio.

Unlike so many environmental activists who came of age in the seventies, Reynolds never became jaded about the movement, or the legal system. He remained a true believer in the power of people—especially in league with creative lawyers—to save the planet. Many of his law school professors loved the law for its intellectual elegance and exactitude. For Reynolds, the law was only a means to an end. He reserved his love for the shrinking wild places of California, and for the animals that depended on wilderness to survive. His devotion to the land gave Reynolds the stamina he needed for long, drawn-out battles. And it fed his outrage at the arrogance of greedy corporate polluters and the complicit government agencies that abetted them.

His secret weapon was his temperament. If the engine that drove him was outrage at environmental injustice, his success lay in his ability to cloak his anger in California cool. Even in the heat of legal combat, he never lost his temper. When facing off against adversaries, Reynolds led with the same kind of low-key manner, lanky grace, and self-deprecating good humor that served actor Jimmy Stewart so well. He was the sort of guy who could beat you eight games in a row at horseshoes, and still manage to convince you that he just got lucky. Among the top tier of successful litigation attorneys—a stratum that typically attracts and enables aggressive, even obnoxious personalities— Reynolds stood apart as a genuinely nice guy. His opponents couldn't help but like him personally. They didn't recognize that his protective California coloring of authentic geniality camouflaged a relentless drive to win.

The Baja campaign became a case study in what NRDC—and Reynolds in particular—did best: improvise methodically. Without legal standing in Mexican courts, Reynolds and Scherr reasoned that the only way to save the lagoon was to shame Mitsubishi and the Mexican government into doing the right thing.

Environmental campaigns have a lot in common with the Napoleonic Wars. They're prolonged and punishing offensives fought on multiple fronts, with success often determined by the strategic alliances you forge and the foot soldiers you mobilize. And they cost a lot of money. Like most large environmental groups, NRDC's programs were funded by membership, foundations, and large donors. Reynolds and Scherr tapped all those sources to build a war chest and recruit an army of activists. One major donor pledged start-up money. A foundation provided matching funds. NRDC's crackerjack direct mail group activated its membership, which contributed money and generated over 1 million letters to Mitsubishi.

To focus international media attention on the whale lagoon, Reynolds and Scherr enlisted movie stars—particularly Pierce Brosnan, who became the face and the voice of the campaign—and celebrity lawyers like NRDC's longtime staff attorney Robert Kennedy Jr. They recruited Jean-Michel Cousteau, the son of Jacques-Yves Cousteau and heir to the family filmmaking franchise, who agreed to bring a film crew to shoot at the lagoon. Reynolds reached out to marquee scientists, like Roger Payne, who'd jumpstarted the Save the Whales movement back in the early seventies with his discovery and promotion of humpback whale songs. Payne, in turn, recruited dozens of other internationally renowned scientists and persuaded them to sign an open letter denouncing the saltworks project.

Reynolds and Scherr brokered a crucial strategic alliance with the International Fund for Animal Welfare (IFAW), a deep-pocketed animal protection partner that was founded in 1969 to stop the commercial seal hunt in Canada. IFAW paid to have the scientists' letter published in full-page newspaper ads around the world, which generated more waves of letters and petitions.

The coalition partners embarked on a worldwide tour to spread the gospel of saving the whale lagoon, beginning with a trip to Mitsubishi's corporate headquarters in Tokyo to deliver a mountain of letters and petitions, then on to Kyoto for the UN World Heritage Commission meeting to lobby for the lagoon's "in danger" status. A year later, they made another pilgrimage to the commission's meeting in Marrakesh, Morocco.

Back in the States, they launched a consumer boycott of Mitsubishi businesses, from cars to banks. They knew they couldn't afford to mount a nationwide boycott, so they launched one in California and threatened to take it national. They deployed operatives across Mexico to drum up grassroots support, bought billboard, radio, and print ads in Mexico City, educated fishermen in Baja about the pollution threats from the saltworks, and convinced Mexico's most popular Telemundo soap opera to write the gray whales of Laguna San Ignacio into its storyline and shoot an episode on location. By the winter of 2000, five years after the Mexican government entered into partnership with Mitsubishi, polls showed that 70 percent of Mexicans opposed construction of the saltworks.

In the end, it may have been the whales' face-to-face charisma that tipped the balance. In late February, Mexican president Ernesto Zedillo made his first visit to the lagoon, along with his wife and children. After just a few minutes on the water, the whales began to approach the president's *panga*. The children ran to the bow of the boat to greet them. When Zedillo's wife leaned out of the boat to kiss one of the whales, the president snapped a souvenir photo.

In early March, just days before the whales came ashore in the Bahamas, Reynolds was preparing to board a plane to Baja for the latest round of media offensives when he got the news: President Zedillo had canceled the saltworks. Reynolds, Scherr, and their coalition partners decided to continue on to Laguna San Ignacio as planned. When they got off the plane in Punta Abreojos, they were met and serenaded by the local schoolchildren. School was canceled, and the whole town threw a fiesta to celebrate the victory.

It was a sweet win. Now, for the first time since the campaign had begun five years earlier, Reynolds could stop fighting for the lagoon and simply enjoy the whales.

When he came ashore from his afternoon on the lagoon, Reynolds was looking forward to a cold beer and a game of horseshoes. The camp manager met him on the beach to say he had a call on the satellite phone, the camp's only link to the outside world. Reynolds groaned. A satellite call was never good news. As he slouched toward the tent where the satellite phone was housed, Reynolds scanned his mental checklist of where each of his three children should be this time of day in Los Angeles. Warily, he raised the phone to his ear.

"Joel, this is Michael," Jasny announced. So it was work, not a family crisis.

Reynolds tried to imagine which lawsuit in his caseload might have gone off the rails. "How are the whales?" Jasny asked.

"The whales are wonderful. Go ahead and spoil my day."

"There's been a mass stranding. In the Bahamas." While Jasny briefed him on the incident, Reynolds stared out at where two whale spouts punctured the lagoon's surface. As Jasny described the sequence of strandings, Reynolds visualized the arc of color-coded pushpins spread across the map on Jasny's office wall back in Los Angeles. He tried to imagine what could cause whales to strand along a 150-mile stretch of island beaches.

Before Reynolds could ask if there were any sightings of naval vessels in the area, Jasny reported that he'd been making calls all day, but the Navy's press office was in lockdown. No one he knew there would talk to him about the Bahamas. "But my friend at Fisheries sent me a permit that the Southeast Office issued last month to the Office of Naval Research. It's for a sea test near the Bahamas for something they're calling Littoral Warfare Advanced Development. I'm still figuring out what that is."

"We obviously don't have enough facts," Reynolds said. "We need to know more about what the Navy was doing there—a timeline of events and locations. And soon, before the Navy starts narrating the story for us."

Jasny agreed and promised to keep digging. He looked across the NRDC office, already empty on a Friday evening, and he could see the rest of the weekend flattening out in front of him. Reynolds suggested he start by drafting a letter to the Secretary of the Navy; hopefully something that the Humane Society would co-sign. "I'd like to have something we can send out on Monday," he said. Jasny said he'd already started drafting one.

Jasny had saved the good news for last. "There's a whale researcher in the Bahamas—on Abaco Island—who posted a report on MARMAM. He says he and his team collected heads from two of the whales."

For six years now, Reynolds had been shadowboxing with the Navy over its sonar exercises. Six years of researching case law and cultivating science experts and wrangling with Navy lawyers. After all that time and effort, he still lacked a trail of physical evidence to support a lawsuit. Perhaps, he hoped, that trail might begin in the Bahamas.

Jasny waited out the silence until Reynolds spoke. "I'll try to get back on tomorrow's plane," he said. "Until then, keep up the spadework."

Reynolds hung up the satellite phone, opened a cold Pacifico, and squinted at the sun that was setting over the lagoon. A whale breached, defied gravity for a moment, and then fell back with a soundless crash.

He turned away from the lagoon and ambled toward the horseshoe pit, where a couple of the *panga* drivers were already pitching perfect, lazy loops that clanged against the stake. Reynolds hoped that with a bit of luck he could win a game or two before dinner, before the storm approaching from the Bahamas drowned out the dream of Laguna San Ignacio.

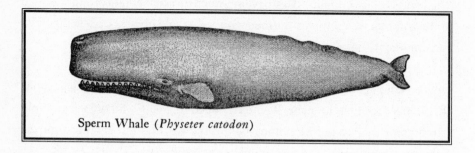

Sperm Whale (*Physeter catodon*)

10

The Whale Coroner Arrives

DAY 4: MARCH 18, 2000
Freeport, Grand Bahama

After the tumult of the stranding and the days spent collecting heads, flying over to Grand Bahama to meet Darlene Ketten's plane felt to Balcomb like a vacation. He hitched a ride with another pilot friend for the hourlong hop to Freeport.[1] The northernmost island in the archipelago, Grand Bahama lies just 56 miles offshore from West Palm Beach. On a clear day like this one, Balcomb could just make out the Florida coastline from the cockpit of the plane as it began its descent.

Inside the airport, Balcomb was confronted by the dueling the front-page headlines of the *Freeport News* and the *Nassau Tribune*:

"Whale Beached at High Rock," declared the *News*.

"Whales Come Ashore in the Bahamas!" shouted the bigger, bolder-faced *Tribune*, above a page one photo of a beached whale, and an article that began:

Ten whales were beached or stranded in shallow waters in the Bahamas during the last two days in a phenomenon that has baffled fisheries experts. While various whales have beached in the Bahamas from time to time, this is the largest number to occur at one time.

Freeport veterinarian Dr. Alan Bater said he never heard of so many beachings at one time in his 30 years in the Bahamas. "It seems very strange to me that nine should beach in one day. We don't get nine in a year."

As he walked toward Ketten's arrival gate, Balcomb realized that he was nervous about meeting her. The two occupied opposite positions in the universe of marine mammal research. He labored in the shadows of photo-identification field surveying, recognized primarily for his long-running orca census and his chapter in the *Handbook of Marine Mammals*. Ketten was a bright star in the constellation of elite bioacousticians who lectured at international conferences and published in the most prestigious journals.

Their paths had crossed only once, after a lecture Ketten delivered on beaked whales' hearing at the marine mammal biennial four years earlier. She'd presented with flair, punctuating her impressive data analysis with witty asides that reminded the serious scientists that they could still get excited by the miracle of cetacean anatomy. Balcomb had waited for her entourage of grad students to thin out before introducing himself and asking her about the source of one of her PowerPoint slides—the one illustrating the ear canal of Gervais' beaked whales. It was a brief exchange between two beaked whale nerds. What he remembered best was that she quoted a passage from his Baird's beaked whale chapter back to him, verbatim. Ketten asked him when he was publishing his Bahamas research, and he mumbled something about wanting to compile a more complete data set. Then he invited her to come down to see the Cuvier's and Blainville's herself. "I'll get there eventually, as soon as there's a volunteer," she replied with a smiling reference to her stranded research subjects.

As he waited outside her arrival gate, Balcomb wondered whether she'd remember their meeting four years ago. He decided not to bring it up unless she did.

Darlene Ketten was accustomed to being on call. Rather like a country doctor, she thought, who answered the night bell whenever a child decided to arrive into the world or, on the other end of the life cycle, when the family of a recently deceased patient required certification of cause of death.

Ten weeks before the Bahamas stranding, Ketten had been celebrating New Year's Eve at a party in Hyannis, on Cape Cod. The partygoers were joking nervously about Y2K, laying wagers on whether or not their computers would reboot the first morning of the new millennium. Two hours before midnight, she got a cell phone call reporting a stranding on Nantucket Island. Darlene enjoyed a good party as much as the next person, but the minute she heard that a dead sperm whale had stranded on Surfside Beach, she put down her champagne glass, borrowed a hammer and chisel from her host, and bolted for the airport. Everything else she needed—including knives, specimen jars, formalin and foil, flashlights and energy bars—was stowed in the dissection kit she always carried in the trunk of her car.

Darlene was three years and six ear bones into her study of sperm whale hearing. Three years of impatiently waiting for the next "volunteer" to wash ashore. If she delayed investigating this stranding until first light, the tide would roll back in, and she'd find herself working in three feet of surf. Worse, some human or animal scavenger might get there ahead of her and contaminate the evidence trail. An unthinkable outcome.

By two in the morning, the high school students who had discovered the whale during an impromptu New Year's Eve beach party had long since departed Surfside. Had they lingered, they would have witnessed a remarkable moonlit tableau: a 50-foot-long sperm whale lay on its side in the sand, the surf knocking against its tail—while at the other end of its massive expanse, a petite, 40-year-old woman in a black velvet minidress and down parka seemed to be disappearing into the side of the whale's head. The light of a nearby Coleman lantern glinted off the blade of her flensing knife as it tunneled deeper into blubber and tissue.

Ketten had been hard at work for more than an hour. Her feet were wet and cold, her hands numb beneath thin latex gloves. It was all she could do to keep from gagging from the rank plume of steam that poured out of the head cavity, where 98-degree tissue met the frigid night air.

She was in heaven.

Inch by inch, moment by moment, she drew closer to her prize: the tympano-periotic bulla—the ear bone that houses the exquisite, intricate labyrinth of the sperm whale's inner ear.

When Ketten reached the bony structures guarding the bulla, she switched from flensing knife to hammer and chisel. Then, when she finally exposed the ligaments behind the bulla, she used a handsaw to cut it loose. Slowly, she lifted the bulla out of the whale's head and cradled it in her hands. Though the ear bones are the smallest bones in any mammal's body, a whale's bulla— particularly in low-frequency baleen whales—can be as large as a grapefruit and heavier than rock. After examining its contours by lantern light, Ketten injected formalin through a crevice in the bony vault to preserve the cochlear structures that were locked inside.

By dawn, Ketten had extracted the other ear bone and had driven back to the airport in time for the early-morning flight to Boston, her treasures tucked safely inside her carry-on bag. By lunchtime, the ear bones would be nestled together on the bed of her CT scanner back at Harvard, ready to give up all their hidden secrets.

In the weeks that followed her Nantucket scavenger hunt, Ketten logged thousands of air miles in pursuit of other specimens stranded on distant shores. When Bob Gisiner tracked her down the day after the Bahamas strandings, she was consulting with colleagues at the Navy's marine mammal research station in Point Loma, California, and preparing to guest-lecture at Scripps in La Jolla. She couldn't cancel her lecture, but she skipped the reception afterward and caught the red-eye to Miami.

No one could ever accuse Balcomb of being a groupie. But over the past decade, he had followed Ketten's publications closely. She was the first researcher to study the internal structures of beaked whale phonation and hearing, and the first to trace the path of sound waves all the way from their source in the ocean to the beaked whale's auditory cortex.

There were a few guys, like Jim Mead at the Smithsonian, who knew as much or more than Balcomb about beaked whale evolution, based on the fossil and bone records. But Ketten was fluent in the esoteric language Balcomb had learned in the Navy: marine acoustics. Now that she had finally found her way to the Bahamas, Balcomb was excited at the prospect of an on-site tutorial from the world's leading expert in beaked whale hearing.

Like Balcomb's own career path, and those of so many of his cetologist colleagues, Ketten's arrival at the apex of her arcane subspecialty had been accidental. "Serendipitous" was the adjective she preferred. She hadn't started out wanting to be a whale coroner. Like most young whale researchers, she'd planned to study live cetaceans. When she graduated from MIT in 1980 with a master's degree in biological oceanography, she wanted to investigate how dolphins used their vocalizations to communicate compared with how they echolocated with sound while hunting.

She applied to the Johns Hopkins University School of Medicine—not to become a physician but because the medical school's behavioral ecology department had a research affiliation with Baltimore's National Aquarium. The aquarium's half dozen dolphins doubled as stars of the twice-daily dolphin show and as research subjects. When the dolphin tank became contaminated the summer before her first semester, the dolphins were loaned to another aquarium for the next two years during renovations to their Baltimore home. So Ketten arrived at Hopkins without a research project.

She was despondent but, as always, resourceful. As long as she was at a major medical center, she reasoned, she might as well study anatomy—cetacean anatomy. In the absence of live subjects, Darlene studied specimens harvested from stranded marine mammals around the country. One day someone sent her a block of frozen tissue containing a sperm whale ear. She was new to whale anatomy and didn't know where or how to begin her dissection. When she asked the head of the radiology department if she could use their X-ray machine to take a look inside the tissue block, he suggested she try their new computerized tomography (CT) scanner.

Computerized tomography was a breakthrough technology in 1980. Conventional X-rays produce two-dimensional images on film. CT scanners take thousands of thinly sliced digital X-rays of a three-dimensional object, then compose those X-rays into a 3-D composite model of bone and tissue—the same way you might reconstruct a sliced salami into its original shape. And unlike magnetic resonance imaging (MRI), CT scans can precisely image tissue, fat, bone, and blood as distinct structures.

Watching that first block of sperm whale tissue move through the scanner bed and appear magically on the screen as a fully rendered ear bone was Ketten's eureka moment. The scanner could actually see through the tissue and the protective ear bone to reveal the underlying structures of the whale's inner ear. There was the graceful spiral of the cochlea, as if sculpted out of Italian marble! Ketten realized that she was standing on the edge of an entirely new frontier in medical pathology: digital dissection. No longer would scientists have to destroy a delicate specimen in order to reveal its anatomy or the pathology of its injury.

She convinced the radiology department to let her use the CT scanner after the medical clinic closed each night. By the time she completed her PhD thesis, she'd mapped the inner ear anatomy of 16 species of toothed whales, including harbor porpoises, dolphins, and sperm whales. Her CT models demonstrated how each species had evolved its own specialized auditory structures to hear specific frequencies and wavelengths, depending on the demands of its respective hunting environment.[2]

Unfortunately, by earning a PhD in experimental radiology and neuroethology, Ketten effectively specialized herself into unemployment. Whale hearing was endlessly fascinating to her but too esoteric to attract a postdoctoral research or teaching fellowship. It wasn't until Harvard Medical School launched its first human cochlear implant program—and needed a radiologist who specialized in CT scanning of inner ears—that Ketten found her academic niche.

For the next five years, she conducted human hearing studies at Harvard and moonlighted as a nonfaculty whale ear researcher at Woods Hole Oceanographic. Harvard, like Hopkins, let her use its CT scanners after clinic hours, so most weeks she ferried specimens back and forth between Woods Hole and Cambridge.

Beginning in the early 1990s, soon after he arrived at ONR, Bob Gisiner became the patron who would sponsor Ketten's cetacean research. The Navy also sent her to the Armed Forces Institute of Pathology in Bethesda, Maryland, for formal training in forensic pathology. It was a natural fit. She appreciated the order that forensic protocol imposed on the chaos and incongruity of a whale on a beach. She felt she owed her volunteer subjects that level of dignity in death.

As her experience and reputation grew, Ketten found herself downstream from a steady flow of stranded cetaceans, large and small, who'd met untimely and often mysterious deaths. Increasingly, it fell to her to make a differential diagnosis among the possible causes of cetacean demise that read like a biblical litany: death by ship strike, by net entanglement, by gunshot wound, by underwater explosion, by swallowed plastic bags, by toxic algae bloom, by parasitic infestation, by seismic or acoustic shock.

By the late 1990s, with joint appointments to the faculties of Harvard Medical School and Woods Hole Oceanographic Institution, Ketten had all the requisite assets to excel at forensic pathology: a ravenous curiosity for solving puzzles combined with a passion for detail. She worked hard, wrote well, and published often. She was a gifted, witty teacher who could speak with equal eloquence to lay and professional audiences. And like every good forensic scientist, she was relentless in her search for conclusive evidence. She scoffed at colleagues who published papers based on two or three specimens—a common practice, given the dearth of research subjects. If she didn't have enough data to publish conclusively, she waited for enough volunteers to prove or disprove her hypothesis. She sometimes ruffled feathers by being a stickler for protocol. Balcomb had once seen her stand up at the end of a colleague's presentation and, in front of hundreds of peers, state matter-of-factly, "I think it's important that everyone understand, before they accept your conclusions, that you refrigerated your specimens at thirty-seven degrees Fahrenheit rather than the optimal storage environment of thirty-five degrees."

Regardless of her occasional lapses in professional tact, by 2000 Ketten had secured her status as the go-to whale coroner in the aftermath of an atypical stranding. Her competitors for access to the limited supply of stranded specimens included colleagues at Woods Hole and around the world: zoologists, veterinarians, paleontologists, marine biologists, and toxicologists, as well as hordes of ambitious graduate students. In the area of acoustic trauma and whale ear pathology, Ketten was *the* unassailable expert. Free from the constraints of marriage and family, she could board a plane on a moment's notice, bound for whichever far-flung coastline where her services were required.

If you were Bob Gisiner at ONR, or Teri Rowles at Fisheries, you could trust Darlene Ketten to restore order to the chaos of a mass stranding on foreign shores.

Balcomb spotted Ketten chatting up a white-uniformed Bahamian customs officer. He poked around inside her dissection kit, laughed at something she said, and waved her through. She was traveling light—her dissection kit on one shoulder and an overnight bag on the other—and was dressed in a linen pantsuit set off by a brightly colored silk scarf.

Balcomb waved at Ketten, and she waved back. "I told you I'd get down here, as soon as you found me some volunteers," she said. Balcomb smiled. She *did* remember their last meeting.

On the cab ride to Bater's office, Balcomb briefed her on the strandings and the possible specimens that remained scattered across the islands. Very gently, he probed her about any details she might have heard from her Navy contacts about exercises in the Bahamas.

"I've heard that ONR has been testing sonobuoys northeast of Abaco," she told him, echoing what he'd heard from Gisiner. "But that's been dismissed from the equation. Everyone knows," she said, meaning everyone who knew anything about sound in the ocean, "those transmissions couldn't have been a factor. Not with a twenty-mile landmass between the source and the strandings. I guess we'll just have to wait and see what we can learn from the heads you've collected. Just as soon as we're done here in Freeport."

Balcomb kept the conversation light and local. The weather, culinary treats. He was enjoying the collegiality she'd extended him, and he didn't want to cast aspersions on her naval patrons—so he didn't mention the destroyer. And he didn't talk about the underwater microphone arrays at AUTEC.

Two Cuvier's whale heads that Alan Bater had retrieved from Gold Rock Creek were arranged across an examining table in his veterinary office. By the time Balcomb and Ketten arrived, the aroma in the cramped examining room had become pungent to the point of embarrassment. When he saw Ketten enter, Bater broke off wrestling with a window that was reluctant to open and rushed to introduce himself.

"Welcome to my clinic, Dr. Ketten."

"Please, call me Darlene."

"It's an honor to have you here, Dr.—er, Darlene. A privilege."

Balcomb had met Bater once before at a benefit event in Freeport that Diane had urged him to attend. He recognized Bater now by his tanned, bald head, trim white beard, and less than trim figure. A Brit transplant who'd fled cold, damp England for the warm embrace of the island life and all its consumable pleasures, Bater was known in Freeport as a bon vivant and ardent rugby player, until his love of food sidelined him from active play. He was somewhat less well known as a captive-dolphin doctor who—as Bater took pleasure in informing new acquaintances—had consulted on *The Day of the Dolphin* when it was filmed on Treasure Cay in the early 1970s.

Wedged into the corner of the examining room were Ruth Ewing, a Fisheries veterinarian who had flown in from the Miami office, and Charlie Potter, Jim Mead's research partner from the Smithsonian in Washington. There wasn't room to maneuver around for handshakes, so Ketten and Balcomb made do with head nods of welcome.

Ketten pulled on a pair of latex gloves with two crisp snaps. She leaned in close to the heads and prodded them with her thumb and forefinger. To judge from the expression on Ketten's face, she'd hoped for fresher goods.

"Is there a CT scanner available here, or somewhere else on the island?" she asked.

"I'm afraid not," said Bater. "My practice is mostly cats and dogs. Occasionally a horse, though equines are not my specialty. And, of course, dolphins, though I tend to treat them on-site. Unless they required intravenous antibiotics, in which case—"

Ketten broke in, "What about the local hospital?"

"That would be Rand Memorial, and no, I'm afraid they don't have a CT scanner either. The closest would be in Nassau, but, of course, that's a plane flight away, and we might need permission from Bahamian Fisheries to transport these specimens."

Darlene took a scalpel from her kit and made an incision below the jawline of one of the whales, revealing a layer of acoustic fat that was black with putrefaction. When she resected the other jawbone, a stream of dark green goo oozed onto the floor. "These won't do," she said sternly. "I'll take the ear bones, but there's nothing else I can use, inside or outside the braincase, CT or no CT. Not in this state of decomposition."

Bater was crestfallen, and a bit embarrassed. "I have a blood sample . . . from the eyes."

"How long was it exposed to air?"

"Twelve, perhaps sixteen hours. Not more than eighteen, certainly."

Ketten let his reply hang in the air, allowing her audience to visualize the effect of 18 hours of oxidation on a blood specimen. Balcomb almost felt sorry for Bater.

"Are there any fresher heads on this island?" Ketten asked, looking around the room.

"There's a minke whale at High Rock that I've arranged for you to examine," said Bater. "From what I've heard, it's been well protected from the elements. Other than sharks, which I gather had a rather good go at the bugger before it died. Is a shark an 'element,' properly speaking? I wonder."

Ketten turned to Balcomb. "When can I see your heads?"

"Whenever you like. We can fly over this afternoon."

"His heads are in a freezer. They'll keep," Bater protested. "The minke is the highest priority! I really must insist."

Ketten sighed. Balcomb could imagine the condition of the minke by now. He was already restless to return to Abaco. "I need to get back to my team," he said to Ketten. "I'll keep the heads on ice till you get there."

"Until then," she agreed. She peeled off her gloves and dropped first one, and then the other, into the waste pail.

An hour after fleeing Bater's office, Balcomb tracked down his pilot friend in a sport fishing store downtown. They were aloft and headed home by midafternoon.

As their plane began to descend toward Marsh Harbour Airport, it flew directly over two US Navy guided-missile frigates that were steaming down the center of Northwest Providence Channel. It's hard to hide modern warships the size of American frigates, but it seemed to Balcomb that the Navy wasn't even trying.

He returned to Sandy Point to find Diane and the Earthlings clustered around a TV that someone had set up in the living room. A Miami news station was reporting on the strandings from Grand Bahama. Ken could see the reporter interviewing Bater, posed proudly beside the stranded minke whale at High Rock, while local schoolkids mugged for the camera behind him.

Ken hadn't eaten all day, and he was suddenly very hungry. He rummaged through the refrigerator and found a sandwich that he ate standing in front of the sink. Sometimes it felt as though he'd eaten most of his meals standing up—in ship galleys, on the deck of his house in the San Juans, in sonar stations in the middle of the Pacific.

When Diane joined him in the kitchen, he tried to read her body language as she stood with her arms crossed, leaning back on the kitchen counter. Was she sore that he'd left her behind to babysit the Earthlings?

"Have you been out on the water to have a look around?" he ventured.

"I've been chained to the phone, fielding calls." She picked up a sheaf of handwritten notes and held them out to him. There were reports by local fishermen of naval craft in the channel, and calls from reporters who wanted comments or interviews. National Public Radio, an Associated Press correspondent, someone from the *Dallas Morning News*. "I told them they should talk to you."

Ken couldn't tell whether she was deferring to his seniority or if she was simply wary of being quoted in print. Now that the US Navy was surfacing in the stranding narrative, Ken felt doubly damned in Diane's eyes—as an American and as a Navy veteran. He understood why she resented the way the Americans pushed around the Bahamian government. It made no sense that the US Navy had a 60-year lease on the AUTEC testing range that dominated Andros, the biggest island in the Bahamas. Diane's cousin in the Interior Ministry had told them how the US Navy typically secured the Bahamians' "consent" to conduct exercises in their waters. A day or two in advance, a midstaff lieutenant or civilian contractor would phone the ministry and inform it of the exercises, perhaps suggesting that it post a mariners' notice or have a Bahamian patrol boat handy to keep the fishermen and cruise ships outside the perimeter. Sometimes they'd warn the Bahamians if live fire exercises would be involved. Sometimes not.

Ken never defended the Navy to her. But Diane didn't seem to understand that back when he was serving, there was a war going on. It may have been a Cold War where weapons were rarely fired, but the stakes couldn't have been higher. Civilians never saw the deadly serious game of blindman's bluff going on between Soviet and American submarines, and Ken never spoke about it. No one did. Whether or not anyone even remembered, Americans had relied on their Navy to track every Soviet submarine armed with nuclear missiles, day and night, for 30 years.

He was proud of his seven years of silent service to that mission. What did Diane, with her boarding schools and her summers sailing catamarans around the islands, know about the dead-cold sweat of a Delta-class boomer leaking through the net, loaded with enough kilotons to take out Los Angeles and San Francisco?

He shoved the mayonnaise in the refrigerator and shut the door harder than he had to. As usual, his internal monologue and curt gesture were the closest he came to speaking his mind. Then he retreated to the office.

Balcomb logged on to MARMAM and found that his posting had generated considerable commentary from opinionated parties near and far. Most of it was uninformed speculation, hearsay reports of seismic activity, mariners' warnings pulled from elsewhere on the web, some talk of British navy ships sighted off Eleuthera, to the south.

Scrolling through the chatter, Balcomb found a posting by a well-known Greek correspondent:

Posted by: Dr. Alexandros Frantzis
Subject: Re: Atypical mass strandings and naval exercises

Dear all,

Unfortunately, we didn't have to wait very long since 1996 (when NATO low-frequency sonar exercises and beaked whales mass stranding occurred in Greece). Some people will say it is too early to speak about possible causes for the Bahamas mass stranding. Perhaps they are scientifically right and certainly, we will all wait for the results of the good specialists who went to Bahamas to collect samples and data. Nevertheless, since the news seems to confirm that the US Navy was there at the right time and the right place performing "submarine detection," the Bahamas case seems like another sonar-related stranding. Unfortunately, all this is very difficult to prove scientifically. And we cannot interview the stranded animals asking them "why are you here?"

Let's hope that this atypical mass stranding will be the last and we will not need other strandings to convince the world navies that their games are very dangerous.

Best wishes, Alexandros

Dr. Alexandros Frantzis, Institute of Marine Biological Resources, National Centre for Marine Research, Hellenikon, Greece

Balcomb's email in-box was crammed with interview requests from journalists. He leafed through the phone messages Diane had given him, pulled the first Post-it note off the top of the pile, and dialed the number.

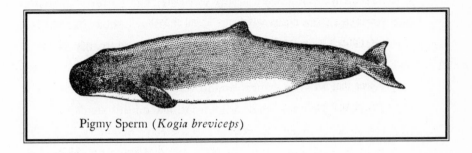

Pigmy Sperm (*Kogia breviceps*)

II

Depth Charges

DAY 6: MARCH 20, 2000
Los Angeles Office of NRDC

Joel Reynolds was pleased to find Michael Jasny's draft letter to the Navy Secretary waiting on his desk Monday morning. As usual, Jasny's research was exhaustive.

As the scientific R&D arm of the Navy, the Office of Naval Research was constantly testing new weapons systems, including sonar. Jasny's list of ONR's newest acoustic and nonacoustic weaponry read like science fiction. Reynolds had no idea what the Channel Probe Pulse Program, geoacoustic inversion, or Multipulse Airgun System were. Neither did Jasny—although Reynolds was confident that by week's end he would. One of the tests—the Directional Command Activated Sonobuoy System—involved floating active-sonar transmitters called sonobuoys that were dropped from aircraft to acoustically search a quadrant of ocean.

According to Jasny's research, the mid-March sea tests were just the first in a series that ONR planned to conduct in the coming months at various "littoral," or close-to-shore, locations up and down the Eastern Seaboard. Ever since the end of the Cold War, the Navy's strategic focus had shifted away from tracking Soviet subs in deep "blue ocean" environments. The new priority engagement scenario was coastal, or "brown water," action in support of ground troops, or to keep critical inland waterways such as the Persian Gulf and the Strait of Hormuz open for international oil shipments.

Reynolds was eager to get the letter off to the Navy Secretary, just to let him know that NRDC was investigating its permit applications and would be scrutinizing its response to the stranding. He spent his morning peppering the letter with the kind of pointed legal language designed to get the attention of the Navy Secretary's attorneys: "In order to cure these legal infirmities the Navy must comport with the following requirements . . . In order to avoid the necessity of NRDC taking further action in this matter . . . The Navy's failure to suspend Sea Test 00-1 only adds to a list of legal violations and other inadequacies through which its project initially received authorization."

Reynolds called Naomi Rose at the Humane Society of the United States to thank her for agreeing to co-sign the letter on behalf of the Society's 7 million members "to express our serious concern about the Sea Test . . . and to urge that this Sea Test and all future Sea Tests be immediately suspended pending an investigation into the mass stranding of cetaceans that occurred March 15 and 16, 2000, within its vicinity."

By enlisting Naomi Rose, Reynolds gained both the partnership of the country's largest animal protection group and a marine mammal expert with a Rolodex of almost every marine mammal researcher *not* on the Navy's payroll. There weren't a lot of American names in her Rolodex, since most cetologists in the United States, or the institutions where they worked, were funded in part by the Navy. But they were all serious scientists with world-class credentials—including her husband, Chris Parsons, a British academic transplant with a conservation focus who was also one of Reynolds' expert witnesses.

Rose was yet another graduate from UC Santa Cruz, where Gisiner had been among her teachers. She wrote her PhD thesis on killer whales in the Pacific Northwest, where she met and befriended Ken Balcomb. Then she moved to Washington, DC, to take over the Humane Society's marine mammal campaign. The Society focused most of its anticruelty advocacy on pets, lab animals, factory farming, and wildlife. But Rose had convinced its leadership to sign on as co-plaintiff in a previous lawsuit that Reynolds had brought against the Navy. Reynolds had come to appreciate Rose's pragmatic, results-oriented style—unusual among animal welfare and animal rights activists, who are characterized more by their passionate intensity than by their ability to work collaboratively with groups on different wavelengths of the "humane movement" spectrum.

Reynolds and Rose agreed to add the Navy's general counsel and ONR's attorney to their letter's recipient list, just in case its legal implications escaped the Secretary. By the end of the day, the letter had been faxed and hard copies mailed by certified post.

5:30 P.M.
Pentagon Office of the Department of the Navy, Arlington, Virginia

Reynolds' letter achieved its intended effect of raising an alarm in the Navy's legal wing. The Secretary of the Navy and his general counsel sat face-to-face across the Secretary's desk, marking up their respective copies.

Like many Navy Secretaries, Richard Danzig had never served in the military. Appointed by his former Yale Law School classmate Bill Clinton, Danzig was an attorney, technocrat, and policy wonk who'd spent his career rotating among corporate law firms, the Defense Department, and Washington-based think tanks. He knew next to nothing about marine mammals, and not much more about sonar. But he recognized a threatening legal letter when he read one.

For the past six years, Reynolds had been a persistent thorn in the Navy's side. As soon as Danzig heard about the stranding, he grasped its legal implications. He understood that any evidence gathered on the ground in the Bahamas might well end up as an exhibit attached to a lawsuit. And he'd been expecting just this kind of letter from Reynolds, demanding that the Navy cease and desist whatever exercises it might be conducting in the Bahamas.

Danzig knew he could expect vehement pushback from the fleet if he were to impose any limitations, even temporarily, on training exercises. But unlike the admirals, Danzig had to balance military considerations against the potential political, legal, and public relations fallout from the stranding, especially if the national media picked up the story and ran with it. As the civilian head of the world's largest navy, who served at the pleasure of a civilian commander in chief, the Navy Secretary's job description encompassed the often-conflicting demands of politics, the law, and national defense.

Before deciding how to respond to Reynolds' letter, the Secretary wanted to be fully briefed on any naval activities in the area, and on all matters related to sonar and whale strandings. He was determined to avoid having the Navy dragged into court by NRDC over the Bahamas incident.

Another Navy Secretary had underestimated Reynolds the first time he sued the Navy. Danzig was too savvy a veteran of Washington politics to repeat that mistake.

SIX YEARS EARLIER: FEBRUARY 2, 1994
Los Angeles Office of NRDC

When Reynolds first heard about the Navy's "ship shock" program, Fisheries had already approved the Navy's application to test the structural integrity of its new Aegis-class destroyer, the USS *John Paul Jones*, with underwater explosives. In less than 30 days, the Navy was scheduled to "shock" the ship's hull by detonating bombs weighing up to 10,000 pounds apiece in the coastal waters of Southern California.[1]

For the first time since the passage of the Marine Mammal Protection Act two decades earlier, the Navy had voluntarily applied to Fisheries for a permit to conduct tests that might "harass or harm" marine mammals. As soon as the Navy's plan was announced, the young director of Save the Whales in Los Angeles, Maris Sidenstecker, began to mobilize public and scientific opposition.[2] The marine sanctuary where the Navy proposed to detonate explosives was home to endangered blue, sperm, fin, and humpback whales, as well as dolphins, seals, and sea lions. But the Environmental Assessment conducted by Fisheries arrived at a Finding of No Significant Impact, and the agency authorized the Navy to detonate 282 underwater explosives over the next five years.

Maris Sidenstecker was desperate to stop the ship shock tests. The day she called Reynolds to ask for help, he was sprinting to meet a filing deadline in his four-year-old fight to block construction of a toll road through the fragile coastal wildlands of Orange County, California. In a variation on the spotted owl defense used to save old-growth forests in the Pacific Northwest, Reynolds had successfully invoked the endangered status of the tiny coastal California gnatcatcher to prevent the toll road from being built across the bird's disappearing sage scrub habitat.

He'd never met Sidenstecker, and he had less than three hours to file his motion in the toll-road case. He'd become expert in enforcing the California Endangered Species Act in defense of animals and their habitats, but he'd never sued to protect marine mammals. The only oceans case he'd ever been involved in was to prevent the Los Angeles Bureau of Sanitation from dumping sewage into coastal waters.

In addition to lack of time, staff, and expertise in relevant law, there was the hard fact that any legal battle against the US Navy would be an uphill slog. California was virtually a Navy company town, with seven bases across the state, including the Pacific Fleet's home port in San Diego. The Navy employed tens of thousands of Californians and spent tens of billions of dollars in the state each year. Judges in every circuit could be expected to give special deference to the armed forces, particularly over a "national security" activity such as ship shock tests.

Reynolds was a strategic activist who often found himself surrounded by passionate idealists. He considered himself the grownup in the room who had to make prudent decisions about when, how, and if to take legal action. He never wanted to launch a high-stakes lawsuit without enough time for planning, research, and careful preparation of legal arguments.

Unless he saw blue.

Every so often, some part of his brain overrode his reason. On first hearing about a habitat or an environment in peril, his mind would very occasionally do a synesthetic backflip. Before he could evaluate the case law and size up his opponent's strengths and weaknesses, his visual field became flooded with color. It was always the same rich cobalt blue. He had no idea whether the phenomenon was related to his childhood eye surgeries or to some more obscure deep-brain anomaly. But he'd come to welcome the calm, cool oasis of that blue. As someone who calculated every decision to the nth degree, it was a relief to override the cautionary "Stop" signs with an emphatic "Go" from his gut.

Five minutes into his first phone call about the Navy's planned explosives test, Reynolds saw a field of deep blue spreading out in every direction.

Reynolds' compulsion to answer calls for help was bred in the bone. Growing up, his brother and four sisters often joked about his messiah complex. By fifth grade he'd already developed a precocious, almost comical obsession with civics—and a determination to fix the world's problems. He set up a pair of card tables in the bedroom he shared with his older brother that he called his "ambassador's desk." Armed with a manual typewriter and a government organization manual that included contact information for all the federal agencies and congressional offices, he embarked on a one-boy letter-writing campaign. He'd write to representatives of both parties to comment on upcoming legislative issues. He typed missives to the US ambassador to the United Nations, Adlai Stevenson, with his thoughts about arms control and world hunger. He clipped articles from newspapers and magazines and pasted them onto lined, three-hole paper, and filed them by topic in binders: Civil Rights, Vietnam War, Space Race, Political Speeches. He revered *National Geographic* magazine as the gospel of globalism and kept the year's issues arranged chronologically on his desk. He tape-recorded local community meetings on his Akai reel-to-reel machine and transcribed his own minutes. In 1964 he memorized all 20 propositions on the California ballot and created a seating chart for his sixth-grade classroom that mirrored the US Senate chamber. In 1966, at age 13, he volunteered to work on Democratic congressman John Tunney's reelection campaign.

Inside the crowded Reynolds household on Spruce Street, all the children felt deeply loved by both their parents. But they believed their mother, Mary Lee, had a special bond with Joel—perhaps because of his chronic childhood eye problems. Both his mother and father expressed effusive appreciation for his accomplishments, and Joel feasted on their attention, always proud to report to them on his latest success, in school, on ball fields, or onstage.

Music was the family's common currency. Joel's father, Bill, was a professor of music and the choral conductor at the University of California, Riverside. Everyone sang and played an instrument. Joel played piano from age six, and his father taught him the violin beginning when he was nine. By high school, he was playing violin in the Riverside Symphony Orchestra and singing in the UC Riverside chorus. Music would remain a lifelong source of pleasure for him. But unlike two of his siblings who went on to become music professors, Joel never considered it more than a passionate avocation. He reserved his professional aspirations for the only mission that really mattered to him: saving the planet.

It's not clear from what wellspring of grandiosity Joel drew his self-confidence. Perhaps it was his special bond with his mother. Whatever its source, his unshakable optimism in the face of steep obstacles persisted throughout his life, despite periodic professional setbacks and marital struggles.

Joel's devotion to preserving wilderness was easier to trace. During his family's summer vacations at his grandmother's house in nearby Palos Verdes, he and his siblings and cousins spent all day bodysurfing at Redondo Beach. As a teenager, he began to explore California's wild places. His father built a cabin in the San Bernardino Mountains with five other faculty families. Whenever he could, Joel holed up in the cabin to practice his violin in seclusion and to hike the mountains. It was a revelation to discover—within a few hours' drive from the smog belt of the valley—the foothills of the southern Sierra Nevadas in full spring blossom, the rugged peaks of Kings Canyon National Park, and the vaulted cathedral groves of Sequoia National Park. He climbed Mount Whitney's 14,505-foot peak and planned a summerlong Mexico-to-Canada hike along the 3,000-mile Pacific Crest Trail—until the necessity of getting a paying summer job intervened.

Among his civic role models, Joel placed the Kennedy family on a special pedestal. He idolized their passion for culture, social justice, and family cohesion. To the 15-year-old Joel, Robert Kennedy personified intelligence, compassion, and street fighter grit in service to social justice. Joel followed the progress of the 1968 Democratic presidential primaries with almost unbearable excitement as California emerged as the likely climax of the march toward nomination. Joel was already looking forward to working on Kennedy's fall campaign.

Kennedy's assassination on the night of his California primary victory in June of 1968 broke Joel's heart, but not his idealism or his activism. In an act of epistolary catharsis, he spent the summer typing letters to each of the 104 delegates and alternates to the Republican National Convention, urging them to nominate the moderate Nelson Rockefeller. He withstood the disappointment of Richard Nixon's nomination, election, and inauguration. He refused to cave in to cynicism.

Two years later, when Joel won a national essay-writing contest sponsored by the National Council of Teachers of English, he attracted the attention of top college recruiters. An admissions officer from Harvard came to town, took him out to lunch, and invited him to visit the university that spring. But Joel's father balked at the idea of sending him to a private college. Joel's older brother Chris, also an excellent student, had continued to share a bedroom with Joel at home while attending UC Riverside, where the tuition was virtually free for faculty members' children.

Joel was valedictorian of his high school in 1971. At graduation, he inveighed against society's casual acceptance of violence in a speech that drew heavily from both Martin Luther King Jr. and Robert Kennedy. Three months later, he followed Chris to UC Riverside, and he lived at home throughout college.

Ironically, it was the Nixon administration that offered Joel a path out of Riverside. During his junior year he landed a seven-month internship at the Environmental Protection Agency, which the president had established, albeit reluctantly, in 1970. While the Watergate hearings wore on during the spring and summer of 1973, the 20-year-old Reynolds cut his teeth alongside the first generation of environmental regulators, who were armed with a growing portfolio of newly enacted environmental laws. A year later, after Nixon had resigned and returned in exile to Southern California, Joel was heading east to Manhattan, and Columbia Law School.

FEBRUARY 17, 1994

Shearman & Sterling Law Offices, Century City, Los Angeles

Every environmental lawsuit has a ticking clock, but the 30-day run-up to the first ship shock test was the steepest learning curve Reynolds had ever faced.

The lunacy of detonating 10,000-pound bombs adjacent to a marine sanctuary seemed self-evident to Reynolds. But common sense is never enough to win a case in court. He had to present fact-based legal arguments. And to do that he had to line up co-plaintiffs, recruit expert witnesses, and learn marine mammal law, all in very short order.

Co-plaintiffs were the easiest box to check off. Reynolds wanted a large national organization and local grassroots activists to join the suit. Naomi Rose convinced the Humane Society to join NRDC as lead co-plaintiff. Save the Whales and Heal the Bay filled out the local slots.

Next came the crucial expert testimony, on which virtually every environmental lawsuit depends. Reynolds' roster was deep in ornithologists and toxicologists, but what he knew about marine biology could fit in a petri dish. Fortunately, Save the Whales had cultivated Hal Whitehead, a respected Canadian-based cetacean expert, and his wife and research partner, Lindy Weilgart. Together they helped Reynolds recruit two expert witnesses from the Hubbs-SeaWorld Research Institute—the research arm of SeaWorld marine parks, based in San Diego. Marine parks had deep roots with the Navy, and none went deeper than SeaWorld's. So Reynolds felt fortunate to have Brent Stewart, a pinniped researcher, and Scott Eckert, a turtle expert, join his team.

Naomi Rose introduced Reynolds to John Hall, who signed on as his dolphin expert. Hall had crossed over to the environmental camp after spending most of his career working with the Navy, SeaWorld, and the oil industry. He'd done it all: trained Navy dolphins to clear mines; served as the chief scientist for SeaWorld during the legal and public relations battles over its wild-capture of orcas; conducted bowhead whale surveys for oil companies that wanted to drill under the Arctic ice. By 1994, he was fed up with turning cetaceans into entertainers and research subjects. He'd decided to move to Hawaii to run deep-sea fishing charters. But on his way out the door, he couldn't resist giving the Navy a parting shot—and the whale huggers a boost—if he could.

To add muscle and mainstream credibility to his legal team, Reynolds reached out to a partner in the Los Angeles office of a Wall Street law firm, Shearman & Sterling. Like many corporate lawyers in Los Angeles, Richard Kendall was eager to get involved in pro bono cases of personal interest. He was a corporate litigation specialist who didn't know anything about marine mammal protection. But he was a highly successful trial attorney, with a stable of smart young associates he could lend to the fight. And he had the kind of corner office that broadcast power and success.

Reynolds boned up on the Marine Mammal Protection Act. Originally passed in 1972, it was unique among environmental protection statutes in codifying the "precautionary principle." In drafting the law, Congress made clear that if there's any doubt about a potential threat to marine mammals, the dispute should be resolved to the benefit of the animal. Where was the precaution, Reynolds wondered, in the Navy's selection of such a biologically rich and sensitive marine environment for hundreds of explosives tests?

Two weeks before the ship shock explosions were scheduled to begin, Kendall invited Fisheries and the Navy to a settlement meeting at the law offices of Shearman & Sterling. Given the high stakes, Reynolds would have welcomed an out-of-court settlement. And if they did end up in court, he wanted the judge to know that they'd made every effort to negotiate a settlement.

Kendall's 32nd-floor office had a commanding view west over Century City. On a clear day, you could see all the way to the ocean. Reynolds hoped that Shearman & Sterling's imposing glass and steel fortress would send a message to the Navy that NRDC wouldn't be outgunned if the case went to court.

The day of the meeting, a squadron of Navy attorneys, marine mammal experts, and admirals crowded into Kendall's office. Frank Stone was there from the Navy's Environmental Readiness Office. Gisiner had worked on the Environmental Assessment but hadn't traveled west to the settlement meeting. Fisheries sent representatives from its Southwest Office, which had approved the Navy's permit.

Reynolds hoped his own marine mammal experts would engage the Navy experts in a dialogue that could lead to a safer location for the tests. But the Navy's contingent was led by Sam Ridgway, one of the founders of the Navy's Marine Mammal Training Program back in the early sixties. He was old school and didn't kowtow to civilian whale huggers. An internationally recognized dolphin expert, Ridgway had edited the multivolume *Handbook of Marine Mammals*, the standard text that every science expert in the room had studied in school—and that included Balcomb's chapter on Baird's beaked whales, which Ridgway had invited him to contribute. Ridgway had also been John Hall's boss back in the late sixties when they trained Navy dolphins together. Marine mammal science was still a very small world in the mid-1990s.

As the meeting progressed, it seemed clear to Reynolds that Hall was reluctant to stand up to his old mentor. Reynolds grew increasingly frustrated with the way everyone was pussyfooting around, waiting for the meeting to end. "We're wasting time," he said. "And we don't have much of it left."

He stood up, walked over to a large map of the Southern California coastline that hung on the wall, and pointed to the deep water beyond the continental shelf. "All our experts believe it would be much less risky to detonate out here, beyond the animals' foraging areas on the shelf. Isn't there some compromise area we can agree to?"

The Navy wouldn't budge. The admirals insisted that they needed to move ahead with the tests on schedule, in waters near their San Diego base. Ridgway asked, skeptically, if Reynolds' experts had any "hard data" to support their theory that deep water explosions would pose fewer risks to marine mammals. Reynolds replied that the consensus opinion of his experts was solid enough for him.

Ridgway lifted a large Sierra Club photo book off of Kendall's coffee table, admiring its heft and colorful cover. "In *my* consensus opinion," he said, "this is what the ship shock test will sound like to the whales, dolphins, and sea lions." He held the book a foot above the oak coffee table and let it drop with a dull thud. "That's about it."

Ridgway looked over at the Navy contingent. They rose in unison from their seats. The settlement meeting was over.

• • •

The day after the failed settlement meeting, Reynolds filed a motion for pre-liminary injunction. US District Judge Stephen Wilson scheduled a half-day hearing. It lasted five days.

Initially, Judge Wilson was skeptical of NRDC's challenge. The Navy pre-sented a lineup of uniformed officers from the Pacific Fleet who explained how crucial these tests were to ensure the seaworthiness of its vessels and the safety of its sailors. Relocating the tests would cost millions of dollars and delay deployment of the destroyer to the Far East. But as the facts emerged about the diversity of marine life in the sanctuary and the impact of 10,000-pound bombs on the entire ecosystem, Wilson began asking the Navy and Fisheries pointed questions that weren't addressed in their Environmental Assessments. By the end of the third day, he urged the Navy to work with Fisheries and NRDC to reach an agreement on a different location for the test.

That night, Reynolds fielded phone calls from his own experts, Stewart and Eckert, urging him to reconsider his lawsuit. Yes, they agreed that there were problems with the Navy's plan, but this was the first time it had ever ap-plied for a permit. Next time, they insisted, the Navy would do a better job. If Reynolds pushed the Navy to the wall, it might retreat from the permitting process altogether. Reynolds assumed his experts were feeling the heat from their ONR sponsors, but he wasn't prepared to reverse course.

Judge Wilson eventually grew impatient with the Navy's and Fisheries' unwillingness to reach a settlement. On the fifth day, he announced that he was prepared to rule. During the recess, the Navy's lawyer approached Ken-dall and Reynolds. "We'll settle," he said, "but only if we do it before the judge issues his decision." Reynolds declined the 11th-hour offer, sensing that the tide had turned in his favor.

After the recess, Judge Wilson granted a preliminary injunction and halted the ship shock tests. He ruled that Fisheries and the Navy had "failed in its obligation to protect marine mammals, that it hadn't prepared a full Environmental Impact Statement, and that it hadn't investigated all reason-able alternative sites and properly mitigated the impact of detonations on marine life."[3]

The Navy immediately filed an appeal. But in the meantime they were prohibited from proceeding with the ship shock tests. That's when the general counsel to the Secretary of the Navy, Steven Honigman, decided it was time to intervene.

Honigman had been a Navy JAG attorney and corporate lawyer before President Clinton appointed him general counsel to the Navy. Like Danzig, Honigman had been a Yale Law School classmate of the Clintons, and he was on the same page as the president about the challenge facing the armed forces following the end of the Cold War. If the Navy wanted to maintain its expensive bases and fleets of battleships and submarines, it would have to serve the public interest—and that included protecting the environment. Transparency and accountability were the new bywords, and they were here to stay. During Honigman's tenure, the Navy had stopped dumping garbage and toxic waste at sea. Ship shock threatened to erase its improved image as a good steward of the ocean environment.

Honigman had a broader perspective than the Department of Justice and Navy JAG attorneys who'd tried the case and now wanted to appeal the injunction. He understood that the peacetime battlefront extended beyond the oceans, to the courtroom and to the court of public opinion. Losing an appeal of the ship shock case in a higher court would undermine the veneer of invincibility that the Navy, and every fighting force, works tirelessly to cultivate. He wanted the Navy to stay out of court and start taking the Fisheries permitting process seriously. When legal challenges emerged, he would reach out to reasonable parties on the other side to find compromises the Navy could abide. At least NRDC was staffed by lawyers who spoke a language Honigman could understand.

Within a few days, Honigman had negotiated a settlement with Reynolds and Kendall. The five-year permit for 280 detonations was withdrawn. After three days of aerial surveillance for marine mammals in areas selected by the Navy and by NRDC, Fisheries opted for NRDC's proposed deep-water location as the lowest-risk site.

On June 10, 1994, 85 miles southwest of Point Mugu, California, a Navy tugboat towed a 10,000-pound charge to within a hundred feet of the guided-missile destroyer *John Paul Jones*. The bomb detonated at a depth of 200 feet, and the *John Paul Jones* withstood the blast. But the aftershocks of NRDC's lawsuit resounded through the fleet for more than a decade.

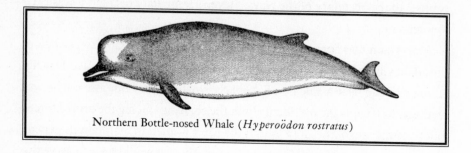

Northern Bottle-nosed Whale (*Hyperoödon rostratus*)

12

Beachside Necropsy

DAY 6: MARCH 20, 2000
Sandy Point, Abaco Island, the Bahamas

To judge by the gaiety, a passerby might have mistaken the necropsy under way outside Ken and Diane's house for a festive beach party. But instead of conch fritters and beer lining the wooden picnic table, it was groaning under the weight of a defrosting Cuvier's head, which was quickly attracting flies.

Much to Balcomb's relief, Alan Bater and Ruth Ewing had stayed behind in Grand Bahama. The Earthlings were in attendance, but they hung back at a respectful distance while Darlene Ketten prepared to conduct her master class in ear anatomy and head dissection. Dave Ellifrit videotaped the proceedings.

Everyone was in exceptionally high spirits, especially Balcomb. The world's leading expert in beaked whale hearing was about to give a tutorial using *his* specimen. Ketten seemed equally elated. It seemed as if every time she rushed to a beaked whale stranding, she was disappointed to find badly decayed remains. She'd certainly never seen anything as fresh as the two heads Ken and Diane had collected. Earlier that morning, they'd decided to dissect the jawbone and the ears from the Cuvier's and leave the Blainville's intact for CT scanning and necropsy back in the States.

Wearing a white smock over her shorts and T-shirt, Ketten flexed her fingers underneath latex gloves and circled the picnic bench in her bare feet, appraising the head from every angle. She asked Balcomb some polite questions about his photo-ID work, which he was pleased to answer. Then she shifted her questioning to the condition of the whale head, which she determined had finally thawed out enough for dissection.

"As you can see, this guy was hit pretty bad by sharks," Balcomb explained. "My guess is he was alive and bleeding when they started to attack, which is why there was so little blood inside when we found him."

"Was there any blood coming out the pinna?" she asked, referring to the vestigial cetacean ear holes, no longer used for hearing. "Or the eyes?"

"No blood from the eyes or ear holes. The eyes were bubbling a little bit. But it was postmortem fluid, mostly, probably juicy from pressure."

"Remarkably fresh specimen. Really extraordinary." Ketten assessed the head with the discerning appreciation that Balcomb remembered seeing on the faces of tuna merchants at Tokyo fish auctions. She selected a green-handled scalpel from her kit and excised a blubber sample from the back of the head. "See how white and smooth this blubber is?" she asked, displaying the specimen for the Earthlings. "You can see the collagen running in white strips, here. That's what makes it so resilient."

After securing the blubber in a plastic sample bag, she selected an entry point at the back of the jawbone. "The acoustic fats along the jawbone are a very different story, as you'll see." She cut a clean slice all the way down the rostrum. "Look at what we've got here. An entirely intact lobe of acoustic fats along the length of the auditory canal! I need a picture of this. Dave, come get a close-up. This is so cool! I've never seen this before. Low-density fats in the auditory canal! Ken, this turned out better than I had dared to hope."

Balcomb was blushing under his salt-and-pepper beard. "You really have Dave to thank for this head." He motioned to Ellifrit behind the video camera. "I'd never have been able to get it off the beach without his help."

Ketten carefully finished resecting the acoustic fat lobe and presented it for all to admire. It was the size and shape of a large salmon fillet but the color of pale ivory. She held up the lobe to her own jaw and moved her head in a lunging motion to mime how beaked whales use the acoustic fats like a receiving antenna for incoming sound waves. "We humans have an internal air cavity to conduct sound from the air to our eardrum," she told the Earthlings. "But whales use these acoustic fats, which are almost precisely matched to the density of salt water. They create a low-impedance channel that conducts the incoming sound straight up the jawbone to the ear bone."

Once the specimen was safely triple-bagged and tagged, Ketten shifted her attention to the ears. "Ordinarily, this would all be greenish and putrefied," she said as she exposed the tissue covering the ear bone. "But see, it looks like teriyaki. Still dark red with myoglobin," she said, referring to the iron-rich protein. "I can't wait to see the ear."

When she got close to the tympanic bone, Ketten motioned the Earthlings to come closer. "Look here, where you can see the stapes tucked in behind the bulla. The stapes is the smallest bone in the body, and it's connected to the largest proportional muscle, the stapedial ligament, which they use to attenuate sound. These animals can put out two hundred twenty decibels at the source, but they can shut down their own receivers before they make that noise. When they know a loud sound is coming, they can turn down the volume, the same way you'd turn down a hearing aid. The problems happen when they don't have time to turn down the volume before a loud sound arrives."

Switching to a flat blade, Ketten slowly, carefully wedged the tympanic bulla free from the ligaments. It was the size and shape of a small conch shell in her hand. "Look at that. This turned out great. A beautiful job," she said, in matter-of-fact appreciation of her own work.

Everyone crowded in to admire the ear bone. "This is beautiful," said Ketten as she rotated the bone in her hand. "Look: this auditory nerve is in perfect shape. It's gorgeous! I love it. The facial nerve is good too; it's huge because there are so many jaw muscles to control. Look at that condition of that nerve—fabulous."

Then her smile gave way to a frown. "Hmm . . . There are two things I don't like about the way this ear looks. The round window is filled with blood. So is the cochlear aqueduct."

An hour later, Ketten had removed the second ear, injected it with formalin, and submerged each ear in a carefully labeled jar of fixative. She was eager to get the Cuvier's head back to the freezer at Nancy's Restaurant, so they swatted away the flies and wrapped it carefully in plastic garbage bags. Then, under Ketten's watchful gaze, Balcomb stowed the formalin jars holding the ear bones in a locked filing cabinet in his office.

Ketten wanted to escort the head back to storage. After inspecting Les' bait freezer, she was satisfied that the specimens were being kept at a constant temperature. But she was unhappy with the fact that it didn't have a lock. After they'd replaced the head, she wrapped the freezer lid with yellow tamper-evident tape and signed and dated the chain-of-custody form. She explained to Balcomb and Claridge that they needed to sign and date the same form when they removed the specimens for transport to Boston. She expressed optimism that Fisheries could clear the import paperwork within a week or ten days.

"I want these two heads up at my lab at Harvard, where we can get a better look at them inside the scanner," said Ketten. "The dolphin too. Then we'll take them down to Woods Hole for a proper necropsy."

Though he didn't want to spoil the collegial mood, Balcomb needed explicit reassurance from Ketten that he and Claridge would be included in the ongoing investigation after they delivered the heads. And as a lifelong collector of beaked whale skulls, he wanted to get the heads back from Fisheries once the final necropsies had been completed. Ketten agreed to his conditions.

They had time for a late lunch before Ketten's flight. She was highly complimentary of the conch salad Les served them on his back porch, comparing it favorably to the octopus she'd recently enjoyed in Greece.

"You've done good work," said Ketten, raising her Kalik beer bottle toward Balcomb and Claridge. "I can't tell you how often I get on a plane to Timbuktu and come back with nothing to show for it. This has been a rare pleasure."

"To the 'volunteers' who brought you here," Balcomb toasted. They clinked their three bottles together as one.

MARCH 20, 2000

Navy Office of Environmental Readiness, Alexandria, Virginia

It had only taken 48 hours from its first reports for the story to go national. Admiral Baucom stared glumly at the clippings that bulged out of his *Early Bird* briefing file. Dozens of papers across the country had picked up a full-length Associated Press article connecting the Navy to the Bahamas stranding. Meanwhile, the headline of the article in the *Washington Post* read: "Whales Became Stranded After U.S. Naval Exercises; Bahamas Incidents Drawing Scrutiny."

The Navy public affairs office, in concert with a cluster of internal lawyers, had crafted an artfully ambiguous response to the incident. Reading the AP article, Admiral Baucom wasn't altogether sure what to make of the Navy statement. It *seemed* to acknowledge that ONR was conducting research on the north side of Abaco Island—while at the same time insisting that it couldn't possibly be related to the stranding. Frank Stone and the Navy JAG attorney assigned to N-45 stood behind Baucom's desk, reading over his shoulder.

FREEPORT, Bahamas—Eight whales beached and died soon after the U.S. Navy conducted anti-submarine exercises off the northern Bahamas, prompting an investigation and calls for an end to the exercises.

The Navy said Tuesday that there was no evidence to link the whale deaths to last week's exercise testing sonar detection of submarines.

Navy Cmdr. Greg Smith said the tests took place from about 1 p.m. to 5 p.m. March 15 off Abaco Island as part of a series of exercises testing "sonar buoys" that were to continue through March 22.

Marine biologist Ken Balcomb of the Earthwatch environmental group said beachings began that same day, and within two days at least 14 whales had grounded themselves on Abaco, Grand Bahama to the north, and Eleuthera to the south. Eight died, prompting investigations by Bahamian and U.S. scientists and authorities.

"A whale beaching in the Bahamas is a once-in-a-decade occurrence," said Balcomb, an American who has been studying whales around Abaco Island for nine years. "We will be making recommendations to the Bahamian government that these sort of exercises be terminated," he said. "The fact that it coincides with the military exercises cannot be just coincidental."

But the Navy spokesman said there was no evidence linking the two events. "My understanding of the actual locations would put the island between the operations where the sonobuoys were located and where the whales eventually beached themselves," said Smith.

He said the exercise had nothing to do with Low Frequency Active sonar, a new and controversial system that transmits sonar pulses so loud they can match the roar of a rocket launch. . . .

The U.S. National Marine Fisheries Service, responsible for overseeing all U.S. actions that could affect the environment at home or abroad, said it approved the Navy's Environmental Assessment for its exercise.

Roger Gentry, coordinator of the service's acoustics team, said the exercises shouldn't have affected the whales. "Yet we have beached whales."

Baucom was still new to his desk job, but he understood that leading the *Early Bird* two days in a row was bad news. National coverage meant the stranding investigation would be conducted in a media spotlight.

"What's the story with this marine biologist?" he asked. "And who the hell is he to recommend that the Bahamians terminate these kinds of exercises?"

Stone explained that Balcomb was the field researcher who collected the whale heads right after the stranding. That's all he knew about him.

Ever since the stranding five days earlier, Stone had been in constant communication with Bob Gisiner at ONR and with Fleet Command in Norfolk. Information was the most valuable currency inside his world, and he'd always tried to be the best-informed person in a crisis room. He'd compiled a detailed diagram of the fleet's movements in the Bahamas on March 15, which appeared to correspond in time and place with the reported locations of the strandings.

What he hadn't discovered was that Ken Balcomb had trained as a Navy pilot at the Pensacola flight school one year ahead of Admiral Baucom. And he didn't know that Balcomb had served as an acoustics expert in Navy sound surveillance for seven years.

MARCH 21, 2000
Sandy Point, Abaco Island, the Bahamas

By the end of the first national news cycle, Balcomb realized that the Navy had outflanked him. He assumed by now that Navy officials knew a lot more than they were saying. Someone had made a calculated decision to let the public affairs office disclose the sonobuoy experiments being conducted by ONR north of Abaco—a red herring that shifted the public's focus away from the site of the strandings and gave the Navy some plausible deniability. Anyone who claimed that sound experiments conducted on the Atlantic side of the island could cause the strandings on the west side, in Providence Channel, would come off sounding like an idiot.

Balcomb had let himself sound like that idiot. He knew that the destroyer and frigates he'd seen in the channel weren't connected to any sonobuoy experiments. But he wasn't ready to talk about the fleet's presence in the canyon. Not yet. He wanted more facts about the stranding. Without them, all he could do was speculate.

Balcomb hadn't been prepared for the rapid-fire questions from reporters angling for a pithy sound bite or an impassioned accusation directed at the Navy. He felt conflicted. He'd served for seven years and was loyal to the Navy's mission. But he'd also learned a healthy distrust of the Navy on an institutional level, especially when it felt exposed. Within the ranks, there was a strict code of accountability, and a rigorous process for after-action investigations when things went awry. But for most of the admirals in the fleet, accountability began and ended with the Navy. They only grudgingly answered to their civilian overseers, and they didn't bother to veil their contempt for the press.

Balcomb wanted to keep the Navy honest and accountable, and he wanted to make sure that people understood what had happened to the whales in Providence Channel. But he hadn't formulated a coherent hypothesis yet, and he didn't want to come off sounding half-cocked. He also wanted to preserve his role in the ongoing investigation. So he decided not to mention the destroyer and frigates he'd seen in the channel, or his own naval history and his knowledge of marine acoustics.

The day the Associated Press story ran, a *60 Minutes* producer called Balcomb from New York. She said she wanted to feature him in an investigative piece and use his videotape of the mass stranding, which she'd heard about from the CBS affiliate in Miami. Balcomb told her he wasn't ready to work with anyone on a story, but she insisted that she was planning to bring a crew down to Abaco whether Balcomb cooperated or not.

As soon as the newspaper stories began to appear, Balcomb started taking flack from ONR and Fisheries. Gisiner fired off an email telling him to sit tight and stop talking to the press. Then came a phone call from the head of marine acoustics at Fisheries, Roger Gentry.

Gentry, Gisiner, and Balcomb had all been grad students together at UC Santa Cruz. They were the young, second-generation marine mammal scientists, a band of brothers who vied like siblings for the attention and patronage of their professors, who were the founding fathers of the field. But Gentry had stood apart from the other grad students, the first among equals. He was tall and movie-star handsome, even amid the seaweed and slime of marine biology fieldwork. By the time Balcomb showed up at school, Gentry was already teaching undergraduates and publishing articles on gray whale distribution in Mexico and California.

Balcomb and Gentry had become friends that year. They spent a long winter together in an unheated hut on the Baja coast with nothing to do but tally the whales migrating along the shore, and nothing to eat but what they could scavenge on the beach. After he earned his PhD, Gentry authored a half dozen books on Steller sea lions and the fur seals of the Pribilof Islands off the coast of Alaska. Then he ran Fisheries' Northwest Regional Science Center for six years.

Rumor had it that Gentry and Gisiner had been up for the same job at ONR in the early 1990s, but Gisiner won out. Although Gentry had more academic chops, Gisiner had deeper ties to Navy research. Then, in the mid-1990s, Fisheries found itself in the middle of acoustic controversies

involving Navy sonar and the oil and gas industry's use of air guns during seismic exploration for undersea deposits. Gentry wasn't a bioacoustics
expert—at least not where whales were concerned—but he was a respected
academic who'd done a good job running the Northwest Science Center.
When headquarters decided it needed a marine acoustics department, Gentry got the nod.

Balcomb had never felt competitive with Gentry or Gisiner—they'd been
on totally different trajectories. Decades after university, Balcomb was still
doing field research, while Gentry and Gisiner had graduated to administrative jobs with big budgets and staffs, piling up co-author credits on the
publications of studies their agencies funded. But now that their paths had
crossed again, he felt a familial tug toward the past. When he heard Roger's
voice on the phone, it was as if the fraternal bonds of grad school had been
embedded in amber.

Gentry spoke to Balcomb as an older, wiser brother would. "You have to
be patient, Ken. Let the process play out." He assured Balcomb that Fisheries
was committed to a full and independent investigation. Hadn't they sent their
top people down there, and wasn't Darlene working with Ken as a partner?
But if Balcomb wanted to be part of the team, he had to act like it. He couldn't
go shooting his mouth off to reporters before the investigation had even gotten under way.

Balcomb couldn't tell whether Roger was being sincere or was simply
naïve. They both knew that the Navy was providing most of the personnel
and funding for the investigation. Balcomb also suspected that Fisheries
would only get the fleet records and acoustic data that the Navy wanted to
share with it. As Balcomb knew from his two tours, the Navy was the most
secretive of all the armed services, and never more so than when things went
wrong. Internally, the Navy was relentless in its search after the facts. But it
tended to erect a firewall between its internal investigation and any public
accounting.

Ketten had agreed to keep Balcomb involved and informed, but he was
glad to have Gentry—someone he had personal history with—working inside
the Fisheries end of the investigation.

• • •

The day after Ketten left Abaco, the Earthlings decamped, and Ken and Diane could finally exhale. Having the volunteers around had been like hosting houseguests during a family crisis. That afternoon, they took the boat out to the canyon to troll for whales. They took along their catalogue of ID photos in hopes of identifying those they'd pushed off the beach the first day of the stranding. They spotted two whales, but none of the ones that had come ashore. The canyon was eerily quiet.

Back at the house in Sandy Point, alone except for Dave Ellifrit, Ken and Diane felt swamped by sadness. For a decade, they had built their life in the Bahamas around the beaked whales—a community that had made its home in the underwater canyon for millions of years. They could only guess at what had driven the whales onto the beaches or, they assumed, to their final rest on the floor of the canyon.

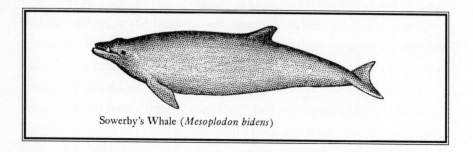

Sowerby's Whale (*Mesoplodon bidens*)

13

Cease and Desist

DAY 7: MARCH 21, 2000
Pentagon Office of the Department of the Navy, Arlington, Virginia

From the moment Navy Secretary Danzig heard about the Bahamas stranding while meeting with Pacific Fleet Command in Pearl Harbor, he knew he'd have his hands full managing the fallout, both inside and outside the Navy. He fully expected to have to deflect attacks, both legal and rhetorical, from groups such as NRDC and the Humane Society—which also meant he'd have to carefully manage the Navy's messaging to the media. And lurking in the background was Fisheries, which might feel pressured by the press coverage to assert its regulatory authority.

Eventually, he'd have to deal with the admirals. Fleet Command's priority was to protect its combat readiness—which meant the admirals would be at loggerheads with the Navy lawyers, both inside the secretariat and N-45's environmental division.

Simply sorting out the facts of the fleet's involvement, if any, would tax all of Danzig's skills as arbiter among the Navy's competing branches. Danzig put his Assistant Secretary for Installations and Environment, Robert Pirie Jr., in charge of interviewing the Atlantic Fleet commanders. As the highest-ranking former commander in the secretariat, Pirie was the obvious person to reconstruct the Atlantic Fleet's movements in the Caribbean.

Pirie was a second-generation blue-suiter—the son of a highly decorated vice admiral and a former submarine commander himself—so he wasn't bashful about butting heads with admirals. The Atlantic Fleet was led by some of the fastest-rising stars in the Navy, many of them poised for their next move up in rank. Danzig had to update his org chart almost weekly to keep abreast of the Navy's ever-changing leadership. The commander of the Atlantic Fleet, Admiral Vern Clark, was due to take over as Chief of Naval Operations in July. His successor as fleet commander, Admiral Bob Natter, and the commander of the Second Fleet in the Caribbean, Admiral Bill Fallon, were widely perceived as being on track to becoming Chief of Naval Operations themselves someday.*

Pirie understood that these men hadn't risen to three- and four-star admiralty simply by seniority. In addition to talent, smarts, and a strong work ethic, they all had robust survival instincts and high levels of testosterone and ambition. None of these admirals wanted a black, or even gray, mark on his record that could slow his ascent to the pinnacle of Fleet Command. Pirie had conducted enough after-action reports to know that when something went wrong during exercises, the cockroaches always came from someone else's compartment.

Like many large organizations, the Navy suffered from "stovepiping." While the name for this syndrome was originally coined by the intelligence community, the problem of vertical, nonshared silos of information was endemic to the Navy. Among the competitive fleet divisions, surface ship commanders didn't always know what the submariners or the aviators were up

---

* Both Admirals Natter and Fallon went on to assume four-star leadership commands in the Navy. Natter became commander, US Atlantic Fleet/Fleet Forces Command, while Fallon became the first naval officer to rise to commander, US Central Command. On March 11, 2008, Fallon announced his resignation from CENTCOM and retirement from active duty, citing administrative complications caused in part by an *Esquire* magazine article that described him as the only thing standing between the Bush administration and war with Iran.

to. And nobody in the fleet paid much attention to Environmental Readiness, since that division reported to Installations, not Operations. The fleet viewed environmental compliance as just another round of paperwork with boxes to check and signature lines to sign and file, a bothersome distraction from its combat mission—which at the time was focused on supporting NATO operations during the Bosnian Civil War in the former Yugoslavia. Meanwhile, a scientific research division like ONR operated in a stovepipe of its own, and its reports rarely rose to fleet level. Other than trying to avoid colliding with right whales, the fleet hadn't been much focused on ONR's marine mammals research.

Pirie's mission was to shine a light down all the stovepipes surrounding the Bahamas incident and reconstruct a coherent, comprehensive account for the Secretary. Danzig had a reputation for being thorough and fair. The more complete Pirie's reconstruction of events, the more influence he could exert over the Secretary's decision making. The final judgment on whether or not to limit sonar exercises was Danzig's, but Pirie knew the admirals would expect him to take their side in any face-off with the civilian Secretary.

Pirie flew down to Fleet Forces Command headquarters in Norfolk, Virginia, to meet with Admirals Natter and Fallon. First on his plate was figuring out why the fleet was conducting exercises in the Bahamas. He soon learned that the trail to the Bahamas stranding led back to another environmental and political fiasco in the Caribbean: the US naval base in Vieques, Puerto Rico.

Since 1948, the US Navy had been using the eastern part of the small Puerto Rican island of Vieques as a missile and bombing range and the western end for weapons storage. Problematically, the middle of the island was still inhabited by 9,000 local civilians. According to the Puerto Rican protesters, the Navy had dumped more than 20 million pounds of industrial waste on the island, including lead paint and acid. The Vieques Fishermen's Association claimed that the Navy had poisoned the reefs and killed off the fish. Puerto Rican health officials reported spikes in cancer rates among the islanders.

The Navy had managed to keep the government officials on its side, until a wayward bomb killed an islander named David Sanes during target practice in April 1999. Within days of his death, demonstrations broke out across Puerto Rico. Soon protesters started coming ashore on Vieques and setting up tents inside the practice grounds. As soon as they were arrested and removed, another group would land and set up camp on the beach.

Eventually it became a badge of honor for Puerto Rican celebrities in the States to get arrested on Vieques. Singer Ricky Martin and actors Jimmy Smits and Edward James Olmos all jetted in, with TV cameras in tow. Al Sharpton and Jesse Jackson flew in to show solidarity. NRDC attorney Robert Kennedy Jr. came down to sue the Navy for toxic dumping, and then stuck around to get busted and hauled off to jail. He even named his newborn son after the island: Aiden Vieques Kennedy.

After more than 200 straight days of protests on the Vieques range, the Navy decided it was time to shut down the media circus. It brought in 1,000 US Marshals and Marines to tear down the shantytown settlement and haul the protesters off the island and into jail. Hundreds of demonstrators were arrested. But days later, hundreds of new agitators came ashore. This time they brought a whole new cast of characters: Hollywood celebrities, members of Congress, priests, nuns, ministers, and the mayors of every town in Puerto Rico. Even the archbishop of San Juan got himself arrested.

Vieques had turned into an international embarrassment for the Navy. But Admiral Natter had a more pressing question to answer in the winter of 2000: Where to stage the Atlantic Fleet's training exercises now that it had become impossible to operate on the Vieques range?

Every Navy carrier strike group had to complete war-game training exercises before deploying overseas.[1] The USS *George Washington* battle group—including an aircraft carrier, three destroyers, two frigates, and three hunter-killer subs—needed to train in a deep-water environment that could simulate antisubmarine scenarios in the Strait of Hormuz and the Persian Gulf, which is where this battle group was headed after completing its sonar training. Specifically, Admiral Natter was looking for a "choke point" training site such as Vieques, which was adjacent to a deep underwater canyon with limited entry points at either end. Providence Channel, which traversed the Great Bahama Canyon, was the obvious choice.

Natter liked that the Bahamas were closer than Puerto Rico to Atlantic

Fleet's home port in Norfolk, Virginia. Any support aircraft needed during exercises could fly out of the Mayport Naval Station in Jacksonville, Florida. Best of all, the underwater landscape of Great Bahama Canyon had been extensively mapped by the Navy, going all the way back to its deep sound channel research off Eleuthera during World War II. Although the Bahama Islands were in foreign waters, the US Navy had a good working relationship with its government, which received tens of millions of dollars a year in rent for the AUTEC submarine testing range off Andros Island.

Natter's planning goal was to avoid the sort of "single-point failure" of the Vieques debacle that threw the entire Atlantic Fleet training schedule into disarray. He envisioned the exercises in Great Bahama Canyon as a test run. If things went smoothly, the Navy could move most of its Vieques-based exercises up to the Bahamas on an ongoing basis.

Things hadn't gone smoothly.

Natter and Fallon confirmed that the Second Fleet had been operating with sonar in the canyon the night before the strandings. But no one on the ships had been alerted to the presence of whales, and none had been sighted during the exercises, either in the canyon or stranding on the beach. Of course, they were nighttime exercises, so visual sightings would have been difficult, if not impossible. Regardless of the coincidence in timing, Natter and Fallon were not willing to concede that the exercises had caused the strandings.

As soon as Pirie got back from Norfolk, he briefed the Secretary's general counsel, Stephen Preston, on what he'd learned from the fleet admirals. After spending most of the 1990s trying to keep Preston's predecessor, Steven Honigman, from "giving away the store to the environmentalists," as he saw it, Pirie was reassured by Preston's more pugnacious style. In light of the briefing he was about to give the Secretary, Pirie hoped that Preston could present a legal rationale for allowing sonar training exercises to proceed on schedule.

MARCH 22, 2000
Office of Naval Research, Arlington, Virginia

Admiral Paul Gaffney was due to depart as chief of ONR in three months to become president of the National Defense University in Washington, DC.

Gaffney didn't want to exit ONR under a cloud. Nor did he want ONR to become the fall guy for the fleet exercises in the Bahamas. Unusual among flag officers, Gaffney was a trained oceanographer who'd devoted the shank of his career to directing the Naval Research Lab and the Office of Naval Research. As a man of science, he wanted to present the Navy Secretary with a science-based defense of ONR's sea tests in the Bahamas.

With more than 500 scientists and other staff working under him at ONR, Gaffney couldn't keep abreast of every field program in every ocean. But he quickly located the acoustics expert in charge of ONR's Littoral Warfare tests in the Bahamas, and called him into his office.[2] Gaffney and the acoustician agreed that ONR's sonobuoy testing on the northeast side of the islands couldn't have caused the stranding on the western coastlines. They both assumed that some sort of acoustic event was to blame. Maybe it was military, or maybe it was something seismic, like an earthquake or commercial explosives. Meanwhile, the Secretary was rattling the cage for hard data, not just theories.

Gaffney directed the acoustician to produce a real-time acoustic model of whatever had happened in the canyon on the night of March 15. The admiral would get him the logs of ship movements and sonar transmissions from the fleet. Gaffney wanted the modeling and analysis to be conducted by a team of expert acousticians from *outside* the Navy—either arm's-length academics or private contractors. If this all ended up in the press or in the courts, the Secretary would need to have an impartial, non-Navy assessment.

The acoustician pointed out that there *weren't* any marine acoustic experts that the Navy hadn't hired or funded at some point. At least not in the United States. And he couldn't imagine the fleet sharing classified ship logs with foreign nationals. Gaffney considered this problem for a minute. "Okay, then just get the best people you can find on it," he said. "I want unassailable experts."

After lengthy discussion, they decided to hire two different research groups to work up independent models, using different algorithms: one at the Naval Research Lab, which had the best Navy acousticians; and another at the Massachusetts Institute of Technology, a longtime Navy contractor that boasted the best computers and software.

Just three days after the stranding, Secretary Danzig had called Gaffney with direct questions about what ONR was doing in the Bahamas and if it could have caused the whales to beach. Gaffney had referred the Secretary to Bob Gisiner as ONR's resident expert in bioacoustics.

Gisiner had been working late at his office on Saturday and was taken aback by the unexpected call from the Secretary. As he reviewed the basics of beaked whale sensitivity to sonar and recounted the details on the Greek stranding in 1996, Gisiner could hear Danzig taking notes on the other end. He was impressed by the Secretary's questions about the underwater topography of the Great Bahama Canyon compared to the Ionian Sea. Danzig told Gisiner to make sure that Darlene Ketten joined the conference call he was setting up with the fleet. In the meantime, he told Gisiner to call him on his cell phone day or night with any important developments from the Bahamas investigation.

SATURDAY, MARCH 27, 2000, MORNING
Woods Hole Oceanographic Institution

The Navy Secretary's conference call wasn't due to begin until 0900 hours, but retired Rear Admiral Dick Pittenger had been pacing his office since dawn. After a decade of civilian life, Pittenger still hadn't adjusted to a nine-to-five regimen.

It had taken time to get used to the casual work style at Woods Hole, where the marine biologists wore shorts and flip-flops and everyone addressed him by his first name. When he'd earned his first star, Pittenger was assigned a personal adjutant to carry his briefcase and open the back door to his car, which came with a driver and a Navy flag on the hood. But it wasn't the trappings of power that Pittenger missed from his days in the admiralty. It was the actual power to make decisions about the future of the Navy and national defense.

For a man who would rise through the ranks of the US Navy to become its Director of Antisubmarine Warfare at the peak of the Cold War, Dick Pittenger had an unlikely and unpromising childhood. He grew up "sickly and dust poor," as he described himself, in Lexington, Nebraska, during the worst of the 1930s Dust Bowl drought. Before his first birthday, he almost died of pneumonia, as his older brother had. After his family lost its farm to the bank and moved to Tacoma, Washington, Dick joined the Sea Scouts— a sailing program of the Boy Scouts—and fell in love with all things marine. At 14, he was a malnourished 80-pound boy who'd never seen a doctor or a dentist. A few years later he enjoyed a growth spurt that raised his weight to a normal range and lowered his voice in the barbershop quartet he sang with from soprano to bass.

Dick joined the Navy Reserves at age 17 during the Korean War and managed to pass the Naval Academy entrance exam by going back to high school for an extra year of study. He scored so high on the Navy IQ test that the Academy was willing to overlook his lung problems, which would persist throughout his life. After squeaking through the Academy physical, and after his first-ever dentist visit, he headed east to Annapolis.

The Academy was like Oz for Dick, who was the first in his family to graduate high school. He couldn't help feeling like a rube alongside his fellow midshipmen, many of whom—such as his classmate John McCain—were born into Navy royalty. But he worked hard at his studies and graduated in 1958 in the top third of his class.

His first assignment out of the Academy was to the same Fleet Sonar School in Key West that Ken Balcomb would later attend. After earning a master's degree in the physics of underwater acoustics at the Naval Postgraduate School in Monterey, California, he skippered a minesweeper off the coast of Vietnam. Then he attended the Naval War College in Newport, Rhode Island, where he wrote his thesis on the history of surface sonar. During his Cold War tour in Europe, Pittenger commanded a fast frigate and led an antisubmarine warfare squadron of destroyers that tracked Soviet subs throughout the Mediterranean. By the end of the 1970s, he had risen to the admiralty and become the Navy's chief sponsor of midfrequency active sonar.

In the mid-1980s, when the Soviet subs became too quiet to track with the passive SOSUS system, the Navy brought Pittenger to the Pentagon as a two-star admiral to direct and revamp its antisubmarine warfare strategy. Faced with a Soviet submarine fleet he described as "virtually silent and underfoot," he devised an intricate system for "acoustic cueing" across wide ocean areas. His master plan for expanding active sonar systems included low and midfrequency platforms on surface ships, sonobuoys, towed arrays, and aircraft. When he became Oceanographer of the Navy in 1988, he continued to promote his antisubmarine warfare plans in the Pentagon and on Capitol Hill.

Then, in 1989, the Soviet empire began to wobble, and soon after, to tear apart. After feverishly "hunting Ivan" in every ocean of the world for four decades, the US Navy was suddenly a fighting force without a mission. Pittenger had spent his entire 35-year Navy career as a Cold Warrior, and now the war was over.

Unless they are tracking toward the very top of the four-star command chain, most two-star admirals, such as Pittenger, retire from the Navy in their fifties, at the peak of their careers. Some move on to academia. Others, who need to better support their families after decades on a military salary, take jobs in defense contracting. An admiral whom Pittenger worked with closely at the Pentagon had retired to become director of Woods Hole Oceanographic Institution. Soon afterward, he recruited Pittenger to join him at Woods Hole to coordinate its arctic research program and upgrade its fleet of research vessels. So in 1990, Pittenger quietly retired from active duty and settled down in Woods Hole, Massachusetts.

Pittenger had served with total devotion to his Navy. But his shoulders sagged when he thought about how he'd shortchanged his family. They'd had to move 22 times over the course of his career, and he'd been at sea much more often than not, missing most of his four kids' birthdays. His wife named their first two daughters, Beth and Meg, after the sisters in Louisa May Alcott's *Little Women*, whose father, Mr. March, was away constantly during the Civil War.

His worst memory was during the Vietnam War. The minesweeper he commanded was stuck in port at Subic Bay riding out a typhoon, while his wife was in labor with their third child back in Huntington Beach, California. Pittenger received a ship-to-shore radio message from the Red Cross reporting that his son had been born. There was no phone on board the ship, but he was able to see a phone booth a hundred yards away on the other side of the storm-driven harbor. He made a run for it, reached the booth, dropped a coin in the phone box, and convinced the operator to put a call through to his wife in California. During the call with his wife, he learned that his daughter

Beth was at the same hospital in a full body cast, having suffered a spiral leg fracture in a bike accident. The storm raging outside the phone booth seemed to mirror his swirling emotions of joy, anxiety, and frustration at being 7,000 miles from his family and powerless to help them. When the call was over, he had to get back onboard his ship to ride out the second half of the typhoon with his crew.

Retired admirals such as Pittenger play an important, though largely unseen, role in Navy policy making. On a logistical level, the fleet relies on its retired admirals to officiate at war games and to review after-action reports, which is why Pittenger had been invited to participate in the conference call from Woods Hole, along with Darlene Ketten, who worked across campus. On a more informal basis, retired admirals network with their far-flung "flag buddies" to exert influence on a range of policy issues—such as keeping Navy leadership from compromising national security in the name of political expediency.

Pittenger had been anxiously awaiting the Secretary's conference call all week. But then, he had spent his entire naval career in a state of chronic, even obsessive anxiety. For decades he had worried about the next generation of Soviet subs growing too quiet for SOSUS sensors to detect. He worried about spies and about any subs that might leak through the global acoustic net the Navy had woven across the oceans. As a ship commander, he worried about the safety of the men under his command. During his time at the Pentagon, he worried about the politicians on Capitol Hill who cut defense funding every time peace broke out, as if national security were a onetime battle that you could win and then forget about. When the Cold War ended and the Soviet navy retreated to dry dock, he worried about where the next submarine threat might emerge—from China or from North Korea, or from any rogue nation with a submarine that might be lurking, unseen and unheard, anywhere in the world's dark oceans.

Long before the Bahamas stranding—and particularly since the Greek stranding four years earlier—Pittenger had been ringing the bell about the need to bring sonar exercises inside the permitting and regulation process. He realized that with its new generations of high-powered active sonars, the Navy was engaged in "acoustic warfare." The sooner it started getting permission through proper channels, he reasoned, the better. His message to his fellow admirals, active and retired, had been dire and direct: "The end of active sonar is in sight unless we do something to change the way we operate." Now he wished he'd rung that bell even louder.

He worried that the active sonar program he'd nurtured, and which he still viewed as crucial to national defense, was imperiled not only by environmental activists, but by the cavalier attitude of many in the Navy leadership. One three-star admiral he'd tried to persuade on the topic had said, "Tell me again, why are we having all this discussion about some fish?" To which Pittenger replied, "Because if we don't it could shut down our Navy." He'd been down this road before. For years the Navy brass had insisted—in defiance of an unstoppable social and legal tide to the contrary—that women couldn't be integrated into the fighting fleet. Now he was girding for what he feared would be another bungled engagement with the media and the forces of social change.

In the days leading up to the conference call, Pittenger had tried to convince both the active-duty and retired admirals he knew that the Navy needed to get out in front of this stranding mess. As soon as the commanders realized that fleet exercises were likely involved, he argued, they should have said straight out and in public, "We've got a problem, and we're going to fix it." Instead, the fleet had placed its battle readiness in the hands of lawyers, none of whom had ever commanded sailors or ships in combat.

The Secretary ran the conference call, though he did very little of the talking. The review was conducted with precision and civility. No one spoke out of turn, as Danzig methodically polled the participants on whether or not he should curtail sonar exercises, and why.

The Secretary wanted to hear first from Ketten, who had recently returned from the Bahamas. Speaking from Pittenger's office, she reported her suspicions of acoustic trauma, based on her beachside necropsy. It was impossible to identify the source of that trauma, and the heads weren't due up at Harvard for another few days. So she didn't want to speculate on what she'd find. Since the underwater topography and acoustics of the Bahamas were unlikely to exist anywhere else, she cautioned against generalizing a sonar threat to marine mammals from this one stranding event, even if it turned out to be sonar related.

Next up was Gaffney. After he ruled out any connection between ONR's sea tests north of the islands and the strandings, he reported that so far his acoustic teams hadn't been able to identify any *nonmilitary* acoustic sound sources in the canyon on March 15. No industrial explosives. No earthquakes or sea storms. He noted that ONR had circulated its cautionary report from the Greek stranding to all the commanding officers in the fleet four years earlier. And since that 1996 incident, ONR had undertaken a more formal permitting process. In this case, it had conducted its Environmental Assessments in collaboration with the Southeast Regional Office of Fisheries, which had issued ONR a permit to conduct tests of its Littoral Warfare weapons.

Admirals Fallon and Natter knew they were in the hot seat. They felt that Danzig was trying to get them to acknowledge that the fleet's antisubmarine exercises caused the strandings. But neither of them was willing to concede the point. Fallon adamantly resisted any curtailment of sonar exercises. Expressing the strongest emotion of anyone during the call, he asserted, "It would be easy to shut down sonar exercises—but doing the easy thing isn't our job." Natter stated his opposition to a shutdown in more muted language. The investigation had just begun, he pointed out, and they'd only been able to eliminate a few of the possible causes of the strandings. Then he punted to Pittenger, in the hopes that the Secretary might defer to the most experienced admiral on the call.

An obsessive student of naval history, Pittenger felt compelled to share his historical perspective on the high cost of nonpreparedness. It had happened time and again: as soon as the US Navy decisively defeated an enemy, the politicians slashed its funding, and the Navy fell behind in the never-ending chase after more rigorous antisubmarine warfare training. At the end of World War II, a war-weary nation cut back on defense spending, while the Soviet submarine fleet swelled in numbers. After the Vietnam War, Nixon sought détente with the Soviets, just as Russia was rolling out its quietest, most deadly class of submarines. When the Soviet Union collapsed in 1989, the politicians in search of savings were delighted to turn a blind eye to the non-Soviet threats in oceans.

By the late 1990s, the navies of virtually every aspiring power in the developing world boasted quiet attack submarines, among them Libya, North Korea, Pakistan, India, and Iran. Forty-three navies worldwide operated submarines—even nations as militarily insignificant as Thailand, Algeria, and Colombia.[3] At any given time, submarines from a dozen different navies might be patrolling the waterways of the Mediterranean and the Persian Gulf, including Turkey, Greece, Egypt, Israel, and Saudi Arabia. And in the Pacific, China was quickly building up a naval force, while the North Koreans had dozens of submarines and Chinese-made midget subs circulating in the waters off the East Asian coastline.

For all their armaments and high-tech sensors, the Navy's warships remained vulnerable to the most destabilizing, asymmetrical force in the ocean: a rogue submarine lying in wait along the side of an underwater canyon. A single torpedo could sink a modern battleship up to frigate size. Cruisers and destroyers could probably withstand one hit, but two well-placed torpedo strikes could split them in half. Even a massive aircraft carrier was at risk. Ships could be replaced, but the real hostages to unpreparedness were the hundreds of crew members serving on each battleship—or the thousands aboard an aircraft supercarrier.

Active sonar remained the only way to track virtually silent diesel-electric subs. "Antisubmarine warfare is hard," he told Secretary Danzig. "Sonar is complicated. You put sound in the water, and it doesn't go straight. It winds its way through shadow zones and convergent zones, around sea mounts and underwater storms." To be effective in combat, he insisted, sonar operators have to train in a full spectrum of battle environments and situations. Once acquired, sonar training is a fragile and perishable skill. If you don't train constantly and in real-world conditions for antisubmarine warfare, you're dead in the water. That's why war games are such deadly serious business.

Pittenger respectfully but emphatically asked the Secretary to maintain the level of fleet training and readiness required for national security. But he also advised the Secretary to take a middle path between caving to the environmentalists and going to war with them. If the Navy wanted to maintain the moral high ground, he said, it should acknowledge that something had gone awry in the Bahamas and resolve publicly to get to the bottom of it. There was no reason, he suggested, why sonar training exercises couldn't proceed in parallel with a vigorous and transparent investigation into the cause of the Bahamas stranding. Stonewalling for weeks after a public incident like this only played into the environmentalists' hands and undermined the Navy's credibility with the public.

When it was Pirie's turn to weigh in, he staked out a position halfway between the intransigence of the fleet commanders and the environmental appeasement he feared the Secretary might be contemplating. Pirie expressed his concern that the fleet might be compromised operationally by a shutdown. He urged the Secretary "not to set a precedent that anytime something went wrong the Navy would turn everything off and only turn it back on when everyone was positive nothing could go wrong again." Pirie was indirectly mocking the "precautionary principle" embedded in the Marine Mammal Protection Act that he felt environmentalists waved like a banner of righteousness every time someone put a microphone in front of them.

As he listened, Danzig was making his own precautionary assessment of the risk and benefit of rejecting versus accommodating NRDC's demands for a sonar shutdown. He asked Frank Stone what kind of environmental precautions N-45 and the fleet had taken in advance of the exercises in Great Bahama Canyon. Stone walked him through the Atlantic Fleet's standard protocol for training exercises: fleet training's internal environmental shop had conducted its own Environmental Assessment of the expected impact of the planned exercises on marine mammals in the area. Since the assessment had arrived at a Finding of No Significant Impact, the Navy was not required to conduct a more detailed Environmental Impact Statement. Fleet training had signed the assessment and sent a copy to N-45. Stone had then filed a memo with Fisheries confirming the report's Finding of No Significant Impact.

When Danzig asked Stone and the admirals what measures were in place to prevent a similar event of "No Significant Impact" from occurring during the next training exercise, no one responded.

Following the call, Danzig reviewed his notes and his options. In the two weeks since the whales had stranded in the Bahamas, the media coverage hadn't let up. There seemed to be an endless supply of gruesome photographs and conspiracy theories circulating on the internet. With the Vieques situation still in the spotlight and international lawsuits pending, Danzig didn't want the Bahamas to become another case study of the US Navy's environmental recklessness.

The Secretary understood it was past time to formulate a formal public response, even though he was still working with incomplete information. Within a few days of the strandings, everyone involved knew that there was no plausible way that ONR's activities could have caused whales to strand on the south side of the island. On the other hand, there was likely some link between the fleet's sonar exercises in the canyon and the whale strandings— though the acoustic modeling of events wouldn't be complete for several more weeks. Danzig had to choose between acknowledging the Navy's probable culpability now, or waiting until he had a complete story to tell about what caused the strandings and what steps the Navy was implementing to prevent future incidents.

Danzig had one strategic advantage: he knew about the fleet exercises, and Reynolds didn't. So far Reynolds and the public were focused on ONR's sonobuoy tests, because there was a transparent paper trail of its Environmental Assessment and the permit issued by Fisheries. This information gap offered Danzig a move that would limit the Navy's exposure without bowing to the demands of his environmental antagonists.

Danzig chose the only decision that would prevent the possibility of another whale stranding before he had all the facts of the Bahamas incident in hand: he issued a confidential all-fleet bulletin suspending sonar exercises in deep-water environments until further notice. To appease the admirals, and to keep Reynolds guessing, he didn't make the sonar shutdown public. He preferred to keep the press and the public focused on ONR's activities in the Bahamas, because ONR could plausibly deny any connection between its tests and the strandings. This would buy Danzig some time to get the Navy's story straight before acknowledging any sonar exercises in the neighborhood of the strandings. In the meantime, his priority was to keep the whales in the ocean where they belonged and the Navy out of court.

A few days later, Reynolds was at his desk early, drinking coffee and reading the latest AP story in that morning's *Los Angeles Times*:

U.S. NAVY SAYS EXERCISE DID NOT PROMPT
BAHAMAS WHALE BEACHINGS

SAN JUAN, Puerto Rico

The U.S. Navy denied Thursday accusations by environmentalists that an anti-submarine exercise in the Bahamas in March caused 11 whales to beach themselves.

Four of the stranded whales were discovered four hours before the exercise began on March 15, and the others were found more than 75 miles away, Rear Adm. Paul Gaffney, Chief of the Office of Naval Research, said in a letter to the Washington-based U.S. Humane Society.

The exercise "could not have been responsible," Gaffney said.

The Navy has said it was testing upgrades of a buoy system used to track submarines. One buoy emitted a sonar signal that was received by another while a submarine moved between the two devices. . . .

He also noted that some whales stranded themselves on the south side of Abaco, the side facing away from the buoys. Gaffney noted the Navy had done an environmental impact study before the test. "The Navy takes its stewardship-of-the-seas responsibility very seriously," he said.

Environmental groups said Thursday they were unconvinced. . . . Naomi Rose, a marine mammal scientist for the Humane Society, and Joel Reynolds, director of the Los Angeles office of Natural Resources Defense Council, said they would press for more information.

Reynolds folded the newspaper and tossed it into the recycling bin. He had the uncomfortable feeling of having been played, without knowing how or exactly by whom.

Balcomb, reading the same article online from Abaco, reacted as a former sonar officer. The Navy's tactic reminded him of a last-ditch evasive maneuver that WWII submariners had occasionally resorted to when they'd been spotted by an enemy's active sonar. The captain would release the ship's garbage from its aft compartment, or even through a torpedo bay, leaving a trail of debris that would disrupt the enemy's sonar—and hopefully the guidance mechanism of any torpedo aimed at the submarine. Balcomb had to smile. It was a desperation tactic, but sometimes it worked.

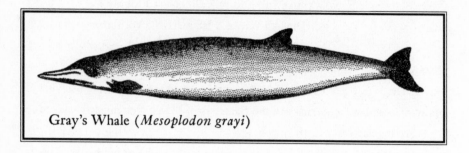

Gray's Whale (*Mesoplodon grayi*)

14

Acoustic Storm

There was a big unspoken X factor in the Secretary's decision to temporarily shut down deep-water sonar exercises. What everyone on the conference call knew—that didn't even bear mentioning because it was so obvious—was that for the past six years, Joel Reynolds had been hounding the Navy over its planned deployment of Low Frequency Active (LFA) sonar. Ever since the ship shock trial, he'd been digging into the Navy's underwater sound projects, including its classified low-frequency sonar program.

The Bahamas stranding couldn't have come at a worse time for the team at ONR, led by Bob Gisiner, that had been shepherding the long-range, low-frequency sonar system through its permit application with Fisheries. Low Frequency Active sonar wasn't being tested in the Bahamas, by either ONR or the fleet. But the publicity surrounding the mass stranding of whales might plant unwelcome doubts about the system's safety in the minds of the public, of regulators at Fisheries, and of any judge who might hear a lawsuit to block its deployment.

No one on the conference call had more invested in Low Frequency Active sonar than Admiral Dick Pittenger. He'd been its godfather back in the late 1980s, and ever since, he'd tracked its growing pains and troubled adolescence. Now that it was finally ready for deployment—and just when the Navy needed to make the case that LFA sonar posed no threat to marine mammals—17 whales had washed ashore in the Bahamas during exercises.

Some had argued, both inside and outside the Navy, that ten years after the end of the Cold War, LFA sonar had outlived its original purpose of detecting Soviet submarines at long range. But Pittenger knew from a naval career devoted to antisubmarine warfare that the race for technological advantage has no finish line. You always have to be innovating and training for the next war, the next enemy. He'd been right there in the thick of it the last time the US Navy got caught napping.

As soon as the SOSUS listening network had been installed in the Pacific and Atlantic basins, in the early 1960s, naval strategists began worrying about its inevitable obsolescence. Soviet submarines were still noisy enough to detect with passive listening sonar. But someday they would become quiet enough to render SOSUS useless and America defenseless against submarine-launched missiles.

By the mid-1960s, even before Balcomb was tracking Soviet subs from the Pacific Beach SOSUS station, the Office of Naval Research had conceived of a countermeasure. When the day arrived that Soviet submarines became too quiet to be heard by wiretapping the deep sound channel, the US Navy would echolocate them with *active* sonar.

The first attempt at a long-range, active sonar system—code-named Project Artemis—ended in failure.[1] The massive array of underwater sound transmitters and receivers that the Navy anchored in the waters off Bermuda was doomed by the primitive state of signal processing in the 1960s, which severely limited Artemis' ability to identify objects hundreds of miles from its sound source. The physical and biological clutter between the transmitters and their distant target made it impossible to read an echo cleanly. After six years of pummeling the oceans with high-intensity sound, the Navy dismantled Artemis and went back to the drawing board.

By the mid-1970s, the Navy faced a genuine crisis in long-range submarine detection. As each generation of Soviet submarines became progressively quieter, the US acoustic advantage gradually eroded. Soon Soviet submarines would be silent to SOSUS. In 1974 the Navy convened its first "Workshop on Low-Frequency Sound" at Woods Hole with the express mission of replacing the passive sonar surveillance of SOSUS with a long-distance *active* system. Since low-frequency sound waves traveled much farther through the ocean, low frequency was the starting point for the development of long-range, "over-the-horizon" submarine detection.

It wasn't until the autumn of 1985 that the Navy finally figured out how the Soviets had been able to build submarines quiet enough to test the limits of SOSUS detection. Two low-ranking Navy communications officers—John Walker Jr. and Jerry Whitworth—were arrested and convicted of having sold top-secret naval intelligence to the Soviets over an 18-year period, compromising both the SOSUS listening system and the US Navy's submarine-quieting technology. The Walker-Whitworth case proved to be America's most damaging intelligence breach of the Cold War and its highest-profile espionage trial since Ethel and Julius Rosenberg's convictions and executions in the early 1950s.[2]

A few months after the trial, the Soviet navy launched its new Akula-class nuclear-powered attack submarines. The aptly named Akula, Russian for "shark," was the quietest Soviet hunter-killer sub to ever roam the oceans—and it was undetectable by SOSUS. Three decades of SOSUS-enabled domination in antisubmarine warfare had ended. The era of active sonar was at hand.

In the wake of the Walker-Whitworth trial, Admiral Dick Pittenger was promoted from chief of staff of the US Naval Forces in Europe to director of the Antisubmarine Warfare Division at the Pentagon. His urgent mission was to transform the acoustic storm of high-intensity active sonar into a precise tool for long-range submarine detection. For help, he turned to the Navy's foremost stormcaster: a playful pixie of a man with an incalculably high IQ.

Walter Munk had earned his reputation as a wizard of underwater weather forecasting during World War II. Having recently emigrated from Vienna, Austria, Munk was a 24-year-old graduate student at the Scripps Institution of Oceanography in La Jolla when America joined the war in 1941. Toiling in a bunker beneath the Pentagon with only weather maps, sea charts, and a slide rule as his guides, Munk was able to track storm-driven waves across the entire Atlantic Ocean and accurately forecast surf conditions weeks in advance of the Allies' amphibious landings on the beaches of North Africa and Sicily.[3]

Munk's highest-stakes prediction of the war was forecasting a 16-hour lull in an Atlantic Ocean storm between June 5 and 7, 1944. At 6:30 a.m. on June 6, the supreme commander of the Allied forces, US general Dwight D. Eisenhower, launched the D-day landing along the beaches of Normandy, France, in maneuverable two- to three-foot surf. The assault caught the Germans by surprise, and the liberation of Europe had begun. Munk went on to successfully forecast surf conditions for American landings on the Pacific islands of Saipan, Guam, Tinian, Palau, the Philippines, Iwo Jima, and Okinawa.

Though Munk's contributions to the war effort went unheralded in public,[4] the Navy was determined to keep its brightest young oceanographer under contract. In 1946 the Office of Naval Research sent Munk on a world tour of Navy-funded research voyages: first aboard a Navy icebreaker to study submarine operations in the Arctic, and then to the South Pacific to observe the underwater impact of the atom and hydrogen bomb tests.

Over the course of the Cold War, Munk divided his time between conducting his own research at Scripps and problem solving for the Navy. Like all inveterate explorers, Munk was drawn to virgin territory, and the ONR was happy to let him follow his curiosity into uncharted waters. Munk's genius lay in seeing the order amid the complexity and seeming chaos of the oceans. He was the first oceanographer to recognize that the interlocking network of internal ocean currents that circulated throughout the globe's oceans were driven by the wind's force against the countless tiny surface ripples. He called them "wind-driven gyres."[5] And when he delved beneath the ocean surface, Munk discovered underwater storm systems directly analogous to those in the atmosphere. His insights turned oceanography on its head and reframed the Navy's thinking about how best to track Soviet submarines.

In 1961 Munk was invited to become the first nonphysicist member of "the Jasons," the Pentagon's newly formed, top-secret think tank.[6] Con-

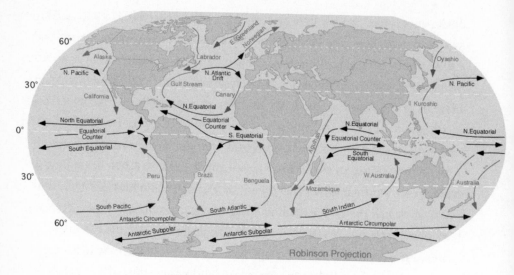

Walter Munk's wind-driven gyres.

ceived as the Cold War's equivalent of the Manhattan Project, the Jasons were a fraternity of academic scientists who spent their summers working in small groups to crack puzzles posed by American military strategists.* The group was christened by Mildred Goldberger, the wife of one of its founding physicists, to evoke Jason and the Argonauts in search of the Golden Fleece.[7]

As the czar of Antisubmarine Warfare Planning, Admiral Pittenger consulted frequently with Munk and his "Jason Navy" on how to use low-frequency sound to light up the dark ocean depths.[8] At a Jason summer study in the late 1970s, Munk proposed a novel method for using low-frequency sound to surveil the ocean. He called it "ocean acoustic tomography" to evoke the recent advent of computerized tomography, or CT, scanning—the same imaging technology that Darlene Ketten would later use to scan whale ears at Johns Hopkins.[9]

Pittenger immediately recognized the potential value of acoustic tomography to antisubmarine warfare. He funded regional demonstration projects

---

* Though the Jasons' summer study sessions continued without interruption throughout the Cold War and beyond, as late as their informal 50th reunion in 2010, no verifiable list of Jason members had ever been published.

for acoustic tomography and granted Munk access to SOSUS listening arrays to use as receivers. Perhaps to cement his already close connection to Navy research, in 1984 Munk was awarded a lifetime appointment as the first Secretary of the Navy/Chief of Naval Operations Chair in Oceanography at Scripps.

It was through a Jason study project that Munk's career-long fascination with marine weather forecasting found a new focus: global warming. At the request of the US Energy Department, Munk forecast how carbon dioxide loads around the world would affect climate change.[10] Based on his research, Munk was convinced that the atmosphere was heating up. But the question remained: How quickly was the climate changing, and how could it be measured?

Measuring temperature change in the atmosphere was difficult with so many variables of latitudes, seasons, and weather patterns. Munk reasoned that since the oceans absorb most of the heat in the atmosphere, taking the ocean's temperature would be the most reliable test of whether the planet was running a fever. But because of the ocean's own variable weather patterns, dipping thermometers over the sides of ships would measure temperature only in specific locations.

When Munk finally seized on the best way to measure the ocean's temperature, he was delighted by the simplicity of his solution. Best of all, he conceived of a single experiment to test both climate change *and* acoustic tomography on a global scale. All he needed was the right equipment and enough money to deploy it across five oceans and seven continents. It would require a high-energy sound source and more than a dozen receivers stationed around the world. He'd have to broadcast the sound signal over a period of years, so it would be expensive to maintain. Even a feasibility test would be costly.

Fortunately, he knew the admiral who could deliver on all fronts.

By 1989, Dick Pittenger had moved from the Pentagon to the Naval Observatory to become Oceanographer of the Navy. Pittenger was delighted to get Walter Munk's invitation for a drink at the Cosmos Club. Though he considered Walter a friend, he understood that it was a business meeting. Pittenger expected that he'd be pitched a wonderful and, most likely, wonderfully expensive idea. Though he no longer had a hefty R&D budget at his disposal, Pittenger was still well connected where it counted: at ONR, at the Pentagon, and on Capitol Hill.

Housed in an elegant nineteenth-century mansion, with its membership reserved for distinguished scientists and statesmen, the Cosmos Club was Munk's home base in Washington and his favorite venue for proposing projects to congressmen and admirals. When Pittenger found him inside the club's wood-paneled bar, Munk was absorbed in arranging sugar packets into a starburst pattern. His elfin figure bent over the carefully arranged sugar packets, and his feet dangled in the air, not quite reaching the floor. Perhaps because of Munk's imposing intellectual stature, it always surprised Pittenger to see how small and boyish he appeared in person.

When he noticed Pittenger in the doorway, Munk scrambled the sugar packets and waved him over. The two exchanged Navy gossip and family news until their gin and tonics arrived. Then they clinked glasses, and Munk began his pitch.

"As you well know, Dick, I've been searching for a way to test acoustic tomography and climate change on a global scale." Munk spoke in a conspiratorial stage whisper, his Viennese accent still strong after five decades in America. "I wanted you to be the first to hear what I've come up with."

It was deliciously simple, Munk explained. Since the speed of sound in water increases with temperature, the simplest way to measure global warming was to time the speed of a constant sound signal across the ocean, over a period of years. If the sound signal sped up over time, it would prove that the oceans were warming, and how quickly. Munk hypothesized that for every 1-degree-Celsius increase in ocean temperature, the speed of sound would increase by four meters per second.

Munk looked at Pittenger to see if he understood. The admiral nodded and smiled. "So," Munk continued, "here's the part you'll particularly appreciate, my friend."

In Pittenger's experience, Munk never needed any presentation props beyond a cocktail napkin and a ballpoint pen. Sure enough, the oceanographer now unfolded a CC-monogrammed bar napkin and quickly sketched out a map of the continents, with the southern Indian Ocean at its center. "This

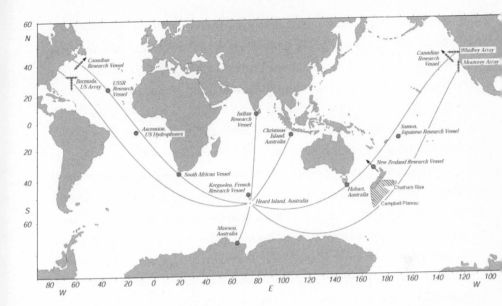

is Heard Island," he said, making a dot halfway between South Africa and Western Australia and marking it "H.I." "It's an uninhabited, glaciated volcano at fifty-four degrees south, seventy-four degrees east." He looked up at Pittenger for a reaction. "Can you guess why I've chosen this location for the sound source?"

By way of illustrating the answer, Munk began to draw ray-paths from the island to Antarctica and the tips of South Africa, India, South America, Australia, New Zealand, and Brazil.

"Heard Island looks to be about equidistant from the East and West Coasts of the US," Pittenger observed.

"Precisely equidistant!" exclaimed Munk, filling in ancillary ray tracings in every direction. "In fact, Heard Island is the only location on earth from which geodesic ray-paths can cross every ocean and reach every continent." He paused for a moment to admire the elegance of his experiment's design. Even in his seventies, Munk's face flushed with excitement. "If we can broadcast a powerful-enough sound signal from Heard Island to reach these sixteen receivers around the globe"—he quickly made a series of Xs to signify SOSUS receivers on various continents—"we'll be able to read temperature and internal wave gradients across all the oceans *simultaneously!*"

Pittenger asked him how powerful a sound source he'd need. When Munk responded that he'd require 2,500 watts of power transmitting at 220 decibels at low frequency, Pittenger saw where Munk was heading with his proposal. There was only one sea-based sound transducer that could transmit underwater at 2,500 watts: the *Cory Chouest*.

Though it had never appeared in any published directory of Navy ships, the *Cory Chouest* was the workhorse of the Navy's Low Frequency Active sonar program. Originally an oil field support tug, the *Cory Chouest* had been retrofitted to ONR's specs with a powerful sound transducer lowered through the center of its hull, enabling it to transmit high-intensity, low-frequency sound pulses in all directions. For the past several years, ONR personnel aboard the *Cory Chouest* had been conducting secret sea tests of Low Frequency Active sonar around the world. Since the *Cory Chouest* had been under his direction at the Pentagon, Pittenger knew that it was currently positioned in the Indian Ocean, not far from Heard Island.

Pittenger found a lot to like in Munk's proposal. On Capitol Hill, the politicians had quickly moved from declaring victory in the Cold War to carving up the Navy's budget. Loaning out the *Cory Chouest* and the network of SOSUS sound receivers to Munk would constitute a perfect "swords into ploughshares" showcase for the bean counters on Capitol Hill, while providing a rationale for continued funding of the Navy's hard-earned Cold War assets.

As Oceanographer of the Navy, Pittenger had a keen interest in climate change—because of the dramatic impact it would have on antisubmarine warfare tactics. Whatever changed the ocean climate would change sound in the ocean, and sonar. Ever since the first compelling evidence of global warming emerged in the late 1970s and 1980s—including from Munk's first study of the effect of carbon dioxide on climate—Pittenger had been particularly focused on the accelerated melting of the Arctic ice cap, since the Artic had always been a strategic submarine battlespace. In 1984, he'd commissioned the Navy's first surface ship expedition to study the problem in the Arctic. And soon after becoming Oceanographer of the Navy—whose duties included working in close liaison with NOAA on climate issues—Pittenger sponsored the purchase of the operational Navy's first Cray supercomputer, for use in acoustic modeling of climate change in the ocean.

Munk was already looking beyond Heard Island to the establishment of an ongoing "acoustic observatory" in the ocean, analogous to an astronomical observatory. Acoustic tomography would enable oceanographers to address fundamental questions about the oceans, in the same way that astronomers had for centuries probed the mysteries of the heavens. Monitoring climate change was just the beginning.

Pittenger had his own vision—of a future when the Navy would have continual access to a real-time sonogram of the oceans. On paper at least—or rather, as illustrated on a Cosmos Club cocktail napkin—acoustic tomography promised to finally deliver the holy grail of antisubmarine warfare: a three-dimensional map of the seven seas that could track submarine movements at any distance and at any depth.

In deference to the Cosmos Club's prohibition on conducting business in the public rooms, Pittenger and Munk retired upstairs to an empty card room. Within an hour, they had worked up a budget for the Heard Island Feasibility Test.

JANUARY 9, 1991
Freemantle, Australia

The Heard Island expedition was on course to become the crowning achievement of Munk's career. It combined all the elements he loved most: a big idea for solving a significant problem, lots of boats and scientists around the world working with state-of-the-art hardware and software, and enough uncertainty to ensure suspense about the outcome. But now, with commencement of the experiment less than three weeks off, Munk was marooned at port on the west coast of Australia, waiting for permission from US Fisheries to proceed. Dozens of researchers were already on-site at Heard Island and positioned at listening stations around the world. With so many moving parts, delaying the experiment's start date would be tantamount to cancellation.

Everything had proceeded apace since the Cosmos Club meeting. With Pittenger running interference, it had taken Munk only a few months to raise the $1.7 million in funding from ONR, the National Science Foundation, the National Oceanic and Atmospheric Administration (NOAA), and the Department of Energy. Though there were four agency sponsors, the Heard

Island experiment was being run out of ONR, if only because it owned the *Cory Chouest*. Global warming was such a timely topic that ONR's role as lead funder and project director escaped notice. And for the first time in his long career, Munk could speak publicly about one of his experiments to scientific colleagues and to journalists. He coined the double-meaning moniker "The Shot Heard Round the World" to describe his Heard Island experiment. No one below Pittenger's pay grade—certainly not the science writers who delighted in profiling the Viennese "Einstein of the Oceans"—grasped the military significance of acoustic tomography.

It was all smooth sailing until *Science* magazine ran an article entitled, "What's the Sound of One Ocean Warming?"[11] It caught the attention of John Twiss, the executive director of the Marine Mammal Commission, an independent federal agency created by Congress to watchdog the provisions of the 1972 Marine Mammal Protection Act. As he read the details of Munk's sound experiment, Twiss grew alarmed: *220-decibel sound pulses transmitting one hour on and one off for ten days at low frequency!* What little research had been conducted on the effects of low-frequency sound showed that marine mammals changed their behavior in response to just 120 decibels. It seemed obvious to Twiss that a global sound experiment of such intensity would likely pose a danger to marine mammals.

Twiss called the project director at ONR,[12] who'd spent most of his career running acoustic projects for the Navy. He had never heard of Twiss, or the Marine Mammal Commission.

"So tell me," asked Twiss after he'd introduced himself and his agency, "has Fisheries granted you permits for Heard Island yet?"

"Permits?" asked the project director. "What permits?"

That laconic exchange marked the end of the era of unimpeded Navy sound experiments in the oceans. The Marine Mammal Protection Act had been on the books for almost 20 years, but the Navy had never applied for a permit—as the law mandated—for any experiment or exercise that might "injure or harass" any marine mammals. Congress didn't invest the Marine Mammal Commission with enforcement powers, but the commission's advisory role to Congress gave Twiss a powerful bully pulpit.

Twiss telephoned the head of NOAA, the parent agency of Fisheries, and pointed out that the area immediately surrounding Heard Island was rich with marine life, including several species of endangered whales. Certainly this experiment merited a thorough scientific review and judicious permitting process.

Fortunately for Munk, NOAA was one of the Heard Island experiment's lead sponsors, and the agency's director had once been a PhD student of Munk's at Scripps.[13] A Fisheries permit would ordinarily take months to prepare and approve, but he was able to secure a special "research permit" in a week's time, just days before the feasibility test's scheduled start date.

The first sound transmission was to commence on January 26, 1991. Munk calculated that the signal would take three and a half hours to travel west to Bermuda and slightly longer to arrive on the Oregon coast, 10,000 miles east of Heard Island. On the night of January 25, Munk wanted to retire early. He was exhausted by the last-minute permit drama and the checking and rechecking of all the instruments aboard the *Cory Chouest*. When the sound engineer insisted that he needed to do one more sound test, Munk waved good night and went belowdecks to sleep.

In the middle of the night, Munk was awakened by the radiophone beside his bed. It was his man in Bermuda, and he sounded irritated. "What's going on out there? We're already receiving a signal!"

It took a moment to sink in. "Oh my God, it works!" Munk shouted. The sound engineer aboard the *Cory Chouest* had jumped the gun by 12 hours, but the test signal had traveled past South Africa and Brazil, all the way to Bermuda! Munk wanted to be alert for the next day, so he went back to sleep. Fifteen minutes later, he was awakened by a call from his station operator on the Oregon coast, where the signal had just arrived across the Pacific, loud and clear. The feasibility of global-scale sound transmission had been confirmed before the experiment had formally begun.

The next day, the transmissions commenced on schedule, and the other stations reported in. The *Cory Chouest*'s low-frequency sound signals were received across five ocean basins by 16 different listening stations. Two weeks later, Munk set sail for La Jolla, California, elated by the success of his mission and excited to launch the implementation phase of his project.

• • •

By the summer of 1992, the Cold War was quickly receding into America's rearview mirror, overtaken by the first Gulf War and a deepening economic recession.

No one ever accused Walter Munk of being a slow learner when it came to fund-raising for his grandiose oceanography experiments. He understood that the rules of the game had changed. "Swords into ploughshares" and "dual-use technology" were the new watchwords of defense appropriations. Fortunately, acoustic tomography fit neatly under the military-civilian "dual-use" rubric being advanced by vice presidential candidate Senator Al Gore. In hopes of endearing his project to the new funding oligarchy, Munk rechristened the implementation phase of acoustic tomography with a more environmentally correct name: Acoustic *Thermometry*.

With his Navy sponsors under pressure to cut their budgets, Munk had to look farther afield to finance the next phase of his project. After 18 months circling the Beltway, he raised the $35 million he needed to install and activate a two-year broadcast of low-frequency, high-decibel sound from transmitters off Point Sur, California, and Kauai, Hawaii.[14]

To deflect the kind of blowback from the marine mammal community that almost scuttled the Heard Island Feasibility Test, Munk agreed to dial down his sound source by 30 decibels, to 195 decibels, and to commit 10 percent of his hard-won budget to marine mammal monitoring. Pittenger—who had scolded Munk for failing to anticipate the necessary permits for Heard Island—suggested that Scripps hire a well-respected marine mammal researcher to run the regulatory gauntlet for Acoustic Thermometry. Chris Clark, the director of the Bioacoustics Research Program at Cornell, was a widely recognized bioacoustician who specialized in how baleen whales such as humpbacks, bowheads, and blue whales used low-frequency sound to navigate and communicate.[15]

Throughout 1993, Clark worked quietly with the Navy to keep Acoustic Thermometry's permit application moving smoothly through the Fisheries bureaucracy and off the radar of marine mammal advocates. Then, in February 1994, just as Fisheries was preparing to issue a permit for Acoustic Thermometry, a postgraduate student in Clark's Cornell bioacoustics lab, Lindy Weilgart, got wind of the program. Weilgart was appalled that Clark would be promoting a high-intensity sound experiment with potentially disastrous consequences for marine mammals.

Weilgart and her husband, Hal Whitehead, were active at the time in the campaign to halt the Navy ship shock test in California. Weilgart was a recent PhD with none of Whitehead's expert credentials and reputation. But she was determined to sound the alarm—as loudly as possible—about the potential threat that Acoustic Thermometry posed to whales. She sent out a stream of faxes and posted impassioned messages on the newly launched MARMAM Listserv in hopes of rousing the conservation community into opposition. But her plea failed to instigate any public protest.

When Joel Reynolds read Weilgart's MARMAM posting, he immediately called her for more information. Reynolds had only recently become involved in the ship shock case and was still learning his way around marine mammal law. Intrigued by the details that Weilgart was able to provide about Acoustic Thermometry, Reynolds conducted some quick research and discovered that he could submit a request to Fisheries for a public hearing on Scripps' permit application—but the deadline was one day away. He quickly drafted the request and faxed it to Fisheries.

The agency agreed to hold a single public hearing in Silver Spring, Maryland, on March 22, just days before its scheduled decision on Acoustic Thermometry's permit. The day of the hearing, the *Los Angeles Times* published a front-page article about the sound experiment that hit all the hot buttons for a California readership that revered its coastline and marine habitats:

"One set of loudspeakers would be located twenty-five miles offshore in the Monterey Bay National Marine Sanctuary, where rare blue whales, humpbacks, and other whale species gather.

". . . Sponsors of the project at Scripps estimate that the noise off the California coast could affect 677,000 marine mammals."[16]

Weilgart was the sole scientist interviewed for the article, which quoted a lengthy list of ways she believed Acoustic Thermometry's high-decibel sound signal might harm whales and render them unable to navigate or find food. But one particular pull-quote would galvanize public opposition to Acoustic Thermometry: "A deaf whale is a dead whale."

By day's end, both California senators, Barbara Boxer and Dianne

Feinstein, had called on Fisheries "to proceed cautiously" with its permitting process. Feinstein asked the agency to consider other locations for the project, while Boxer demanded it hold public hearings in California and recommended that congressional approval be required for Acoustic Thermometry. Reynolds wrote to Fisheries, urging it to require Scripps to prepare a full Environmental Impact Statement to assess the harm its sound source could pose to marine mammals.

Besieged by phone calls and faxes from outraged Californians, Fisheries delayed its permitting decision and extended the comment period to include public hearings in Santa Cruz and Kauai. Both hearings were well attended, and both went badly for the Scripps team. Munk was shouted down as a heartless whale killer. "A deaf whale is a dead whale!" became the opposition rallying cry from California to Capitol Hill. Fisheries' two public hearings turned into a dozen meetings up and down the California coast and in Hawaii. For Munk, who attended each meeting until the bitter end, it was a torturous series of humiliating public rebukes. Virtually his only defender was a young Darlene Ketten, who flew out west with a sperm whale ear bone on her lap as a teaching prop to explain why Acoustic Thermometry's low-frequency sound waves would likely prove harmless to whales. But no one seemed willing to trust Ketten's and Munk's assurances.

In reality, no one could predict the impact of Acoustic Thermometry on whales or other marine life. No one had ever broadcast 195 decibels of low-frequency sound for years on end, generated inside a marine mammal sanctuary and audible across an entire ocean basin. With bioacoustic experts reduced to speculation on both sides of the argument, Acoustic Thermometry became a test case for the precautionary principle. Oceanographer Sylvia Earle summed up the position of the skeptics in the written statement she submitted to Fisheries: "If you further damage the patient, the earth, while you try to take its temperature, then maybe the method is flawed."

When Fisheries decided to table its decision on a permit, Acoustic Thermometry was at an impasse. ONR brought in a new project director, Bob Gisiner, to try to revive the permitting process. But at that late date, Gisiner could do little more than watch the Scripps team move through the five stages of grief for its formerly grand, now stranded, project.

Munk was dismayed at being cast as an environmental villain after conceiving an ingenious method for measuring climate change. A man who could predict the movements of underwater weather systems across the oceans had failed to anticipate the tsunami of opposition that had overwhelmed his global sound experiment.

Meanwhile, Reynolds—who felt emboldened by his recently won injunction against the Navy's ship shock test—pressed Scripps to move its sound experiment outside the Monterey Bay National Marine Sanctuary. NRDC sent a direct mail letter to its members who, in turn, unleashed a torrent of letters to Scripps asking why the West Coast's leading oceanographic institute would be endangering whales.

Munk was galled by Reynolds' attacks, particularly since Scripps and NRDC scientists had recently collaborated on a nuclear-nonproliferation project to monitor underground explosive tests. In a fit of pique, Munk called NRDC Executive Director John Adams in New York to ask him to get Reynolds off his back. Or at least to agree not to sue Scripps. Wasn't NRDC concerned about global warming? Munk asked.

Adams explained as diplomatically as possible that while he valued Scripps' expertise and partnership, ocean noise was an important issue for NRDC, and it was going to see it through. "I don't tell my senior attorneys how to do their job," he told Munk, "and as far as I'm concerned, Joel Reynolds is just doing what I hired him to do."

After he got off with Munk, Adams called Reynolds to tell him not to worry about Scripps or Munk. "Fuck 'em," he said with characteristic bluntness. "Just keep doing what you're doing. And don't look over your shoulder."

When Munk realized that Adams wasn't going to rein in Reynolds, he called Sylvia Earle and asked her to broker a peace. She was the obvious person to bridge the chasm between physical oceanographers and marine biologists, having divided her career between both disciplines.[17]

Earle liked Munk personally. He had an irresistible continental charm, and he was unassailably a genius when it came to decoding the internal structures of the ocean. But she resented the arrogance of Munk's generation of physical oceanographers, who turned a blind eye to marine life. She'd recently resigned her position as chief scientist at NOAA—a stint she referred to as her "US Sturgeon General" period—to become a more vocal activist on behalf of ocean conservation. Her book *Sea Change: A Message of the Oceans*, published that same year, was a clarion call to rescue the oceans from "death by debris" and "death by a thousand cuts," including noise pollution.

Munk distrusted Earle's recent tilt toward environmental advocacy. But he was out of options. Earle had collaborated with Scripps on a number of research projects over the years, and she currently sat on NRDC's board. The day after she heard from Munk, Earle got a call from John Adams with a parallel request that she coax the two sides toward a compromise. She agreed to try.

Earle convened a meeting in San Francisco where researchers on both sides could express their views and try to find common ground. No press was allowed. Neither was the general public. The goal was to move the discussion from the vitriol of a public debate to a closed-door meeting among scientists—and their lawyers. The hoped-for result would be a process for moving forward with Acoustic Thermometry without resorting to lawsuits—though NRDC clearly stood ready to go to court if the parties failed to reach an agreement.

Earle opened the meeting by expressing her own cautionary view of deep-sea sound experiments: "Listen before you leap, because you can't undo damage once it's done." Otherwise she hung back and let the invited guests do the talking. Reynolds simply took notes as the scientists articulated their views.

By the end of the session, a framework for a settlement had emerged. Munk and his team would devote phase one of Acoustic Thermometry, including a third of its funding, to studying the effects of low-frequency sound on marine mammals. Phase two would proceed only if monitoring of phase one demonstrated that the sound source posed no threat to the whales in its path. Munk would move the California sound source from the ocean floor off Point Sur in the Monterey Marine Sanctuary up the coast and farther offshore, where there were fewer marine mammals. Reynolds and the Scripps attorneys agreed to work out the details in a follow-up meeting.

Munk watched in dazed disbelief as his prized program drifted farther and farther out to sea. After years of painstaking mathematical calculations and logistical planning, after endless rounds of grant writing and fund-raising, after all the abusive public hearings where he'd been treated like a war criminal, it had come to this: a roomful of lawyers who understood less about underwater acoustics than his first-year grad students were haggling over his Acoustic Thermometry assets like so much community property in a divorce settlement. It was simply too much to bear.

Munk shoved back his chair and glared across the table at Reynolds. When he spoke, his voice had none of its usual courtly lilt. "I really don't understand why you've gone after us like this," said Munk, clearly strained by fatigue and exasperation. "The Navy is putting so much more sound into the ocean, right here off the California coast."

Reynolds sat stock still, waiting for Munk to continue. He'd conducted enough depositions to know when to ask questions and when to shut up and let a witness do the talking. "Magellan II was transmitting up and down the coast just last summer."

With as little inflection as he could, Reynolds intoned, "Magellan II . . ."

"Yes, Magellan II is much louder than our sound source," Munk continued. "Two hundred thirty-five decibels." He also quoted a frequency range of 250 hertz, which Reynolds scribbled on his legal pad. "Next to Magellan II," Munk insisted, "Acoustic Thermometry sounds like a humming refrigerator."

Reynolds scanned the room, but no one else seemed to register that Munk was detailing the acoustic specs of a code-named Navy operation—except for Sylvia Earle, who gave Reynolds a questioning glance. After the meeting adjourned and everyone else had left for the airport, Earle turned to Reynolds. "What was Munk talking about?" she asked. "Magellan II?"

Reynolds shrugged. He had no idea. But he was determined to find out.

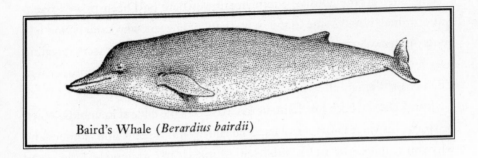

Baird's Whale (*Berardius bairdii*)

15

The Sonar That Came In from the Cold

JULY 10, 1994
Los Angeles Office of NRDC

The morning after the Acoustic Thermometry settlement meeting, Reynolds was still puzzling over his handwritten notes: "Magellan II" . . . "sound source level: 235 decibels" . . . "transmission frequency: 250 hertz."

Walter Munk had opened the vault of the Navy's secret underwater sound experiments. But only a crack. The longer Reynolds stared at the figures on his yellow legal pad, the more mystified he became.

Everything Reynolds knew about marine mammals and underwater acoustics he'd crammed during the prior six months of the ship shock and Acoustic Thermometry controversies. He understood the basics of how sound behaves in the ocean, and how whales and dolphins use acoustics to communicate, hunt, and navigate. But his knowledge of sonar and anti-submarine warfare began and ended with episodes of *Sea Hunt* he'd watched on TV as a kid.

Internet and public database searches for "Magellan II" came up empty.

Reynolds asked the nuclear disarmament wonks at NRDC's office in Washington, DC, if they'd ever heard of it. They hadn't. All they knew was that it must be a classified program, which meant it wouldn't be mentioned by name in public documents or peer-reviewed journals.

Over the next six months, Reynolds kept digging for leads in dry holes. Then one day in May 1995, a plain manila envelope arrived in his office mail. No return address. Inside he found the latest issue of *Sea Technology*, an esoteric trade magazine that billed itself as the "worldwide information leader for marine business, science & engineering." A Post-it note pasted to the table of contents read, "Thought you'd find this interesting—John." Reynolds knew it must be from John Hall, the former Navy dolphin trainer who'd coached him on all things Navy during the ship shock trial and Acoustic Thermometry negotiations.

Reynolds scanned down the list of articles to "Low-Frequency, High-Power-Density Active Sonar," written by a commercial contractor for the Navy's experimental Low Frequency Active, or LFA, sonar program. The article provided detailed specs of the system's powerful sound transducer and the array of passive sensors towed behind to capture the return signals. It also described thousands of hours of sea tests, named Magellan I and II, which the Navy conducted between 1992 and 1995, around the world and off the California coastline, aboard the research vessel *Cory Chouest*—which Reynolds recognized as the same ship that Admiral Pittenger had loaned to Munk for the Heard Island Feasibility Test.

Armed with a raft of new search terms, Reynolds uncovered a US General Accounting Office report that outlined the Navy's plan—conceived by Admiral Pittenger in the mid-1980s as part of his master plan for expanding active sonar—to install LFA sonar aboard dozens of newly commissioned ships and deploy it worldwide. John Hall filled in the gaps in Reynolds' understanding of the technical specs of the system, including his personal observations of low-frequency sound experiments he'd witnessed while working for the Navy.

Munk was correct in his assertion that Acoustic Thermometry's sound level didn't compare to the intensity of the Magellan transmissions. Since decibels progress logarithmically—much like the Richter scale that measures the intensity of earthquakes—Low Frequency Active sonar's 235 decibels cre-

ated a sound pressure wave *10,000 times more powerful* than Acoustic Thermometry's 195-decibel transmission. And its omnidirectional, low-frequency
signal would carry for hundreds of miles across the ocean—*thousands* of
miles if it entered the deep sound channel.

Reynolds' subsequent outreach to acoustic experts confirmed the Navy's
interest in long-range active sonar technology, as well as its geographic range
and intensity. As one of them described it to Reynolds, LFA sonar would
"light up literally hundreds of thousands of square miles of ocean at a time."
What must 235 decibels feel like, Reynolds wondered, to the humpback, blue,
and gray whales that lived and migrated along the California coastline? Or,
for that matter, to a recreational swimmer or diver?

By mid-August 1995, Reynolds had completed a six-page letter of inquiry addressed to the Secretary of the Navy and the head of Fisheries. He catalogued
the "significant and unknown" risks that LFA sonar posed to the whales, dolphins, and seals of the California coastline. After describing the legal implications of those risks, he asked pointedly if the Navy had complied with the
Marine Mammal Protection Act, the US Endangered Species Act, and the
National Environmental Policy Act—all of which this sonar system appeared
to violate. If the Navy was not in compliance, Reynolds asked Fisheries to
order the Navy to cease testing and deployment of LFA sonar "until all required permits have been obtained, legally adequate biological opinions have
been issued, and a full Environmental Impact Statement has been prepared
and certified."

Reynolds knew less than his letter implied about the specifics of LFA
sonar. But he wanted to make sure he got the attention of the Navy brass.

Reynolds was working in his office when he received a call from the San Diego
field office of the Naval Criminal Investigative Service. They were sending an
agent over to interview him—as soon as his schedule permitted.

The interview lasted only a half hour. In a courteous but quietly menac-
ing tone, the investigator explained that Reynolds' letter of inquiry contained
classified information related to Navy projects that were critical to the national defense. Whoever had shared them with him had likely violated the

Defense Secrets Act. The investigator acknowledged that Reynolds wasn't bound by an oath to protect state secrets, but he could surely understand the Navy's interest in learning how he'd come into possession of classified information.

Reynolds had no intention of identifying Walter Munk as his original source, though it remained a puzzle to Reynolds as to why Munk, who'd worked on classified Navy programs his whole career, would disclose the existence of Magellan to an environmental attorney.* Reynolds simply told the investigator that the letter was the end product of a lengthy investigation during which he'd spoken to a lot of people. As to the source of the technical specs, he handed the investigator a copy of *Sea Technology*, which, he noted, was available at several branches of the Los Angeles Public Library.

Three weeks after he sent his letter, Reynolds got a call from Navy General Counsel Steve Honigman, inviting him to the Pentagon for a personal briefing on Magellan II. Honigman was the same general counsel who had stepped in to negotiate a settlement to the ship shock injunction 18 months earlier. He wanted to avoid a repeat of that debacle and preferred to negotiate with Reynolds across a Pentagon conference table rather than place the fate of LFA sonar in the hands of a civilian judge.

After so many months of searching for details about LFA sonar, Reynolds was eager to be briefed inside the citadel. He invited Peter Tyack, a bioacoustician from Woods Hole who'd been a friendly advisor during the Acoustic Thermometry negotiations, to serve as his wingman and marine mammal expert.

When they arrived at the Pentagon, Reynolds and Tyack were seated on one side of a long conference table. On the other side was a battalion of Navy and Fisheries personnel, including uniformed brass, lawyers, and scientists. Leading the marine biology side of the Navy's briefing was Chris Clark, who had flown in overnight from a SOSUS listening station in the Pacific North-

---

* During a 2010 visit to Washington, DC, to attend a 50th-anniversary "working celebration" of the Jasons, Munk was asked by the author why he would disclose the name and specs of a secret Navy acoustics program in a roomful of environmental lawyers and activists. Munk replied, "If you want to keep something secret, you don't broadcast it at two hundred and thirty-five decibels."

west where he'd been conducting research. (Clark was one of only two civilian scientists afforded access by the Navy to SOSUS stations for whale research.) Like Clark, Whitehead, and Weilgart, Tyack had come of age as a researcher on Roger Payne's humpback whale expeditions in Argentina and Hawaii. Tyack and Clark had gone on to become rival bioacousticians at competing research centers. Now they found themselves facing each other across a table in an arena that was more political than scientific.

Alongside Clark and Honigman sat a cast of characters who were familiar to Reynolds from the ship shock case, including Bob Gisiner from ONR, Roger Gentry from Fisheries, and Frank Stone from Environmental Readiness. They were flanked by a dozen naval officers of varying rank, including six admirals in blue dress uniforms, their jacket lapels heavy with medals.

Reynolds was accustomed to dealing with corporate CEOs, powerful politicians, and Hollywood celebrities. But it was hard not to feel a bit shabby and underdressed in the presence of the admiralty. The admirals' demeanor was courteous; their erect, almost royal bearing, imposing. They spoke very little during the meeting. They didn't have to. Their presence sent the clear message that when it came to safeguarding the country's national security, they were in charge. The scientists and lawyers were mere functionaries.

General Counsel Honigman explained that the Magellan II exercises off the California coast were the latest in a series of 22 sea tests of LFA sonar that ONR had conducted around the world since the late 1980s. Like the program's namesake, Portuguese explorer Ferdinand Magellan, the *Cory Chouest* had circumnavigated the globe to test LFA sonar in every ocean environment of tactical significance to the US Navy's antisubmarine warfare effort. Honigman contended that since each of the internal Environmental Assessments of the sea tests had arrived at a Finding of No Significant Impact, the Navy hadn't been required to apply for permits from Fisheries. Reynolds was skeptical that the fig leaf of internal assessments would stand up to a legal challenge. But rather than contradict the Navy's general counsel in the presence of the admiralty, he decided to hold his peace.

Over the next several months, Reynolds and Honigman continued to talk and to negotiate. In order to forestall an NRDC lawsuit over LFA sonar, Honigman agreed to have ONR conduct a program-wide Environmental Impact Statement, rather than a perfunctory Environmental Assessment, for its LFA permit application to Fisheries. The Navy had never before undertaken this much more time-consuming, transparent, and rigorous level of risk–assessment for a sound experiment in the ocean.

Reynolds counted it a major victory when, as part of its Environmental Impact Statement, ONR agreed in 1997 to sponsor a three-phase scientific research program to study the impact of low-frequency sound on whales off the coasts of California and Hawaii.[1] Previously, there had been very little research on the subject, and much speculation. During the Acoustic Thermometry debate, many marine mammal researchers, including Clark and Tyack, had expressed concerns that low-frequency sound signals could interfere with the hearing-based behaviors that were critical to whales' survival, including migration, navigation, communication, hunting, and mating. LFA sonar transmissions might cause whales to abandon their feeding grounds, alter their migration patterns, or cease vocalizing. If their auditory environment was swamped by ambient noise, whales could have trouble locating their prey, their predators, or their mates.

As soon as Reynolds felt he had gained some ground, the Navy seized it back. Bob Gisiner, who was in charge of ONR's research program for its Environmental Impact Statement, appointed Chris Clark as his principal investigator. Gisiner's nomination of Peter Tyack as co–principal investigator caught Reynolds off guard. When Tyack subsequently decided to accept the position, it was a setback for Reynolds. Not only had he lost his lead scientific advisor but also an expert witness if he decided to challenge Low Frequency Active sonar in court.[2]

The Navy's hope of moving beyond the chant of "A deaf whale is a dead whale" ran aground before its research program even began. In November 1995, at the very beginning of the first phase of Acoustic Thermometry that Munk had agreed to devote to monitoring the impact of low-frequency sound on marine mammals, three dead humpback whales washed ashore on the California coastline at Half Moon Bay. One of the whales was buried quickly, and the other two drifted back out to sea, so no cause of death was ever determined. When the media reported the whale deaths—and when Scripps soon resumed the testing—an already aroused public turned its outrage on the Navy's proposed scientific research program. The most vocal dissidents denounced the research, which would use the *Cory Chouest* to test the behavioral effect of low-frequency sound on gray, blue, fin, and humpback whales, as irresponsible and dangerous.

The confrontation between the public and the Navy came to a head in Hawaii, where activists organized to halt the Navy's offshore sound tests. A coalition of animal welfare and environmental groups went to court to prevent the experiments during the local humpback breeding and calving season. They urged NRDC to join their lawsuit.

Reynolds was reluctant to sue to prevent a research program he felt might yield important missing information about the impact of low-frequency sound. More to the point, he didn't believe there were strong-enough legal arguments to win an injunction. As a result-oriented litigator, Reynolds never undertook a lawsuit merely to generate publicity. He was determined to build the strongest possible science-based case he could marshal before going to court against Low Frequency Active sonar. If not suing to block the Navy's scientific research program meant that he had to take flack from hard-core activists on his left flank, Reynolds accepted it as a small price to pay for moving Navy research out of the Cold War shadows and into the daylight of the Fisheries permitting process.

As Reynolds had predicted, a district judge ruled against the Hawaiian lawsuit. That's when the nonlawyers took up the fight. Ben White of the Animal Welfare Institute called on the public "to join me in harm's way by forming a human wall of divers between the Navy and the whales." White proclaimed, "The time has come to literally put our bodies on the line to stop this unprecedented sonic attack on humpback whales. If the United States Navy insists on going forward," he said, "they may well kill their own citizens as well as whales."

As a safety precaution, Clark's and Tyack's research protocol required that the LFA sound signal be shut down whenever swimmers were sighted in the water within a mile of the *Cory Chouest*. Back in 1993, during Magellan I sea tests in the Mediterranean, the French government complained to the US Navy that LFA sonar had disturbed recreational divers 220 miles away and might be implicated in the death of another diver. Subsequent diver studies by the US Navy found that exposure to LFA transmissions above 130 decibels induced vibration in the lungs, abdomen, head, and arms. One diver exposed to 150 decibels said he "felt like being between two catapults on an aircraft carrier" and that it was "much greater in intensity" than any of his previous exposures to active sonar.[3]

Ben White failed to recruit a "human wall of divers." But he did find a few stalwarts to heckle the *Cory Chouest* from small boats and dive into the water with him when it started transmitting sonar. The Navy had to postpone the tests and reduce the phase-three exercises from 21 days to 10. The shortened test produced very little data and no apparent deaths, either cetacean or human. Reynolds appreciated that Ben White's style of gonzo activism energized public opposition. And by staking out an abolitionist position, activists like White motivated the Navy to negotiate with mainstream legal groups such as NRDC.

NRDC had a history of being the first to confront an environmental threat, only to subsequently be perceived as an inside player and rebuked by younger, more radical wings of the movement. Sometimes it was a useful distinction. Back in the 1980s, both NRDC and Greenpeace were pressuring Office Depot to stop sourcing its paper products from old-growth forests in the Pacific Northwest. NRDC was trying to reach a settlement with top management rather than file a lawsuit that could drag on for years. During a critical phase in the negotiations at Office Depot's Atlanta headquarters, Greenpeace demonstrators climbed to the roof of the building and unfurled an enormous banner reading, "Office Depot out of the Forest!" Then they chanted the slogan through bullhorns as a crowd of onlookers and journalists gathered on the sidewalk. While Office Depot management watched the melee unfolding outside the conference room window, the NRDC attorney told them, "You can deal with me, or you can deal with them." Office Depot decided to accept NRDC's proposed settlement.[4]

When the Navy started releasing its LFA sonar research findings in the late 1990s, it only added fuel to the controversy. The meaning of the data varied depending on which scientists interpreted them. Gray whales swam away from the low-frequency sonar signal but appeared to resume their migration a few miles upcoast from the sound source. Blue and fin whales vocalized less in the presence of sonar sounds; humpback whales suspended their singing during transmissions but resumed singing when the noise stopped. Low-frequency sonar appeared to change the migration and communication behaviors of baleen whales, at least temporarily, but the significance of the disruption was open to debate. Not surprisingly, the Navy researchers minimized its impact.

The Navy's efforts to portray LFA sonar as benign and nonlethal collided head-on with the stranding of 12 beaked whales along the Greek coast during NATO naval exercises in 1996. NATO's internal investigation disclosed that its exercises included both low- and medium-frequency sonar transmitting at up to 228 decibels. In 1998 Alexandros Frantzis, the Greek veterinarian who had examined the best-preserved organs among the stranded animals, published his conclusion regarding the cause of the strandings in the journal *Nature*: "Although the available data in 1996 could not directly prove that the use of active sonars caused the mass stranding in Kyparissiakos Gulf, all evidence clearly pointed to the Low Frequency Active sonar tests."

The US Navy dismissed Frantzis as "merely a veterinarian"—despite the fact that its own leading marine mammal expert, Sam Ridgway, was also a doctor of veterinary medicine. What the Navy couldn't deride or ignore was the growing concern among marine scientists that naval sonar posed a potential threat to whales.

Reynolds hoped the Greek stranding would mobilize the public and the scientific research community in opposition to military sonar. To raise awareness of the issue, he began accepting invitations to speak at scientific conferences such as the Acoustical Society of America and the Society for Marine Mammalogy. Scientists were initially suspicious of an attorney in their midst. If naval sonar had been causing mass strandings, they insisted, researchers in the field would have made the connection. What did Joel Reynolds, a lawyer, know about whales, and what was he doing at a scientific conference? Most were uneasy about taking a definitive position in a new area of inquiry, preferring to withhold judgment on LFA sonar until there was consensus among their peers. And since the majority of them relied on Navy funding for their research, they were understandably reluctant to bite their sponsor's hand without indisputable evidence.

Reynolds felt stymied by how invisible and inaudible ocean noise remained to everyone but the animals it was imperiling. No one had ever compiled an accessible and comprehensive survey of how much industrial noise was being dumped into the oceans, from what sources, and at what cost to marine life. He realized that if he wanted to arouse the public, the policy makers, and the scientific community to action, he needed to educate them first.

Reynolds gave the assignment to the best researcher and writer on his small staff, Michael Jasny: write a report on noise in the ocean that is authoritative enough to pass muster with scientists, but keep it accessible to journalists and citizen activists. Jasny dove in. A year later, in 1999, NRDC published *Sounding the Depths: The Rising Toll of Sonar, Shipping and Industrial Ocean Noise on Marine Life*. It was the PhD thesis that Jasny never got around to writing at UCLA. In it, he managed to synthesize all the available research on the three most prevalent sources of man-made ocean noise: commercial shipping; oil and gas exploration; and military sonar.[5]

Jasny's report documented how chronic noise pollution in the ocean—what Chris Clark dubbed "acoustic smog"—had been doubling every decade. The biggest contributor was international shipping. As global trade proliferated in the second half of the twentieth century, so did the numbers of propeller engines and increasingly large cargo vessels in the ocean. Ten thousand supertankers crisscrossed the oceans, each emitting up to 190 decibels of sound at their source. Another 40,000 large cargo vessels created a cacophony of low-frequency noise. An armada of container ships, ferries, ocean liners, hydrofoils, tugboats, motorboats, and Jet Skis blanketed the oceans with a steady drone that threatened to mask the ability of whales to hear and be heard by each other.

After shipping, the most significant source of chronic sound pollution was the oil and gas industry. Early in the twentieth century, oil and gas prospectors set off underwater explosives to identify reserves hidden beneath the ocean floor. By midcentury, high-powered air guns had replaced dynamite as their explosive of choice. Rows of air-gun arrays were towed behind boats on milelong cables, and then fired repeatedly toward the bottom of the ocean in search of subterranean oil. The acoustic blast of the air guns ricocheted off the ocean floor, rebounded again off the surface, and back and forth and up and down until the sound energy finally dissipated. The noise from the air-gun arrays reached 260 decibels, making them the highest-intensity industrial sound on the planet. By the end of the twentieth century, every corner of the world's oceans was besieged by the volleys of air guns, their continuous thud audible hundreds and even thousands of miles away. Once the air guns located oil reserves, the noisy work of extraction began: platform construction, pile driving, dredging, and oil drilling and pumping and processing and shipping. Each step in the production chain dumped more noise into the ocean.

By comparison with the shipping and oil industries, naval sonar had been an acute, rather than chronic, source of noise in the ocean. But now with the US Navy's planned deployment of Low Frequency Active sonar across the globe, and the proposed deployment by several European navies as well, the oceans were about to be subjected to another chronic source of low-frequency noise pollution. *Sounding the Depths* was the first layperson's explanation of how military sonar operated, which national navies were deploying it, and how much acoustic energy it added to the oceans' acoustic load.

Sounding the Depths also catalogued the ways that industrial and military noise threatened whales and other marine life. In addition to chronicling the growing number of mass strandings linked to naval sonar, the report detailed the range of nonlethal harm caused by sound in the sea. Emerging research suggested that every manner of marine life was vulnerable to noise pollution, including fish, invertebrates, and even coral.

Reynolds was delighted that *Sounding the Depths* garnered significant attention from the media and the scientific community. But it did nothing to change the fact that he had very little recourse to stem the rising tide of industrial noise pollution in the ocean through legal action. With no ocean noise statutes on the books, and no international enforcement agencies, intercontinental shipping was immune from any lawsuits NRDC could bring. Meanwhile, oil and gas companies had armies of lobbyists on Capitol Hill, close ties with Fisheries, and a bottomless legal war chest.

As he geared up for what felt like an inevitable legal confrontation with the Navy over LFA, Reynolds was glad he'd added Jasny and Wetzler to his team.

Between monitoring Navy sonar and managing the rest of his caseload, he worried about becoming overextended. He didn't want his second marriage to fail from neglect as his first one had.

As soon as he'd moved to Los Angeles in 1980, he'd married his college sweetheart, Linda—and promptly immersed himself in the years-long battle to defeat Diablo Canyon. While Joel hopscotched between administrative trials in San Luis Obispo and circuit court appeals in Washington, Linda sat alone in their apartment in Venice, California, watching him being interviewed on the evening news and wondering if she would ever get her husband back. As months and years passed, she watched their marriage recede into a sea of depositions and hearings. Even when he was home, Joel's head was filled with filing deadlines and trials. Everything had become a blur of work. Joel's work.

When Joel surveyed his life after Diablo Canyon, it was hard for him to mark the point where Linda had become lost to him. It was all a blur. He'd resisted her overtures to have children because he wasn't ready. He hadn't even been around and available for the big breakup scenes. Eventually Linda had accepted reality and moved on to a better marriage to someone less subsumed by his work.

Reynolds met his second wife, Susan, shortly after he joined NRDC in 1990. They married six months after their first date, following a torrid courtship between Los Angeles and New York, where Susan worked as director of publications in NRDC's headquarters. Like many organizations, NRDC had a policy against married couples working together. So Susan resigned her position and moved to Los Angeles.

As often happens, the "opposites attract" physics of courtship became the focus of tension early in their marriage. Susan was a consummate East Coaster. Having grown up on the Upper East Side of Manhattan, she attended the exclusive all-girls Spence School before moving on to Middlebury College in Vermont. She then returned to Manhattan to work at the *New York Review of Books*. Joel was enamored of her beauty, brains, and literary passion. To Susan, his blend of equanimity, affability, and intense idealism personified the best of the West Coast.

But the move to California, where she knew no one, left Susan feeling lonely and depressed. Joel remained immersed in his cases, as well as what felt to Susan like an endless stream of work retreats, NRDC benefits, and donor cultivation trips—none of which included spouses. Though she was proud of his accomplishments, Susan felt excluded from Joel's work life, and insecure about him hobnobbing with Hollywood movie stars and studio heads, several of whom served on NRDC's board. She struggled to establish herself professionally while juggling the demands of mothering their three young children.

When she finally secured a staff position as a book reviewer and columnist for the *Los Angeles Times*, one of her colleagues asked her, "What's it like to be married to Neil Armstrong?" To Susan, it sometimes felt as though her husband *was* an astronaut. He certainly orbited in a loftier social realm than she did. In truth, she was temperamentally ill suited to be the wife of a celebrity lawyer in a glitzy town like Los Angeles. She dreamed of the family moving back east, but Joel insisted that California was where he needed to be for his work.

The mood at home grew increasingly tense and argumentative. Their fights became more frequent and more punishing. Joel had always been a fixer, but he didn't know how to fix his marriage. More and more, he compartmentalized his emotional life, walling off the pain of his fractious marriage from the good times he managed to preserve with his kids. Though he continued to work long hours, he was committed to being home for dinner and putting his children to bed at night. He adored his two daughters and son, and reveled in sharing his passions with them: music, sports, and the glory of California's wild places.

His colleagues understood that he had "problems at home," but no one knew the depths of his despair. Joel poured even more of himself into his work and became more determined than ever to rescue whatever he could of the planet's dwindling natural treasures.

By the winter of 2000, after five years preparing its Environmental Impact Statement, the Navy was finally ready to apply to Fisheries for a permit to deploy LFA sonar around the world. Then the whales came ashore in the Bahamas—and the Navy's carefully constructed case for safe sonar was thrown into disarray.

From the moment he heard about the whale researcher collecting fresh specimens on the beach, Reynolds hoped that those frozen whale heads might provide the forensic evidence he needed to bolster his legal case against naval sonar. What he hadn't anticipated was the power of the *visual* evidence that Balcomb had collected: indelible images of dead and dying whales on the beach.

"A deaf whale is dead whale" was arguably more of a rallying cry than a scientific pronouncement. But a *beached* whale was indisputably a dead whale. Photographs of stranded whales with blood leaking from their eyes fed a growing wave of public indignation that even the world's most powerful Navy couldn't contain.

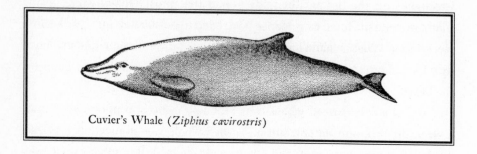

Cuvier's Whale (*Ziphius cavirostris*)

16

Heads That Tell Tales

DAY 15: MARCH 30, 2000, DAWN
Nancy's Restaurant, Abaco Island, the Bahamas

"Here you go, man," said Les Adderly as he switched on the overhead fluorescents. "Take any boxes you want."

Balcomb and Claridge surveyed the cartons of beer, ketchup, and napkins piled along the wall of the restaurant storeroom. "This one should work for the Cuvier's," he said, grabbing a 100-roll box of paper towels. "And this one"—he pulled out a big box of toilet paper rolls and measured it against his outstretched arm—"looks big enough for the Blainville's."

It was early morning on moving day. Time to pack up the heads and the dolphin for the trip to Boston. After two weeks of wrangling between the US and Bahamian departments of Fisheries, all the paperwork had been arranged to allow the whale specimens to leave the country. If everything ran according to plan, they'd deliver them safe and still frozen to Darlene Ketten's radiology lab at Harvard Medical School by early evening.

Balcomb cut the tamper-evident tape from around the freezer lid and wrote the date and time on the chain-of-custody form. Balcomb signed, and Claridge countersigned as witness. With Les' help, Balcomb hoisted the Cuvier's, and then the Blainville's, head out of the freezer chest. Claridge had to help them negotiate the frozen dolphin.

They double wrapped each head in 40-gallon garbage bags and then covered them in a thick layer of bubble wrap. The Cuvier's went into the paper towel box, along with the two jars containing whale ears submerged in formalin that they'd brought from the house. They wedged the somewhat smaller Blainville's head into the toilet paper box. It took three rolls of duct tape to secure the boxes to Balcomb's satisfaction. Ketten had shipped them a metallic silver body bag for the dolphin. At six feet long, it fit snugly inside. They had to coax the zipper to close around its dorsal fin.

Les helped them load everything into the back of their pickup, while his daughter, Mercy, cooked them scrambled eggs with crawfish and hot sauce. With a daylong sprint from Abaco to Miami to Boston to Harvard still ahead of them, Balcomb figured this could be their only chance to grab a meal.

Bob Gisiner had promised to reimburse Balcomb the $900 it cost to charter an Abaco Air six-seater for the flight to Miami. There was just enough room on board for the three human and three cetacean passengers.

As soon as they hit the ground in Miami, everything shifted into sped-up Keystone Kops mode. They ferried their frozen cargo on dollies across the overheated tarmac to Agricultural Inspection, and then to customs, and finally to the passenger terminal for the flight to Boston, with the departure time drawing closer with every delay. The paperwork they had to process was mind numbing. There were Agriculture Inspection manifests, Bahamian and US Fisheries export and import papers, and chain-of-custody signatures every step of the way. There were inspectors on break, and inspectors who had to confer with supervisors to figure out how to properly categorize "whale products; ears" and "whale products; heads" and "dolphin; deceased."

No one had told Balcomb and Claridge that Miami International Airport was the largest airfreight terminal in the United States—and the most notorious port of entry for drug shipments from South America and the Caribbean. Every package was given a close going-over at every inspection station.

As they waited in one line after another, Balcomb couldn't stop visualizing drops of moisture beading on the whale heads as they began to thaw in their boxes.

At length, they reached the front of the customs line. "Any firearms, alcohol, or tobacco products to declare?" the agent asked.

"No, nothing like that."

"Any currency, US or foreign, in excess of ten thousand dollars?"

"No," Balcomb said. "We're declaring two beaked whale heads, two ear bones, and a spotted dolphin. And we're in a hurry."

That got the agent's attention. Of course, he then wanted them to untape the boxes and to explain why they were importing frozen whale heads into the United States. They unzipped the body bag all the way down to the dolphin's tail, and the customs agent fished his hand around in the corners of the bag, searching for contraband. "Just last month we intercepted five kilos of coke stashed inside a sealed coffin," explained the agent. "Inside the corpse, actually. In the stomach cavity."

When it was time to sign the customs forms and transfer custody of the heads to US Fisheries, Balcomb hesitated. The heads were the most important physical evidence of the stranding. Once he handed over custody to Fisheries, he'd lose control of the specimens and become expendable to the investigative team. But he had no choice. He signed the transfer documents.

He and Claridge were merely couriers now. And they were dangerously behind schedule. They piled their cargo back onto dollies and jogged toward the American Airlines passenger terminal. The flight was scheduled to take off in 45 minutes, and there were a dozen passengers ahead of them at curbside check-in.

Balcomb collared the nearest redcap and pleaded for his help. "We *have* to make this flight," he said with an urgency that he hoped would convey authority rather than naked panic.

The redcap shook his head as he surveyed their cargo. "These boxes are too big to fly as baggage. They have to go as freight, and freight check-in for this flight closed"—he checked his watch—"fifteen minutes ago."

"We're carrying crucial evidence for a federal investigation," said Balcomb, patting the body bag for emphasis. The redcap tilted his head to one side.

"It's true," said Claridge. "Here's the paperwork." She pointed to the Fisheries seal on the transfer documents. The redcap scanned the manifest.

"Are you folks involved with those beached whales I've been hearing about?"

"Yes, we are," said Claridge. "We're the directors of the Bahamas Marine Mammal Survey."

The redcap laughed. "You're not going to believe this, but my daughter is a marine biology major at U. of Florida. She's *crazy* about dolphins."

Claridge unzipped the top of the body bag far enough to reveal the dolphin's rostrum. "This is an Atlantic spotted dolphin that stranded on Powell Cay under suspicious circumstances. Dr. Darlene Ketten is standing by at Harvard Medical School to examine these specimens."

"Alison—that's my daughter—she's going to go bananas when I tell her about this." The redcap chuckled to himself and then checked his watch again. "You'll never make it through this cattle line. If you hustle inside and upgrade your tickets to first class, that will get you each a cargo allowance. I'll check the dolphin through as golf clubs." With that, he levered the body bag onto his trolley. "Then I'll wheel the boxes over to the cargo bay myself and make sure they get loaded on the plane."

The redcap waved away Balcomb's offer of a tip. "I just want to tell Alison I played a part in the whale investigation."

Balcomb was nervous about letting the heads out of his sight. And he hated shelling out $400 a ticket for first-class upgrades. But he gave the ticket agent his credit card and held his breath while he waited to see if the upcharges busted his credit limit. The charge went through.

He sent Claridge ahead to board the plane while he hung back to watch the cargo being loaded. Just as the cabin door was about to be sealed, he caught sight of the duct-taped boxes and the silver body bag as they rumbled up the conveyor belt ramp and disappeared into the cargo hold.

After six sweaty hours of wrestling their unwieldy cargo off the island and onto the Boston-bound jet, Balcomb and Claridge suddenly found themselves deposited into plush first-class thrones. "Look, a swag bag!" Claridge exclaimed, pulling fluffy cotton booties and a satin eye mask out of a drawstring bag. A steward poured complimentary glasses of sparkling wine. Another one offered them moist, perfumed hand towels.

Claridge sipped her wine, slipped on her booties, and reviewed the movie options. Balcomb was still worrying about how he'd explain the $800 upgrade to Gisiner, and whether he'd be good for it.

One of Ketten's grad school assistants met their flight at Logan International Airport and helped them load their cargo into a Massachusetts General Hospital van. The sun was setting over the Boston skyline as they approached the hospital and descended into the basement service entrance. Three empty gurneys stood sentinel on the loading dock.

The underground arteries of the night hospital were virtually empty of patients and staff as the three of them guided their heavily laden gurneys through the dark hallways. Eventually they pushed through swinging double doors marked "Computerized Tomography Lab" into a cold, brightly lit room. A gleaming white CT scanner dominated the middle of the lab.

Ketten emerged from the rear office dressed in pale blue surgical scrubs, her hair pulled back into a tight bun. "I hope my volunteers had a gentle transit." She smiled at the three gurneys, barely looking up to acknowledge Balcomb and Claridge.

There was no confusion about who was in charge of the investigation now. Ketten's beachside dissection had been in Balcomb and Claridge's backyard, replete with island gaiety, blood, and guts. Ketten's lab, by contrast, was immaculate and silent, save for the whir of the air-conditioning and a faint buzz from the banks of fluorescent lights.

"Before we begin," Ketten said, "let's take care of paperwork."

Claridge presented her with the packet of permits, which Ketten read page by page. "Excellent. These all appear to be in order." She time-stamped and signed the chain-of-custody forms, held them for Balcomb and Claridge to countersign, and then handed them to her assistant. "Carl will file these in a secure cabinet." Carl disappeared into the back office.

"Hope you don't mind," said Balcomb, raising his camera bag off the floor, "but I brought my video camera. To record the proceedings."

Ketten stiffened. She said that she'd need to get permission from the department chief before Balcomb could use recording equipment in the lab, but he'd left for the day. She'd invited Ken and Diane to stay for the scanning out of professional courtesy. Since neither of them had forensics accreditation, they could participate only as observers, not as investigators.

"That's what I'm here to do," said Balcomb, indicating his camera bag. "Observe."

During his two Navy tours, Balcomb had navigated his share of face-offs with bureaucrats who wielded protocol like a sword. As he began to slowly, methodically unpack his camera gear, he reminded Ketten that the specimens remained the property of the Bahamian Ministry of Fisheries and that as the photo-identification expert on the team, he needed to document the proceedings, as well as archive copies of the CT scans. He was bluffing. Ketten could kick him out of her lab or even call security if she wanted. But he wagered that she wanted to show off her imaging expertise to another beaked whale aficionado, someone who would share her excitement at the scans.

"Give me a moment, please," she said and then retreated to her back office. Balcomb could hear Ketten talking to someone on the phone. A moment later, she emerged from the office with a document for Balcomb to sign.

"It's a waiver. It says you agree to consult with the attending—that's me—on any use of recorded material, including the CT scans, which remain the property of Mass General."

Balcomb signed the waivers. Ketten countersigned and handed Balcomb one copy. Balcomb wished he'd had the presence of mind to get his own agreement with Ketten in writing when she was in the Bahamas. But that ship had left port.

"Carl will help you scrub in," she said crisply, returning to her office to file the waiver.

Soon they were all identically attired in blue cotton scrubs and white latex gloves. As Ketten cut open the box holding the Cuvier's whale head, Balcomb leaned over her shoulder to peer inside. When they'd claimed their cargo at Logan, he'd checked to make sure that nothing nasty was leaking through the cardboard and duct tape. But he hadn't had a look inside the boxes since customs, six hours earlier. He prayed the specimens were still frozen solid.

Ketten cleared her throat and began dictating notes into a tiny digital recorder that hung from her neck. "The frozen *Ziphius cavirostris* head was transported in"—she looked at the paper towel box and withdrew some of the bubble-wrap batting—"an insulated box, by charter and commercial airlines from"—she consulted the chain-of-custody document—"Abaco Island via Miami to Boston on 30 March, 2000, with a total transit time of"—she checked her watch—"twelve hours, with specimen examination beginning at 7:34 p.m."

She peeled away the plastic garbage bags and probed the head with her gloved hand. "The *Ziphius cavirostris* head is well preserved, with little evidence of freezer artifact," she said, nodding in approval. "There is no evidence of thawing of any but the most superficial layers." She favored Balcomb and Claridge with a slight smile.

Ketten removed the two specimen jars containing the whale ears. "The head was dissected in a fresh state, on-site in Abaco, the Bahamas, on March 20, 2000," Ketten continued. "The ears of the animal were extracted and secondarily examined with ultrahigh-resolution computerized tomography."

Carl positioned the whale ears side by side on the scanner bed, two feet apart. "The left ear on the left," Ketten intoned, "the right on the right. Just as nature intended." She motioned Balcomb and Claridge to follow her into the glassed-off observation area and sat down at a computer terminal in front of a bank of monitors. She typed in the species, sex, estimated age, and the location where the Cuvier's stranded. When she pushed a button on the console, the bed began moving slowly through the donut hole opening of the scanner, emitting a short, clipped buzz with each thin-slice X-ray exposure. Line by line, a two-dimensional image of the inner ears began to form. At first it looked like something drawn on an Etch A Sketch toy, monochromatic and low resolution.

As soon as the image began to take shape on the screen, the tension went out of the room, and the chill departed from Ketten's voice. "This is my favorite part," she said, "when I get my very first look inside. It's wonderful, isn't it?"

It *was* wonderful. Balcomb and Claridge were transfixed. The lines of pixels gradually grew in detail to reveal the structure of the ear bone in all its elegance: the spiral nautilus shape of the cochlea leading to the three small ear bones of the auditory ossicles. Ketten manipulated the computer's mouse like a digital scalpel to pare away layers of tissue and fully articulate the bony structures.

"Now watch this: it's so great!" With a few keystrokes, the two-dimensional image began to rotate and reveal itself in three dimensions. The ear bones revolved like a jeweled tiara in a Cartier display window.

"Now, here's the coolest part of all," she said in a hushed voice, as if speaking too loudly might break the spell. "We can colorize the specimen by density." With another keystroke sequence, Ketten transposed the monochromatic model into vivid greens and yellows. "The CT can differentiate the density range of bones, soft tissue, and fluids—even air pockets," she explained.

Ketten pointed at red lines in both ears. "Look what we have here: the pattern of hemorrhaged blood is almost identical bilaterally. If we saw the blood only in one ear, that would suggest a postmortem trauma, or simply evidence of the whale lying on one side postmortem. But this bilateral hemorrhage is a clear sign that the ears were traumatized *before* the whale hit the beach."

They replaced the ears with the Blainville's head, which took a full hour to image.

"Look," she said, when the details were filled in and colorized. "The same hemorrhagic bleed pattern in these ears." After the Blainville's, they scanned the Cuvier's head and found blood pooling around the brain.

It was well after midnight when they hoisted the dolphin onto the scanner. Claridge reached out to touch the dolphin through her latex glove. It was utterly transformed from the warm, smooth animal that convulsed and died in her arms two weeks earlier. Now it was stiff and lifeless, an ice sculpture of a dolphin.

An hour later, digitally rendered on the CT's monitor, the dolphin was reincarnated as a white skeleton floating inside a pale blue shell of skin. A close-up of the head showed its brain in pink, suspended above two orange lobes of auditory fat along the jawbones. Nestled underneath the lobes, the inner ears stood out as bright red knobs. Claridge, who had observed dolphins in the wild all her life, had the eerie feeling that she had never truly seen one before this.

By three in the morning, they had completed their work, and Carl had packed all the specimens into the lab's freezer. Ketten was still dictating her findings. "The patterning of the hemorrhages therefore suggests strongly that a cerebrospinal fluid 'squeeze' from an intense pressure event was the source of inner ear blood in these animals . . . The inner ear pathologies demonstrated on the scans are consistent with observed pathology in ears exposed to exceptionally intense impulsive sources . . . The pattern of damage is consistent with acoustic trauma, but a number of other causes are equally possible and cannot be ruled out at this stage of analysis."

Just before dawn, the four of them drove the specimens down to Woods Hole, two hours south of Boston. They were giddy with exhaustion by the time they reached the Redfield Laboratory on Water Street. When they'd moved the specimens inside the walk-in freezer, Ketten closed the freezer door and sealed it with a padlock. Final chain-of-custody papers were signed all around. "And we're done," said Ketten, sealing the documents into a large envelope. With a mock ceremonial bow, she presented Balcomb with another envelope containing a full set of CT scans. She told them she'd be in touch as soon as they had a date scheduled for the full physical necropsy.

Balcomb would have liked to linger in Woods Hole and tour the facilities. But they had a noon flight back to Miami, and Ketten had a class to teach in an hour. They said their good-byes on the steps of the lab, and Carl drove them back to Logan Airport.

Before her class began, Ketten called Bob Gisiner to report her preliminary findings. She confirmed that the heads were now in secure custody at her Woods Hole lab, and that Balcomb and Claridge would soon be on a plane back to the Bahamas.

SANDY POINT, ABACO ISLAND, THE BAHAMAS

A week after his return to Abaco, Balcomb couldn't stop thinking about the heads back in Woods Hole. He'd tried calling Ketten to find out the date of the necropsy, but he couldn't catch her in. And she didn't call him back. Gisiner wasn't taking or returning his calls either. The only person he could reach was Gentry, who was sounding more and more like an assigned handler, counseling patience and team play and trust that things would come out right in the end.

Without the whales to survey, Balcomb and Claridge were at loose ends. Each of their daily trips to the canyon in search of beaked whales had ended in disappointment.

Sitting on the back porch at the end of another restless, purposeless day, Balcomb gazed out across the canyon in the direction of the AUTEC testing range. He wondered what sounds the Navy hydrophones mounted on the sea floor had recorded the night of the stranding. He was haunted by a memory from his final Navy tour in Japan. His wife at the time, Camille, was researching the 400-year-old dolphin fishery at the small coastal town of Taiji. Though it was normally closed to Westerners, he and Camille had arranged to witness the seasonal dolphin drive hunt.

A flotilla of a dozen small boats arranged itself into a straight line just outside the mouth of the cove. A short time later, a large pod of dolphins approached, and the line of boats opened out to herd them inside the cove. Then the boats closed formation, sealing the mouth of the cove. Each boatman lowered a steel pipe halfway into the water and began banging the top half with a second steel pipe. From the shore, Ken and Camille could hear the steel pipes clanging loudly in unison. Balcomb knew that underneath the water's surface, the sound was converging into a wall of high-decibel noise. Then the boats began to move toward the shore, driving the dolphins ahead of them and into the shallows.

Ken and Camille watched in horror as the men leapt from their boats into the churning waters. They culled a few young females for export to foreign marine parks. They stabbed the remaining dolphins with spears, dragged their thrashing bodies onto the beach, and slit their throats. The men didn't wait for the dolphins to die before butchering them into steaks bound for fish markets across Japan. The shallows turned dark red with blood, and the air filled with the shrieks of dozens of dying dolphins.

Twenty-five years later, standing on another beach a world away from Taiji, Balcomb could still hear the knell of the steel pipes, could still see the panicked dolphins fleeing ahead of the acoustic storm, rushing toward the oblivion of the beach.

PART THREE
THE RELUCTANT WHISTLE-BLOWER

What if the catalyst or the key to understanding creation lay somewhere in the immense mind of the whale? . . . Suppose if God came back from wherever it is he's been and asked us smilingly if we'd figured it out yet. Suppose he wanted to know if it had finally occurred to us to ask the whale. And then he sort of looked around and he said, "By the way, where are the whales?"

—*Cormac McCarthy*, Of Whales and Men

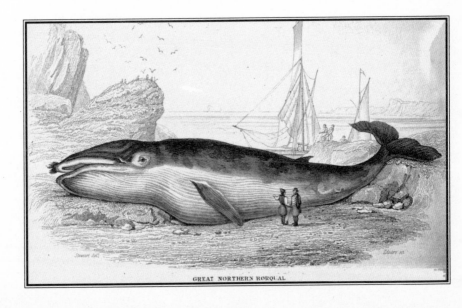

GREAT NORTHERN RORQUAL

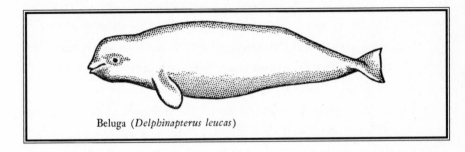

Beluga (*Delphinapterus leucas*)

17

A Mind in the Water

When the Navy began studying cetacean biosonar in the late 1940s, the only people who cared about saving the whales were whalers.

By the end of World War II, it had become clear to everyone in the whaling industry that 50 years of unbridled slaughter had decimated populations around the world. Many commercial species were already depleted and threatened with extinction. Two late-nineteenth-century inventions by the Norwegian whaler Svend Foyn had reduced even the most gigantic whales to helpless prey. In 1863 he introduced the first steam-powered whaling ship that could overtake even the largest and fastest of the great whales: blues, fins, and seis that could outswim any ship under sail. A few years later, he demonstrated how his deck-mounted harpoon canon, firing explosive grenades, could stop the heart of a 100-foot-long leviathan.

Things got progressively worse for whales in the twentieth century. Demand for whale oil to manufacture glycerin bombs spiked during World

War I, and after the war, the process of hydrogenating whale oil created a boom market for its use in margarine. By the 1920s, fleets of floating factory ships were killing and processing whales at sea with lethal efficiency. Throughout the 1930s, tens of thousands of great whales were harvested each year. In 1939 alone, whalers killed almost 40,000 blue whales.

Whaling was suspended during World War II, as shipping lanes shut down and many whaling ships were drafted into service as military cargo vessels. Still, the war took a deadly toll on whales caught in the cross fire of major sea battles in the Atlantic and Pacific. Millions of tons of explosives were detonated in the oceans, including hundreds of thousands of antisubmarine depth charges. Air forces and navies on both sides of the conflict made a practice of using passing pods for target practice. In the aftermath of the war, industrious whalers adapted military sonar to locate, drive to the surface, and herd their prey—but there were indisputably far fewer whales left to hunt.[1]

In 1946, 15 whaling nations established the International Whaling Commission with the stated goal "to provide for the proper conservation of whale stocks and thus make possible the orderly development of the whaling industry." The idea of preserving whale populations for purposes other than killing and processing them into margarine and motor oil was still 20 years in the future. And it would be fully 40 years before the International Whaling Commission called a halt to commercial whaling worldwide in 1986.

During those intervening four decades, whales would undergo a radical cultural transformation from commercial commodity to entertainment superstars and revered icons of the New Age, environmental, and animal rights movements. Where once their value was measured in the price per barrel of their oil, whales and dolphins would suddenly become box-office sensations, drawing millions of admiring customers to movie theaters, aquariums, and theme parks, and, in time, to open-sea whale-watching venues around the world.

One of the unlikely catalysts of this cultural sea change was the cadre of scientific researchers—almost all of them funded by the US Navy—who first studied and appreciated whales as more than mere casks of oil. Some of these early investigators were so transfigured by their close encounters with whales and dolphins that they abandoned their research careers to become public advocates for whale conservation, and even liberation.

• • •

The impetus for the Navy's decades-long investment in whale research was a bat-obsessed biology student named Donald Griffin. In 1940, while still an undergraduate at Harvard, Griffin conceived an experiment to solve a 200-year-old zoology puzzle known as "Spallanzani's bat problem." Lazzaro Spallanzani had been an eighteenth-century Italian naturalist who hypothesized, after alternately blinding and deafening bats, that they navigated in the dark using sound rather than sight. But because bats transmitted their high-frequency sound signals *above* the human hearing threshold, they *appeared* to be flying in silence. This conundrum left Spallanzani unable to explain precisely how bats navigate in pitch-black caves.

When Griffin learned that Harvard's physics department had recently invented an ultrasonic sound detector, he hoped this new technology might be the key to unlocking Spallanzani's "problem." He constructed an elaborate maze of hanging wires in a blacked-out basement laboratory, which he then equipped with ultrasonic sound receivers. The bats successfully navigated the maze in total darkness, and the ultrasonic receivers enabled Griffin to record the squeaky clicks of their ultrahigh-frequency sound emissions. He deduced correctly that the bats were navigating by the echoes from their clicks, a method that he named "echolocation." Griffin later demonstrated that bats also employed echolocation to hunt in the dark, using different frequency transmissions depending on the size of the insects they were hunting.

The Navy, always on the lookout for ways to improve its radar and sonar capabilities, immediately took an interest in Griffin's findings. After ONR began supporting his research into animal behavior, Griffin speculated that mammals *other* than bats might navigate by echolocation—*notably, whales in the lightless ocean depths.*[2] This provocative supposition encouraged the Navy—in service to its antisubmarine warfare mission—to embark on a decades-long effort to confirm, describe, decode, and deploy cetacean biosonar.

There was nothing novel about the idea of recruiting animals into warfare. Elephants, camels, and horses had conveyed soldiers, supplies, and arms into battles for centuries. Soldiers had long trained dogs to attack enemies, sniff out bombs, guard facilities, and, in the case of the Soviet army in World War II, to run under enemy tanks with explosives strapped to their backs.

During the same war, the British Air Ministry Pigeon Section deployed a quarter million homing pigeons as military messengers—32 of which were awarded the Dickin Medal "for conspicuous gallantry and devotion to service." Not to be outdone by its ally across the Atlantic, the US military developed the Bat Bomb Project, which hoped to use bats as flying incendiary devices for the firebombing of Tokyo.[3]

But Griffin's discovery of animal echolocation transformed the quest to harness an animal's unique sensory talents for military advantage. Instead of merely training animals to fight, Griffin inspired naval engineers to renew a centuries-old tradition of looking to biology for design inspiration. Leonardo da Vinci modeled ship hulls on the fish and marine mammals he illustrated. The Wright Brothers adopted a fixed-wing design for their first airplane after observing that large birds glided with almost no wing movement. In the 1950s, engineers called animal-inspired technology biomimetics and biomimicry, derived from the Greek *bios*, for "life," and *mimesis*, for "imitation." However, it was the term "bionics," the compound of "biology" and "electronics," that the Navy adopted to describe its research and development of technology that could rival the biosonar talents of a dolphin.

Before the US Navy became the leading patron of modern cetology, whale science had relied primarily on whalers' observations of the behavior of their prey. The only research expeditions of any note had been the Discovery Investigations in the 1920s and 1930s led by British scientists who culled anatomical specimens from the decks of whaling ships working the waters near Antarctica.

The Navy chose a tamer setting to test Griffin's hypothesis of cetacean biosonar. Marine Studios, originally built in the 1930s as a film set for underwater movies, was stocked with dolphins, seals, and sharks captured from the waters near St. Augustine, Florida. After closing during the war, it reopened as Marineland, the nation's first marine park.

Marineland's live shows starring trained dolphins gave tens of thousands of visitors their first close-up view of small whales. Just a decade earlier, dolphins had been despised by fishermen who derided them as "pig fish" and "herring hogs" for poaching fish from their nets. But with the rising celebrity of Flippy, Splash, and Zippy—whose balletic performances were broadcast live on CBS-TV's *Marineland Carnival*—dolphins began a long run as America's marine mammal sweethearts.

A marine park turned out to be a good laboratory for conducting dolphin research. Man-made tanks bore little resemblance to a dolphin's natural habitat, but compared to the dark oceans, they offered early investigators a transparent and controlled research environment. Dolphins, highly social and responsive to training, could provide direct feedback to stimuli much the way that a human subject could, pressing levers in response to commands and even vocalizing. Navy-funded studies at Marineland marked cetology's transition from a "dead science," based on examination of scavenged remains from beaches and whaling stations, to a "life science" of controlled experimentation and observation, first in captive settings and later in the wild.

The young biologist-psychologist who served as the curator of Marineland, Arthur McBride, became fascinated by the extraordinary range of sounds emerging from the dolphin tanks. Aristotle had recorded his observations of dolphin vocalizations thousands of years earlier in his *Historia Animalium*, but McBride was the first scientist to remark on the biosonar possibilities of their barks, grunts, clicks, whistles, moans, and distinctive "creaking door" sound. Having heard from local fishermen about the dolphins' ability to evade their nets in Florida's opaque St. John's River, McBride noted in his journals that "this behavior calls to mind the sonic sending and receiving apparatus which enables the bat to avoid obstacles in the dark." In 1947, with the aid of "a supersonic sending and receiving apparatus" provided by the newly formed Office of Naval Research, McBride began to measure dolphin responses to ultrasonic frequencies.

In 1951 ONR dispatched William Schevill and his research partner and wife, Barbara Lawrence, from Woods Hole to Marineland to test Griffin's and McBride's hypothesis of dolphin echolocation. After recording the full range of dolphin vocalizations and verifying the acuity of their hearing, Schevill and Lawrence transported one of the animals back to Woods Hole for further tests. Working at night in a pond, they confirmed the dolphins' ability to navigate around nets in the dark, muddy water.

At the same time, ONR was funding research by Winthrop Kellogg, a psychologist at Florida State University. With the assistance of then under-graduate marine biologist Sylvia Earle, Kellogg established that dolphins consistently swam around a transparent Plexiglas wall, even in darkness. By 1953, Kellogg and the Schevills had independently published research demonstrating that the dolphins' "rusty-hinge" vocalization was actually a series of rapid clicks with a wideband frequency spectrum that they used to navigate, hunt, and communicate.

Finally, Ken Norris, a World War II Navy veteran and curator of Marineland's newly opened sister park, Marineland of the Pacific, in Southern California, conclusively proved dolphin echolocation. Norris, who would later mentor Balcomb, Gisiner, and Gentry at UC Santa Cruz, outfitted a bottlenose dolphin named Zippy with suction cup blindfolds to demonstrate that he could navigate a maze of pipes suspended in a tank. Zippy accurately echolocated objects at a distance of 30 feet. Later research revealed that dolphin biosonar far outmatched the Navy's active sonar technology in every dimension. Dolphins could detect a target the size of a tangerine from 300 feet away, and could distinguish between an aluminum and an iron plate, a hollow tube and a solid one, and ball bearings of microscopically different sizes. Dolphins could discriminate 5,000 individual clicks per seconds, compared to a human's ability to detect 30 per second.

Kellogg expressed the consensus view of his research colleagues when he reported to ONR, "What these animals can do has a definite bearing on our national defense, as a means of improving man-made sonar."

The improbable ascent of whales from raw material for dog food to cultural icons and prized naval assets was propelled, as much as anyone, by an eccentric neuroscientist who tirelessly promoted his passion for small whales and their big brains. John Lilly was the progenitor of two parallel and, eventually, intersecting crusades: the Navy's drive to decode cetacean communication and the conservation community's campaign to save the whales.[4]

In many ways, Lilly's career mirrored Walter Munk's. They were both fugitives from successful banking families—Lilly hailed from Saint Paul, Minnesota; Munk from Vienna. Like Munk, Lilly ran away to California and ended up at the California Institute of Technology, where he immersed himself in physics, biology, and human physiology. Coincidentally, their paths crossed during their senior years, when Lilly and Munk were co-presidents of the CalTech ski club that Munk had founded the year before. When Munk moved on to graduate school at Scripps, Lilly went east to medical school at Dartmouth College, where he studied brain physiology and began inventing medical instruments. During the war, the US Army Air Forces recruited Lilly to study problems of high-altitude flight at its aeromedical lab in Columbus, Ohio. By the war's end, Lilly had migrated to the top of the "preferred list" of scientists compiled by the War Manpower Commission.

Like oceanography, neurology was in its infancy in the 1950s, the brain as uncharted and unexplored as the ocean depths. Lilly's training in neurophysiology, combined with his aptitude for electronic engineering, placed him in the front ranks of neuroscientists who were parsing the boundaries separating the brain, the mind, and the psyche. To prepare himself for what he called his "implorations" of human consciousness, Lilly underwent psychoanalysis and earned his certification as a psychoanalyst.

During a decade of neurological research at the National Institutes of Health, Lilly created the first atlas of the primate central nervous system. While Munk was deconstructing ocean wave patterns, Lilly was inventing the first electrical waveform that could stimulate brain cells. He also engineered a narrow-gauge stainless-steel sleeve that could penetrate a primate skull without anesthesia. By inserting a thin tungsten electrode through this guide, Lilly could stimulate the deep structures of the brain—specifically, the brain of the macaque monkey, Lilly's animal model for cortical mapping.

Lilly strapped the monkey into a chair and clamped its head securely in place. With a single strike of a claw hammer, he pounded the sleeve guide through the monkey's skull, and then lowered the tungsten electrode through the cortex and into the deeper regions of the brain. Once the electrode was in place, Lilly delivered an electric pulse to the "primitive" areas controlling pleasure and pain, evoking telltale expressions of excitement or fear. While the image of a monkey with hundreds of wires protruding from his skull was ghoulish in the extreme, Lilly took pride in how little pain and risk of infection his insertion technique caused.

Within two years, he had completed a blueprint of the neural pathways of pleasure, pain, sex, hunger, thirst, aggression, and fear in the primate brain. But Lilly was frustrated by his finding that the monkey brain seemed to be nothing more than a fuse box of on-off switches for pleasure and pain. What good was mapping the primate brain, he wondered, if it didn't reveal the secrets of consciousness that lay hidden inside the folds of its gray matter? Lilly was eager to explore a more expansive brainscape.

When Lilly arrived at Marineland in the spring of 1957, he wasn't interested in dolphins' prodigious talent for echolocation. He'd come in search of a big-brained mammal whose cortex he could chart with the same precision that he'd applied to the brains of cats, rabbits, and monkeys. At a time when scientists considered brain weight to be the primary measure of intelligence, the dolphin appeared to be an Einstein-like species. Compared to the paltry mass of a macaque monkey's three-ounce brain, the bottlenose dolphin's gray matter weighed almost four *pounds*—heavier than a human brain and essentially equivalent to human brain weight in relation to total body mass. The biggest-brained mammal of all, the sperm whale, boasted a brain weight of nearly 20 pounds. But there were no captive sperm whales available for experimentation.

The first several dolphins that Lilly anesthetized drowned when the respirator he designed malfunctioned.[5] After refining his sleeve-guide technology to penetrate a nonanesthetized dolphin skull, Lilly eventually succeeded in implanting an electrode into a dolphin's deep brain. As he gradually increased the electrical current to the probe, the animal began vocalizing in what Lilly called "a dolphinese fashion." Deeper penetrations and increased voltage evoked "more exuberant vocalizing than ever I'd heard before. Whistles, buzzings, raspings, barks, and Bronx cheer–like noises were emitted . . . One time, he mimicked my speaking voice so well that my wife laughed out loud, and he copied her laughter."

Lilly constructed a lever that the dolphin could push with its rostrum to activate the electrical charge itself. After pushing the lever faster and faster, the dolphin went into an epileptic seizure and died. Lilly later reported, "This death made us very sad, and we went through a period of mourning for this delightful animal . . . Despite the disappointment and sadness, we had to go on with the research: our responsibilities lie with finding the truth."

The "truth" Lilly uncovered in the course of his experiments was that dolphins not only learned the reward response much faster than his monkey subjects. They were also able, when properly stimulated, to mimic human speech—a response never evoked in his macaques, and to which Lilly assigned great significance. Lilly left Marineland convinced that he had tapped into the whispering chamber of interspecies communication. Listening to the whistles, laughs, and barks of the electrically neurostimulated dolphin, he heard a voice calling to him across what he termed the "air-water boundary" separating humans from their cetacean cousins. Lilly had come to Marineland in search of a big brain of humanlike complexity. What he discovered was "a mind in the waters."[6]

Lilly presented his findings at the 1958 annual meeting of the American Psychiatric Association in San Francisco. Just six months after the Soviet Union's successful launch of the first satellite, Sputnik, as the superpowers embarked on outer-space exploration, Lilly chose this gathering of consummate inner-space voyagers as the first audience for his proclamation that dolphins offered us a gateway to what he termed "cosmic consciousness."

Sputnik had fixed everyone's sights on the sky and on the unseen world of outer space. For some, it raised the specter of Soviet missiles raining down from the heavens. For others, it heralded the opening of a new age of space exploration and possible contact with extraterrestrials. The science-fiction realm of interplanetary travel and first contact with extraterrestrials was suddenly being presented as scientific possibility on the covers of newsweeklies—and from the podiums of scientific conferences.

As he rose to make his predinner address, Lilly felt like an explorer reporting back to the members of a geographical society. Dolphins, he began, were true extraterrestrials from our unexplored oceans and from the black lagoon of our untapped consciousness. Unlike our primate cousins, they didn't look human. But their brain was human sized, and their convoluted frontal cortex was ripe with language and communication hardware that dwarfed our own. Might not a capacity for language, he proposed, indicate that dolphins were also endowed with logic, thought, and a sense of self—perhaps even a soul?

If we are ever going to communicate with a nonhuman species of this planet, the dolphin is probably our best present gamble . . . Before our man-in-space program becomes too successful, it may be wise to spend some time, talent, and money on research with dolphins; not only are they a large-brained species living their lives in a situation with attenuated effects of gravity, but they may be a group with whom we can learn basic techniques of communicating with really alien intelligent life forms.

His San Francisco speech marked Lilly's debut in the popular press, a forum that would outlast his tenure as a neuroscientist. Newspaper editors across the country were quick to translate Dr. Lilly's pronouncements into tabloid headlines: "Scientist Has Shaggy Dolphin Tale." "Psychiatrist Wants to Make Dolphins Talk." "Shock-Happy Porpoise Laughs with Scientist . . . Dies."

Only a month after making a big splash at the San Francisco convention, Lilly landed a contract to write a book about his work with dolphins. When Doubleday published *Man and Dolphin* in 1961, it inspired a generation of young marine mammal researchers and military engineers, while providing the Age of Aquarius with its first aquatic emblem of peace, love, and understanding. *Man and Dolphin* proclaimed, "Within the next decade or two, the human species will establish communications with another species: nonhuman, alien, possibly extraterrestrial, more probably marine."

In hopes of speeding the advent of interspecies dialogue, Lilly began promoting what his grant proposals described as "the world's first laboratory devoted to the study of the intellectual capacities of the small, toothed whales." He conceived of an aquatic research center—far removed from the sterile confines of academic labs and marine parks—where he could bridge both the "air-water boundary" and the linguistic divide separating mankind from dolphins.

By 1963, Lilly had raised the money to launch his Communications Research Institute in the Virgin Islands. Lilly's first funder was the Office of Naval Research, which sent a Navy demolition team to Saint Thomas to blast a dolphin cove out of a rock and coral promontory overlooking Nazareth Bay. His other funding came from the Department of Defense, the National Science Foundation, and the National Aeronautics and Space Administration (NASA).

Earthwatch volunteers set out to observe beaked whales off of Abaco Island.

Diane Claridge on the lookout for marine mammals in the Great Bahamas Canyon, where she and Ken Balcomb studied the beaked whale population from 1991–2000, and where she continues to conduct research.

Ken Balcomb on his porch in Smugglers Cove, San Juan Island, Washington. He has conducted an annual summer survey of the resident orca community since 1976.

4

Cuvier's beaked whales dive to depths of greater than a mile for more than an hour at a time, surfacing only briefly to breathe. Individual Cuvier's beaked whales can be identified by the scratches on their backs and dorsal fins from mating competitions.

5

Blainville's beaked whales are smaller than Cuvier's, but have similar diving and hunting behaviors. The "beak" refers to the rostrum or snout of the whale, which is elongated rather than blunt-headed. Individual identification, once considered impossible, is facilitated by the light oval scars from the bites of cookie-cutter sharks.

Blainville's beaked whale that stranded in the lagoon behind Cross Harbor, March 16, 2000. Subsequent necropy and CT scans revealed a subarachnoid hemorrhage and blood in the cochlear aqueduct.

6

3D reconstruction from CT scans of the Blainville's beaked whale from Cross Harbor. The skin and skull are rendered transparent to show key features: pooled blood inside the skull on the left side (dark red), the brain (pink), two brain ventricles (blue), the ear bones (yellow), acoustic jaw fats (orange).

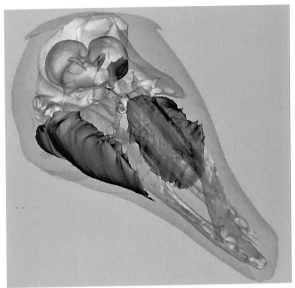

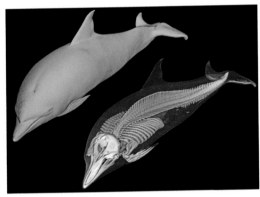

3D reconstruction from CT scans of a whole Short-beaked Common Dolphin (*Delphinus delphis*) showing the animal's external surface and below, with a transparent skin, the skeletal anatomy.

13a

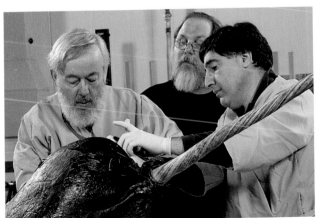

Jim Mead (*left*), at the Osteo-Prep lab at the Smithsonian's National Museum of Natural History in 2002, dissects a narwhal whale specimen with Ted Cranford of San Diego State University and Martin Nweeia of Harvard University.

14

Ken Balcomb's family in 1942 (*left to right*): his uncles Douglas and Edward Balcomb; his grandmother Katherine; Ken at age one and a half; his father, Kenneth, Jr. (known as "Blue"); his grandfather Kenneth, Sr.; and his uncle Robert.

15

Ken, on left, with half-brothers Howie and Rick Garrett, 1948.

16

17

Barbara Balcomb Bales, Ken's mother, in her days as a piano bar singer.

Ken's father, Kenneth "Blue" Balcomb, Jr.

18

During Balcomb's first whale-tagging trip aboard the *Lynnann*, January, 1964. From left to right: Captain Bud Newton, Engineer John Dietrich, Dr. Masaharu Nishiwaki, Cook Bob Young, Dale W. Rice (Expedition Leader), Crewman Ernesto Gonzales, and Ken Balcomb.

19

Aboard the *Lynnann*, armed with a whale-tagging shotgun and a camera.

21

Bird banding on Hull Island in the North Pacific, 1966.

20

While bird banding on Swain's Island near American Samoa, 1966.

22

23

24

ABOVE LEFT: Ken's second wife, Julie, pinning on his naval aviator "wings" after graduation from flight school in Corpus Christi, Texas, August 1968.

ABOVE RIGHT: Lieutenant Balcomb with his son, Kelley, during a visit to Midway Island, the Pacific, 1970.

RIGHT: Hitchhiking with half-brother Howie Garrett (*left*) on Highway 101 along the Washington coastline, summer 1972.

25

26

The *Regina Maris* under sail in April 1979, off Magdalena Bay, Baja California, Mexico. Balcomb was chief scientist on this research ship for twelve winters, from 1976 to 1988.

27

Diane conching during a camping trip to Schooner Cay, Bahamas, February 1991.

28

Diane and Ken in Lichtenstein for her sister's wedding, 1993.

Hiking over Muir Pass in the Sierra Nevadas, June 1976.

Joel Reynolds graduating from Columbia Law School, May 1978 (with classmate Roger Morie).

Joel Reynolds in his twenties, preparing to play in a string quartet with his sister, Martha, and father, Bill Reynolds.

March 1997 at Laguna San Ignacio, Baja California, Mexico, with Pierce Brosnan during the campaign to block a proposed salt works project planned at the site of gray a whale nursery.

32

33

With his son, Sam, greeting a "friendly" Pacific gray whale in Laguna San Ignacio.

Camping with daughters, Amelia and Eleanor, at Laguna San Ignacio, March 2007.

34

Four of the 14 beaked whales that stranded on the Canary Islands during NATO sonar training exercises, September 24, 2002.

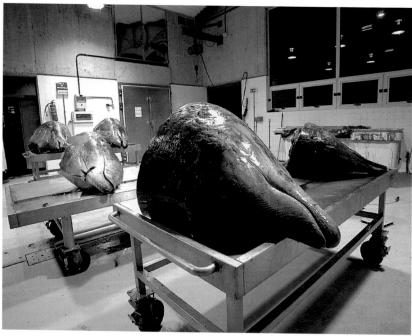

Severed beaked-whale heads awaiting dissection at the Veterinary School of the University of Las Palmas, Canary Islands, September 2002.

Orca from L Pod breaching in Smuggler's Cove, San Juan Island, Washington.

37

38

May 5th, 2003: Smuggler's Cove, San Juan Island, Washington. Ken Balcomb photographs and videotapes the guided-missile destroyer *USS Shoup* as it conducts a sonar sweep of Haro Strait. Foreground: whale-watching vessels and the orcas of J Pod.

Reynolds at a UC Riverside Distinguished Alumni Award ceremony, spring 2007.

At Tejon Ranch, Lebec, California, Reynolds announces the agreement he negotiated with the ranch and state of California to preserve 90 percent of the 270,000-acre Tejon Ranch—with California Governor Arnold Schwarzenegger in the background, 2008.

Being interviewed by Nina Totenberg on the steps of the US Supreme Court following oral arguments in the sonar case, November 8, 2008.

41

42

Reynolds and Balcomb at Smugglers Cove, San Juan Island, Washington, September 2013.

Ken Balcomb on the deck of his house—and headquarters of the Center for Whale Research—Smugglers Cove, San Juan Island, Washington, 2010.

Once installed at his Virgin Islands research center, Lilly enjoyed his first flush of mass media celebrity. He was featured in a *Life* magazine photo-essay alongside his dolphins, interviewed on *The Tonight Show* by host Jack Paar, and courted by the literati and glitterati of the day, many of whom traveled to Saint Thomas to visit his now-famous dolphins. To shore up the linguistic credentials of his communication research, Lilly recruited British anthropologist, social scientist, linguist, and semiotician Gregory Bateson from Stanford University to help deconstruct dolphinese.

During this same period, Lilly consulted with producer Ivan Tors on a dolphin movie shot mostly at the newly opened Miami Seaquarium. When it was released in 1963, MGM's *Flipper*—and the TV series of the same name that ran from 1964 to 1967—cemented the dolphin's status as a boy's best friend. With *Flipper*, the dolphin completed its redemptive journey from nuisance "herring hog," to adored performer, to neoclassical helpmate.

In 1964 producer Ivan Tors' wife turned Lilly on to LSD. After an injection of 100 milligrams, Lilly found himself hot-wired to a party line of Guides and Beings that would redirect the trajectory of his dolphin research and his career as a New Age apostle. When Lilly began including LSD in the research protocols for his NIH grant proposals, nobody inside the federal bureaucracy raised any objections. At the time, LSD was still legal and widely used in research. Since the 1950s, the CIA had deployed LSD in its clandestine Project Artichoke as an interrogation tool and espionage countermeasure. And in the early 1960s, researchers were investigating the therapeutic potential of LSD and other hallucinogens as a treatment for alcoholism and other social ills.[7] During the same period, the Navy and other federal agencies were funding communication research involving gorillas, dogs, and fish dosed with LSD.

During his years at NIH, Lilly had invented the isolation tank to study the effects of sensory deprivation on the human brain and consciousness.[8] To simulate the buoyant environment in which dolphin consciousness had evolved, Lilly built an isolation tank and suspended it over a dolphin pool in Saint Thomas. When he dosed both his dolphins and himself with LSD, Lilly soon found that ingesting hallucinogens both expanded and distorted the traditional boundaries of scientific inquiry. "During a session in an isolation tank constructed over a pool where dolphins were swimming," Lilly wrote, "I participated in a conversation between dolphins. It drove me crazy, there was too much information, they communicated so fast."

Another notable experiment studied the effect of long-term cohabitation of a male dolphin and a young female researcher in a flooded compartment. For months on end, the young woman spent all her waking hours in the water interacting with the dolphin and slept in a hammock suspended just above the pool. With Lilly's encouragement, her interactions included responding to the dolphin's sexual overtures with an underwater hand job.[9]

As news of Lilly's unconventional experimentation bubbled up from the Virgin Islands, the marine mammal research community began pushing back. Thanks to ONR's support of basic research, marine mammalogy was finally gaining traction as a bona fide scientific discipline. The First International Symposium on Cetacean Research convened in Washington, DC, in 1963. The next year marked the inaugural "Conference on Biological Sonar and Diving Mammals" at the Stanford Research Institute. Navy-contracted researchers were successfully applying metrics to dolphin biosonar and hydrodynamics, and marine mammalogy courses were now being taught as part of standard marine biology curricula. By throwing scientific method to the winds, they complained, Lilly undercut his colleagues who were working inside rigorous research protocols. Where, they asked, were the data to support his grandiose claims of interspecies communication? Instead of submitting his research to peer review for publication in serious journals, Lilly's wild pronouncements appeared in the boldfaced headlines of tabloids.

When Lilly began adding ketamine, another powerful psychotropic drug, to his LSD regimen, he went off the deep end—at least as far as his institutional funders were concerned. ONR repossessed the advanced computers they'd loaned him. His five-year National Science Foundation grant was in danger of being revoked. His second marriage—to the former wife of a psychiatrist he'd met at the San Francisco conference—was foundering. In 1968 Lilly abruptly denounced captive dolphin research, proclaiming to the press that his dolphins had "deprogrammed" him. He released his animals into the Caribbean and walked away from his institute. Soon he had relocated to California, where he preached the gospel of better living through chemistry and Zen Buddhism.[10]

Lilly continued to write and publish his metaphysical musings for a loyal following of New Age enthusiasts. But he remained persona non grata among his former peers in the research community. While some grudgingly acknowledged his groundbreaking "early work" in neurology and cetology, most marine mammalogists considered Lilly an embarrassment who had undermined the credibility of their fledgling discipline.

Despite the opprobrium of his fellow cetologists, Lilly's legacy resounded for decades on both sides of the emerging divide between the Navy and environmentalists. His exalted vision of cetacean intelligence and cosmic consciousness helped kindle the global movement to Save the Whales. Meanwhile, his speculations about the potential for deploying dolphins as wartime combatants would shape the Navy's Marine Mammal Training Program for decades to come. These opposing waveforms, which Lilly set into motion in the 1960s, would collide on the beaches of the Bahamas, and in American courtrooms, 40 years later.

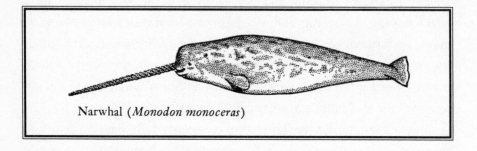

Narwhal (*Monodon monoceras*)

18

The Killer Turned Tame

DAY 30: APRIL 14, 2000
Smugglers Cove, San Juan Island, Washington

Ken Balcomb cut the engine on the skiff and let it glide to a stop. Just as he mounted a long lens onto his Nikon, a group of orcas emerged as if on cue from the early-morning fog that shrouded the still surface. Their black barreled bodies rose and fell in graceful arcs. He counted seven dorsal fins, one as tall as a man, knifing through the water.

The orcas passed within a stone's throw of Balcomb's boat, columns of mist whooshing out of their blowholes with each exhalation. They were part of J Pod, one of the three distinct pods of the Southern Resident Community of killer whales, or orcas, in greater Puget Sound. L Pod and K Pod were still migrating back from their winter hunting grounds on the Oregon and California coastlines. By June, they'd all be assembled in the strait to intercept the Chinook salmon returning to spawn in the inland rivers. He knew each of the 88 killer whales intimately, having photographed them continuously over the past 25 summers of surveys. He knew every scratch and scar on their dorsal fins, every distinctive mark on the gray saddle patch behind their fins.

He knew the family dynamics of each maternal group, the sound signature of their calls, their hunting habits, and favored prey. They were his extended family, and their annual reunion filled him with renewed hope each spring. Especially this spring.

For the first time in a month, Balcomb felt like he could finally clear his head of all the turmoil back in the Bahamas. Smugglers Cove was his home port, the safe harbor he returned to each summer to continue his survey of the Southern Resident Community of orcas. His house, perched on the bluff above the beach, was the repository of his most prized possessions. Whale skulls adorned the walls. Bones and fossils lined the shelves. His photo archive of slides and prints going back decades filled a wall of cabinets on the lower floor. And outside, stashed in sheds around the yards, were a half dozen antique cars he'd collected since his teens.

Balcomb had arrived the day before to open up the house and flush out the boat engines in advance of the summer orca survey. No one else was up here yet—not the summer interns or staff, not the Earthwatch volunteers, not even the whale-watching boats that would be clogging the inland strait between San Juan Island and Victoria, Canada, by early summer. For a few more days, before he returned to Abaco to help Claridge shut down their winter station, it would be just him and J Pod.

The archipelago of the San Juan Islands, tucked into the extreme northwest corner of the country, was the perfect antipode to the Bahamas. Unlike the flat, dry, and ceaselessly sunny Caribbean, the San Juans were wet, green, and lush, their rocky shorelines swathed in cool clouds and fog. While the beaked whales were elusive deep divers, orcas hunted near the surface and close to shore, making them much easier to observe and photograph. And they had undeniable magnetism, drawing tens of thousands of whale watchers to the Pacific Northwest each summer. Balcomb's various wives and girlfriends had come and gone over the many summers, along with the research assistants, the volunteers, and the project funders. But the orcas always came back. And they were always spectacular.

In 1976, following his Navy undercover assignment in Japan, Balcomb returned with Camille to the Northwest. They arrived on the scene just as an aroused public was rallying to the defense of the orcas of Puget Sound.

A decadelong spree of wild captures—some of them grossly illegal and highly publicized—had depleted the local population of orcas. When the regional office of Fisheries solicited proposals for a census of the local whale community to assess its sustainability, as it was required to do under the recently passed Marine Mammal Protection Act, Balcomb applied for the contract.

The contagion of orca captures had begun, by accident, in 1964. The Vancouver Aquarium considered orcas too violent to display alongside its dolphins and performing seals. But it wanted to acknowledge their central importance to indigenous cultures. So the aquarium director, Dr. Murray Newman, commissioned a local sculptor to collect an orca specimen as a model for a life-sized courtyard sculpture. Whatever his talents as an artist, the sculptor was a lousy gunner. He set up a harpoon gun on Saturna Island, south of Vancouver, and managed to shoot a young orca at the base of its dorsal fin. He reeled in his catch and tried to finish it off with several rounds of rifle shots. But the animal wouldn't die. Dr. Newman ordered the wounded animal towed back to the aquarium, using the line attached to the harpoon as a towline. He housed the animal in a concrete tank and named the first-ever captive orca "Moby Doll," a revealing hybrid of Melville's feared white whale and a child's plaything.

Moby Doll became an instant celebrity, drawing thousands of visitors and dozens of researchers to the aquarium. William Schevill and Bill Watkins flew in from Woods Hole to record her vocalizations for their catalogue of biological sounds and to confirm that she echolocated like her dolphin relatives. What confounded marine biologists was Moby Doll's docile, even playful disposition. Where was the storied ferocity of the bloodthirsty man killer?

Until the 1960s, the public perception of orcas was based on an amalgam of misinformation, myth, and legend. In the first century, Roman natural historian Pliny the Elder observed, "A killer whale cannot be properly depicted or described except as an enormous mass of flesh armed with savage teeth." Swedish naturalist Carolus Linnaeus—the father of taxonomy—classified the two kingdoms of plants and animals into groups according to their form. In the tenth edition of his *Systema Naturae*, published in 1758, he named the species *Orcinus orca*, Latin for "Belonging to the realms of the dead." And a century later, retired whaling captain Charles Scammon would write, "Whatever quarter of the world Killer Whales are found, they seem always intent upon seeking something to destroy or devour." As recently as the mid-1970s, a US Navy diving manual warned that a killer whale will "attack human beings at every opportunity." And yet, paradoxically, no one had ever observed an orca attack a human.

There is good reason why orcas are also known as killer whales.* Though properly classified as dolphins—the largest species of the family Delphinidae—orcas are among the world's most voracious carnivores. In the Pacific Northwest, "resident" pods feast on Chinook salmon, with each three- to five-ton orca devouring hundreds of pounds of fish a day. The biologically distinct "transient" pods of orcas prey on seals, sea lions, dolphins, porpoises, and other cetaceans. Hunting in packs like wolves, they can wear down and overtake whales many times their own size, including blue whales. Their two interlocking rows of conical-shaped teeth can grab seal pups off beaches or rays out from under rocks on the ocean bottom. Cunning and specialized hunters, orcas have been videotaped ramming great white sharks with their rostrums and then devouring them.

Top predators such as sharks, wolves, and orcas have always aroused fear and hatred among humans altogether out of proportion to any direct threat they pose. Unlike dolphins, which are plentiful around the world, orca populations are small and besieged by their only predator: man. Though they never had enough oil or blubber to interest whalers, orcas have often competed with humans for food in coastal regions, which made them perennial targets of retribution; sometimes even prompting a military response. In 1956, for instance, the Icelandic government asked the US Navy to attack killer whales that competed with its herring fishery. The United States dispatched an antisubmarine air squadron to target the Icelandic orcas with 50-caliber machine guns, aircraft rockets, and depth charges. During that same decade, salmon fishermen in British Columbia lobbied their government to mount heavy artillery guns on hillsides overlooking the inland straits frequented by orcas. In the absence of direct military intervention, and with the tacit encourage-

---

* "Orca" and "killer whale" are interchangeable and correct names for the whale species *Orcinus orca*.

ment of their governments, fishermen on both sides of the Canadian border routinely fired on orcas from boats and the shoreline.

Moby Doll's winning personality was chronicled in *Life* magazine and *Reader's Digest*. When she died after three months of captivity from a skin disease she'd contracted in her tank, she was eulogized in newspapers around the world—even after a postmortem exam revealed that Moby Doll was a juvenile male. Aquarium director Newman sought to tamp down the public's effusive killer-whale hugging. "I worry about this sentimentalizing," he told a reporter from the Vancouver *Province*. "It was a nice whale but still a predatory, carnivorous creature. It could swallow you alive." But Moby Doll's friendliness to humans turned out to be typical, not aberrant, orca behavior.

Given our primal reaction to killer whales, it was perhaps inevitable that we'd demonstrate our dominance by training orcas as entertainers. Displaying exotic marine mammals to a ticket-buying public was nothing new. A century earlier, in 1861, showman P. T. Barnum captured two beluga whales in Newfoundland, packed them inside seaweed-lined crates, and shipped them by railcar to his American Museum in lower Manhattan. They both died after just two days of display inside a freshwater tank, but the enthusiastic response of New Yorkers foretold the future popularity of marine mammal acts at aquariums and marine parks around the world. A century after Barnum debuted his belugas, orcas were poised to step up in social class from abhorred "blackfish" to adored matinee idols.

Moby Doll's runaway success at the Vancouver Acquarium box office spurred a killer-whale grab that soon spread across the Canadian border and around the world. The head of the Seattle Aquarium, Ted Griffin, was particularly avid to have one. But he soon discovered how hard it was to snare an orca without recourse to harpoons and rifles. And he had competition. When he hopped into a powerboat and tracked the local community of killer whales in Puget Sound, hoping to lasso one by the tail, he kept crossing paths with another orca hunter, Don Goldsberry, who was stalking the same pod from a helicopter.

Griffin's big break came in 1965 when a 24-foot, five-ton orca became entangled in nets near the fishing town of Namu, British Columbia. Griffin recruited his rival, Goldsberry, to help him bring the whale home alive. They built a 40-by-64-foot floating cage to enclose Namu—named for his place of capture—during his 450-mile swim to Seattle. When they returned home a month later, the docks were lined with cheering spectators and journalists. Five thousand visitors paid to view Namu his first day at the aquarium.

Griffin didn't just display his prize catch. He swam with him and trained him to perform the tricks he'd taught his dolphins, only with a much bigger splash. Namu proved to be a gentle and intuitive playmate. During Namu's year in captivity, 120,000 paying customers lined up to behold "The Killer Turned Tame!" as Griffin billed him.

After 334 days of twice-daily shows at the Seattle Aquarium, Namu contracted a bacterial infection that soon drove him to delirium. He repeatedly crashed into the walls of his tank for two days, and then sank to the bottom and drowned. A necropsy found a decade-old .30-06 Springfield rifle slug nested in his flank. Fully a quarter of killer whales captured in Puget Sound during the late sixties and early seventies had visible bullet wounds.

Before Namu died, he was immortalized in the movie *Namu the Killer Whale*, starring Namu in a fictionalized account of his relationship with Griffin. Released in 1966, it introduced the world to a bigger and better icon of interspecies friendship than Flipper, the dolphin pop star. "Make room in your heart for a six-ton pet! He's the biggest hero in the whole wide world of adventure!" the movie poster exalted.

Marine parks around the world took note of Namu's charisma, trainability, and box-office magnetism. SeaWorld in San Diego was looking for a headliner for its performing dolphin and seal acts. So Griffin and Goldsberry incorporated their partnership as Namu Inc. and went orca hunting. After harpooning a mother orca from a helicopter, they captured her calf, which would be easier to transport to San Diego than its full-grown parent. Griffin refused to sell the rights to the name Namu, so SeaWorld called its female orca Shamu, a contraction of "She" and "Namu." Shamu was such a big hit for SeaWorld that it institutionalized "Shamu" as the stage name for all the killer whales it subsequently acquired for its various marine parks. When one Shamu died, a successor Shamu was slotted seamlessly into the Shamu Show.

By the time the original Shamu died in San Diego, SeaWorld had purchased ten more orcas for its new marine parks, SeaWorld Ohio and Sea-World Orlando. Meanwhile, Griffin and Goldsberry had grown their capture operation into a highly profitable enterprise. They refined a technique of herding whole pods of orcas into inlets, closing off the cove with seine nets, and then culling the juveniles and calves for sale to SeaWorld and other marine parks around the world. Over their ten-year hunting partnership, Griffin and Goldsberry captured 262 whales in Puget Sound, released the adults, and culled 50 juveniles for transport to marine parks in the United States, Canada, Japan, France, and Argentina. More than a dozen orcas died during capture operations, mostly by drowning in nets. Sixteen of the 50 whales they captured died during their first year of captivity.

The dark side of Namu Inc. remained hidden from public view until a 1970 roundup in Washington State's Penn Cove. A flotilla of small boats, backed by helicopters dropping explosives into the water, chased the entire population of Southern Resident orcas into Penn Cove. Among the 80 corralled, Griffin and Goldsberry chose seven juveniles to fulfill orders from SeaWorld and other marine parks. One adult and four juveniles died during the capture. Hoping to anchor the evidence at the bottom of Puget Sound, Griffin and Goldsberry slit open the bellies of the four juveniles, stuffed them with stones, and wrapped them in steel chains. When a fishing trawler accidentally raised the four dead whales in its nets a few weeks later, it created a furor among the public and local politicians.

Namu Inc. was finished. Griffin retired from the business, and Goldsberry became SeaWorld's corporate director of collections. By the mid-1970s, orcas were inextricably linked to SeaWorld's brand and entertainment offerings. In honor of the US Bicentennial in 1976, SeaWorld trained its Shamus to reenact scenes of the founding fathers, complete with George Washington wigs and tricornered hats. SeaWorld's logo featured a breaching orca, and orca-themed paraphernalia was the top seller in its gift shops.

Meanwhile, the purchase price of a wild-captured orca had spiked from $20,000 a decade earlier to $150,000. After the passage of the 1972 Marine Mammal Protection Act, any marine park that wanted to collect an orca from the wild needed a capture permit from Fisheries, which was now charged with monitoring and sustaining populations of orcas and other marine mammals. But SeaWorld was committed to keeping its theme parks stocked with orcas, and its captive breeding efforts had failed to produce new generations of performers.

In February 1976 Goldsberry was hunting orcas for SeaWorld under a Fisheries-issued permit. When he was caught using seal bombs and buzzing aircraft to herd six orcas into Budd Inlet, the Washington State attorney general sued Goldsberry for violating his permit. Eventually the charges were dropped when Goldsberry and SeaWorld agreed to never again capture whales in Puget Sound.[1] Public outrage over the Budd Inlet incident prompted Fisheries to conduct a census of the orcas of greater Puget Sound to establish how significantly wild captures had depleted the population.

Balcomb proposed a novel method for his orca census: counting each individual whale by photographing its distinctive dorsal fin. Previous whale censuses had relied on population estimates based on local surveys extrapolated over entire migration routes. Until recently, the premise that each killer whale could be differentiated visually was considered as laughable as photo-identifying every salmon in the Salish Sea between Washington and Canada. But for the past several years, a team of researchers to the north—led by the marine mammal director of the Canadian Department of Fisheries and Oceans, Michael Bigg—had been doing just that.

When Balcomb proposed conducting a photo-identification census of the orcas in greater Puget Sound, marine biologists still largely derided Bigg's approach. But the first time that Balcomb examined Bigg's catalogue of black-and-white photographs, he was convinced. Each magnified image of the left side of a dorsal fin revealed unique patterns of nicks, scratches, and scars, as individual as a human fingerprint. Balcomb managed to persuade Fisheries of the merit of the method, beating out the University of Washington for the seven-month survey contract.

That first season, Ken and Camille worked alone in a Boston Whaler they bought with the first Fisheries check, using the same Nikons that Ken had been carrying with him since his first expeditions on the *Lynnann*. They rented the house on Smugglers Cove, with its commanding view of Haro Strait, and worked nonstop through that first spring, summer, and fall.

First they distributed questionnaires to boaters, lighthouse keepers, and fishermen throughout Puget Sound, asking them to record all killer-whale sightings. Then they were out on the water at first light, every morning, tracking and photographing orcas until dark. Each night they developed and printed the day's pictures, and then catalogued them. After collapsing into bed for a few hours of sleep, they'd be up at dawn again to begin the next day's survey.

Bigg had assigned a letter to each pod in the Northern Resident Community, A through I, and he gave each individual whale a number. Balcomb began his survey with J Pod, and he and Camille identified the distinct K and L pods. By October, they were convinced that they'd documented each of the orcas in greater Puget Sound and had sorted them by sex and family grouping.

Their total was 70 killer whales. Balcomb calculated that the 50 juveniles that Griffin and Goldsberry had collected and sold in the preceding decade, plus the 13 orcas killed during capture operations, had depleted the Southern Resident population by almost 50 percent.

Balcomb's bleak results were not welcomed by Fisheries or by the local aquariums, universities, and marine parks that had applied for permits to collect more orcas. If Fisheries accepted Balcomb's assessment that the local orca population had been severely depleted, it would be obliged under the Marine Mammal Protection Act to implement a recovery and protection plan. No further capture permits could be issued until the species had recovered to sustainable levels. Fisheries declined to renew Balcomb's contract.

That same fall, Michael Bigg submitted his final report to Canadian Fisheries. Prior estimates had put the Northern Community's population in the thousands. Bigg's count came to just 252. When he concluded that ongoing orca collections from British Columbian waters were unsustainable and recommended strict limits on wild captures, Canadian Fisheries shut down his survey and reassigned Bigg to other projects. Universities and aquariums on both sides of the border attacked Bigg's and Balcomb's methodology and results.

The following spring, John Twiss of the Marine Mammal Commission in Washington, DC, awarded Balcomb a $7,000 grant to conduct a confirmation study. That was the last federal or state funding Balcomb's survey would receive for 28 years. Canadian Fisheries didn't renew funding for the Northern Community survey until after Bigg's death in 1990. But by the end of 1976, Balcomb and Bigg had resolved to combine and continue their annual surveys of the Northern and Southern populations of orcas, with or without government funding.

Each summer, from 1976 onward, Balcomb found a way to keep his survey boats in the water and film in the cameras, despite his lack of funding. The orcas themselves proved to be powerful magnets for volunteers. Local islanders and far-flung whale enthusiasts would simply walk up the road at Smugglers Cove in early summer, knock on the door to his house, and offer to help. Balcomb enlisted other volunteers during his winter cruises aboard the *Regina*, and he covered gas and photo expenses by selling orca buttons and T-shirts and calendars in town. In the leanest summers, he resorted to eating roadkill rabbits.

The summers were always tight financially, but there was no shortage of camaraderie among the survey partners. The researchers on both sides of the Canadian border were constantly helping one another get by, sharing data and volunteers—including Naomi Rose, who was conducting her graduate research with Michael Bigg's group. After Camille left that first winter, during the *Regina Maris'* maiden voyage, Balcomb recruited his half brother Howie Garrett to be his boat buddy. Best of all, Balcomb's son Kelley, now a teenager, started spending summers on San Juan Island photographing whales alongside his father.

In 1979 Balcomb launched the Whale Museum in Friday Harbor, at the tourist end of the island. He wanted to educate the public about orcas, build support for the ongoing census, and have a permanent repository for all the bones and skulls that were piling up at his house. A few years later, Balcomb founded the nonprofit Center for Whale Research to support his research. As his local reputation grew, he attracted a few high-dollar donors who contributed money and boats to the survey. Earthwatch began sending paying volunteers, which gave him a little breathing room. In the 1980s, whale watching started up in earnest as a local commercial enterprise, introducing the public to wild orcas and injecting tens of millions of dollars into the community each year.[2]

Summer after summer, the census continued, and the database grew into one of the most complete profiles ever compiled of a wild animal population: births, deaths, diets, social associations, and complete family trees across two distinct communities and 18 pods in British Columbia and Washington. Balcomb's and Bigg's research offered the first science-based understanding of orca behavior and communication, and an appreciation of a mammal group whose social complexity equaled that of elephants and great apes. Perhaps most significantly, their census had uncovered one of the only matrilineal societies among whale populations. Male orcas stay with their mothers and maternal relatives throughout their lifetimes, and the matriarchs maintain a central position in the pod as multigenerational transmitters of the pod's culture.

In 1979 Balcomb and Bigg presented their findings at the third biennial meeting of the Society for Marine Mammalogy in Seattle. The rousing reception they received from their peers was unimaginable just a few years earlier. In 1984 Balcomb and Bigg were invited to present their findings to the scientific committee of the International Whaling Commission in Eastbourne, England, signaling to Balcomb the final acceptance of photo identification by the worldwide whale conservation community. That was the same spring he met Diane Claridge aboard the *Regina Maris*. Somehow he always linked those two happy events in his mind. Two years later, in 1986, the International Whaling Commission banned commercial whaling worldwide.

His orca surveys had continued every summer since, the last 12 of them with Diane. Now that the beaked whales of Abaco had been battered and scattered, Balcomb felt even more determined to safeguard the Southern Resident Community of orcas that he'd been watching over for the past quarter century.

A continent distant from the Bahamas, he struggled for perspective on the catastrophic event he and Diane had witnessed. After all the winters spent cataloguing the beaked whales, they had been powerless to protect them. Had they been lulled into complacency, he wondered, by the idyllic Caribbean seascape, blinded to the dangers that had lurked below the blue waters? Their efforts to document the mass stranding might turn out to be the most meaningful legacy of their work in the Bahamas. If so, had they done enough to force the answers to the surface?

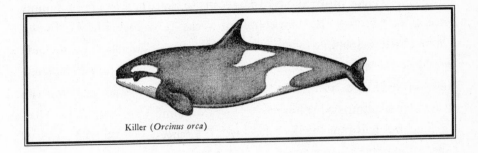

Killer (*Orcinus orca*)

19

A Call to Conscience

DAY 35: APRIL 19, 2000
Smugglers Cove, San Juan Island, Washington

Spending a few days on the water with the orcas was tonic for Balcomb. But by the third night alone in his house above the cove, he began to feel isolated and anxious. He kept trying to imagine what was going on back east at Woods Hole, at Fisheries, and at ONR. Ever since he'd handed over the heads to Darlene Ketten, he had a queasy feeling he couldn't shake.

Then his friend Jim Mead at the Smithsonian emailed to say that the necropsy had gone forward at Woods Hole without him, with just Ketten and Ruth Ewing attending. Balcomb didn't have the heart to share the news with Diane, who was 4,000 miles away on Abaco welcoming a new group of Earthwatch volunteers.

That evening, Balcomb sat out on the deck eating some leftover lunch that passed for dinner, watching the last light fade on the cove. The underwater hydrophones were hooked up to the deck-mounted speakers, so he could hear the chatter of J Pod moving out toward Eagle Point. When the phone rang, he hoped it was Diane.

It was Michael Jasny from NRDC, calling to invite him to a press conference in Washington, DC, in a couple of weeks. It was being hosted by the Animal Welfare Institute to publicize the Bahamas strandings. Joel Reynolds would be there from NRDC, and Naomi Rose from the Humane Society. They wanted Ken to come talk about what he had witnessed and screen whatever video his team had recorded.

Balcomb told him thanks for asking, but he was tied up with work in Abaco and here on San Juan Island.

"You know," said Jasny, "Ben White is flying in for the press conference."

"I'm sure he is. Ben never met a press event he didn't love."

"Maybe you two could come together."

"I'll think about it," was all Balcomb said.

Ben White lived down the road from Balcomb on San Juan Island. He was a no-holds-barred eco-warrior, a one-man band of environmental and animal rights activism. Balcomb liked Ben. Everyone did. He was smart, big-hearted, and an effective instigator of protests that got press attention. Rarest of all in the world of animal rights, Ben had a sense of humor.

Part prankster, part hard-core ideologue, White had perfected the stage-craft of guerilla street theater. He understood that if you wanted to protect the environment or animals, you had to give the media something to lead the six o'clock news. When he joined the campesinos' "peasant protest" against a porpoise hunt in Cancun, Mexico, he brought along 350 handmade dolphin costumes to make sure that Mexican television covered the event. And when he dressed hundreds of demonstrators in full turtle regalia to protest the World Trade Organization's policy on turtle catches, papers around the world ran front-page photos. Humor was his favored tactic, but for White, having skin in the game was more than a figure of speech.

Long before he dove into the water during the Navy's low-frequency sonar tests in Hawaii, White was scaling New York City skyscrapers to unfurl huge antifur banners during Fashion Week. Before he began defending animals, he was putting his body between ancient forest and loggers. A college drop-out turned arborist and tree surgeon, White launched the first tree-sitting campaigns, perched 200 feet off the ground for four days to save redwoods in Humboldt County, California. Then he masterminded a blockade of logging roads using RVs to keep logging crews out of the Oregon forests.

White traced his special connection to whales and dolphins to a face-to-face encounter while swimming with a herd of wild dolphins off Hawaii in the 1970s. As he wrote to a friend at the time, "I had never seen such complexity, humor, and recognition in the eyes of any creature other than humans, and rarely enough in those." On the subject of captive dolphins and orcas, White was an unyielding abolitionist. Balcomb had often heard him rail against SeaWorld's Shamu Shows as pointless displays of dominance that degraded humans as much as orcas.

"What does it do to us to become so violent that we grab these animals out of the wild and then starve them until they're willing to eat dead fish out of our hands and let us stand on their faces and brush their teeth with oversized toothbrushes? What does that do to our humanity?"

When White got arrested—for the 20th time, by his own count—for liberating captured dolphins in the Florida Keys, he used freedom of religion as his courtroom defense. He had recently incorporated his Church of the Earth and sanctified the defense of wildlife as its sacrament. When he moved to San Juan Island, he founded the Natural Guard, a tree care company that trained teenagers as organic arborists and organized protests against development projects that threatened the local orcas.

Balcomb respected Ben's all-in commitment and his willingness to get arrested for what he believed. But civil disobedience and dressing up in costumes weren't Balcomb's style. Neither were press conferences. He was determined to keep up the pressure on the Navy and Fisheries to investigate what had happened in the canyon. But he wasn't ready to carve "whistle-blower" across his forehead. He'd worked hard to earn the respect of his peers for his surveys on orcas and beaked whales. He worried that if he stepped onto a podium with Reynolds and Rose, he'd put his credibility as a researcher—and the orcas—at risk.

Despite having spent decades under the spell of whales and working to protect the orcas of Puget Sound, he'd always been wary of the Save the Whales movement—or, for that matter, save-the-anything movements. Animals, he revered. It was the humans who rushed to their rescue with their political agendas that Balcomb often had trouble with. In his experience, the animal rights crowd tended to look down on the "humane" community as mainstream sellouts who cared only about cat-and-dog rescue. Meanwhile, the humane players called the conservation groups "species-ists" because they were enthralled by charismatic megafauna such as elephants and pandas that looked good on refrigerator magnets. And the animal liberationists thought that anyone who wasn't ready to break and enter to liberate a captive animal was a hypocrite.

Balcomb only met John Lilly once, at a 1977 marine mammal conference where Lilly was shunned by his colleagues. But he was well acquainted with several other Navy-funded researchers who had crossed over to become public advocates for whales. He always found it ironic that the Save the Whales movement was jump-started by a SOSUS acoustician like himself. Frank Watlington was a legendary figure in the secret world of SOSUS and something of a mentor to the acoustic analysts of Balcomb's generation. Since 1950, he'd run the first proof-of-concept sonar station constructed offshore from Bermuda. Like Balcomb and every other SOSUS operator listening for Soviet submarines, Watlington heard lots of whales calling to each other. Over the years, he became an aficionado of the eerie vocalizations of the Atlantic humpbacks that wintered in the Bermuda waters, compiling their distinctive calls on hundreds of hours of audiotape. As whaling continued to deplete the North Atlantic humpback population throughout the fifties and sixties, Watlington worried that his personal archive of recordings would soon be the only surviving record of this dwindling species and their unique calls. When he met a bioacoustics researcher named Roger Payne in 1967, Watlington decided to draw back the curtain of SOSUS just enough to show the world what it risked losing forever.

Payne had studied bat biosonar under Donald Griffin at Harvard, earned a PhD in biology at Cornell, and conducted ONR-funded research into whether or not owls echolocated during their nocturnal hunts. He determined that owls used acute night vision rather than hearing for hunting and navigating in the dark.

In 1966 Payne read an article in *Scientific American* that reversed the direction of his research. "The Last of the Great Whales," written by one of Lilly's bioacoustics disciples, Scott McVay, was a cri de coeur against the lethal toll of international whaling on endangered species of cetaceans, including the Atlantic humpback population, which had dwindled to barely 5,000. When

Payne learned that the closest resident humpbacks were based in Bermuda, he persuaded the New York Zoological Society to sponsor a study.

Soon after arriving in Bermuda, Payne and his wife and research partner, Katy, were introduced to Watlington by a mutual friend. Watlington played them the tapes he'd been recording for the past decade from the SOSUS hydrophone array mounted on the ocean floor 30 miles off the coast. Roger Payne was taken immediately with what he described as the humpbacks' "exuberant, uninterrupted rivers of sound." Watlington lent him a copy of a tape to analyze.

Payne brought the tape to Scott McVay at Princeton University, where the biology lab was using sonographs to analyze bird songs—the same type of sonographs that Balcomb had used at his SOSUS stations to diagram the sound signatures of submarines. McVay graphed the humpback whale calls, and he and his mathematician wife, Hella, and Roger and Katy Payne assembled to analyze them. They reached a startling conclusion: the whale calls featured discrete phrases that were repeated regularly, revealing an underlying musical syntax and composition. Payne concluded that the humpback's chorus of baleful moans were songs, perhaps some sort of mating aria performed exclusively by male humpbacks. Later, when he studied humpback populations in the South Atlantic and the Pacific, he discovered that the songs differed from one whale community to another.

In 1971 Payne and McVay published their findings as the cover article of the journal *Science*. The article stirred considerable academic debate and interest. But Payne wasn't content to make waves merely in academic circles. He wanted to rescue humpback whales from extinction. So he did something rare, and professionally risky, for an academic researcher. Like Lilly before him, Payne decided to promote the whales' talents directly to the public.

Instead of writing a book, Payne produced an album of their music. While the *Science* article was crawling through the peer review process, he convinced a small California record company to release Watlington's recordings as an LP entitled *Songs of the Humpback Whale*. It was an immediate sensation, selling hundreds of thousands of copies and joining the Beatles' *Let It Be* and the Grateful Dead's *American Beauty* as iconic albums of 1970. Near the end of the decade, in the largest album pressing ever, *National Geographic* inserted ten million flexible vinyl sound sheets in its magazine. Payne proved a tireless evangelist for the wonder of whale songs. He traveled the talk-show circuit, from *The Tonight Show* to *The David Frost Show*, while McVay delivered the message of singing humpbacks to the whaling industry's ports of call in Japan.

Rock, pop, and jazz critics debated the musical merits of the humpback songs, whose ethereal melodies resonated with the New Age genre of electronic music. Kids who had grown up on the theme song from *Flipper* could now clamp on their Koss headphones and tune in to the vibes of a 40-ton contralto. The album's cover featured a humpback breaching against an all-white background, and the liner notes included an antiwhaling manifesto calling on listeners to help save the humpbacks.

Whale scientists, for their part, were divided on whether or not humpbacks were actually singing, and if so, what about and to whom. But there was no disputing the influence of humpback whale sounds on the listening public and on the burgeoning movement to save the whales. The album was released two years before passage of the Marine Mammal Protection Act, when whale oil was still a heavily promoted ingredient in many American consumer products, from motor oil, to cosmetics, to soaps. Sperm whale oil, the highest-viscosity substance on the planet, was used as a lubricant in US nuclear-powered submarines. The breakout success of *Songs of the Humpback Whale* went a long way toward stigmatizing whale oil in consumer products—and elevating whales from by-the-barrel commodities to rock star celebrities.

In 1977, when Voyager I was launched into space to probe the outer solar system for intelligent life-forms, its cargo included a gold-plated audio disc engraved with greetings from the secretary-general of the United Nations and the president of the United States, as well as a medley of musical works by Beethoven, Chuck Berry, and—courtesy of Frank Watlington and the Navy's SOSUS hydrophones—the songs of the humpback whales. John Lilly, no doubt, was smiling up at Voyager I from his hot tub atop the cliffs of Big Sur.

If Payne used whale melodies to win the hearts and minds of the public, it was another bioacoustics researcher—a colleague of Balcomb's in the Pacific Northwest—who aroused more militant opposition to whaling.

Paul Spong, a neuroscientist from UCLA's Brain Research Institute, was hired by Dr. Newman of the Vancouver Aquarium to study two wild-captured orcas it had acquired in the late 1960s. Spong quickly grew fascinated by their vocalizations and their responsiveness to sound and music. Just as quickly, he lost interest in trying to evoke conditioned responses with dead-herring rewards. Like so many whale and dolphin researchers, the intense personal bond Spong formed with his study subjects eventually turned him against research on captive animals. During a 1968 lecture at the University of British Columbia, Spong declared his research subjects "intelligent and articulate communicators unfit for captivity." When he recommended relocating them to a semiwild penned environment in Vancouver Sound, he was fired.

Spong later moved to nearby Hanson Island and launched the nonprofit OrcaLab devoted to the observational study of orcas in the wild. Spong's ethos of "research without interference" was modeled after the noninvasive, long-term studies of gorillas and chimpanzees in the wild conducted by Dian Fossey and Jane Goodall. It was a novel approach to whale research in the late 1960s. By the mid-1970s, whale researchers at international meetings were debating both the scientific and ethical merits of studying whales and dolphins in captive settings versus wild environments.

For Spong, it was a natural progression from opposing captive research to confronting the whaling industry. Greenpeace began its first oceangoing protests in 1971, when a handful of young activists in the Pacific Northwest plotted to disrupt nuclear bomb tests on the Alaskan island of Amchitka and subsequent bomb tests in the South Pacific. A few years later, Spong convinced Greenpeace to redirect its oceangoing protests at the Russian and Japanese whaling fleets.

In April 1975, with a rousing send-off by 30,000 supporters gathered at the Vancouver docks, Spong and a small Greenpeace crew launched Project Ahab aboard a vessel Spong had equipped with hydrophones and underwater speakers so he could soothe the whales with his flute playing. A month out, they intercepted a Soviet ship chasing a pod of whales. Armed with bullhorns and video cameras, they boarded inflatable Zodiac rafts and inserted themselves between the whalers and the whales. In the midst of the hunt, they captured dramatic and gory footage of a sperm whale being harpooned.

Two weeks later, a somber Walter Cronkite broadcast the video clip on the *CBS Evening News*, detonating what Greenpeace co-founder Bob Hunter called a "mind bomb" in the American psyche. Overnight, Greenpeace became a media darling. "For the first time in the history of whaling," spouted the *New York Times*, "human beings had put their lives on the line for whales." When the next Spong-directed Greenpeace expedition sailed from Hawaii, it was trailed by a crew from ABC's *Wide World of Sports*.

Greenpeace's direct-action antiwhaling campaigns would remain a staple of network news for the ensuing decade, until the International Whaling Commission announced its worldwide moratorium on commercial whaling in 1986.

APRIL 20, 2000
Smugglers Cove, San Juan Island, Washington

Balcomb was awakened early the next morning by the sound of a chain saw. He didn't have to guess whose it was. Whenever Ben White came to visit, he carried a chain saw in the back of his Natural Guard pickup, just in case Balcomb had some trees that needed pruning.

When he crawled out of bed and went outside to look, Balcomb could see White hanging from a safety line strung between two 80-foot firs behind his house. The trees were full of dead branches, and White was perched atop the tallest one, cutting away the bad wood. He worked his way down the topmost layer of the first tree, and then fastened the chain saw to his belt and swung across to the other.

Balcomb guessed that White was showing off his blue-collar cred, perhaps to establish parity with Balcomb, who could dismantle and rebuild any kind of car, truck, or boat engine ever made. For the next hour, Balcomb tried to focus on pasting photos into his J Pod catalogue and ignore the chain-saw racket and the acrobatic figure outside his window working his way back and forth between the two trees. An hour later, White had reached the ground and reduced the dead timber to a neat stack of firewood.

When the chain saw went quiet, Balcomb hoped that White would leave him in peace. But a few minutes later, he found White in his kitchen, rummaging through the refrigerator.

"You really ought to stop eating animals, man," White said, holding up a dried-out handful of sliced salami. He stuck his head back inside the refrigerator and pulled out a sorry-looking apple. "How can you be so in love with orcas and still eat pigs?"

"Come on in, make yourself at home."

"So, did you hear about the press conference in DC? You coming?"

"You know Jasny already invited me," said Balcomb. "You could have just called me and saved yourself all the hard work," he said, gesturing to the wood piled outside. Balcomb put some day-old coffee on the stove to warm.

"You've got to be there, man," said White. "Without you, all we have are talking heads. But you"—he pointed at Balcomb and grinned through his full beard—"you've got video! That's all the networks care about."

"So that's why *60 Minutes* has been calling me," said Balcomb. "I thought they cared deeply about beaked whales."

"I heard through the grapevine that you're stiff-arming that *60 Minutes* producer. I hope I heard wrong. You know how many eyeballs tune in to that show?" He bit into something nasty inside the apple and spit it out in to the sink. "Remind me to bring my own food next time I visit. You live like a frat boy."

"Only when I have a few days to myself."

And so it went for the next half hour. White pushing, Balcomb trying to deflect him. It was like wrestling a bear. White agreed with Balcomb that if he attended the press conference, Fisheries and the Navy would probably never do business with him again, and that he'd likely be smeared by the academic crowd, who were all in the pay of the Navy anyway. It was a sure bet that some admiral would call him a pawn of the environmental lobby. But so what? Why had he been self-funding his orca and beaked whale surveys for 25 years? To make pretty posters and calendars to sell to the tourists? So he could present his data sets at a science conference and bask in polite applause? If he really gave a damn about the whales, White insisted he had to step up and bear witness to what happened in the Bahamas.

Balcomb mumbled something about White not knowing everything that was involved.

White stared him down. "I know about you and the Navy, Ken." Balcomb didn't know how much White knew, but he'd learned not to underestimate him. "And I know all about the Navy. All that bullshit about how blue and thick Navy blood runs. I was born in Portsmouth, Virginia, right in the deep, dark shadow of the Atlantic Fleet. My old man was military intel. I learned all the secret handshakes before I left the playpen. That's what this is all about, don't you see? It's all about the secrets and who gets to keep them. You and me, we've got to drag those nasty Navy secrets out of Davy Jones' locker, and put 'em on TV. Until then, the Navy's just going to keep stonewalling, and the whales are just going to keep washing up on the beach."

Balcomb told White that he had work to do. Alone. On his way out the door, White pointed to another stand of firs that needed attention. "I'll just swing by next time I'm in the neighborhood and give them a little TLC."

J Pod was spouting up a storm out in the cove. But Balcomb didn't feel like getting in the boat today. He tucked a photo of the new calf's dorsal fin into the catalogue, below its mother. No sex determination yet. Just an alpha-numeric tag: J-36.

Balcomb was annoyed by White's diatribe. Just because he'd grown up as a military brat and rebelled against his father, it didn't mean that White understood what it meant to have served. Balcomb was 60 years old, a proud veteran of two tours—too old and too loyal to call out the Navy in public. He'd taken oaths. He knew how to keep secrets, and he understood why the Navy had to keep some things hidden.

When he checked his email that afternoon, Balcomb found a message from Ben White with the subject line "Secret Handshakes." There was no message, just an online link to a Navy press release dated that same day, en-titled "Navy Supports Investigation of Whale Strandings in the Bahamas." Five weeks after the stranding, this was the Navy's first formal response. Most of it was standard press office boilerplate: "The U.S. Navy takes its role as a steward of the seas very seriously . . ." and "Navy peacetime operations and training events are designed to fully comply with U.S. environmental laws and regulations . . ." Then, buried deep in the second page, Balcomb found the first acknowledgment that the fleet had been conducting exercises in the Bahamas:

The Commander in Chief, U.S. Atlantic Fleet, is reviewing the tran-sit of seven ships and three submarines through the area during the morning and afternoon of March 15th in an effort to determine if any action by these vessels could have created an environmental hazard to the marine mammals.

Balcomb wondered how many Navy lawyers had helped coin that bloodless hypothetical: "if any action by these vessels could have created an environmental hazard to the marine mammals." He'd seen that "environmental hazard" up close, in the dead eyes of a shark-ravaged Cuvier's and in the perfectly preserved body of the Blainville's that beached in a shallow lagoon—just before he cut off its head and stuck it in a bait freezer. He wondered: Now that those heads had given up their secrets to ONR and Fisheries, would anyone ever hear the truth?

Balcomb didn't believe in fate. It was just a coincidence that he was the only person in the Bahamas that day who knew enough about beaked whales to properly collect and preserve the specimens. But if it had been just chance—if he had just happened to be there with cameras and flensing knives at the ready, and Bob Gisiner's business card in his desk drawer, and four decades on beaches and in boats studying beaked whales—if that was all simply random, then what happened *next* was up to him. The stranding had happened on his watch. And now he had to decide what to do about it. He could wait to see if the Navy and Fisheries followed through on their investigation, or he could try to put public pressure on them to do the right thing.

Balcomb knew he'd given up most of his leverage when he handed over the specimens. Fisheries had the heads now, and the Navy's press office spin machine was up and running. But he still had the photographs and the video of the whales on the beach, and of the destroyer in the canyon. If he hoped to challenge the Navy's sanitized version of the Bahamas stranding, he decided, it was time to step up and speak out.

Balcomb emailed Jasny, saying that he'd come to the press conference. Then, before he could change his mind, he also emailed the *60 Minutes* producer in New York and told her he'd be back in Abaco in a week, if she still wanted to bring down her crew.

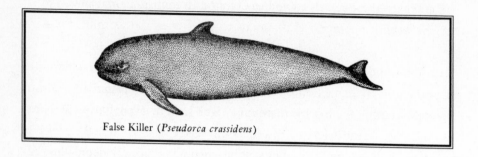
False Killer (*Pseudorca crassidens*)

20

The Dolphins That Joined the Navy

1961

Navy Marine Bioscience Division, Point Mugu, California

The clandestine Navy program that aroused the darkest public speculation and fueled the animal rights community's deepest distrust was its decades-long Marine Mammal Training Program.

Balcomb didn't know about the program when he was working inside the classified Sound Surveillance System. Even Walter Munk, who conducted highly classified Navy research throughout his career, didn't know that alongside their intensive funding of oceanography and marine acoustics research, his Navy sponsors were making a parallel investment in studying cetacean biosonar, navigation, and communication.

In setting its sights on militarized marine mammals, the Navy took a page from John Lilly's book *Man and Dolphin*, which presented two opposing visions of whales: as beacons of higher consciousness who could lead us toward interspecies communication, and as aquatic biowarriors who could be trained to assist humans in specialized naval operations.

After its opening-page paean to dolphins as ambassadors from a higher realm, *Man and Dolphin* shifts focus to their potential as military assets. "Many people have asked me if it is possible to teach these animals to detect submarines and to communicate their detection to human beings," Lilly wrote. "I don't think we need to teach them to detect submarines; I think they detect submarines already. . . . They may be highly military types. Let us try to find out."

He went on to itemize a range of promising venues for deploying dolphins: "Cetaceans might be helpful in hunting and retrieving nose-cones, satellites, missiles, and similar things men insist on dropping in the ocean. They might be willing to hunt for mines, torpedoes, submarines, and other artifacts connected with our naval operations. They might also be willing to do some scouting and patrol duty for submarines or surface ships, and they might carry their protagonist activities to the point where they can be used around harbors as underwater demolition teams operators."

Lilly's musings on dolphins' potential as marine sentries, minesweepers, deep-water object retrievers, and, perhaps, bombardiers, was a virtual blueprint for the Navy's subsequent development of operational "marine mammal systems."[1]

The Navy's Marine Mammal Research Program began as a straightforward physics experiment. Dolphins had long been observed to be among the fastest swimmers in the sea, so the Navy had a natural interest in studying their hydrodynamic properties, from their streamlined fuselage to the drag-reducing properties of their skin. The Naval Ordnance Test Station (NOTS) at China Lake was a dry lakebed in the Mojave desert, 100 miles inland. But its satellite facilities on the Pacific Coast concentrated on improving torpedo propulsion, speed, and accuracy.

In 1961 NOTS purchased a female white-sided dolphin it named Knotty from Marineland of the Pacific. For the next year, until Knotty died, NOTS researchers conducted a variety of tests to measure her speed and propulsion through the water. The impact of those studies on submarine design is evident in comparisons of before-and-after diagrams of their hulls, which became markedly less boatlike and more cetacean in shape after 1962.

The research program soon expanded to include animal training. In 1961 the Navy lost out to the Air Force for contracts in support of the man-in-space program. This was particularly galling to the Navy, since its "right stuff" test pilots had been recruited as NASA's first astronauts.

In an effort to grab back some of the public spotlight, the Navy launched its man-in-the-sea initiative. While NASA was promoting its celebrity astronauts as new world explorers, the Navy tried to focus the public imagination on the deep inner space of the oceans. Sealab, conceived as an ocean-floor research lab analogous to a space station, was to be manned by human "aquanauts," who would be supplied with food and other essentials by dolphin couriers. The Navy code-named the dolphin component of Sealab "Project Arion," after the mythical Greek poet who was rescued from drowning by a passing dolphin.

To train the dolphins for Sealab, the Navy constructed a large concrete tank, affectionately known as "the porpoise pool," just up the coast from Malibu at Mugu Lagoon. But the three white-sided dolphins it purchased from a fisherman in Santa Monica died within weeks of their arrival. So the Navy borrowed a veterinarian from a nearby Air Force base to try to figure out how to keep its dolphins alive in captivity.

Until he was recruited to treat the Navy's dolphins, Sam Houston Ridgway's veterinary experience had been confined to treating Air Force sentry dogs. He was an avid fan of Lilly's just-published *Man and Dolphin*, but growing up in South Texas, he'd never seen a marine mammal. His first encounter with a dolphin was dissecting the dead whitesides the day he arrived at Point Mugu. When Ridgway opened up the dolphins, he was at a loss to comprehend their physiology. William Schevill and Barbara Lawrence had diagrammed the dolphin skull in an attempt to understand how it echolocated, and Lilly had created a cortical map of its neural pathways. But there was no published literature on dolphin respiratory, digestive, and circulatory systems.

The Navy turned to its long-standing partnership with Marineland in Florida for help. Marineland's curator and head veterinarian, Forrest Wood, came aboard as director of the nascent Marine Mammal Training Program at Point Mugu. Wood brought along a new supply of dolphins, his own expertise in dolphin health care, and several trainers who had tutored animals for Marineland shows and for Hollywood movies such as *Doctor Dolittle*. Wood taught Ridgway how to keep the Navy dolphins alive in captivity, while the animal trainers instructed him on how to train dolphins to respond to sound signals and food rewards in much the same way that guard dogs are trained. Sam Ridgway would remain the scientific director of the Navy Marine Mammal Program for the next four decades.

In 1964 the Navy produced a feel-good documentary about its program to train dolphins as man's faithful helpmate in the deep ocean. Narrated by movie star and former Navy officer Glenn Ford, *The Dolphins That Joined the Navy* was a 30-minute tribute to the Navy's dolphin program and a promo for its upcoming Sealab expedition. Among the gee-whiz technologies showcased in the film was a John Lilly–inspired "human-dolphin translator," which converted human voice commands into a high-frequency register presumed optimal for communicating with dolphins. "These dolphins are calling to each other," Glenn Ford intoned over footage of a pair of chirping bottlenoses. "We can hear them, but we don't know what they're saying—yet. The United States Navy intends to find out."

Sadly, there would be no Hollywood ending for Sealab. The director of the human-dolphin translator program died in a mysterious laboratory accident, and during a Sealab training exercise, aquanaut Berry Cannon developed a problem with his breathing gear and drowned in the arms of his fellow divers. Sealab was scrubbed, and Congress pulled its funding for the Navy's broader man-in-the-sea program.

Then, in 1967, CIA satellite surveillance discovered that the Soviets had undertaken their own dolphin research program, headquartered in an old hotel on the shore of the Black Sea. Russian science articles purloined and translated by US naval intelligence documented extensive research into dolphin bioacoustics, physiology, anatomy, radiotelemetry, and hydrodynamics. Fearing an imminent "dolphin gap," Congress ramped up funding for the Marine Mammal Training Program, shifting its focus to operational "animal systems" that could directly support naval operations.

Almost overnight, all of the Navy's marine mammal research and operations became classified and would remain so until the end of the Cold War.

Navy Marine Bioscience Division, Point Mugu, California

In the 1990s, John Hall would become Joel Reynolds' indispensable tutor in marine biology, bioacoustics, and sonar. But back in 1967, all John Hall knew about dolphins was what he'd read in John Lilly's books. He had just earned his master's degree in marine science from Humboldt State University in Northern California and was looking for a job when Sam Ridgway hired him to help train dolphins and whales at the Navy's research facility in Point Mugu.

The month after he arrived at Point Mugu, John Hall was cleared to high-security level and assigned to mine-detection training. Enemies could easily blockade a harbor by laying mines in shallow water or tethering them to the seabed, set to detonate in response to any acoustic or magnetic impulse from an approaching ship. Another mine-laying technique was to litter a harbor with dozens of decoy mines interspersed with a few live ones. It would take a conventional minesweeping crew days to distinguish the live mines from the decoys.

Ridgway entrusted Hall with his best open-water-trained animal, Tuffy, to test dolphin proficiency in identifying sea mines. Hall planted 48 mines in Beacher's Bay in the Channel Islands. Within two hours, Tuffy located all 48 mines, plus five World War II–era mines that had gone astray 25 years earlier. Tuffy and other Navy dolphins could also distinguish real mines from decoys. They could even detect mines buried under six feet of sediment on the ocean floor. After just a few weeks of training, dolphins were consistently outperforming human and mechanical minesweepers.

Hall's next assignment was to train marine mammals in Deep Ops recovery. Because the Navy frequently lost expensive equipment and weapons in deep water, it attached acoustic "pingers" to anything of value that might fall overboard as a guide to divers during recovery missions. But humans are poorly equipped to retrieve objects from the deep ocean. They can't dive deeper than a few hundred feet; they don't tolerate the cold temperatures at depth very well; and they can't work for more than 12 minutes at depth before having to surface slowly and decompress. Human divers can't see well underwater, and they have poor directional hearing, so even with the aid of an acoustic beacon, they have trouble distinguishing the location of the sound source. Dolphins, by contrast, are perfectly engineered for the task. They can hold their breath for 7 minutes and dive repeatedly to hundreds of feet with minimal decompression time at the surface between dives. Their underwater hearing is excellent, and their echolocation skills enable them to find objects hidden behind vegetation or buried in mud.

Early on in the Marine Mammal Program, the Navy investigated whether seals and sea lions could echolocate.[2] Though they turned out not to possess biosonar, sea lions proved to have acute low-light eyesight and very sensitive directional hearing underwater. And like dolphins, they are very responsive to training. One advantage that sea lions had over dolphins on recovery missions was portability. Moving dolphins to a distant dive site was an elaborate operation involving saltwater tanks and slings and several human attendants to ensure their safe transport. Sea lions could follow a trainer around on a leash like a dog, even walking on land and sitting upright alongside drivers in small motorboats en route to recovery locations.

In support of Deep Ops and Operation Quickfind, Hall trained dolphins and sea lions to first locate lost equipment on the ocean floor, and then attach lift lines or self-inflating lift bags to bring the objects to the surface. Historically, recovering torpedoes meant dispatching teams of Navy divers, recompression vans, and medical personnel. Hall trained his sea lions and dolphins to recover torpedoes lost at depths of up to 800 feet.

For recovery missions at greater depths, the Navy turned to deeper-diving marine mammals. Following the debut of orca shows at marine parks in California early in 1968, Ridgway commissioned Ted Griffin of Namu Inc. to capture two killer whales for the Navy Marine Mammal Program. In October a Navy transport plane flew Ahab and Ishmael to Point Mugu, where they became the first orcas to be trained in the open ocean. Ridgway also bought a deep-diving pilot whale named Morgan from a local fisherman who had snared him off the coast of Catalina Island.

Hall soon trained Ahab to locate and retrieve objects from depths of 800 feet. Morgan, the pilot whale, could dive twice as deep. While their

biosonar was just as discriminating as that of dolphins, orcas proved less
obedient to commands in the open water. Ahab had a habit of disappearing at sea for days at a time, and Ishmael finally went AWOL one afternoon
during training exercises, never to return. Since killer whales were judged
too unreliable to handle torpedoes, Hall designated the pilot whale for the
Deep Ops retrieval program. On one notable occasion, Morgan located a
torpedo at 1,800 feet and attached a hydraulic lift bag that raised it safely
to the surface.

In 1969, North Vietnamese frogmen were infiltrating the port at Cam
Ranh Bay and attaching explosives to the sides of American ships. As a
countermeasure, Hall trained the Point Mugu dolphins for "swimmer
interdiction."

Hall, equipped with a snorkel and a rebreather, played the enemy swimmer trying to penetrate Mugu Lagoon without being detected by the bottlenose sentries. Once he'd trained the dolphins to ram intruding swimmers
with their snouts, Hall never made it anywhere close to the beach before
being intercepted. Several cracked ribs later, Hall flew eight of the bottlenoses
and one pilot whale to Hawaii aboard a specially equipped cargo plane, and
then on to Guam for final operational training.

In early 1970 the five best-performing guard dolphins arrived at Cam
Ranh Bay. The Navy anchored three catamarans with netted dolphin pens
hanging between the pontoons across the mouth of the wide bay at 9:00,
12:00, and 3:00. The dolphins were trained to continuously scan their sector
of the bay and to press a black or white paddle with their snouts every two
minutes: white for "all clear," black for "swimmer in the water." When a dolphin pressed the black paddle, the door to the pen would open and release the
animal into the bay. Before leaving the pen, the dolphin would press its snout
into a custom-fitted fiberglass nose cone armed with a barbed steel hook that
protruded from the front. The dolphin was trained to quickly track down the
swimmer, stab him in the buttocks or the upper thigh with the barbed hook,
pull out of the nose cone, and return to its pen. The nose cone was designed
to rapidly inflate and jettison the swimmer to the surface, where Navy SEALs
in high-powered black speedboats would swoop in for the capture. The swim-

mer saboteurs, drawn from the ranks of North Vietnamese army officers, were considered high-value interrogation subjects.

The system worked flawlessly for the first few interdictions—until the swimmers began carrying hand grenades and tossing them into the approaching speedboats. The SEALs eventually designed countermeasures to prevent grenade attacks, and, after losing several highly trained saboteurs to the dolphin/SEAL patrols, North Vietnam stopped sending swimmers into Cam Ranh Bay.

While its "swimmer nullification" program remained classified, rumors and reports continued to circulate about the Navy training "kamikaze dolphins" to kill enemy swimmers with antishark explosive devices and .45 caliber "bang-sticks." The Navy denied using dolphins to target enemy swimmers with lethal force. But over the decades since the end of the Vietnam War, interviews with former Navy animal trainers and CIA operatives detailing these programs appeared periodically in newspapers, magazines, and books—as well as a Navy SEAL who described working with dolphins to plant limpet mines in North Vietnam's Haiphong Harbor.[3]

One reason rumors of these extreme kamikaze dolphins persisted is that Lilly proposed just such a scenario in *Man and Dolphin*:

If they are military types they could be very useful as antipersonnel self-directing weapons. They could do nocturnal harbor work, capture spies let out of submarines or dropped from airplanes, attacking silently and efficiently and bringing back information from such contacts. They could deliver atomic nuclear warheads and attach them to submarines or surface vessels and to torpedoes and missiles.

Both the popular media and contemporary politics lent credence to stories about dolphin dark ops. The 1973 Mike Nichols film *The Day of the Dolphin* featured a fictionalized John Lilly character, played by George C. Scott, whose Caribbean research center is subverted by shady intelligence officers who train his dolphins to plant explosives under enemy boats. Two years later, the Church Senate Committee hearings into extralegal CIA operations

uncovered plans that were developed—although never deployed—to assassi-
nate Fidel Castro by training dolphins to deposit explosive-filled conch shells
in a cove where the Cuban leader liked to snorkel each morning.

1973
Marine Corps Air Station, Kaneohe Bay, Hawaii

Bionics had finally come of age, at least in popular culture. From 1974 to
1978, actor Lee Majors reigned as the first bionic TV superstar in *The Six Million Dollar Man*. His character, US astronaut Steve Austin, had been critically
injured in a crash and was "put back together again" with bionic replacement
parts that endowed him with superhuman vision, strength, and speed.

After the United States withdrew from Vietnam in 1973, the focus of the
Navy's marine mammal research shifted from "What can they do?" to "How
can we build technology to replicate what they do?" As Hall and Ridgway
had demonstrated, dolphins consistently outperformed human divers and
existing sonar technology for guarding harbors and detecting mines. But
dolphin crews were expensive to maintain and difficult to transport around
the world.

The Navy hoped it could gradually replace its high-maintenance dolphins
with bionic drones. On a broader level, it wanted to reverse engineer dolphin echolocation to improve existing sonar technology. In 1970 the Navy
drained the porpoise pool at Point Mugu and relocated its marine mammal
biosonar research to the Marine Corps Air Station at Kaneohe Bay in Hawaii.
Sam Ridgway moved to San Diego to oversee cetacean physiology research,
while John Hall decamped to graduate school at UC Santa Cruz, where he
befriended Ken Balcomb and Bob Gisiner.

In Hawaii, an electrical engineer and experimental psychologist directed
a team of acousticians and statisticians to develop bionic sonar.[4] The more
they learned about dolphin biosonar, the more daunting their bionic design
challenge appeared. Dolphins could collect, assimilate, and interpret an as-
tounding amount of data, and they could do it amid the acoustic complexity
of the open ocean. And dolphin signal processing exceeded anything that
computers could replicate in the 1970s.

Research into dolphin hunting behavior in the wild offered tantalizing clues for designing the kind of short-range, high-frequency sonar systems that might someday replace dolphins as minesweepers and harbor sentries. Dolphin biosonar operates in a highly mobile and adaptive fashion, with decisions about next actions flowing out of real-time assessment of streaming information. When the Navy searched the sea, it ran a grid in straight lines on a regimented schedule. But a dolphin continues to adjust its swimming pattern and sonar algorithm as it goes, circling an unknown object, scanning it from different angles to create a three-dimensional model, sorting relevant data from extraneous data, and, finally, extrapolating historical data points to arrive at accurate judgments about a target: Is this fish going to taste good or make me sick? Is this an armed mine, or a decoy?

Navy researchers confirmed Lilly's early observation that dolphin sleep occurs in one brain hemisphere at a time, while the other hemisphere continues to scan the environment for data—in much the same way that an antivirus program continues to scan a hard drive even when the drive is "sleeping." But duplicating the dolphin's continuous learning cycle required a level of artificial intelligence design that lay decades in the future.

Another avenue of biomimicry research examined the group-learning dimension of dolphin biosonar—what today would be called "crowd-sourced intelligence." As herd animals, dolphins in the wild are constantly pooling and exchanging their search data. The closest analogy would be the modern internet search engine, which scans oceans of data using specific terms, tags, and criteria, while simultaneously incorporating a steady stream of user search requests, past and present.[5]

In the eighties, the Navy moved closer to deploying its dolphin drones, which it called Autonomous Underwater Vehicles, or AUVs. They *looked* like dolphins in size and shape, and were equipped with multibeam sidescan sonar that approximated dolphin biosonar. But the AUV had a gaping hole in its motherboard where a real dolphin's "wet brain" lives and works. After a quarter century of close observation, Navy researchers had learned a lot about the dolphin's physical and neural anatomy but very little about its mind and how it made judgments. Despite the early confidence of naval engineers that they could manufacture a bionic dolphin, the "advanced biologicals," as the Navy referred to its marine mammal recruits, had been evolving their biosonar for 30 million years—too big a head start, it appeared, to overcome in just a few decades.

In 1986, in the wake of the John Walker–Jerry Whitworth spy trial, the Navy persuaded Congress to amend the Marine Mammal Protection Act to allow the Navy to collect dolphins in the wild for unspecified "national defense purposes." The Navy's marine mammal menagerie swelled to more than 100 dolphins, dozens of sea lions, and a supporting cast of beluga whales recruited for deep dives in Arctic waters.

In 1987, for the first time since the Vietnam War, the Navy redeployed dolphins as seagoing sentries—this time in the Persian Gulf. When Iran began mining the harbor in Bahrain to disrupt oil tanker traffic, the Navy dispatched six dolphins to clear mines, protect US warships against enemy swimmers, and escort Kuwaiti tankers in and out of the harbor. Many of the dolphins couldn't handle the sudden transition from the cold water of San Diego to the extreme warmth of the Gulf. One named Skippy died of a bacterial infection. The Marine Mammal Program was still classified at the time, but news of the dolphin deployment in the Persian Gulf leaked to the media.

When the *New York Times* and other outlets reported that the Navy was endangering dolphins to protect Arab oil tankers, the animal rights movement mobilized in protest. A year later, the Navy proposed deploying dolphins to guard the Trident missile submarine base at Bangor, Washington. When animal advocates sued the Navy over the health risks of moving the San Diego–based dolphins to cold northern waters, a judge ordered the Navy to study the issue, and the Navy abandoned the project.

After the Cold War ended with the Soviet Union's dissolution in 1991, the Marine Mammal Program was among the first American military projects to be downsized.[6] The Navy donated its Kaneohe Bay station to the University of Hawaii—on condition that its research team could continue its dolphin work as university faculty—and moved the remainder of its "advanced biologicals" to its facility in Point Loma, California, for ongoing training and research under the direction of Sam Ridgway.

The Navy dolphins would not be called up for active duty again until the outbreak of the second Gulf War. When the Navy deployed its Autonomous Underwater Vehicles for mine-clearing operations, the AUVs worked only where the sea floor was sandy and flat. In more complex environments, they proved unreliable. Without a fully functional dolphin drone, and with new underwater enemies to combat, the Navy turned once again to its porpoise pool for help.

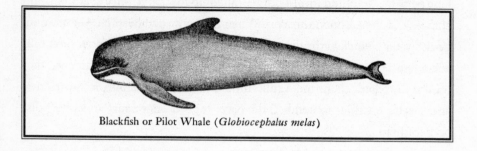

Blackfish or Pilot Whale (*Globiocephalus melas*)

21

Mr. Balcomb Goes to Washington

MAY 5, 2000
Sandy Point, Abaco Island, the Bahamas

Things had been tense between Diane and Ken during the week since he'd returned from Smugglers Cove. She was clearly upset that he'd decided to talk to *60 Minutes* and appear at the DC press conference without consulting her. It never seemed to occur to him, she noted, that his decisions affected both of their lives, and both of their careers. She was plenty angry about the way the US Navy operated in the Bahamas, but the risk of calling them out in public was greater for her, since she was just getting started in her research career. Balcomb always talked about how they were equal partners, but then had taken it upon himself to torpedo any chance that either of them would ever get research money from ONR. He may have invited *60 Minutes* to their research station and agreed to hand over their videotape, but she had no intention of appearing on camera for an interview.

The night before the *60 Minutes* crew arrived, Balcomb stayed up late reviewing the videotape from the stranding and its aftermath. He indexed each tape by time, date, and location, including the footage of the destroyer in the channel, Darlene Ketten's beachside necropsy, and the late-night CT scanning up in Boston. After all the years he'd spent behind the camera photographing and videotaping whales, it was eerie to see himself on-screen, wading out into the shallows to examine the stranded whales. Stranger still were the video images of deep-diving beaked whales lolling in three-foot surf and lying inert on beaches.

Balcomb drove up to Marsh Harbour Airport to meet the TV crew. First off the plane were producer Mary Walsh and on-camera correspondent David Martin, who together covered the Pentagon beat for *60 Minutes*. On the drive to Sandy Point, Walsh laid out her "Navy versus the whales" angle. She wanted to interview Balcomb and shoot some "B-roll" footage of the local scene for color. But as Ben White had predicted, what she seemed most focused on was the video footage of the stranding and its aftermath. Talking heads were necessary filler for any segment, and it was Martin's job to elicit something quotable from his interview subjects. But the emotional hook, line and sinker for this story had always been the images of whales on the beach, and the volunteers fighting valiantly to rescue them.

Dave Martin wanted to interview Balcomb where the first whale had stranded in front of the house. Martin stood on the beach in pressed chinos and an expensive-looking but tasteful polo shirt. Balcomb wore a faded Earthwatch T-shirt, shorts, and flip-flops. He declined the producer's offer of makeup. While the sound engineer hooked up and tested Balcomb's lapel mike, Ken tried to pretend that he'd be having a one-on-one conversation with Martin. He wished that Walsh hadn't already told him that every Sunday night, 17 million Americans tuned in to the loudly ticking stopwatch on *60 Minutes*.

Martin began his interview by introducing Balcomb as "a marine biologist who worked for seven years for the Navy tracking submarines." Balcomb had agreed to this intro in advance. Under the circumstances, it seemed relevant. After 25 years of silence, the *60 Minutes* broadcast would mark his first disclosure, public or private, of the secret sound surveillance he'd conducted for the Navy. The funny thing, he realized, was that Diane had made a point of going grocery shopping during the interview, so she still didn't know what he'd done during the Cold War.

Balcomb quietly and methodically narrated the series of whale strandings on March 15, the daylong rescue efforts, and the next day's rush to collect fresh specimens. He held up a photograph of the destroyer they'd seen in the canyon late the second day. Martin leaned in to ask the question he'd come to the Bahamas to ask:

"Do you think the Navy is responsible for the strandings?"

Balcomb wasn't surprised by the question. He'd seen the segment title, "Who Killed the Whales?" taped across the clapsticks during the sound check. If he rendered a verdict publicly, before Ketten published her findings, he knew the Navy would go after him with a vengeance. Diane was right to worry about being caught in the cross fire.

Martin waited in silence for Balcomb's response. The cameraman zoomed in for the trademark *60 Minutes* close-up of the whistle-blower's moment of truth.

"I believe the Navy did it," Balcomb answered.

MAY 9, 2000
Washington, DC

Balcomb loved to fly, but he hated flying into cities. The air, the traffic, and the noise were all toxic to him. It had been 34 years since he'd last visited Washington, DC. In the summer of 1966, he'd landed a six-week job at the Smithsonian between his bird-banding trip and his induction into the Navy. Back then the only air-conditioning was in movie theaters and supermarkets. There was no subway yet, and Reagan National was simply called National Airport. But he suspected that one thing hadn't changed: the strong stink of politics that hung over the city.

Although he preferred to travel light, Balcomb hauled a large suitcase and a duffel bag out of the terminal, both of them filled with videotape cassettes and an editing deck. He clambered aboard the subway for the ride to Silver Spring, where he had an appointment with the Office of Protected Resources at Fisheries headquarters. He'd offered to preview the tape he was planning to screen at the press conference the next day, in hopes that he might preserve enough goodwill to retain a role in the investigation.

Those hopes were dashed as soon as he walked into the conference room. Not one of the ten people seated around the conference table rose to greet him. The only friendly face he knew at headquarters, Roger Gentry, had pointedly left the building for another meeting.

While Balcomb screened his video, the suits around the table watched in silence. When it ended, he asked if there was anything they objected to his sharing with the press. Someone muttered, "All of it." No one laughed. The head of the division asked him to delete some slides ONR had published in its preliminary Environmental Impact Statement for Low Frequency Active sonar. Balcomb agreed to make the cut. Then he nodded to the stony faces around the table and left.

He took the subway to a Motel 6 out on Route 1 that he'd booked online from Abaco. Even by Balcomb's Spartan standards, it was a dump. He ate dinner next door at the Pizza Hut and spent the evening deleting ONR slides from each of the dozen videotape copies he'd brought with him. Before going to bed, he tried on the clothes he'd brought for the press conference: a brown blazer he purchased to wear at his brother's wedding six years earlier and a white collared shirt that some Earthling had left behind in Abaco. His khaki pants had a pizza stain that he rubbed clean with a damp towel. Looking at himself in the bathroom mirror, Balcomb saw a heavily bearded castaway stuffed inside a too-tight sport jacket. He should have gotten a haircut, he realized. Diane always cut his hair, and it was too late to look for a barbershop. He borrowed a pair of scissors from the girl at the front desk and trimmed his beard over the bathroom sink, wondering to himself when it had gone so gray.

MAY 10, 9:00 A.M.
Zenger Room, National Press Club

Balcomb squinted into the television lights. His mouth was dry, and his head ached. He poured himself another glass of water from the pitcher in front of him on the table, and gulped it down.

He scanned the audience, looking for a friendly face. Finally, he caught sight of Ben White crouched behind a video camera in the center aisle. Ben looked up from the eyepiece long enough to smile and wave at him with a broad sweep of his hand. That put Balcomb at ease for a minute, until he spotted a contingent from his Fisheries meeting. They all seemed to be glaring at him. When he recognized Roger Gentry sitting with them, dressed in a suit and tie with his arms crossed, Balcomb avoided making eye contact.

Joel Reynolds stepped to the podium and welcomed the assembled reporters. He introduced Balcomb and the other panelists seated on the raised dais: Naomi Rose from the Humane Society, Marsha Green of the Ocean Mammal Institute, and Chuck Bernard, a retired director of several Navy defense labs whom Reynolds had invited to critique Low Frequency Active sonar from an engineering perspective.

Balcomb had met Reynolds for the first time just a few minutes earlier. He impressed Balcomb as very comfortable in his skin; someone who felt at home in any room talking to any audience, including this assembly of reporters and cameramen. Reynolds had a beard, but unlike Balcomb's, his was trim and professorial. His suit wasn't flashy, but his red tie was smartly knotted, and he spoke without a script in clear, declarative sound bites:

"We're here today to call for an end to the indiscriminate and illegal testing and deployment of intensive long-range sonar that threatens our oceans and everything in them. We're particularly concerned with the growing use of active sonar that depends on generating extraordinarily intense noise over vast expanses of ocean, without regard to its effects on marine life and the integrity of the oceans—and most importantly, without legally required permits and environmental review mandated by federal law."

As he watched the journalists jotting notes, Balcomb worried that he should have rehearsed his own remarks. Too late for that now. He glanced at the all-caps phrases he'd scribbled down the night before on the Motel 6 pad he'd found on the night table. Then he stuffed them back in his jacket pocket.

"We're calling for full review and investigation of the Bahamas incident by Fisheries," Reynolds continued. "And we're calling for congressional oversight hearings to review these sonar systems and their environmental impact. Now, I'm going to turn the podium over to Ken Balcomb, a marine biologist and seven-year Navy veteran, who will tell us what he witnessed in the Bahamas."

Balcomb took a final gulp of water, and then stepped up to the lectern to begin his narration of what he described as "the most unusual event of my life." He switched on the videotape deck and glanced back at the screen to make sure it was projecting properly. At first he was disoriented to see the enlarged images of himself in shorts and T-shirt wading out to the first Cuvier's that had run aground at Sandy Point. He watched along with the audience as the beaked whale repeatedly circled back toward shore each time it had been guided out to deeper water. "This whale was not hit by a ship or a propeller," he began. "He was hit by a pressure wave of sound."

In a subdued but clear voice, Balcomb detailed the strandings, the rescues, and the necropsies. It helped to look at the screen behind him while he spoke, instead of at the reporters and the Fisheries staff sitting out beyond the TV lights. It took his mind off the dryness of his mouth and the strangeness of hearing his voice echoing through the speakers. When he'd ended his narration, he paused the tape on the image of the USS *Caron* frozen in place in the middle of Providence Channel.

Balcomb turned back to face the reporters and told them that he had copies of the videotape they could take with them. He started to sit down but then returned to the lectern and leaned in toward the microphone.

"I just wanted to say one other thing." He paused, searching for the right words and peering through the lights to connect with someone. When he found Ben White, he was standing upright behind his video camera, not smiling but nodding his head just enough for Balcomb to see. "I was proud to be a military officer in defense of our country during the Vietnam War. But as I see these active sonar systems developing, I'm not even proud to be an American if we're going to be destroying our whales and dolphins like this in the name of national defense."

Later, when everyone on the dais had spoken and the reporters had asked their follow-up questions, Reynolds stepped forward and offered the press a parting sound bite:

"There are still many questions about the impact of sound on marine animals. But there is no dispute about how little we know. We cannot allow the Navy to play Russian roulette with our oceans. The question that remains is this: Does the US Navy plan to enter this new century as an environmental steward or as an environmental outlaw? We're still waiting for their answer."

Someone killed the TV lights, and Reynolds stepped off the dais to but-tonhole a pair of AP reporters. White turned to talk to a TV reporter, and soon they were both laughing aloud at a story White was telling. Naomi Rose invited Balcomb to join her and Reynolds for dinner that night. Balcomb said thanks, but he had an afternoon plane to catch back to Miami.

Balcomb scanned the room for an exit. Ben White and Joel Reynolds were still working the room. Roger Gentry was huddled with his Fisheries col-leagues in a far corner. Balcomb grabbed his duffel bag and slipped out the side door.

He hit the street feeling like a beaked whale breaking the surface to breathe after an hourlong dive. All he wanted was to get back to the airport and onto the next plane home to the islands. But he'd promised a friend—his only real friend in Washington—that he would drop by before leaving town.

Jim Mead was working in his windowless office in the subbasement of the Smithsonian's National Museum of Natural History. Mead looked less like a museum curator than he did an undersized, bearded woodsman out of a fairy tale. He favored plaid flannel shirts, red suspenders, and a fly fisherman's vest. After growing up in the old-growth forests of the Pacific Northwest, where he worked alongside his father, an itinerant logger and a contract "high climber," Mead was desperate to escape the logging life. On a dare from a friend, he applied to Yale University and won a full scholarship to study botany, then biology, then geology, then paleontology, and, eventually, cetology. The first person to hire him out of graduate school was S. Dillon Ripley, the head of the Yale Peabody Museum of Natural History and the future director of the Smithsonian Institution.

As he searched for his friend in the catacombs below the Smithsonian exhibit halls, Balcomb wandered through a series of ill-lit basement corridors that were crammed to the rafters with cetacean skulls and vertebrae—some catalogued, many not, dating back years, decades, and centuries. Balcomb finally found Mead's office, marked by an enormous papier-mâché mold of a Cuvier's head mounted like a trophy over the door. Mead was typing away on a manual Smith-Corona, barricaded behind shelves full of books and artifacts collected over four decades of marine mammal research. Flensing knives from whaling countries around the globe hung across his office walls. His bookshelves were piled high with research papers and dog-eared chapbooks on every aspect of whale evolution, morphology, and taxonomy. When Mead greeted him with a warm smile framed by a square-cut white beard, Balcomb felt at ease for the first time since arriving in DC.

Their friendship had been forged three decades earlier in blood, sweat, and vomit. They met during the waning days of Canada's whaling industry, when they were recruited to survey fin, sei, and humpback whales off the Newfoundland coast. Mead still winced at the memory of that first whale-tagging cruise. Though he'd been studying whale bones for almost a decade by then, he'd never been to sea. Balcomb, by contrast, had three seasons of whale tagging off the California coast under his belt, a year of banding birds in the South Pacific atolls, and two full tours with the Navy.

As soon as their round-bottomed boat headed out of the memorably named seaport of Dildo for the Atlantic crossing to Greenland, Mead became violently seasick. He proceeded to retch into the wastepaper basket in their shared cabin for the next three days and nights. Every few hours, Balcomb would empty the wastebasket, pat Mead on the back, and offer him a few words of comfort and a handful of saltines from the galley. When Mead finally got his sea legs, Balcomb taught him how to shoot Discovery tags from the deck of the boat. At night, Mead tutored Balcomb on the morphology of whale skulls and toothed-whale evolution. By the cruise's end, their friendship was sealed.

Given his proclivity for seasickness, it was probably no accident that Mead made his mark as a shore-based researcher. A few years later, when he became curator of marine mammals at the Smithsonian's Museum of Natural History, Mead and his field partner, Charlie Potter, plastered the beaches of the mid-Atlantic with leaflets soliciting calls from anyone with news of marine mammal strandings. When the phone rang, Mead and Potter jumped into their pickup truck to scavenge the remains of the beached creatures. Over the next three decades, Mead built the museum's collections of mammal specimens into the world's largest, filling subterranean storerooms with whale brains and pinniped penises, sirenian specimens preserved in vats of formaldehyde, and rows of shelves stacked with boxes of whale bones from cetaceans toothed and baleen, great and small. Mead also co-founded the Society for Marine Mammalogy and was elected as one of its early presidents, created the first regional stranding networks, and served as the Marine Mammal Commission's scientific advisor. All the while, he regularly published his research on beaked whale evolution, anatomy, and morphology.

Mead and Balcomb only saw each other occasionally, catching up over drinks at academic conferences. But they shared a passion for beaked whales, followed each other's publications, and respected each other's expertise. Mead was not an activist. By remaining aloof from the political push and pull among the environmentalists, the animal advocates, and the Navy research establishment, Mead had carved out a reputation as an unassailable and nonpartisan expert.

Ever since Charlie Potter returned from the Bahamas the week after the stranding, Mead had begun to rethink his carefully cultivated neutrality. He followed the fallout from the Bahamas stranding on MARMAM and sifted through the emails bouncing between the Washington-based agencies. He deemed most of the speculation about the stranding to be ill informed: 10 percent science and 90 percent politics. As a longtime observer of the Washington policy-and-power game, he knew how quickly the whirlpool of slander and innuendo could pull you under, particularly if, like Balcomb, you lacked the institutional armor of the Navy or, in Mead's case, the Smithsonian. When he heard that Balcomb was going to challenge the Navy and Fisheries, on their home turf and in front of the press, Mead decided to throw his friend a lifeline.

"I'm sorry to have missed your press conference, Kenneth," said Mead as he pulled the sheet from his typewriter and tamped it even with a short stack of papers. "But I was finishing a time-sensitive task."

When Balcomb had settled into the office chair facing his, Mead handed him a manila envelope. "Here's some reading for your plane ride home. I was going to submit it to *Nature*, but their peer review takes six to eight months, which is much too long to wait, under the circumstances. Or, I should say, under *your* circumstances."

Balcomb pulled the article out of the envelope and read the title page aloud: "Historical Mass Mortalities of Ziphiids."

"It's drawn from a database I've been compiling since 1974," Mead explained. "Something of a pet project of mine. But twenty-five years is long enough to be noodling around with a data set, don't you think? I've decided to publish it in the gray literature, under the Smithsonian letterhead."

Usually authored by the most respected researchers inside the most prestigious institutions, "gray literature" is published directly by academic institutions or governmental agencies under their own letterhead, rather than being submitted for time-consuming peer review and publication in a journal. When published by the right author at an opportune time, gray literature can play an influential role in shaping policy and influencing scientific opinion.

"I'm thinking that in addition to the usual federal registries, I'll post it on MARMAM. That's probably the quickest way to get it into circulation."

When Balcomb started to scan the article, Mead gently took it back and pressed it inside the envelope. "Save it for your plane ride home," he said. "Enjoy it with a stiff drink. You look like you could use one."

As instructed, Balcomb waited until the flight attendant brought him his rum and Coke before pulling Mead's paper out of the envelope. It was a meta-analysis of the 50 known mass strandings of ziphiids—or, beaked whales—beginning with the first recorded stranding back in 1834 in Norway, all the way through the recent mass stranding in the Bahamas. The study's primary finding, indented halfway down the first page of the 26-page article, highlighted a striking anomaly in the 166-year data set:

> There have been six strandings of ziphiids which involved more than one species . . . In all six events there were naval maneuvers present in the area, and all six took place on islands.

It was a simple-enough observation, and rigorously documented in the pages of charts and citations that followed. But no academic researcher had ever before established a direct historical connection between naval exercises and mass strandings of beaked whales. Since the 1996 Greek stranding, the Navy and its handpicked scientists had dedicated significant resources to disavowing any evidence trail of a causal relationship. Had anyone other than Jim Mead written the article, his findings would have been attacked as inflammatory. But Mead was a singular figure in his field. Everyone knew and respected his work, and, more remarkably in a polarized discipline dominated by eccentrics and iconoclasts, Jim Mead was universally well liked.

One notable mass stranding of beaked whales *didn't* appear in Mead's data set—because it occurred the same day as the press conference and hadn't yet been reported in the media.

On May 9, 2000, NATO naval forces commenced antisubmarine exercises inside the 3,000-meter-deep canyon between the islands of Madeira and Porto Santo, off the coast of Morocco. The joint task force included one aircraft carrier, three submarines, and more than 40 surface vessels, including warships, logistic vessels, and landing craft.

The next day, four beaked whales stranded on the beaches of Madeira. The stranding of individual beaked whales is a rare event in the Madeira archipelago, according to the historical records. A multiple stranding had never been recorded before.

Scientific investigators found that the whales' injuries, and the pattern of their stranding, suggested that a pressure event similar to the one in the Bahamas had precipitated or contributed to the strandings. As Darlene Ketten later wrote, following the necropsies and CT scans she subsequently performed on the beaked whales that stranded on Madeira:

> Several observations on these beaked whales are consistent with the findings on the Bahamian specimens. In particular, blood in and around the eyes, kidney lesions, pleural hemorrhage, lung congestion, and in the one preserved head, subarachnoid and ventricular hemorrhages, were found which are consistent with Bahamian pathologies that are consistent with stress and pressure related trauma. The coincidence of pathology and the stranding patterns in both sites raises the concern that a similar pressure event precipitated or contributed to strandings in both sites.

As Balcomb's plane cruised southward, high above the Eastern Seaboard, Jim Mead selected "Historical Mass Mortalities of Ziphiids" from the document list on his desktop computer and uploaded it to the Smithsonian mainframe.

Then he logged on to MARMAM and posted the article "For General Circulation."

With those few keystrokes—and with the evidence emerging from the strandings in the Bahamas and Madeira—Mead upgraded the sonar threat to whales from an unsubstantiated rumor to documented science.

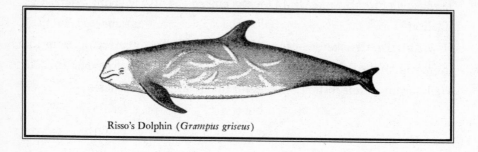

Risso's Dolphin (*Grampus griseus*)

22

The Mermaid That Got Away

MAY 11, 2000

Sandy Point, Abaco Island, the Bahamas

Balcomb didn't feel his usual relief on returning to Abaco. Now that he'd stepped in front of the *60 Minutes* cameras and mounted the podium at the Washington Press Club, his island life no longer felt like a sanctuary from the whirling world.

When he logged on to MARMAM, the tightness moved from his stomach up into his chest. There was already some lively discussion in response to Mead's article, and the first reports of the Madeira stranding were beginning to appear in bits and pieces. Roger Gentry had emailed to tell him Darlene Ketten was furious that he'd distributed video of her beachside dissection in Abaco and her CT lab in Boston to the media. She considered the CT scans the property of her ongoing Fisheries investigation, and Balcomb's unauthorized distribution to the press was a breach of professional ethics.

Tougher to take was the one-line email Bob Gisiner sent to him and cc'd to Gentry: "Norris would be ashamed of you." Ken Norris, who had died in

1998, was a revered teacher and mentor to a generation of young researchers, including Gisiner, Gentry, and Balcomb.[1] He was a father figure to all of them at Santa Cruz. Gisiner knew precisely where to insert the blade.

The next day brought a volley of slurs and smears that friends forwarded to him. Emails between staff at Fisheries and ONR called Balcomb "a grandstander" and not a "real" scientist but merely a photographer. Somebody suggested that he had it in for the Navy because his research had never received funding from ONR.

Balcomb tried not to take it personally. He'd expected this kind of response when he called out the Navy. But his professional reputation was all he had to bolster the credibility of his field research. He didn't have a PhD or any academic affiliations. In addition to bearing witness to the Bahamas stranding, he was 25 years into his orca survey in Puget Sound, and getting closer every year to winning them threatened-species status and the protections that came with that recognition. If his objectivity was called into question over the stand he'd taken on the Bahamas stranding, the orcas would pay the price.

Meanwhile, he wasn't getting any support on the home front. The day he got back to Sandy Point, Diane was busy cleaning up the house after the Earthlings, who had left that morning. She asked how the press conference went but offered no sympathy or support.

He knew something was off kilter when the phone calls began. Unlike his other wives, Diane rarely spoke on the phone for longer than a few minutes.

Until that week in May.

Each night after dinner, the phone would ring. Diane would jump up to grab the cordless extension and disappear onto the back deck, sliding the glass door closed behind her. The calls would go on for a long time. When Ken asked her who she was talking to, she answered, "No one."

When he pressed her, Diane explained that it was a woman from the recently departed Earthling group who had fallen hard for the whales and the island life. Her name was Pam. She worked in Los Angeles as an electrical engineer, and she wanted to change her life. She was thinking about moving to Abaco and joining their research team. She had money, so she wouldn't need a stipend.

They had seen this happen before. One-weekers would have a road-to-Damascus moment out on the water with the whales and feel as though they couldn't return to their life on the mainland. Back in the late 1970s, a woman showed up to volunteer at Smugglers Cove. She'd come all the way from Holland, where she worked as a medical doctor and professor of informatics. She fell in love with the orcas that summer, returned every summer thereafter, and over the years became a senior member of their survey team.

Still, it wasn't like Diane to get so wrapped up in an Earthling's midlife crisis. One night after watching her animated silhouette on the back porch during a marathon conversation, Ken confronted her. Did she and this woman have something going on? He wanted to know. Some kind of girl crush?

"Relax," she responded. "They're all incoming calls, so I'm not running up a big phone bill. I'm just trying to help Pam make some important life decisions."

It was time to close up the house at Sandy Point and move camp to Smugglers Cove for the summer. Dave Ellifrit had flown out ahead of them to field the first wave of summer interns. Those few days at the end of each season—in May in the Bahamas and in October in Smugglers Cove—were the only times they had alone together in the two houses. Ordinarily, Ken looked forward to it as a romantic interlude, like parents whose kids had gone off to summer camp. He and Diane could stay up late at night, make love on the beach, or simply sit on the deck together and stare out at the sea.

This year it didn't feel romantic. And it felt wrong somehow to be leaving the island when so few whales had returned to the canyon and there were still so many unanswered questions. But with the hurricane season starting up in June, they didn't have a choice. They pulled the boats out of the water and towed them up to the Yamaha dealer for summer storage. They stowed the linens, locked up the desktop computers, and secured all their files and photographs in waterproof filing cabinets set well up off the floor. Finally, they shuttered all the windows to protect the house against storms. In the morning they would drive up to Marsh Harbour, leave the car and the truck in a friend's garage, and catch the flight to the mainland.

It was late when Diane climbed into the big claw-footed bathtub for a hot soak. Ken grabbed two cold Kaliks from the fridge, tuned the kitchen radio to a funky mix of calypso and reggae on Radio Abaco, and joined her in the tub. They sat facing each other, their legs intertwined. Ken leaned his head back against the tub's rim and held the cool beer bottle against his forehead. Finally, he thought, a moment of peace and stillness.

Then Diane dropped the depth charge: "I'm not going to Smugglers Cove with you."

Ken opened his eyes and stared up at the flaking paint on the ceiling rafters.

"Once we get to Miami, I'm heading to LA. To visit Pam."

"Why?" was all he could manage. He sat up straight to face her.

"Ken." She moved her foot away from his on the floor of the tub. "It's been really good. It's been great. But it's over. The marriage is over."

A wave of vertigo knocked him sideways. It felt like being in a fighter jet during a sharp turn when the g-force knocks the crystals in your inner ear loose, and your balance goes haywire.

"I may stay in LA for a while," she explained. "I don't know for how long."

Balcomb held up his hand to stop her from talking, as if it couldn't be true unless she said it out loud. He couldn't bear to hear anything else, at least not until the dizziness and nausea passed. He drew up his knees and tucked his head. As soon as he got his balance back, his shoulders began to shake, and he felt himself sobbing. Diane didn't move to comfort him. Sitting in the tub with his heart cracked in half, Ken looked up to see Diane's face composed in a mask of resolve.

Smugglers Cove without Diane was agony. Everywhere he looked, he saw reminders of happier times: their barefoot wedding on the beach, dancing in the moonlight on the deck, kayaking together through the glassy waters just after dawn, alongside a pod of majestic orcas.

Diane called to tell him that she and Pam were heading off to hike in Joshua Tree National Park. Then no word for ten days. When she finally checked in, she was back at Pam's house in LA. She was planning to stay there. She couldn't say for how long. She only said that she was happy.

Diane didn't have a cell phone, so the only way to reach her was to call Pam's house. Ken couldn't bear to hear Pam's voice, so he tried not to call. He began writing letters: his "I hope it's not too late" letters. He'd never been the kind of guy to tell people he loved them. Even Diane, whom he'd loved more than anyone in his life. Now he let it all pour out. He apologized for not being a better partner, for making decisions without consulting her. He promised to let her steer the boat if only she'd come back to him.

After two weeks of unanswered letters, Ken drove the Volkswagen mini-bus onto the Friday Harbor ferry, disembarked on the mainland north of Seattle, and headed south for the 1,200-mile drive to LA. He drove in silence, rehearsing the speech he planned to make when he got there, stopping only twice for a few hours' sleep at roadside rest stops.

He'd only passed through Los Angeles before on his way to Baja, so he had to buy a map to find his way to the gated community on the west side of town where Pam lived. When he called up from the gatehouse, Diane sounded shocked and unhappy that he'd come. After some negotiation, she agreed to meet him at a tea shop a few blocks away on Wilshire Boulevard. When she showed up an hour later, she was stiff and aloof, refusing to eat or even order a cup of tea. She repeated that she was happy. Their marriage was over, and there wasn't anything else to talk about. When he pressed her to meet him again, she said she'd come only with Pam. She agreed to meet him the next day on the Venice boardwalk.

That scene was even worse than the tea shop. How was he supposed to win her back in the middle of the Venice boardwalk freak show? There was a nonstop parade of tattooed fortune-tellers and Rasta vendors stinking of weed, and every manner of roller skating nut job. They talked standing next to a phone card kiosk because Diane refused to sit down in a restaurant or even walk with him on the beach. Pam stood back a few paces, pretending to peruse a rack of sunglasses and exchanging intense glances with Diane every few minutes. Ken stammered through the speech he'd rehearsed all night, determined to try to connect with her somehow. But Diane wouldn't budge. She handed Ken a list she'd compiled of the personal effects she'd left the past season at Smugglers Cove. She asked Balcomb to ship them back to her, either here in LA or care of her sister in the Bahamas. Suddenly, incredibly, there was nothing left to say, except good-bye.

The drive back north felt like a one-car funeral procession. He'd spent most of his 14 years with Diane disbelieving his good luck at having this young superwoman in his life. Now that his luck had run out, he had nothing left to fight for, except the whales.

After a week back at Smugglers Cove without Diane, with no hope of reeling her back into his life, Balcomb was emotionally spent. He tried to lose himself in the daily drill of tracking orcas in the strait. The best he could manage was to wake up early, stay out on the water all day, and hope that none of the interns asked him when Diane was planning to arrive for the summer survey.

Balcomb was actually relieved at the prospect of returning to Washington, DC, for a Fisheries investigative meeting. He wasn't invited, and they clearly didn't want him there. But the agency couldn't keep him from attending, since he had relevant evidence to present. He tried to convince Roger Gentry to cover his airfare and lodging, but Gentry told him that if he wanted to attend, he'd have to travel on his own dime. Balcomb estimated the trip would cost him at least $600, which ordinarily would have been a deal breaker. But he'd heard that the day after its own investigative session, Fisheries was expecting to be briefed by the Navy. He still hoped to find a way to get invited to—or crash—that briefing.

When Balcomb showed up at the Fisheries meeting in Silver Spring, he felt like the pariah in the fifth-grade lunchroom. Darlene Ketten refused to acknowledge him. Gentry gave him a curt nod, nothing more. Janet Whaley, the assistant head of the Fisheries Office of Protected Resources, began the meeting by admonishing everyone in attendance to keep the proceedings confidential. "Whatever is said in this room stays in this room. This is an investigation, not a press event. Understood?" She slowly pivoted her gaze around the conference table until each attendee had nodded assent. She glared straight across the table at Balcomb, her hands folded, her mouth set in a tight smile.

Ketten presented her preliminary forensic findings on the ears and heads she'd examined. She reported on the beachside necropsy, the CT scans, and the eventual dissection at Woods Hole. She referred to evidence of a pressure event, the presence of subarachnoid hemorrhages in the cranium, and blood in the ear canal. But she insisted on citing the cause of death as "dehydration and cardiac collapse" subsequent to stranding. The word "sonar" was never mentioned. Any conclusions about what caused the strandings, she cautioned, would have to await the slow decalcification of the outer ear bones. It would take months before the hard bone dissolved away in the weak acid solution and allowed her to obtain thin slices of the inner ear for direct examination.

Next, Ruth Ewing described her findings from examination of the organ specimens that Balcomb had harvested from the whale in Cross Harbor. Her report reinforced Balcomb's belief that she'd made a critical pathology error. She'd embedded the organ specimens in paraffin, which was by-the-book histology. But paraffin dissolves all the fat tissue, which is where you'd look for nitrogen bubbles from the bends.

Balcomb presented his testimony about the events on the ground on March 15 and 16, including warships he and others observed in the channel in the days following. Then he submitted into evidence his videotape of the strandings. As to cause of death, he noted that if you stampede a herd of buffalo over a cliff, what kills them is the impact of the fall. But the cause of death is whatever drove them off the cliff. Some of the stranded whales he examined had died from shark attacks. But in ten years of field study, he'd never seen a healthy beaked whale venture into shark-infested waters outside the canyon. To figure out what caused the whale deaths, he insisted, they first needed to discover what happened inside the canyon that would have sent the whales fleeing to the beach.

Balcomb submitted one other piece of evidence: a document that contradicted the notion that the Navy had no prior knowledge of the presence of beaked whales in Providence Channel. Six months earlier, at the Maui marine mammal conference, Balcomb had befriended a biologist from the Naval Undersea Warfare Center, the naval intelligence agency that administered the submarine test range at AUTEC. The biologist was in charge of the environmental planning and biological analysis division. As part of AUTEC's internal environmental review in 1997, he conducted a comprehensive assessment of marine mammals in the Bahamas, including data from Balcomb and Claridge's ongoing Bahamas Marine Mammal Survey. The assessment included protocols for avoiding harm to marine life during testing on the range, including specific allowable decibel thresholds by species, including beaked whales.

Balcomb pushed the report across the table to Janet Whaley. "If the Navy group at AUTEC knew all about the beaked whales in Providence Channel," he wondered aloud, "why weren't they mentioned in the Environmental Assessment the fleet conducted before the sonar exercises?"

The most compelling new evidence presented that morning came from the tapes at AUTEC that Balcomb had urged Gisiner to track down the first day of the stranding. Now, ten weeks later, he finally found out what they recorded. There were two hydrophone arrays recording in the vicinity of Abaco that day. One was *east* of the Bahamas: an old SOSUS array moored in the deep sound channel. Originally installed in the 1960s to track Soviet submarines as they transited the Atlantic, this array was currently being deployed by geological surveys to monitor underwater earthquakes and other seismic activity in the North Atlantic. Although numerous earthquakes had been detected from around the Atlantic the week of the stranding, there were no unusual sources of low-frequency acoustic energy emanating from the Bahamas region—meaning, the tissue damage observed in the beaked whales couldn't have resulted from an explosion or geological event.

The other hydrophone array was located 100 miles *south* of the strandings, a mile deep on the floor of the AUTEC range. A storm tracker named John Proni from the National Oceanic and Atmospheric Administration happened to be recording in the AUTEC range the morning of March 15. There were no submarine tests being conducted on the range from March 15 to March 18, which was why Proni had access to the arrays those days. On the morning of March 15, he recorded bursts of 135- to 150-decibel sound waves at between 3.5 and 6 kilohertz.

Using the basic algorithm he'd learned in Fleet Sonar School, Balcomb quickly calculated that the sound level 100 miles to the north, where the whales stranded, would have been about 230 decibels! When he looked around the table, he saw Roger Gentry working his own equations on a pad.

After the meeting adjourned, Balcomb hurried to catch up with Gentry in the hallway. "Did you get the same sound source level as I did?" he asked. "Two hundred thirty decibels must mean 53-Charlie," Balcomb said, referring to the nickname for the ANSQ-53c active sonar mounted on the hulls of most Navy destroyers.

Gentry looked around to see who might be watching him. He was unhappy to be having a conversation with Balcomb that might be construed as friendly. "I'm just a civilian, Ken. I know bioacoustics, not Navy hardware."

Balcomb asked him what he knew about the meeting scheduled the next morning between Fisheries and the Navy. Gentry confirmed that, yes, the Navy was scheduled to brief Fisheries, and, yes, Gentry was attending. But even if he wanted to help Balcomb get inside the room—which he didn't—there was no way the Navy would give him a seat at that meeting. Not after the press conference. Not after giving his videotape to *60 Minutes*.

The next morning, Balcomb was already boarding his flight back to Seattle by the time the large Navy team filed into the conference room at Fisheries headquarters. The whole crew showed up: the admirals from Atlantic Fleet Command, the scientists from ONR, the acousticians from the Naval Research Lab, and the leadership from the Office of Environmental Readiness and the Navy Secretary's office. They all brought their lawyers.

In addition to Gisiner from ONR, there were marine mammal specialists from Woods Hole, Florida, and California. The gray eminence among them was Sam Ridgway, who still directed the dolphin training center in Point Loma, San Diego. In the four decades since he was recruited to Point Mugu as the Navy's first veterinarian and dolphin trainer, Ridgway had continued to plumb the mysteries of dolphin anatomy, echolocation, and hearing. By 2000, he was the Navy's longest-serving cetologist, and virtually the last of the first generation of cetacean investigators that included John Lilly, Bill Schevill, Bill Watkins, and Ken Norris.

Ridgway's research into the impact of noise, including sonar, on dolphins and other small whales had established a 180 decibel "safety" threshold for temporary hearing loss. The Navy and ONR had adopted this threshold for their Environmental Assessments, but many non-Navy scientists criticized 180 decibels as much too loud a threshold for safety, since hearing loss was the most extreme consequence of noise, and whales had been shown to change their migration paths and other important behaviors when subjected to just 120 decibels.

The Fisheries contingent was smaller than the Navy's: the leadership from headquarters in Silver Spring and the Southeast Office in Florida, plus the few individuals from the Office of Protected Resources, including Gentry, whose security clearance allowed them to sit in on a classified briefing.

An admiral from the Atlantic Fleet led off by explaining how the political upheaval in Vieques, Puerto Rico, had forced the battle group to conduct its first-ever antisubmarine exercise in Providence Channel. Then Admiral Paul Gaffney, the head of ONR, introduced the acoustic modeling of the sonar exercises in the canyon that he'd commissioned. Someone dimmed the lights and lowered a screen from the ceiling. An acoustician stepped forward to narrate a PowerPoint deck illustrating the progress of the battle group as it transited the 150-mile length of the canyon from midnight on March 15 until four o'clock that afternoon.

As the icons representing the ships moved through the canyon, bands of yellow, red, and green—symbolizing sound waves of varying decibels and frequencies—spread out in front of their bows. Two of the ships proceeded in a zigzagging pattern, while three others followed down the middle of the channel. By the 6:00 a.m. interval in the slide show, the cross-section view of the canyon was flooded with color. The peak-intensity sound, in red, was concentrated in a surface layer, with yellow-to-green-to-blue layers of decreasing sound spreading out at lower depths.

Shifting to an aerial view, the acoustician showed how the advance of the battleships through the canyon coincided with the presumed times and reported locations of the whale strandings, which were represented by white X marks along the shore of Abaco and nearby islands. The acoustician used his laser pointer to indicate how the surface layer of warm water had amplified the sound to levels in excess of 180 decibels within a radius of 30 miles of the ships. By the time he reached the 4:00 p.m. coordinates in the slide show, the sonar exercises were complete, and each of the stranded whale locations had been traversed.

"That's all of them," he said, pointing to whale number 17, which had stranded at Gold Rock Creek in Grand Bahama. He added, incidentally, that no whales or other marine mammals had been sighted by the battle group in the course of the exercise.

The simulation of the 16-hour war game and 17 whale strandings had taken less than ten minutes to reenact.

When the lights came up, there was much throat clearing and fiddling with paper and pencils.

Sam Ridgway pushed his chair away from the table and pulled himself slowly to his feet. "Well, gentlemen," he said with what seemed like an exaggerated South Texas drawl, "that was a very *informative* presentation. I guess we can all go home now." Nervous laughter rippled through the room. Ridgway looked around the conference table, feigning dismay that there might be anything further to discuss or conclude.

Nonetheless, scientific experts from the Navy and Fisheries presented acoustic and biological analysis throughout the morning. But the decision makers had seen what they needed to see, and soon they were slipping away from the table to conduct sidebar conversations in the hallways. During coffee breaks, the Fisheries leadership and its lawyers swirled around one another like a school of bait fish. Navy JAGs and general counsels spoke quietly into the ears of admirals. By late morning, the Navy lawyers were conferring with the Fisheries lawyers, and the Navy Secretary with the NOAA and Fisheries administrators.

When it was time to break for lunch, Gaffney thanked the scientists for their presentations. The Navy brass and their counterparts at Fisheries, along with their respective attorneys, convened to a smaller conference room with better chairs.

Gentry hoped that Fisheries would hold the Navy's feet to the fire. But once he saw the admirals filing into the closed-door conference—"Where the elephants go to play," as Gisiner remarked to him with a smirk—he realized that the idea of Fisheries dictating terms to the Navy was laughable. The Navy had all the acousticians, most of the marine mammal experts, and all the other resources that counted, including money and computers. It also owned virtually all the acoustic and operational data related to the event, and Fisheries had neither the political clout nor the clear legal mandate to compel the US Navy to make it public.

The fleet commanders, for their part, opposed the notion of sharing their closely guarded trade secrets with Fisheries. The details of naval training exercises were classified, including the specific frequencies, source levels, and ranges of its sonar. Any evidence submitted to an investigation or published in a public report would have to be cleared in advance by the Navy. It defied the admirals' comprehension that they had to kowtow to a roomful of lawyers and regulators. They had built and trained the most powerful Navy in the history of maritime warfare, had outlasted the fearsome Soviet armada during a four-decade Cold War, and now they were being called to account because a dozen whales had stranded during a training exercise?

But the civilians in the room—the Secretary of the Navy and the administrators of NOAA and Fisheries—understood the need for accommodation. An unfortunate sequence of events had forced the Bahamas incident into public view and was now forcing them into bed together. For a peacetime Navy intent on promoting itself as a good steward of the environment, pictures of dead whales on a beach with Navy warships offshore demanded a thorough and transparent investigation. So did a relentless environmental lawyer in Los Angeles—who was no doubt preparing at that very moment to sue both the Navy and Fisheries—and a former naval officer turned rogue whale researcher who wouldn't stop talking to the press. By the end of a long afternoon of negotiation, the lawyers had agreed on the rules of engagement for the first-ever joint investigation conducted by the Navy and Fisheries.

When the Navy's "letter of cooperation" with Fisheries was released to the press a week later, Gentry knew he was in for a long ordeal. The lawyers, predictably, had weasel-worded it so badly that you couldn't tell who was admitting to what. The Navy acknowledged that the stranding was "an unusual and significant event," and pledged that if the investigation ultimately determined that sonar could cause trauma to whales, "the Navy will reassess its use of sonars in the course of peacetime training and implement measures to ensure the least practicable adverse effect on beaked whales."

What came through loud and clear to Gentry was that by announcing a joint investigation, the Navy had wrapped its arms around its supposed regulator, and it now had a stranglehold on him as well. Gentry had been named as Fisheries' point person and as liaison with the Navy acousticians. Teri Rowles of Protected Resources was assigned to work with Darlene Ketten on the biological investigation.

The day they announced their partnership, Navy and Fisheries offered Ketten to the press to discuss her findings to date. She characterized the Bahamas strandings as "a red flag" and "a reason for concern," then speculated that the animals that died would have experienced the equivalent of a "really bad headache."[2] She cautioned, however, that there wasn't enough evidence yet to link the strandings to Navy sonar, and the biological investigation would take months to complete.

The week after the joint investigation was announced, Admiral Gaffney left the Office of Naval Research to become president of the National Defense University. Before leaving, he authorized Gisiner to earmark $3 million for the purchase of a Siemens CT scanner for Ketten's Woods Hole lab. Ketten heard the news in Adelaide, Australia, where she and Teri Rowles were briefing the International Whaling Commission on their investigation of the Bahamas stranding.

Balcomb, whose contributions to recovering and preserving the evidence trail of the stranding were relegated to a footnote in Ketten's and Rowles' presentation, was back on San Juan Island considering how he might keep the pressure on the Navy and Fisheries to make good on their promise of a thorough and transparent inquiry.

Reading the "letter of cooperation" in his Los Angeles office, Joel Reynolds was deeply skeptical about the outcome of this "cooperative" investigation, which he doubted would shed any light on the Navy's midnight exercises in Providence Channel.

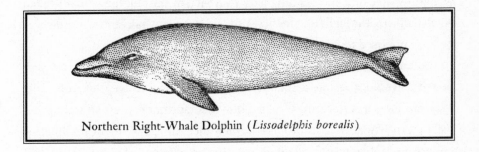

Northern Right-Whale Dolphin (*Lissodelphis borealis*)

23

In the Valley of the Whales

Ken Balcomb spent the summer back on San Juan Island writing letters to members of Congress, speaking to the handful of powerful businesspeople he'd come to know over the years in the Pacific Northwest, talking to any journalist who would listen—doing whatever he could to keep the pressure on the Navy to fully investigate the Bahamas stranding and change the way it used sonar in training exercises. Balcomb worked on his own, rather than allying himself with NRDC, the Humane Society, or any of the conservation groups that were starting to engage on the issue. He was past caring whether he was perceived as an environmentalist, an activist, or a whistle-blower. But he'd always been a lone wolf, and he felt too old to start running with a pack.

By mid-September, all the summer interns had left Smugglers Cove, and by early October, the orcas had begun their migration south toward the Oregon and California coasts. Ordinarily, October was when he and Diane would be folding up camp and heading back to Abaco to start up the winter beaked whale survey. That fall, for the first time in memory, Balcomb had nowhere he was supposed to be.

When the *60 Minutes* segment finally aired in early October, Balcomb hoped it would generate a chain reaction of public outrage. But to his dismay, millions of Americans watched his videotape of the mass stranding and listened to David Martin of CBS News indict the US Navy as the likeliest culprit—and then went back to speculating on whether or not the New York Mets and the New York Yankees would face off in the first Subway Series since 1956. Except for a few calls from journalists, the *60 Minutes* broadcast didn't seem to move the meter.

Ken heard from Dave Ellifrit that Diane was back in Abaco after spending most of the summer in Los Angeles. Dave had joined her in mid-September to help get the boats back in the water and restart the survey. Ken and Diane had communicated only a few times over the summer, in awkward phone conversations that were mostly about Ken's shipping her some personal effects from Smugglers Cove. He'd left behind gear in Abaco, including a couple of precious beaked whale heads he'd salvaged from around the Caribbean over the years. But he was afraid that asking Diane to ship them back to him would slam shut a door he still hoped to keep ajar.

The only follow-up contact he had with Diane was to co-author an article for the *Bahamas Journal of Science* titled "A Mass Stranding of Cetaceans Caused by Naval Sonar in the Bahamas."[1] Their meticulously detailed account documented the time, location, and condition of each stranded animal, provided preliminary analysis of the specimens they collected, discussed the acoustic threat that military sonar posed to whales, and offered suggestions for reducing the risks to marine mammals. It was a bittersweet collaboration, executed through dispassionate emails and a few stilted phone conversations over the course of several months.

For years after its publication, their article would remain the most cited primary reference for the Bahamas stranding. It also served as a somber epitaph for their research subjects.

"None of the Cuvier's beaked whales that we had documented in our nine-year study have returned since the March 15 naval exercise, and none of the 'rescued' whales has been seen again, either . . . Mitigation of naval activities during peacetime exercise appears to be the only reasonable solution to this problem."

OCTOBER 12, 2000
Port of Aden, Yemen

Six months after its ill-fated antisubmarine training exercise in the Bahamas, the USS *George Washington* battle group had deployed to the Persian Gulf. After transiting the Atlantic and Mediterranean, the USS *Cole* led the battle group through the Suez Canal and into the Red Sea. On October 12, while the *Cole* was refueling at the Yemeni port of Aden, a small motorboat packed with 500 pounds of explosives pulled up, unchallenged, along the port side of the destroyer. Two suicide bombers aboard the boat detonated their payload, blowing a 40-by-40-foot hole in the ship's hull and flooding the ship's galley and engineering spaces. The USS *Hawes* and the USS *Donald Cook* arrived soon to assist in the rescue and evacuation of the injured. Seventeen sailors were killed and 39 were injured. The *Cole* narrowly escaped sinking and had to be towed all the way back to the United States for repair.

The *Cole* bombing dashed any illusions the US Navy may have held about its invincibility in the post–Cold War era. It was painful proof of just how vulnerable its warships were to a low-tech suicide attack, despite highly sophisticated sensors and unparalleled firepower. Arleigh Burke–class guided-missile destroyers were designed for deployment in the open ocean against Soviet planes, ships, and submarines. But operating inside narrow gulfs in other countries' territorial waters, where they were hamstrung by politically driven rules of engagement, battleships were almost impossible to defend.

For the Navy, the *Cole* bombing marked a clear escalation in America's tit-for-tat war with Islamic terrorists. Al Qaeda claimed responsibility for the *Cole* attack as revenge for ship-based cruise missiles launched two years earlier against Al Qaeda training camps in Afghanistan—which President Bill Clinton had ordered in retribution for the deadly Al Qaeda attacks on US embassies in Kenya and Tanzania. Al Qaeda's founder, Osama bin Laden, had planned for two years to retaliate against an American cruise missile destroyer, before the USS *Cole* arrived in the Gulf. US Navy and intelligence services girded for the next attack on a soft target, military or civilian.

SEPTEMBER 11, 2001
Smugglers Cove, San Juan Island, Washington

A year after the *Cole* attack—and another year into the snail-paced Navy
and Fisheries investigation of the Bahamas stranding—Balcomb heard the
news of the four hijacked commercial airliners crashing into the Twin Towers, the Pentagon, and a field in Pennsylvania. He understood immediately
that America was at war—a hot war unlike the tense cat-and-mouse drama of
tracking Soviet subs he knew firsthand. Like so many Americans, particularly
veterans, Balcomb had a powerful urge to jump to the defense of his country.
It was instinctive.

He had spent the past year bird-dogging the Navy and Fisheries' joint
investigation. A few weeks after 9/11, he went back to writing letters to politicians and lobbying journalists to keep the forgotten joint inquiry in the news.
Despite his horror at the terrorist attacks, he resolved not to let the Navy
off the hook for the acoustic storm its sonar training exercises continued
to unleash inside whale habitats. Balcomb felt no contradiction between his
patriotism and his conviction that the Navy needed to walk the walk when
it came to its proclaimed commitment to being responsible stewards of the
ocean environment.

DECEMBER 21, 2001
Washington, DC

Eighteen months after announcing their joint investigation, the Navy and
Fisheries released what they titled an "interim report" on their long-delayed
investigation of the Bahamas stranding. Following the time-honored dictum
of Washington politics that the best way to bury a story is to release it after
5:00 on a Friday afternoon, the Navy and Fisheries waited until 5:30 on December 21, 2001—the last day of the federal work year and the beginning of
the Christmas weekend, when virtually the entire news media was heading
out of town on vacation.

Rick Weiss, a science reporter at the *Washington Post* who was working
the Death Valley shift between Christmas and New Year's, found his lead on
page one of the report's executive summary:

"The investigation team concludes that tactical midrange frequency sonars aboard US Navy ships that were in use during the sonar exercises in question were the most plausible source of the acoustic or impulse trauma suffered by the whales."[2]

Weiss didn't have any trouble tracking down Balcomb, who was spending the holiday alone on San Juan Island. For 15 years, he had celebrated Christmas with Diane's family in Eleuthera. But he hadn't been back to the Bahamas since the stranding, and now he was marking his second solo Christmas in Smugglers Cove, the loneliest week of the most solitary stretch of his life.

He spent Christmas Day reading a copy of the Navy and Fisheries' report that Rick Weiss had emailed to him on Christmas Eve. His only Christmas present, Balcomb mused to himself. He accepted the fact that this carefully worded interim report, released in the midst of the Christmas holiday, was the closest to a mea culpa the Navy was likely to offer. It might seem slender satisfaction to a man who had lost so many pieces of his heart to the Bahamas stranding. But Balcomb knew that when you're trying to turn a wheel as big as the US Navy, you should expect to get only a small turn out of it. The Navy's grudging admission of responsibility for the Bahamas stranding may have been a small turn, but it was a turn in the right direction.

Balcomb called Roger Gentry at home and asked him when a final report was likely to be released. Gentry told him, in friendship, not to hold his breath. In all likelihood, there would never be a final report. Gentry made a point of telling Balcomb that if he hadn't stuck it to the Navy, there never would have been even an interim report. He said as much to the *Washington Post* reporter when he called him for comment on the report he'd helped shepherd past legions of Navy and Fisheries lawyers over the past year and a half.

Gentry had agonized while watching the Navy and Fisheries navigate sideways for 18 months to arrive at essentially the same conclusions it had reached three months after the stranding. He had felt for a long time that Balcomb got a bum rap from the Navy, from Fisheries, and from his peers in the research community—including Gentry himself—all of whom had their own reasons for fearing or resenting a whistle-blower in their midst. It relieved Gentry's guilt a bit to tell Rick Weiss that he credited Balcomb for sticking his neck out for the whales.

Balcomb didn't so much mind the personal smears he'd had to endure; he'd fully expected to be attacked from the moment he stepped up to the lectern at the DC press conference. What made him angry, and a bit sad, was the realization that in all likelihood Fisheries would never return the beaked whale heads to him, despite Ketten's promise to him back at Nancy's Restaurant.

After he finished talking to Gentry, Balcomb went back to his computer screen and printed out the entire 58-page report, including full-color acoustic modeling charts that were similar to the ones presented at the closed-door Navy meeting 18 months earlier—the meeting he had been barred from attending.

Beyond the five-page executive summary, the report was written in technical jargon that would be incomprehensible to a lay reader. But for a beaked whale expert and seasoned veteran of antisubmarine warfare like Balcomb, it all made for a deeply immersive read: the details of the forensic evidence from the necropsies,[3] the movements and sonar transmissions of each warship in the battle group, and the elaborate acoustic modeling of how the pressure waves from the sonar moved through the underwater canyon. Taken together, they filled in all the blanks that had remained in his imagination about the Bahamas stranding narrative.

Every day for the past 20 months, Balcomb had speculated on precisely what had transpired that night on the surface of Providence Channel and in the underwater depths of the Great Bahama Canyon. Now, as he studied the acoustic models and the ships' sonar logs, he could visualize the entire drama as it must have unfolded across the northern Bahamas.*

This is what he saw:

MARCH 13, 2000, 1030 HOURS
High above the Southeast Atlantic Coast

Viewed from the Navy's Keyhole spy satellites 30 miles overhead, the *George Washington* battle group looked almost puny as it steamed out of its home

* See map of Navy ship movements and whale strandings in the Bahamas on the back endpaper of this book.

port in Norfolk, Virginia, en route to the Bahamas. The unmanned surveillance planes flying cover at 15,000 feet had a more realistic view of the strike force's scale.

The battle group maintained a defensive formation around its highest-value vessel, the Nimitz-class supercarrier *George Washington*. More than 1,000 feet long and 20 stories high, it housed a crew of 6,000 sailors and 90 aircraft. Escorting the carrier were three destroyers, the *Cole*, the *Caron*, and the *Donald Cook;* and two guided-missile frigates, the *Hawes* and the *Simpson*. Each warship was longer than a football field and armed with the latest cannons, missiles, torpedoes, radar, and sonar. For added antisubmarine reach, each destroyer had a Seahawk helicopter parked on its back deck. And this was merely the visible portion of the battle group. Six hundred feet below the sea's surface, two fast-attack submarines scouted ahead for enemy submersibles.

This war game was the battle group's dress rehearsal before it could be certified battle ready for its scheduled deployment to the Persian Gulf in July. As the group entered Bahamian waters, its commander received his final battle problem:

"Intel indicates there are two enemy submarines hiding out somewhere in the underwater canyon below Northwest Providence Channel; search and sanitize this choke point so that the carrier can transit safely through it."

The war game's goal was to replicate real-world battle conditions and to stress the battle-group crews with as many unknowns as possible. The narrow, deep-water passage through the Bahamas resembled the Strait of Gibraltar and the Strait of Hormuz, which the battle group would soon be transiting en route to the Persian Gulf. Two hunter-killer submarines from another strike group were playing the role of enemy targets.

Nothing about the training exercises was simulated except the live fire of "target acquisition." Search, detection, classification, and targeting were performed under actual battle conditions. The final measure of the group's combat readiness was simple: Could it find and kill the enemy submarines before coming under attack?

MARCH 15, 2000, ZERO HOURS (MIDNIGHT)
Northeast Providence Channel, the Bahamas

As the battle group entered Providence Channel between Eleuthera and Abaco Islands, the squadron commander directed all battle crews to switch over to encrypted communication. With only a slender new moon hanging over the channel, the squadron began its search for the two enemy submarines lurking somewhere in the 20-mile-wide-by-100-mile-long canyon.

Locating silent and stationary submarines is extremely difficult, even with a broad spectrum of sensors. The cloak of darkness gives the submarines an added advantage. In daylight and in calm seas, a surveillance plane can make out the subtle surface wake from a submerged submarine—if the sub is moving. The squadron commander understood that the only way to locate enemy subs in the dark was to light up the channel with whatever acoustic sensors he could bring to bear.

He radioed the destroyers *Cole* and *Donald Cook*—using their call signs "Fox" and "Zebra"—to dispatch their helicopters up and over the top and lay a "picket fence" of passive sound buoys on both sides of the advancing battle group.

The choppers released their sonobuoys 300 feet above the water. A small parachute slowed the sonobuoys' descent before they splashed down and sank to a depth of 20 feet before leveling off. The Seahawks continued dropping sonobuoys at two-mile intervals until the fence was complete. If the passive sound buoys picked up a potential target, the Seahawks could lower their active dipping sonar by a cable and get a more precise fix before launching their antisubmarine torpedoes.

Miles ahead of the surface ships and 700 feet below them, the battle group's two escort subs advanced along their preassigned search paths. To protect themselves from friendly fire, the hunter-killer subs made sure to stay inside the sonobuoy picket lines. Submarines are the most effective passive sonar platform for detecting other submarines because they can search at variable depths, and they emit very little noise that can clutter the sound field. In good conditions, a submarine can hear another sub's movement within 50 miles, about twice the listening range of a sonobuoy.

But passive sonar has a fundamental limitation: it can hear an enemy sub only when it's moving. If a submarine is hiding motionless along a canyon wall, 600 feet below the surface, the only way to "see" it is with active sonar. Of course, the squadron commander knew that once the destroyers and frigates turned on their active sonar, they would be broadcasting their location to the enemy submarines, making them easy torpedo targets. But he also knew that only a suicidal submarine—or a sub that had been detected and feared attack—would fire on a warship in a battle group. If he located an enemy sub, the commander would have a brief interval to decide whether to take defensive countermeasures or attack.

The commander ordered the two frigates to turn on their omnidirectional active sonar and proceed between the picket fence of sonobuoys in a zigzag pattern, creating a moving search field. The destroyers followed five miles behind the frigates, advancing in a straight line down the middle of the channel, sweeping their directional active sonar beams at different depths and frequencies than the frigates'.

The sonar transmitters mounted on the front hull of the warships emitted a "ping" every 24 seconds. But it only sounded like a "ping" from inside the ship. In the water, each "ping" created a pressure wave of 230- to 240-decibel sound that hurtled through the channel at a mile per second—five times the speed of sound in air.

Ordinarily, the decibel level dropped off geometrically as the sound moved away from the ship. But that night in the channel, a stronger than normal surface duct of warm water trapped the sound energy in the upper 500 feet of the channel, focusing the sound the way a Fresnel lens amplifies a lighthouse beam in air. Meanwhile, other sonar sound waves angled toward the steep canyon walls before bouncing back toward the ships. Minute by minute, mile by mile, the choke point canyon filled with reverberating sound.

The sonar supervisor's display panel alerted him that the active sonar on one of the frigates had detected two moving objects near the surface. Shipboard radar had also made a contact. The undersea warfare evaluator radioed the ensign stationed on the deck of the *Hawes*. "Possible submarine contact bearing zero-two-niner, range five hundred feet. Confidence low. Can you provide visual confirmation?"

The ensign swiveled his tripod-mounted "big-eye" binoculars 12 degrees to his left and scanned the surface, which appeared in grainy green through the night vision scope. A moment earlier, he might have spotted two beaked whales surfacing to breathe. But by the time he panned across the horizon line, they had already ducked back under the water, leaving barely a ripple in their wake.

"Negative visual confirmation at zero-two-niner," the ensign radioed back. "Continuing to scan."

As soon as the whales descended for their hunting dive, they were buffeted by a pressure wave from the frigate's sweeping sonar. They quickly rolled away from the sound and retracted their small pectoral fins into concealed pockets in their flanks. With their drag reduced, they fluked downward through the water column, absorbing the oxygen from their lungs into their blood and muscle tissue.

At 200 feet, the water pressure compressed their lungs and contracted their hyperflexible rib cages. With their buoyancy reduced and their fuselage further streamlined, the whales stopped fluking and glided downward like birds falling through the air, conserving energy as they plummeted through the water.[4]

At 500 feet, the whales slowed down their heartbeat and diverted blood from skeletal muscles to the brain and heart muscles, which require steady oxygenation. To cope with the increasingly intense pressure of the water column, the whales continuously calibrated the pressure of the air sacs in their ears and sinuses.

At 600 feet, the whales entered the twilight zone and began to hunt for squid. Four miles to the east, one of the "enemy" subs hovered motionless along the east canyon wall, listening to the sonar clicks of the beaked whales seeking prey and the chirp-and-bark patter they used to stay in contact with each other.

In the target-rich environment below 1,000 feet—well beneath submarine depth now—the whales deployed a click-buzz sonar pattern to locate and capture their prey. In search mode, the whales emitted two midrange clicks a second that cast a narrow-focused signal, like a flashlight beam. To increase their search field, the whales rolled in a spiral pattern as they descended, turning their heads from side to side. Once a whale indentified a desired target by its echo profile—not too big, not too small, not too spiny—it homed in on its prey with a high-frequency buzz pattern of 250 to 300 clicks per second, approached to within a meter of its prey, and then sucked the squid into its mouth.

After ingesting squid for the next half hour, and with the lactic acid from oxygen debt building up in their tissue, the whales began their ascent to the surface. By ascending slowly and gradually, decompressing in sync with the decreasing hydrostatic pressure, they could reabsorb nitrogen back into their bloodstream. If they ascended too quickly, the nitrogen could form painful and potentially lethal bubbles in their muscle tissue and fat. Normally, on returning to the surface, the whales would make a half dozen shallow recovery dives to allow the dissolved nitrogen in their blood to diffuse into the lungs, and the accumulated lactic acid in their muscle tissue to slowly absorb back into their bloodstream—much the way that marathon runners walk off their oxygen debt and lactic acid buildup after finishing a race.

But on this night, nothing was normal. At 500 feet below the surface, the ascending whales collided against a ceiling of sound waves trapped in the surface duct of warm water. Instinctively, they dove back down to where the pressure waves were less intense. They tried to gather intelligence from other whales in their pod, but all their normal communication frequencies were jammed with intense, head-rattling pressure waves that pounded the tiny air pockets inside their sinuses and ears. They couldn't distinguish their own panicked calls from those of the whales around them, couldn't find the early-morning light above the water's surface, couldn't tell up from down. They were drowning in sound.

The whales that couldn't penetrate the surface duct of funneled noise were overcome by oxygen debt and a lethal buildup of lactic acid. Without air in their lungs, their bodies surrendered to free fall, and they swooned downward through the perpetual darkness of the midnight zone, finally settling four miles below on the canyon floor, alongside the bones of their ancestors.

Some of the whales were able to fight their way through the surface duct to the open air. But then the oxygen in their lungs competed for absorption with the nitrogen bubbling in their blood and tissue. There seemed to be no escape from the acoustic storm—except the shallow shelf beyond the canyon walls.

A female Blainville's separated from her hunting party, fluking frantically away from the hammering noise in the canyon. The water turned warm and shallow, and though her ears still pounded, she could steer by the sunlight that shimmered off the white sand bottom. She was too tired to avoid the clusters of sharp-edged coral that sprouted up around her.

She didn't see the shark until after it hit her tail and circled away through the reddening water. The whale turned to flee back toward the canyon. The shark hit her again, higher up on her trunk this time. Another shark darted in and retreated, its jaws filled with flesh.

Five miles away, another whale fled from the sound storm in the canyon. As he entered the shallows, he was disoriented by the warmth of the water and the unfamiliar sight of sand beneath him. His head ached, and his eyes stung from the bright sun. When he felt his belly lodge against the sandy bottom, he tried to break free. But his fluking only drove his belly deeper into the sand.

He could hear waves lapping on the beach nearby, but it wasn't a sound he recognized or understood. He couldn't see anything but the glare reflecting off the white sand, couldn't feel anything but the sun baking his back and the blood running hot in his veins.

A shape moved through the water nearby. It loomed above him, blocking the sun, and then lowered itself into the water beside him. The whale felt something gentle touch his head, just behind the blowhole.

"What in the world are you doing here?" Balcomb murmured, as much to himself as to the whale.

PART FOUR
WHALES V. NAVY

This is a court of law, young man, not a court of justice.

—Oliver Wendell Holmes Jr.,
U.S. Supreme Court Justice; 1902–1932

BELUGA or WHITE WHALE.

Southern Right-Whale Dolphin (*Lissodelphis peronii*)

24

God and Country v. the Whales

DECEMBER 31, 2001
Los Angeles Office of NRDC

On the day before the new year, a holiday, Joel Reynolds was the only person working in NRDC's Los Angeles office. He was never eager to leave his family during Christmas vacation. But he felt an urgency to get a head start on the battle that he knew was looming. The *Washington Post* was spread open on his desk to Rick Weiss' article about the Navy and Fisheries' interim report:

WHALES' DEATHS LINKED TO NAVY'S SONAR TESTS

December 31, 2001: Washington, DC

The mysterious mass stranding of 16 whales in the Bahamas in March 2000 was caused by U.S. Navy tests in which intense underwater sounds were generated for 16 hours, according to a newly released government report compiled by civilian and military scientists.

The report's conclusions mark the first time that underwater noise other than from an explosion has been shown to cause fatal trauma in marine mammals. The military's acknowledgment of responsibility also marks a sharp departure from earlier statements by the Navy, which had denied responsibility for the Bahamian beachings and other mass strandings of marine mammals that coincided with sonar exercises.

Experts said the study—which relied on an elaborate airlift of frozen whale heads from the Bahamas to a Harvard Medical School X-ray facility—places the Navy on notice that it will have to balance more carefully its need to conduct underwater sonar tests against the need to protect marine mammals. The report, approved by Navy Secretary Gordon R. England, concludes that the Navy should "put into place mitigation measures that will protect animals to the maximum extent practical" during peacetime training and research efforts.

But the report also allows for the suspension of such protections in the interest of "national security," a broad exemption that has yet to be defined in practice. And it does not answer the contentious question of whether marine wildlife may also be imperiled by a different kind of sonar test proposed by the Navy, one that would involve much lower-frequency sound waves in the ocean. . . .

The cause of death in the Bahamian strandings may have remained unsettled had it not been for Ken Balcomb, who with his wife, Diane Claridge, ran the *Bahamas Marine Mammal Survey* on the Bahamian island of Abaco. . . .

"There's no question that these tactical midrange sonars were the sound source that caused the trauma," said Roger Gentry, who heads the acoustical research team for the National Marine Fisheries Service, an agency of the National Oceanic and Atmospheric Administration.

Navy spokesman Patrick McNally said the Navy believes that the injuries were caused by the unique characteristics of Bahamian underwater topography and other factors, and that similar tests may still be appropriate in other waters. Meanwhile, the Navy is instituting new policies to prevent such injuries, he said, and will increase funding of marine mammal research to $9 million in the coming year.

It was the final line of the article that jumped out at Reynolds:

> The Navy is expected to get federal permission to conduct tests of a low-frequency sonar system early next year—permission that environmental groups have promised to fight.

As one of the environmentalists who had "promised to fight" the Navy's low-frequency sonar systems, Reynolds had no trouble reading between the lines of the Navy spokesman's remarks. "The Navy believes that the injuries were caused by the unique characteristics of Bahamian underwater topography" was the Navy's way of trying to put the Bahamas stranding into an "act of God" category that would never recur. "Similar tests may still be appropriate in other waters" was code for "We intend to continue to conduct training exercises where and when we see fit."

For Reynolds, it was the worst possible time to consider filing a lawsuit against the US Navy. No matter how incriminating the interim report might appear, he knew that the recently transformed political landscape had strengthened the Navy's hand immeasurably. Three months earlier, immediately following the 9/11 attacks, President George W. Bush had launched the war on terror. American armed forces were deployed across Afghanistan and the Persian Gulf, and every American embassy and military base around the world was on high alert. In October the US Senate had voted 98–1 to pass the Patriot Act—an acronym for Providing Appropriate Tools Required to Intercept and Obstruct Terrorism—which dramatically expanded the government's power to gather intelligence abroad and at home.

To a degree that Reynolds had never witnessed in his lifetime, American citizens were united by fraught bonds of fear, anger, and patriotism. American flags were on display everywhere, and "America the Beautiful" became the new national anthem, kicking off every NFL football game. For the first time since World War II, the vast majority of Americans embraced a foreign war and the soldiers and sailors fighting overseas. In deference to the prevalent patriotic mood, NRDC—and virtually every other advocacy organization—had suspended communications and direct mail that targeted federal agencies, including the military.

As if to highlight its "all hands on deck" approach to the war on terror, the Navy had redeployed its dolphin mine-clearing unit to the Persian Gulf for the first time since the 1980s. And it wasn't being bashful about it.

"For thousands of years, man has made use of the capabilities of animals; their strength, extraordinary senses, swimming or flying ability," wrote the public affairs spokesman for the Navy Marine Mammal Program in the *Stars and Stripes* newspaper. "Dolphins are naturally suited to perform undersea jobs that would be far more time-consuming and dangerous for human divers." In the same article, Commodore Brian May of the British navy invoked the deity on behalf of the dolphin deployment: "The Lord God decided to give the dolphin the best sonar ability ever devised. We can only aspire to their ability."

The Humane Society and People for the Ethical Treatment of Animals (PETA) denounced the use of dolphins in war zones and appealed to Secretary of Defense Donald Rumsfeld to withdraw them from the Gulf. But their protests bounced harmlessly off the Navy, which was running with the winds of war at its back, its sights trained on defending against better-armed and more-threatening adversaries.

Reynolds was content to let the animal rights and humane groups agitate in the media. He needed to concentrate on a legal strategy to deny the Navy a permit to unleash LFA sonar around the globe.

In April the Navy applied to Fisheries for a five-year permit to operate LFA sonar in 80 percent of the world's oceans—everywhere except in the Arctic and Antarctic Oceans. Three months later, Fisheries granted the Navy permission to deploy its sonar in 75 percent of the oceans, excluding only a waterway circling the Antarctic and a handful of marine sanctuaries in the South Pacific.

Reynolds wasn't surprised. He knew that federal regulators face an inherent conflict of interest when policing other federal agencies—and that Fisheries in particular had a history of accommodating the Navy's requests. That's why nongovernmental watchdogs like NRDC were created in the first place.

After seven years of auditing the Navy's every move on LFA sonar, it was time for Reynolds to either play his hand or fold it. And he didn't like his hand. Lawsuits, he had learned, are a crapshoot. You could have a good case and draw a bad judge. Even with a strong case and a good judge, there is always the risk of a bad outcome. Considering the country's preoccupation with defending against another terrorist attack—and in light of how much time and money the Navy had spent preparing its Environmental Impact Statement—this didn't feel to Reynolds like a strong case to take to court.

He would have preferred to sit down with the Navy and try to work out a settlement. But that wasn't an option. Navy General Counsel Steve Honigman had been replaced by a Bush-appointed successor who clearly wasn't interested in engaging with NRDC. Meanwhile, Reynolds had spent seven years mobilizing marine biologists and NRDC members to confront a threat to whales that—as the *Washington Post* reporter had noted—he'd promised to fight. If NRDC didn't go to court to contest the permit that Fisheries had issued, it would concede the Navy's right to flood every ocean on the planet with high-intensity sound regardless of its impact on whales.

In anticipation of litigation, Reynolds and his team had spent much of the winter preparing. After enlisting a roster of local, national, and international conservation groups as co-plaintiffs,[1] they needed to assemble a legal and scientific team equal to the challenge of a major litigation battle with the Navy, Fisheries, and the US Department of Justice.

In April he traveled to San Francisco to discuss the case with a friend, former Justice Department trial lawyer who had joined the law firm of Morrison & Foerster. In addition to adding some muscle to his legal team, working with corporate firms enhanced NRDC's credibility with conservative judges. By the end of the day, he had successfully recruited the firm to join forces with NRDC on a pro bono basis. Andrew Sabey, a partner with a good courtroom manner who specialized in environmental litigation on behalf of developers, was assigned to lead the law firm's team.

With co-plaintiffs and co-counsel in place, all Reynolds needed was a winning legal strategy. In addition to the adverse political climate, his biggest problem was the lack of legal precedent for defending marine mammals against acoustic threats. Congress passed the Noise Pollution and Abatement Act of 1972 to protect human health and minimize public annoyance from noise pollution in the air and on land. But the legal concept of noise pollution had never before been applied to the oceans. And no one had ever framed noise pollution or acoustic trauma as a threat to animals under the Endangered Species Act or as "harassment" of marine mammals under the Marine Mammal Protection Act. If he hoped to make his case to a federal judge, Reynolds would have to break new legal ground, which always reduced the odds of success.

He had other steep hills to climb. The Navy had spent seven years and $10 million building a science-based case for Low Frequency Active sonar as a low-risk antisubmarine weapon. For the first time, the Navy had agreed to abandon its pro forma Environmental Assessments and conduct a comprehensive Environmental Impact Statement. Its centerpiece was a three-part scientific research program co-directed by the country's two leading bioacousticians, Chris Clark and Peter Tyack. Judges understood the law, not marine science, so Reynolds couldn't expect to prevail by contesting the Navy's scientific experts on a topic as complex as marine acoustics.

Finally, and most problematic for Reynolds, there was the time-honored doctrine of judges deferring to the military in disputes that bear on national security, even in peacetime. If Reynolds hoped to persuade a federal judge to rule against the Navy in the middle of an international war on terror, he'd have to present a compelling rationale.

Reynolds had developed a number of arguments to level the playing field and enable a judge to uphold the interests of whales over the Navy's. One of those was the precautionary principle, embedded in the Marine Mammal Protection Act. When that law was drafted in 1972, there was considerable uncertainty about which human activities threatened the survival of whales and other marine mammals. Whaling and wild capture posed obvious mortal threats. So did underwater explosions, which is why ship shock had been a relatively straightforward case to win. But there were other, less understood dangers, such as toxic contamination of habitats, and industrial and commercial development. Given the precarious state of marine mammal populations, the Marine Mammal Protection Act directed judges and regulators, in close cases, to resolve doubts about credible but unproven threats *in favor of marine mammals*. Acoustic threats to marine mammals were not yet recognized, much less understood, when the law was drafted. Thirty years later, there were still more questions than answers about the impact of high-intensity sound on whales and other marine life.

Never before had the Navy sought and received approval for so sweeping an activity on a global scale. Reynolds planned to highlight how the permit violated legal limitations on geographic range, numbers of animals affected, and overall impact on individual species. None of these limitations, in his view, would impair the Navy's national security mission, and he was careful to craft his arguments to underline that point. He understood that to succeed in court, he would have to persuade the judge that environmental compliance and national defense were compatible objectives.

Reynolds had spent enough time in front of judges to understand that beneath their robes and honorific titles, they were individuals. Their job was to interpret the law, but their legal decisions were inevitably informed by their emotions, politics, and personality—particularly in a case like this one, pitting national security against the marine environment.

The one concern shared by all judges was the credibility of the evidence presented. To make his case, Reynolds would have to show "arbitrary and capricious" disregard for the permitting process by the Navy and Fisheries, a high legal standard of proof. But to convince a judge to issue an injunction to prevent the deployment of LFA sonar, Reynolds needed to cast doubt on the Navy's fundamental contention that it posed no danger to whales.

The Bahamas stranding, which the Navy's own interim report admitted was likely caused by sonar, upended all of the Navy's carefully calibrated algorithms that "proved" the safety of high-intensity, low-frequency sound. Reynolds hoped to show how the Bahamas stranding made a mockery of the "safe buffer zones" and "allowable decibel thresholds" that the Navy proposed for LFA sonar. Reynolds had solicited the assistance of a number of scientific experts to make this case, including Hal Whitehead and Naomi Rose. But one, in particular, was central to this line of attack, because he was the only expert *eyewitness* to the Bahamas stranding: Ken Balcomb.

Balcomb's academic credentials couldn't compete with those of Navy experts such as Chris Clark and Peter Tyack. But he was a Navy-trained acoustician and an acknowledged beaked whale specialist who had witnessed the stranding and preserved the crucial evidence trail. And perhaps most significantly, Balcomb had challenged the Navy's initial denial of the role of sonar in the event. The interim report vindicated Balcomb's assertions and made Fisheries look more like a lapdog than a watchdog.

Reynolds fully expected Fisheries and the Navy to argue that evidence from the Bahamas investigation was irrelevant to LFA sonar. As the executive summary of their interim report stated clearly: "Low Frequency Active, another Navy sonar, had no involvement in this event." High-intensity sonar may have caused the mass stranding in the Bahamas, the report conceded, but that was a different kind of high-intensity sonar operating in "unique" waters. Reynolds had encountered this tactic of "compartmentalization" before, during his seven-year fight to keep PG&E from bringing its Diablo Canyon nuclear power plant online. Yes, there was a partial core meltdown at Three Mile Island, PG&E admitted, but that was a *Babcock & Wilcox* reactor. Our *Westinghouse* reactors are *safe* nuclear technology.

Reynolds believed that he didn't have to prove that low-frequency sonar was as dangerous to whales as the midfrequency sonar used in the Bahamas. He simply needed to use Balcomb's eyewitness account to amplify the judge's doubts about the safety of the Navy's new sonar system. What Reynolds couldn't predict was how a judge would weigh Balcomb's testimony against the expert scientists and highly decorated fleet commanders that the Navy would bring to court. Assuming, of course, that Balcomb was willing to testify.

Balcomb had no hesitation about working with NRDC on its sonar lawsuit. He wanted to help publicize the interim report's findings, since, as Gentry predicted, there was no final report in the offing, and the Navy and Fisheries had succeeded in burying their interim report in the news graveyard of New Year's Eve. He welcomed the chance to testify in an open courtroom, rather than at a press conference or in a closed-door agency meeting.

On a personal level, collaborating on a high-impact legal case offered Balcomb a way to reconnect with his father, who'd spent his legal career trying water rights cases in Colorado, including a successful argument before the US Supreme Court. Balcomb hoped that his father might finally signal his approval, or at least his acknowledgment that his son's obsessive chase after whales had finally added up to something.

By 2002, "Blue" Balcomb had retired and moved into a creekside home in Arizona. Father and son met over lunch in the dining room of a local golf course. Though now in his eighties, with bad knees and a heart condition, Blue still had a piercing gaze and an upright posture.

While sipping their soup, they shared notes on how much the Southwest had changed in the 50 years since they'd each moved away. Over dessert, Balcomb told his father about the written declaration he'd prepared for NRDC's lawsuit and the oral testimony he planned to give in court. He explained the sonar case as best he could, though his legal lexicon was limited, and he struggled to answer some of his father's questions about the relevant statutes at issue. Balcomb showed him copies of the interim report and the *Bahamas Journal* article, which Blue flipped through while he finished his fruit cup. Then he stacked the documents in a neat pile and pushed them back across the table.

"I know you're trying to do a good thing," Blue said, shaking his head, "but you're on the wrong side of this fight. God and country come first."

Balcomb wanted to ask him what God had to do with it. He wanted to remind his father that he wasn't the only one who'd served his country in uniform. Instead, he appealed to Blue's respect for due process, for equal justice under the law, even for legally protected wildlife. Surely he didn't think the Navy was above the law. No one was.

"The law isn't the point," Blue insisted, tapping the table for emphasis with the butt of his spoon. "Not during wartime." If Ken really cared about justice, Blue said, he'd get off the Navy's back and let it do its job, which was to hunt down the bastards who'd attacked America on its own soil. They crashed a passenger plane into the Pentagon, for chrissakes!

Balcomb started to explain about the whales that had beached in the Bahamas; about all the whales that had never been seen again after the sonar exercises. When his father just stared back at him and shook his head, Balcomb realized that he'd come on a fool's errand. He should have known better than to expect a former Marine and lifelong hard-ass like Blue to put his son before his conservative politics. Before God and country.

Balcomb steered the conversation back to neutral ground. He didn't want to end this visit, perhaps their last, with an argument. They talked about Arizona's new baseball team, the Diamondbacks, who had beaten the Yankees in the World Series the previous fall. Blue said the D-backs would have to trade for a better relief pitcher if they hoped to make the playoffs this season, and Balcomb said he was probably right. When he said he needed to be heading out, Blue thanked him for making the trip. Balcomb collected his papers, shook his father's hand, and said good-bye.

Reynolds and his team canceled or cut short their summer vacations. They sprinted through July and early August, working nights and weekends to complete their complaint and accompanying motion for an injunction, including a 100-page brief and thousands of pages of supporting declarations and exhibits.

On August 8, 2002, they filed suit against Fisheries and the Navy on behalf of NRDC and its co-plaintiffs, asking the court to reject the Fisheries permit as illegal and to issue a preliminary injunction to prevent the Navy from deploying Low Frequency Active sonar. Reynolds decided to file in San Francisco, where he calculated their chances were greatest to draw a sympathetic judge.

It was still a game of chance. Of all the variables that can determine the success or failure of a lawsuit, none may be more crucial than the judge assigned to hear the case. And nothing better embodies the unpredictable outcome of litigation than "the wheel." In a tradition dating back to colonial times most federal courts assign judges to cases by spinning a wheel—or, more precisely, turning a solid wooden box with a crank, like a bingo cage— before withdrawing a sealed envelope with the name of one of the judges on the court's panel.

NRDC drew Magistrate Judge Elizabeth Laporte on the wheel. As soon as Reynolds heard the news, he dug into Judge Laporte's background. She had a reputation as ideologically moderate, smart, thorough, and fair minded. He knew their case presented difficult legal issues, so he was glad to have a judge who would be focused on the law rather than on politics. Before becoming a magistrate, Laporte had been a partner in a private law firm and then ran the tobacco unit in San Francisco's Office of the City Attorney. Reynolds felt good about her background, reasoning that she had litigation experience in matters of scientific complexity, presented through expert testimony. And perhaps it wouldn't hurt that she was once a summer associate at Sabey's firm, Morrison & Foerster.

Judge Laporte promptly scheduled the court hearing in San Francisco for October 18, with briefs due by the middle of September.

Then, just weeks before the hearing—not long after Reynolds and his team had submitted their opening brief—another population of beaked whales washed ashore 6,000 miles from California.

SEPTEMBER 24, 2002
Canary Islands, Spain

Early-rising tourists on the islands of Lanzarote and Fuerteventura emerged from their cabanas to find 14 beaked whales stranded on the shore. Throughout the day, the vacationers did their best to shield the whales from the sun and keep them hydrated with wet towels. But by sunset, all the whales had died on the beach.

Clearly visible on the horizon were dozens of NATO warships from member nations participating in joint naval exercises. The archipelago of volcanic islands off the Atlantic coast of Morocco was a frequent site for sonar trainings by NATO and Spanish navies. As in the Bahamas, the steeply sloped underwater canyon abutting the Canary Islands provided an ideal setting for antisubmarine "choke point" sweeps. Between 1985 and 1991, there had been four mass strandings of beaked whales in the Canary Islands, all in close proximity to naval exercises using antisubmarine sonar.

Researchers from the nearby Veterinary School of the University of Las Palmas collected the heads and organs from six of the whales as soon as they died. In addition to bleeding around their brains and ears, the necropsies revealed lesions in their livers, lungs, and kidneys, as well as nitrogen bubbles in their organ tissue—classic symptoms of the bends, a rapid-decompression syndrome that marine biologists had previously believed beaked whales were immune to, due to their specialized evolution for deep diving.

The *New York Times* reported the strandings and the necropsy findings of ear and brain damage "consistent with acoustic trauma." Asked to comment, the spokesman for the US Navy contingent at the exercises said, "It would be inappropriate to speculate on the cause of the stranding."

The findings from the Canary Islands strandings would eventually lead to strict limits on sonar exercises in the Canary Islands and Mediterranean waters. Back in California, in the run-up to the sonar hearing, Reynolds could only hope that the media coverage of the stranding reached Judge Laporte's chambers, where she and her clerks were poring over the opposing legal briefs.

Common Dolphin (*Delphinus delphis*)

25

"It Is So Ordered"

On October 17, the day before the hearing, Reynolds, Jasny, and Wetzler decamped to Morrison & Foerster's San Francisco office, where they were joined by Andrew Sabey and his team of associates for a full-day run-through of the oral argument. As a seasoned courtroom litigator with the establishment credentials of a large corporate firm, Sabey seemed to Reynolds like the best choice to lead off. He also understood that pro bono attorneys need some tangible incentive for donating their time and their firm's resources to a case.

After an hour of moot court rehearsal, Reynolds saw that Sabey was lost. Instead of focusing on the legal requirements of the statutes and the agencies' failure to meet them, he began his argument with a dramatic recitation of the physical harm sonar might cause and an attack on the Navy's science. And he wasn't clear on the provisions of the various environmental laws around which their legal briefs had been constructed. Whatever deference Reynolds had previously shown toward his pro bono co-counsel quickly evaporated.

After seven years of painstaking preparation and careful development of their most compelling legal case, no way was he going to let someone fumble it at the goal line—not when their only hope for success lay in flawless execution.

"This isn't going to work," Reynolds told Sabey during a break. "If we spend our limited time during the hearing arguing the science, we lose. Let the other side wander in that wilderness. We can only win if we keep the judge focused on the Navy's and Fisheries' failure to meet the statutory requirements for the permit."

Reynolds drilled Sabey repeatedly on the talking points he needed to highlight from their brief: the legal limits on "small numbers" of animals that can be harmed, "specified geographic regions" where sonar can be deployed, and "practicable mitigation" to reduce risk to marine mammals. They then ran Andrew Wetzler, NRDC's expert on the Endangered Species Act, through similar paces, peppering him with questions about alleged violations of that federal statute. By the end of the day, Reynolds felt confident that both Sabey and Wetzler were on message.

When Balcomb arrived in San Francisco that afternoon, Reynolds explained to him why his written declarations and oral testimony were crucial to making their case. As a former Navy sonar officer with decades of experience studying beaked whales, Ken's firsthand description of the Bahamas strandings would make a strong impression on the judge.

Balcomb's testimony would also draw attention to the Navy's exclusion of beaked whales from its safety studies for LFA sonar. Beaked whales were the species most clearly at risk from military sonar, including during the Greek stranding where LFA sonar *had* been deployed. If beaked whales were the most vulnerable of all whales, why had the Navy studied only LFA sonar's impact on grays, blues, and humpbacks?

Reynolds listened to Balcomb rehearse his description of the broad distribution of beaked whales across the global range of the Navy permit. He was clear and precise, but Reynolds wanted him to have a visual presentation prop. Late in the afternoon, he and Balcomb hurried down the street to the Rand McNally store, just before closing time, and bought the largest world map it had.

That evening, Balcomb moved all the furniture into the corner of his hotel room and unfurled the map across the floor. Late into the night, he crawled around the edges of the map, hand marking every known beaked whale community in the coastal waters of every continent in the world.

OCTOBER 18, 2002, 9:00 A.M.
United States District Court, Northern District of California,
San Francisco

The sonar hearing was held in a small federal courtroom near the Civic Center in downtown San Francisco. Animal rights groups had planned to stage a protest outside the courthouse, but Reynolds persuaded them to call it off. He didn't want anything to distract the media or the judge from his carefully prepared legal case.

When Reynolds and his team arrived, the courtroom was already crowded with uniformed military personnel, research scientists from inside and outside the Navy, and lawyers from the Department of Justice, the Navy, and Fisheries. Though there were a handful of friendly faces from NRDC's San Francisco office, it was hard for Reynolds not to feel outnumbered by the opposition. Apart from his co-counsel, he was accompanied only by Balcomb and Naomi Rose. He had several science experts available by speakerphone if the judge wanted to ask them questions about their written declarations. But Balcomb would be his only witness to testify in person.

As was his custom, Reynolds walked over to greet the opposing counsel. When any federal agency is sued, attorneys from the Department of Justice typically represent them in court. Reynolds introduced himself to the two women lawyers from Justice, but the Navy and Fisheries lawyers hung back in a group. Reynolds lingered to say hello to the researchers he'd come to know well over the previous years: Gentry, Gisiner, Clark, Tyack, and others. Reynolds' geniality usually succeeded in defusing some of the tension that builds up between legal adversaries. But the energy in this courtroom was tense.

When he approached Darlene Ketten, she took his hand and smiled up at him, almost mischievously. "I'm going to bury you," she said in a stage whisper. Reynolds tried to laugh it off. He didn't know whether she was being serious or flippant. But he'd had enough encounters with Ketten over the years to know that her demeanor could shift quickly and unpredictably from charming to antagonistic, or from chilly to accusatory. He also knew that in the two years since the Bahamas stranding, she'd often had to respond to hostile questions about the length and secrecy of her investigation. She complained to her colleagues about the time it had taken away from her other research, and that some of her funders now viewed her as "radioactive." She felt as though she'd been treated like a chew toy by her antagonists in the conservation community and on Capitol Hill. And she never forgave Balcomb for releasing forensic evidence to the public before she'd completed her investigation.

The judge's law clerk strode into the courtroom bearing a large stack of briefing binders and exhibits that he deposited on the judge's desk. Everyone rose as Judge Laporte entered carrying her own armload of document binders. When she set her stack of papers alongside the other documents, Reynolds could see that each of the binders was flagged with color-coded tabs.

Laporte was a petite, middle-aged woman with a no-nonsense haircut and glasses. She acknowledged the crowd with a nod. "Why don't we all sit down and get started," she said.

Reynolds had appeared before all kinds of judges over the years. Brilliant legal scholars, not-so-smart political hacks, respectful inquisitors, bullies and blowhards who liked to intimidate from the bench, and silent ciphers who kept you guessing. Laporte reminded him of the organized and buttoned-up law professors who always came to class prepared to teach, not to tell entertaining stories. As soon as the judge began her opening remarks, it was clear that she had done her homework over the past six weeks. She had an impressive command of all the briefs, as well as the statutes and regulations at issue.

At the outset, she expressed several of her concerns about the legality of the permit and explained that she wanted to use this one-day hearing to answer a list of questions she'd compiled. Reynolds was pleased to hear her make cautionary reference to the Bahamas stranding, as well as the recent stranding in the Canary Islands, which she said she wanted to hear more about from the expert witnesses. She invited both sides to present their arguments, but asked them not to rehash their briefs, saying she'd already studied them carefully.

Sabey led off for the plaintiffs, summarizing the points of law that he and Reynolds had agreed on. He quickly established rapport with the judge, watching her reactions to his line of reasoning, responding to her questions directly when she interrupted with a query, and then seamlessly returning to the thread of his argument. Sabey, and then Wetzler, took aim at the safeguards the permit proposed: a 12-mile coastal exclusion zone, a 180-decibel threshold for harm to marine mammals, visual surveillance for marine mammals from ships. After whittling away at the efficacy of these measures, they turned to Balcomb to topple them.

Balcomb was sitting in the front row of the gallery with his enormous map rolled into a tight cylinder, pointed skyward like a ship's mast. He came forward to be sworn in, and then introduced himself to the judge as "someone familiar with both the sound and the whale side of this discussion." After describing his seven years of service in Navy sound surveillance, he stated, "I do not dispute for a moment the Navy's need for this sonar system. Nor do I dispute that training is necessary. I *do* dispute that one hundred eighty decibels is a safe level of acoustic energy for any marine mammal, certainly in the case of beaked whales. I dispute that the numbers of 'takes' at levels below one hundred eighty decibels are negligible and small. And I dispute that the mitigation methods and the areas authorized are adequate to protect marine mammals."

Reynolds had seen Balcomb speak only at their joint press conference, where he'd addressed a roomful of reporters in the glare of television lights. Balcomb was much more at ease talking one on one with Judge Laporte. He was soft-spoken but authoritative, polite but firm in his opinions. Balcomb walked the judge through the Navy's own acoustic modeling of the Bahamas stranding, explaining how the battle group created a force field of sound that was lethal to whales at distances of hundreds, not dozens, of miles and at sound levels well below 180 decibels. Watching the judge react to Balcomb's narration of the Bahamas stranding, Reynolds was reminded of the persuasive power of expert and compelling eyewitness testimony.

Next, Balcomb explained how Jim Mead's historical analysis of beaked whale strandings showed that the Bahamas incident was part of a consistent pattern of mass strandings during sonar exercises—not an anomaly, as the Navy claimed. The recent Canary Islands stranding, he pointed out, was just the latest example of how deadly high-intensity sonar could be to beaked whales.

When Balcomb struggled to unfurl his oversized map to its full breadth,

Wetzler and Jasny stepped forward to hold it open while he spoke. Balcomb showed the judge how beaked whales, which the Navy had excluded from its safety study, were ubiquitous throughout the global range approved under the Fisheries permit. Future collisions between beaked whales and Navy sonar were inevitable, he said, if the Navy was granted a permit to deploy LFA sonar across the world's oceans. The map was entered into evidence, and Balcomb returned to his seat.

When the two Department of Justice attorneys followed with their presentation, they were immediately on their heels.[1] They seemed flustered by the concerns that the judge had voiced during her preliminary comments. Instead of defending the legal requirements of the permitting process that NRDC had attacked, they walked through their brief in some detail. The judge kept interrupting them to say she'd already read their submissions and was familiar with their arguments. The two attorneys ended up deferring most of their allotted time to their expert witnesses. Clark and Tyack argued that the Navy's scientific research program demonstrated that low-frequency sonar's impact on marine mammals would be negligible. Joe Johnson, the sonar program director, explained why LFA sonar was important to national security and tried to rebut the written declaration from NRDC's military expert highlighting the technical problems that had plagued the LFA system since its inception.

Darlene Ketten was obviously eager to be heard, but her testimony came off as tone-deaf. She began rather strangely by saying, "I have not testified officially before, and I'll try to do it right, but I also would appreciate some instruction on how to do so."

To which the judge replied sardonically, "Just tell the truth."

Ketten proceeded to dismiss the claims of sonar-related strandings in the Bahamas. She insisted, as she had in congressional hearings and to reporters for the past two years, that sonar hadn't killed the beaked whales she examined. Rather, they had died of exposure to the elements and the crushing weight of their own bodies on the beach after stranding alive. Judge Laporte pressed her to acknowledge the causal link between sonar and the strandings that the Navy's interim report had already conceded. Ketten stood firm behind her seemingly obtuse reasoning.

As to the whales that recently stranded on the Canary Islands, Ketten expressed skepticism about the findings of acoustic trauma. "The head analyses were not done with the same rigor as they were in the case of the Bahamas. They do not have appropriate experts there. And there was no brain damage in these animals," she said. "There was bleeding in the spaces *around* the brain. That's not at all the same thing."

It seemed clear from the judge's expression that she was put off by Ketten's peculiar parsing of the causes of death. Reynolds could see that in her attempt to "bury" him, Ketten was hurting the Navy's case. Expert witnesses are supposed to testify to findings of scientific fact. When an expert becomes prosecutorial and starts to try the case for the lawyers, it undermines the credibility of her testimony and the competence of the legal team.

At the judge's suggestion, the hearing continued through lunch in order to conclude that afternoon. By three o'clock, the Justice Department lawyers were visibly sagging in their seats. The naval officers in attendance seemed agitated and impatient with the pace and direction of the hearing. As the crowded courtroom emptied out onto Golden Gate Avenue, Reynolds had to struggle to keep a lid on his optimism. Despite all the positive signals from the judge's comments and questions, Reynolds knew that he'd have to await her formal ruling before he could relax. In the meantime, he permitted himself and his team a celebratory meal and congratulated them all on a job well done.

Three weeks after the hearing, Reynolds received a call from Judge Laporte's clerk alerting him to stand by for a fax of the judge's ruling. Reynolds and Wetzler hovered over the fax machine, grabbing each of the 37 pages and speed-reading them as they came through.

It was a lengthy and detailed decision. The judge reviewed the arguments on both sides, point by point, noting the strengths and weaknesses of each argument, as well as the statutory mandates that drove her ruling. Finally, on the last page, the judge ruled on the motion for a preliminary injunction:

The plaintiffs have shown that they are likely to prevail on establishing violations of the Marine Mammal Protection Act, the National Environmental Policy Act and the Endangered Species Act. They have also shown the possibility, indeed the probability, of irreparable injury . . . It is undisputed that marine mammals, many of whom depend on sensitive hearing for essential activities like finding food and mates and avoiding predators, and some of whom are endangered species, will at a minimum be harassed by the extremely loud and far traveling LFA sonar . . .

The Court has also balanced the hardships and considered the public interest. The public interest in the survival and flourishing of marine mammals and endangered species, as well as a healthy marine environment, is extremely strong. Indeed, Congress enacted the Marine Mammal Protection Act and the Endangered Species Act in recognition of this compelling public interest, not only to the American public but to the international community, and not only to present generations but to future generations to come . . . Stewardship of the world's precious oceans and the marine life within them is undoubtedly of utmost importance.

At the same time, the Navy has shown that a total ban on use of LFA sonar for training and testing would pose a hardship. More broadly, the public has a compelling interest in protecting national security by ensuring military preparedness and the safety of those serving in the military from attacks by hostile submarines . . .

Balancing the harms and weighing the public interest, the Court concludes that a preliminary injunction should issue, but that it should not impose a complete ban on peacetime use of LFA sonar. Rather, the preliminary injunction should be carefully tailored to reduce the risk to marine mammals and endangered species by restricting the sonar's use in additional areas that are particularly rich in marine life, while still allowing the Navy to use this technology for testing and training in a variety of oceanic conditions.

In particular, the preliminary injunction will extend the coastal buffer zone beyond 12 nautical miles in those coastal areas where LFA sonar can effectively operate at that distance, and will include additional, interim Offshore Biologically Important Areas that are reasonable candidates for permanent status . . . Defendants have acknowledged that they can restrict operations in certain parts of the ocean, during particular seasons, where LFA-equipped vessels are more likely to encounter marine mammals and endangered species. A tailored injunction will help ensure that they do so in compliance with the statutory mandates, including the Marine Mammal Protection Act's mandate that LFA sonar has only a negligible impact on small numbers of marine mammals.

Accordingly, the parties are ordered to meet and confer on the precise terms of a preliminary injunction consistent with this opinion.

It Is So Ordered.

Judge Elizabeth D. Laporte
United States District Court for the Northern District of California

"It is so ordered," Wetzler intoned with quiet satisfaction.

Reynolds returned to page one and reread the whole decision. He was impressed by the way that Laporte constructed her ruling to defend it against being overturned by a higher court. She deferred to the military's national security concerns, as well as to the government's scientific experts, but she managed to rule against the Navy and Fisheries on almost every substantive issue. She was careful to rule within the limits of the statutes, while taking full advantage of protections that each law afforded marine mammals.

Reynolds still had to negotiate the terms of the injunction. Judge Laporte had directed NRDC and the Navy to meet with a court-appointed mediator and reach a settlement as to where and when LFA sonar could operate and what safeguards would have to be implemented.[2] As important as NRDC's briefings and oral arguments had been to securing an injunction, the outcome of the settlement negotiations would be the most tangible measure of its success in limiting the risks of LFA sonar to marine mammals. Reynolds took the lead for the plaintiffs in the settlement talks, as he had more historical knowledge of the case—its origins, legal underpinnings, and technical aspects—than anyone on either side.

The mediation was a multistage, multiday process that included opening statements, arguments, and counterarguments. From the start, Reynolds' strategy was to make the Navy declare the precise areas where it needed to operate for reasons of national security. The Justice Department lawyers balked at this, insisting that the negotiations begin from the 75 percent of the world's oceans that Fisheries had initially approved. That was a nonstarter for Reynolds. Negotiations stalled.

Reynolds held important leverage in the negotiations. Without a settlement on geographic and seasonal exclusion areas, the Navy was barred by the preliminary injunction from operating LFA sonar anywhere. On the other hand, if he refused to agree to some sort of compromise, the judge would impose her own resolution.

For their part, the Department of Justice lawyers continued to behave as if they expected the Navy to eventually get its way, as it had always done. Under pressure from the mediator, they eventually offered to limit the geographic scope of deployment to the Pacific Ocean—65 million square miles, or fully half of the world's ocean area. For Reynolds, that was another nonstarter. They were once again at an impasse.

LFA sonar's program director, Joe Johnson, was beside himself with frustration. Reynolds may have waited seven years for his day in court, but Johnson had been working on Low Frequency Active sonar since its inception in the mideighties, and he'd been directing the program since the midnineties. He and Bob Gisiner spent years building an Environmental Impact Statement that they hoped would stand up to any legal challenge.

Then he'd suffered through the aftermath of the Bahamas stranding, watching the Navy, in his opinion, make a mess of the investigation *and* look guilty in the process. From Johnson's perspective, the Navy had an agenda from the start of the investigation—to keep operating as it wanted without interference from regulators or watchdog groups—and it had constructed a narrative of the stranding that would sustain that agenda. But the Navy's initial denials, its delaying tactics during the investigation, and the interim report with its backhanded admission of culpability only undermined the Navy's credibility and tainted Johnson's LFA sonar program.

Johnson had been forced to sit in court and watch NRDC dance circles around the Justice Department lawyers. Now those same government attorneys were keeping his sonar vessel, the *Cory Chouest*, locked up in port while they postured behind legal concepts that Judge Laporte had already ruled against. The Justice Department's entire investment in Navy sonar was the six months it had spent arguing and losing its case. Johnson wasn't going to let them play chicken with NRDC over the fate of a program he'd nurtured for 15 years. It was high time, he believed, to get back out on the water and operate.

Johnson knew that if Steve Honigman had still been the Navy's general counsel and Richard Danzig the Secretary of the Navy, the settlement talks would be over by now. But Danzig and Honigman were long gone. The new Navy Secretary, H. T. Johnson, was a former four-star Air Force general who'd raised a lot of money for Bush's 2000 campaign. He called the Secretary and explained the urgent need to reach a settlement that would allow the Navy to operate LFA sonar in strategic areas. Johnson was relieved when the Secretary gave him his proxy to cut a deal with NRDC.

Joe Johnson may have had another motive for intervening in the settlement negotiations, to which neither the Justice Department nor NRDC was privy. Once the preliminary injunction was ratified by the judge, there would be a "discovery" period during which NRDC would gain access to internal emails and other communications between Fisheries and the Navy during the permit application and review period. Johnson may have assumed that NRDC would discover, among other things, that the Office of Naval Research and its contractors had engaged in inappropriate collaboration on Fisheries' drafting of the "final rules" of the permit. There was also a clear email trail showing that the Navy had failed to disclose a British navy study that concluded that low-frequency sound was likely damaging to fish populations. And Johnson himself had conveyed strong doubts, in writing, about the viability of the Navy's 180-decibel safety threshold. Once brought to light, those incriminating documents would torpedo the Navy's already suspect credibility and drive the judge even further into NRDC's camp. Better to negotiate terms now, Johnson may have reasoned, while he still had a quantum of leverage.

Johnson and Reynolds sat down together, and within a few hours, they cut to the nub of the issue: the Navy wanted to be able to operate wherever and whenever it chose. But where did it *need* to deploy LFA sonar for national security? Johnson designated the Navy's "need to operate" area along the eastern seaboard of Asia and in the deep ocean waters off the Philippine Sea, just outside the Taiwan Strait. Now that China had supplanted the Soviet Union as America's primary naval rival in the Pacific, the US Navy wanted to bring every possible system to bear on monitoring China's offshore waters.

The calculation for Reynolds was straightforward: Joe Johnson was willing to settle for between 1 percent and 2 percent of the world's oceans, rather than the 75 percent that Fisheries had granted. He was also willing to agree to seasonal and geographic exclusions to avoid migration routes, feeding areas, and breeding grounds for the West Pacific gray whales and humpbacks, and to exclude the marine protected area around the Mariana Islands. By the end of the day, the two sides had hammered out the terms of a settlement agreement, which Judge Laporte quickly approved.

After a lengthy discovery period—which indeed uncovered the incriminating trail of inappropriate emails between the Navy and Fisheries[3]—Judge Laporte issued a permanent injunction extending the terms of the negotiated settlement for five years.

The next day, Reynolds convened a press conference on the Santa Monica bluffs overlooking the Pacific Ocean. Flanked by Jean Michel Cousteau, International Fund for Animal Welfare president Fred O'Regan, and actor and marine mammal activist Pierce Brosnan, Reynolds announced the launch of an international campaign to stop the proliferation of high-intensity sonar in oceans around the world.

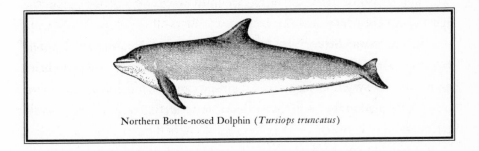

Northern Bottle-nosed Dolphin (*Tursiops truncatus*)

26

Counterattack

It didn't take long for the Navy to regroup and counterattack. If the courts
ruled that the Navy was violating environmental statutes, it could go to Congress to change the laws. And within months of the Low Frequency Active
sonar decision, the Navy did just that. In rapid succession, the Pentagon's allies on Capitol Hill introduced and passed amendments to the Marine Mammal Protection Act that deleted the "small take" and "specified geographic
region" requirements and added a "national security exemption" that the Secretary of Defense could invoke at his sole discretion. Hoping to ride a wave of
promilitary sentiment in Congress, the Defense Department also proposed
national security exemptions to the Clean Water Act, the Clean Air Act, and
the Migratory Bird Treaty Act.

Meanwhile, NRDC aimed to make up the ground it lost on Capitol Hill by
mobilizing the advocacy and scientific communities. Winning the sonar case,
Reynolds learned, turned night into day when it came to recruiting partners.
Previously unpersuaded conservation groups were now eager to join NRDC's

campaign. Many of the fence-sitting scientists were emboldened to join the fight against high-intensity sonar.

NRDC's sonar victory, and media reports about it, also raised public awareness of the threat that military sonar posed to whales. Now, when whales stranded on beaches, people trained their sights on the horizon line. With increasing frequency, they noticed battleships conducting midfrequency sonar exercises:

In June 2004 six beaked whales stranded in the Gulf of Alaska during "Northern Edge" joint exercises between the US and Canadian navies.

In July 2004 four beaked whales stranded during "Majestic Eagle" NATO exercises in the Canary Islands, not far from the site of the 2002 stranding.

Later that same month, during US-Japanese joint exercises conducted near the Hawaiian island of Kauai, 200 melon-headed whales fled into Hanalei Bay and milled about for hours in tight, frantic circles. Local volunteers in kayaks and canoes were eventually able to herd them back out to open water.

In January 2005, 37 whales stranded along North Carolina's Outer Banks following US Navy sonar exercises.[1] Scientists working under federal contract conducted necropsies and tissue analyses to determine the causes of death. The government refused to release the scientists' findings despite a Freedom of Information Act lawsuit filed by NRDC.

On January 26, 2006, following midfrequency sonar exercises by the British Royal Navy, four Cuvier's beaked whales stranded on the Almerían coast of southern Spain, with the same suite of bends-like symptoms seen in whales that stranded in the Canary Islands in 2002 and 2004.

But of all the mass strandings during the period following the LFA sonar case, the one that gained the most attention and notoriety occurred—once again—in Ken Balcomb's front yard. For the second time in three years, Balcomb documented and publicized a mass stranding during US Navy sonar exercises.

MAY 5, 2003
Smugglers Cove, San Juan Island, Washington

After testifying at NRDC's sonar hearing in October, Balcomb had returned to San Juan Island, content to resume his orca survey and leave the courtroom dramas to the lawyers.

The whales returned to Puget Sound in April, on schedule. Just before noon on May 5, 22 members of J Pod, ranging in age from 60 years to three months, were foraging for salmon in the cove behind Balcomb's home and research station. Standing on his deck and watching the whales through the zoom lens of his video camera, Balcomb could see a harbor porpoise and a minke whale hunting alongside the orcas. Two whale-watching boats bobbed in the water nearby. He switched on the underwater hydrophones to hear if he could distinguish the orcas' chirping from the harbor porpoise's and minke whale's calls.

Within a few minutes, the three-way cetacean conversation was overwhelmed by pulses of loud, shrieking noise. Balcomb immediately recognized the sound as sonar—probably midfrequency, to judge by the whining pitch of the "pings." He scanned the horizon with the big-eye binoculars mounted on his deck and soon locked in on the outline of a battleship 12 miles offshore in Haro Strait, the narrow channel separating San Juan Island from the Canadian mainland. It was too far away for him to tell whether it belonged to the Canadians or to the US Navy.

Back in the cove, J Pod grouped tightly together and hovered close to shore. Clearly agitated, they milled in circles, first in one direction and then the other. In decades of observing killer whales in the cove, Balcomb had never witnessed this kind of panicked behavior. As the battleship drew closer to the mouth of the cove, the intensity of the sonar noise increased, along with the animals' distress. The minke whale took off like a shot toward the far end of the cove. The harbor porpoise zoomed across the surface in the same direction. The mouth of the cove was 20 miles wide, but the pod of killer whales seemed to be trapped inside. They broke into two groups and began slapping their tails against the surface.

When the warship approached to within three miles of shore, Balcomb could make out the markings on its side. It was a guided-missile destroyer, the USS *Shoup*. Balcomb called the US Coast Guard and the regional Fisheries office and told them they needed to get hold of the *Shoup*'s commander and tell him to shut off its sonar. Twenty minutes later, the sonar storm subsided.

Balcomb called a Seattle TV station, KOMO 4 TV, which dispatched a helicopter news crew to the scene. When it contacted the Navy for a response to the incident, a spokesman denied that any Navy vessels were operating in the strait. That evening, KOMO 4 broadcast Balcomb's video of the *Shoup* in Haro Strait and the audio of its piercing sonar.* In the foreground, the killer whales looked tormented, and many of the whale watchers nearby were hysterical. Interviewed for the evening news, they described the terrifying din of the sonar, which was audible in the air *above* the water.

By the next morning, the Navy amended its statement. For five hours the previous day, the *Shoup* had conducted minesweeping exercises in the Strait of Juan de Fuca and Haro Strait while transmitting 235 decibels of midfrequency sonar. The sound Balcomb recorded on tape was the *Shoup's* SQS-53C sonar. The *Shoup's* Destroyer Squadron 9, operating out of the naval station in Everett, Washington, often conducted maneuvers in Puget Sound. But after the Bahamas stranding and the interim report, Balcomb assumed that the Navy knew better than to conduct sonar exercises in a narrow channel. Especially inside Haro Strait, which was world famous as a whale-watching destination. Apparently, the *Shoup's* commander didn't get the memo.

The day after the incident, dead harbor porpoises began floating ashore. Ten landed on the US coastline, and six stranded on the Canadian side of the border. When a freshly dead harbor porpoise drifted into nearby False Bay with blood leaking from its eye, Balcomb wrapped the animal in plastic and stowed it in the six-foot freezer chest in his basement.

Balcomb's video of the *Shoup* incident quickly went viral on the internet. Whale watchers were used to seeing wild orcas knifing majestically through the water, not cowering in the shadow of a US destroyer. Most people had never heard the sound of military sonar, and they were horrified to see a US Navy destroyer bearing down on a pod of terrified whales.

The ensuing uproar over the strandings and the videotape forced Fisheries to launch an investigation. Soon six porpoises lay in a freezer at the regional Fisheries headquarters. Fisheries wanted to CT scan the animals before necropsy but said it couldn't reserve time on a local CT scanner for two months. Balcomb found a private clinic that offered to scan his harbor porpoise as soon as he could bring it over. The scans, which he copied before turning

---

* To view the original video and sound recorded by Ken Balcomb in Haro Strait, go to: http://vimeo.com /35584781.

them over to Fisheries along with the frozen porpoise, showed the same signs of acoustic trauma and hemorrhaging around the brain that he'd seen in the scans of the Bahamas specimens.

Fisheries put Darlene Ketten in charge of its forensic investigation and barred Balcomb from the necropsies, even though he had contributed one of the specimens. He showed up at Fisheries the day of the necropsies anyway and was blocked from entering by two guards. So he stood in the press gallery and observed the proceedings through a telephoto lens.

In October the Navy's Pacific Fleet published a report exonerating itself of culpability in the Haro Strait stranding. A panel of experts from the Navy's Marine Mammal Training Program, led by Sam Ridgway, had reviewed Balcomb's videotape of the incident and suggested—in defiance of the videos' alarming visual and audio evidence to the contrary—that the whale-watching boats were more likely to have distressed the killer whales than the *Shoup*'s sonar transmissions. The Navy report concluded: "The *Shoup* operated its sonar on 5 May 2003 in a manner consistent with established guidelines and procedures."[2]

Months later, Fisheries released its report on the stranding incident, citing "inconclusive evidence of causation," due in part to the "advanced stage of decomposition" of the specimens.[3] According to a local colleague of Balcomb's who participated in the necropsies, the Fisheries freezer had been set to "auto-defrost" mode, so the specimens had been continuously thawing and refreezing during the two months between the stranding and the necropsies. The reports by the Navy and Fisheries were widely perceived as flying in the face of reality—and of the most damning documentation ever preserved on videotape of whales caught in the cross fire from a sonar training exercise.

Sonar wasn't the only man-made threat to the Southern Resident Community of orcas. Two decades after the wild capture spree of the sixties and seventies, the killer whales had rebounded to a healthy and stable population of about 100. Then, in the nineties, the community went into steep decline. With their wild salmon prey dying off from dammed rivers and overforested streambeds, orcas were forced to feed on contaminated bottom fish. Fecal samples from killer whales revealed the highest concentrations of toxins, including

PCBs and the banned insecticide DDT, found in any animals ever tested. By the turn of the century, the Southern Resident Community had declined to fewer than 80 whales.

In 2002 Balcomb reported the alarming population drop-off to the government review committee of biologists that met each year to assess the threatened and endangered status of animals under the Endangered Species Act. But it wasn't until Balcomb filed declarations on behalf of a 2003 lawsuit by the conservation group Earthjustice that Fisheries finally agreed to designate the Southern Resident Community as "threatened." A year later, based partly on Balcomb's updated census data, Fisheries moved the local orcas onto its "endangered" list—the first and only killer-whale community to achieve that designation. Once listed as endangered, the orcas won a host of protections. Fisheries was required by the federal Endangered Species Act to designate a protected habitat and to closely monitor the community's health and population size.

Those protections were long overdue, in Balcomb's view. But he had the satisfaction of knowing that three decades of self-funded summer surveys had finally benefited the whales. In 2005, 30 years after his first and only Fisheries-funded census in 1976, Balcomb and his Center for Whale Research was awarded a five-year Fisheries contract to survey the Southern Resident Community.

With so much public attention focused on whale strandings in the presence of naval sonar, the Office of Naval Research was under pressure to fund basic behavioral research—particularly the little-understood diving behavior of beaked whales. The interim report on the Bahamas stranding included a list of research initiatives proposed by Bob Gisiner, most of them focused on beaked whales in the Bahamas. Beginning in 2003, Gisiner funded Chris Clark and Peter Tyack to lead a series of tagging expeditions in the Bahamas to chart the diving and noise-response patterns of beaked whales.

The shotgun-delivered steel darts of Balcomb's early tagging expeditions had been replaced by high-tech electronic sensors designed by Mark Johnson, an engineer at Woods Hole Oceanographic. The challenge lay in attaching those sensors via suction cups to skittish beaked whales when they briefly surfaced for air. Clark and Tyack needed a local beaked whale expert to help them locate and tag the elusive creatures who lived near the AUTEC range, 100 miles southwest of Abaco. They approached Diane Claridge for help and offered her co-author credit on any resulting publications. She accepted.

Infused with new funding and with forthcoming publication credits, Claridge launched the newly named Bahamas Marine Mammal Research Organisation in collaboration with her new research partner, Charlotte Dunn.

In 2004 Balcomb was diagnosed with advanced prostate cancer. He'd gone without health insurance ever since leaving the Navy in 1975, and he had no savings. His doctor estimated the out-of-pocket expense of the recommended radiation treatment at $42,000. Balcomb wasn't about to sell his house and boats to pay for the treatment. They were his bequest to the Center for Whale Research. His only other assets were the antique cars stashed in sheds around the property. Even if he could sell them for enough cash, he couldn't see spending that kind of money on himself. One of his wives had called him penny *and* pound foolish, and he supposed she was right. But it just didn't seem worth the expense.

When word got out about his diagnosis, two donors to the Center for Whale Research offered to help. A Seattle-based radiologist, whom Balcomb had previously persuaded to conduct CT scans of stranded whales, offered Balcomb free radiation treatment for his cancer. Another sponsor donated the use of his small plane to ferry Balcomb back and forth to the mainland. Balcomb agreed, but only on condition that he could pilot the plane himself.

2005
Los Angeles Office of NRDC

The accumulation of evidence from Haro Strait and the other mass strandings around the world increasingly pointed to *midfrequency* sonar as the culprit. But Reynolds knew that restraining the Navy's use of midfrequency sonar would meet with intense resistance, both legally and politically.

LFA sonar remained an experimental, long-range submarine detection system operating from just a few research vessels. Midfrequency sonar, by contrast, was the primary tactical submarine detection system mounted on virtually all the Navy's warships—thanks to Admiral Dick Pittenger's efforts in the 1980s. Details of its sonar capabilities were among the Navy's most closely guarded secrets, which was one reason that the Navy had never submitted its training exercises for environmental review. If Reynolds went after midfrequency sonar in court, he assumed that the Navy would mobilize all of its resources to derail the litigation and would do everything in its power to defy a court-ordered injunction.

But with consensus finally building in the scientific community about the link between sonar and mass strandings, it was hard for Reynolds to see an alternative to legal action.

A 2004 report by the International Whaling Commission's Scientific Committee concluded: "The accumulated evidence is very convincing and appears overwhelming, associating midfrequency military sonar with atypical beaked whale mass strandings." Even more remarkably, a 2004 study of mass strandings by the military think tank the Jasons—a study commissioned by the Navy and co-authored by Walter Munk and a dozen other physicists—began by declaring: "We would like to state at the outset that the evidence of sonar causation is, in our opinion, completely convincing and that therefore there is a serious issue of how best to avoid and minimize future beaching events." [4]

Similar conclusions were reached in a 2005 study published by the International Council on the Exploration of the Seas, and another by the National Research Council. Within a few years of NRDC's low-frequency sonar victory, almost all the major marine science organizations were sounding the alarm about sonar and whales.

Europeans were taking coordinated steps to limit sonar exercises in their waters. The European Parliament called on its 25 member states to stop deploying high-intensity active naval sonar until more was known about the harm it inflicted on whales and other marine life. Citing the growing body of scientific research that confirmed "a significant threat to marine mammals, fish, and other ocean wildlife," the resolution called on member states to "immediately restrict the use of high-intensity active naval sonars in waters falling under their jurisdiction." Spain took the lead by banning sonar exercises in the waters surrounding the Canary Islands following the 2004 Majestic Eagle strandings.

Having successfully lobbied Congress for its national security exemption, the Navy showed no interest in negotiating with NRDC over its midfrequency sonar trainings. The US military was waging wars in both Afghanistan and Iraq, so rallying the public to pressure the Navy for reforms was a long shot. But relying on the Navy's internal Environmental Assessments was a certain formula for continued mass strandings. Litigation, Reynolds concluded, was the only stick that could move the Navy toward accountability and outside review.

By 2005, Reynolds faced a fateful go/no-go decision. Filing a lawsuit was likely to instigate a series of actions and reactions inside the Navy, the Pentagon, the Congress, and the White House over which he'd have no control. The Navy had a national security exemption in its back pocket, a virtual "Get out of jail free" card it could play at will. And even if he won a ruling in a lower court, Reynolds could expect the Navy to appeal it, if necessary, all the way up to the US Supreme Court.

Reynolds reached out for assistance to Richard Kendall, the attorney who'd helped him win the ship shock case back in 1994. Ten years on, Kendall was now a senior partner at Irell & Manella, where he represented Viacom, CBS, Paramount Pictures, and a host of other Hollywood heavyweights. Kendall was a successful-enough litigator to charge his clients top-of-the-market rates: at that time, over $700 an hour. But he agreed to help on a pro bono basis and to bring along several of his brightest young associates.

Reynolds had recently bolstered his own legal team by recruiting a young attorney to replace Andrew Wetzler when he moved to NRDC's Chicago office to focus on his own endangered species cases. Cara Horowitz had graduated first in her UCLA Law School class. She was as smart as Jasny and as calm in a storm as Wetzler.

Reynolds also lined up potential co-plaintiffs. His first call was to Naomi Rose at the Humane Society. But despite their successful partnership in opposing low-frequency sonar, Acoustic Thermometry, and ship shock, Rose couldn't persuade her organization to sign on to the midfrequency case. The Humane Society deemed it too risky politically to take on the Navy with such a confrontational and high-profile lawsuit. Fortunately, Fred O'Regan of the International Fund for Animal Welfare and Jean-Michel Cousteau of Ocean Futures Society had no reservations. They were in.

On October 19, 2005, NRDC and its co-plaintiffs filed suit against the US Navy for violations of environmental laws in its midfrequency sonar testing and training around the world. Reynolds decided to file in Los Angeles, where he knew the judges and where the coastline was particularly rich with marine life. US District Judge Florence-Marie Cooper, a Clinton appointee with decades of experience on the bench, was assigned the case from the wheel. When Reynolds filed "discovery" of the Navy's sonar training records, the Navy lawyers protested that NRDC's request was "overbroad and irrelevant." Judge Cooper rejected their objections and ordered the Navy to produce most of the requested documents. As Reynolds had expected, the Navy leadership responded like a tiger jabbed with a sharp stick.

White-sided Dolphin (*Lagenorhynchus acutus*)

27

The Admirals Take Charge

Office of the Chief of Naval Operations, the Pentagon

Early on a Tuesday morning, an attorney from Operations stuck her head into Rear Admiral Pete Daly's office. "You're not going to believe this," she said, "but the legal eagles over in Environmental Readiness are preparing to deliver a ton of sonar data that the California court ordered them to make public. You should take a look." She handed Daly six fat folders filled with ships' logs. "And this is just for the Atlantic ranges."

Daly was incredulous that Navy lawyers were preparing to release five years of classified operational data detailing the locations and capabilities of Navy sonar assets around the world. The 27-year veteran had served as antisubmarine warfare commander aboard a midfrequency sonar destroyer in the Pacific before commanding a destroyer, a destroyer squadron, and a carrier strike group in the Gulf. After commanding the *Nimitz* strike group in support of Operations Enduring Freedom and Iraqi Freedom, he was awarded his second star and assigned to the staff of the Chief of Naval Operations, Admiral Mike Mullen.

By lunchtime, Daly had expressed his concerns to Mullen about hand-ing over the sonar data. Mullen shared Daly's outrage, both at the judge's order and at the willingness of the Navy environmental compliance lawyers at N-45 to, well, comply with such an order. By day's end, Mullen had ar-ranged a sit-down between Daly, himself, and the new Navy Secretary, Don-ald Winter. Ever since Winter's predecessor, H. T. Johnson, gave his blessing to the LFA settlement back in 2002, the admirals had regarded the secretariat with suspicion—and as a potential adversary in Fleet Command's struggle to maintain control over its sonar exercises. They considered Secretary Winter, who had been CEO of defense contractor Northrop Grumman before his appointment by President Bush, as more of a businessman than a comrade in arms.

Secretary Winter was sympathetic to the admirals' expressed concern that the environmental compliance lawyers were "driving the bus over a cliff." But when Admiral Mullen asked him to invoke the state secrets privilege in response to NRDC's discovery motion, Winter demurred. The state secrets privilege was reserved for extraordinary cases where the government refused to turn over evidence to a court on grounds of national security. Winter wanted to develop a detailed rationale that he could defend in court before in-voking the privilege. Otherwise the judge could overrule his request, and the last thing the Navy needed—he was sure they all agreed—was another poke in the eye from the judiciary. Mullen directed Daly to "work it up" with the Navy general counsel—but not with the lawyers at Environmental Readiness.

Ultimately, the Navy invoked the state secrets privilege, which led to an-other round of furious briefings on all sides—and eventually, a compromise settlement was hammered out in Judge Cooper's courtroom.

In the meantime, the Navy responded by filing its own broad discovery motions aimed at NRDC's co-plaintiffs. In particular, the Navy demanded that Jean-Michel Cousteau provide them with access to every foot of film and videotape he'd shot of whales, going back ten years. With each side filing successive rounds of motions and objections, the case soon bogged down into legal trench warfare, with neither side able to gain an advantage.

JULY 1, 2006
Los Angeles

Reynolds' first gut check on litigating midfrequency sonar came a few months later, in the summer of 2006. The US Pacific Fleet was preparing to conduct eight days of joint sonar exercises with the navies of six Pacific Rim allies in the waters off Hawaii.[1] Two years earlier, the same exercises had caused the panicked flight of 200 melon-headed whales into Hanalei Bay—although the Navy still contended that some rare combination of meteorological circumstances may have been to blame. In advance of these latest joint exercises, the Navy had prepared its usual Environmental Assessment, leading to its usual Finding of No Significant Impact. Since the Navy proposed to conduct the joint exercises in one of the most whale-rich environments in the Pacific, Reynolds thought this might be a strong test case for challenging midfrequency sonar.

Reynolds and Jasny debated whether or not they should sue. Jasny worried that if they confronted the Pacific Fleet on the eve of a major exercise, the Navy would set a damaging precedent by invoking its new national security exemption. Their discussions turned into heated arguments. Voices were raised. Jasny had differed with Reynolds over strategy now and again, but this was the first time he believed his mentor was flat wrong. Suing the Navy over imminent international war games felt to Jasny like going over the falls in a barrel. Just the thought of it made him nauseous.

Reynolds conferred with Kendall, who said he was ready to sue the Navy if Reynolds was. In the end, Reynolds decided the potential upside outweighed the risks. They'd have the same moderate federal judge in that jurisdiction as in the case they filed in Los Angeles—Florence-Marie Cooper—who Reynolds bet was strong willed enough to stand up to the military. Given the near-disastrous melon-headed-whale incident during the previous joint exercises in these waters, he thought they had a reasonable chance to make good law and set an important legal precedent. Two days before the scheduled start of the joint exercises, NRDC filed suit, asking the judge to issue a temporary restraining order pending a hearing on a preliminary injunction.

As Jasny had feared, Secretary of Defense Rumsfeld immediately granted the Navy a two-year national security exemption from the Marine Mammal Protection Act. It was the first time the Navy had invoked the exemption that Congress granted it three years earlier.

The long Fourth of July weekend was a blur of speed-written briefs and reply briefs. On Monday, July 3, Judge Cooper stunned the Navy by issuing a temporary restraining order that blocked commencement of the international joint exercises. Judge Cooper ruled that regardless of its national security exemption from the Marine Mammal Protection Act, the Navy had violated another federal environmental statute, the National Environmental Policy Act, by failing to conduct a thorough environmental impact analysis. In issuing the temporary restraining order, she stated that "given the considerable convincing scientific evidence demonstrating that the Navy's use of midfrequency sonar can kill, injure, and disturb many marine species, including marine mammals," NRDC was "likely to prevail" in its lawsuit. The Navy quickly filed an emergency appeal with the US Court of Appeals for the Ninth Circuit.

Meanwhile, Judge Cooper directed the Navy and NRDC to meet immediately to try to negotiate a settlement that would allow the exercises to proceed with increased safeguards in place. While the US and Pacific Rim navies idled in the waters off the Hawaiian Islands, Reynolds and Kendall talked terms with the Navy's lawyers. After several rounds of bids and counterbids, the Navy made its final settlement offer on Friday morning, July 7. If NRDC turned it down, the Navy would pursue its appeal, with a decision requested from the Ninth Circuit by noon.

The Navy's final offer included a 25-mile exclusion zone around coastal areas and the Northwestern Hawaiian Islands Marine National Monument, as well as other operational safeguards such as underwater, aerial, and ship-based surveillance for marine mammals. Reynolds was torn. The Navy's position was less than he thought that NRDC—and the whales—deserved. But it was more than the Navy had ever agreed to for a midfrequency sonar exercise. If he didn't settle for half of what he wanted now, Reynolds worried that he might lose it all in the court of appeals.

The Navy had always claimed it couldn't train under the restrictions of environmental safeguards. Its current willingness, under legal pressure, to submit to even partial limitations on its sonar training methods would set an important precedent, Reynolds believed. After conferring with his team, Reynolds decided to accept the Navy's final offer.

When Judge Cooper entered her settlement order, allowing the exercises to proceed with new safety measures in place, some of the more radical Hawaiian conservationists condemned the deal as a sellout by NRDC. Reynolds wasn't surprised. He reminded himself that while some of his critics might be good at mobilizing public protests and press coverage, none of them had ever successfully sued the Navy over its use of sonar. As he'd learned over the years, the hardest part of his job was deciding when to litigate and when to cut a good-enough deal, which—as in this case—was often on the table for only a brief moment. With this settlement, NRDC had now won significant concessions by the Navy in its deployment of both low-frequency and mid-frequency sonar.

It wasn't his nature to second-guess himself, but Reynolds still held his breath until the newspapers reported on the settlement. To his relief, the press credited the agreement as a major environmental victory.

FEBRUARY 12, 2007
Los Angeles

It soon became clear to Reynolds that contesting midfrequency sonar was going to be a war of attrition, fought in successive Navy ranges around the country and, eventually, around the world. Six months after winning an injunction and sonar safeguards in Hawaii, NRDC faced another midfrequency battle closer to home. The Navy announced 14 major training exercises over a two-year period in the waters off the Southern California coast, including sonar training in and around the Channel Islands National Marine Sanctuary. According to the Navy's own Environmental Assessment, these exercises would result in a "take," or harassment, of 170,000 marine mammals from 30 species, including five species of endangered whales.

The California Coastal Commission informed the Navy of safeguards it would require. When the Navy challenged the commission's jurisdiction and proceeded without those safeguards, NRDC, its co-plaintiffs,[2] and the

Coastal Commission sued the Navy to block the Southern California exercises. Because the Navy's two-year national security exemption from the Marine Mammal Protection Act was still in force, Reynolds had to rely once again on the National Environmental Policy Act, the Endangered Species Act, and other statutes.

Once again Judge Cooper ruled that NRDC had established a "near certainty" that the Navy exercises would cause "irreparable harm to the environment."[3] The judge granted a preliminary injunction that prohibited the Navy from training with midfrequency sonar in its Southern California range for the next two years.

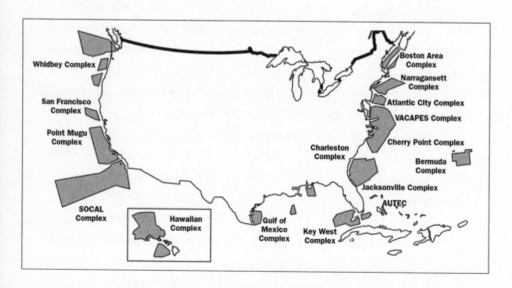

Office of the Chief of Naval Operations, the Pentagon

Being barred from operating on its Southern California range was a clarifying moment for the fleet commanders. With the Vieques range in Puerto Rico no longer in play, Southern California was the crown jewel of the Navy's training grounds. It was the only range left where all the right training elements came together: a land-sea staging area with usable airspace; a shore bombardment range; a naval air station right on the coast, which pilots could use as a "bingo field"; and inshore bombing ranges. The Southern California range had it all.

And now the environmentalists were trying to take it away and give it to the whales.

Admiral Mullen had recently been nominated to become chairman of the Joint Chiefs of Staff. Before he moved up and out, he wanted to make sure that his replacement as Chief of Naval Operations, Admiral Gary Roughead, was engaged with Daly on this issue. The three admirals in the room—Mullen, Roughead, and Daly—were of one mind on the subject. They saw the Navy as a giant deployment machine, constantly working up strike groups and deploying them into forward environments. Everyone, including some inside the Navy, felt free to tell the fleet, "Train less. You're not in a submarine shooting war right now." But never having commanded ships at sea, they didn't realize that the most dangerous submarine is the one you don't yet know about and aren't prepared to kill. The fleet commanders worried that if they let judges and environmentalists dictate conditions for sonar exercises, they wouldn't be able to conduct training realistic enough to certify battle groups as ready for deployment.

The fleet commanders decided they needed to take charge of the Southern California case before the lawyers at Justice and at the Navy's own Office of Environmental Readiness caused irreparable harm to *their* environment. For years now, the admirals had watched the government lawyers argue one elegant and losing legal theory after another, each time giving up more and more of the Navy's autonomy. They'd lost and settled with NRDC on low frequency. Then they'd lost and settled on the midfrequency sonar exercises in Hawaii. Now they'd lost another midfrequency case in the Pacific Fleet's home base of Southern California. The time had come for the folks at Justice and Environmental Readiness to step back and let the fleet make the case for midfrequency sonar on the firmest ground it still held: national security.

What the judges and politicians didn't seem to grasp—perhaps, believed the admirals, because it hadn't been presented to them in plain English— was that without experienced sonar operators who had trained rigorously at sea, American servicemen and servicewomen would likely die in a contested threat environment. To maintain antisubmarine warfare proficiency you need to conduct realistic training in conditions that replicate the threat environment. You never know where you'll have to operate. But if you're not trained and ready to fight in every environment—even in places where whales live—your sailors will be directly in the path of an incoming torpedo or submarine-launched-missile attack.

What crystalized the Navy's dilemma in Daly's mind was hearing a senator tell the Secretary of the Navy, "I am worried about the possibility that any whale may be harmed or killed in the course of Navy sonar training." At no point did she express any concern for the men and women on ships who could die if they weren't properly trained in antisubmarine warfare.

Judge Cooper had directed the Navy and NRDC to try to reach a settlement for trainings in the Southern California range. Admiral Roughead sent Daly out to Los Angeles to replace Environmental Readiness as the lead in those settlement meetings. It soon became evident to Reynolds that Daly had little interest in settling. Reynolds knew that the Navy had appealed Judge Cooper's injunction to the Ninth Circuit Court of Appeals. What Reynolds didn't know was that the admirals were already planning to outflank the judiciary and go straight to the executive branch for help.

Throughout the autumn of 2007, the Southern California case bumped back and forth between the court of appeals and the district court. First an emergency motions panel of the court of appeals lifted the injunction; then a different panel reinstated it but sent the case back to Judge Cooper, instructing her to "tailor" her injunction to allow the training to proceed, subject to whatever safeguards she imposed. Just before New Year's, Judge Cooper toured a sonar-equipped destroyer in San Diego to observe the safeguards that the Navy had already adopted. Then, in the first week of January 2008, she issued a revised injunction, which the Navy once again appealed to the Ninth Circuit Court of Appeals.

The admirals assumed that the liberal Ninth Circuit would uphold Judge Cooper's injunction—which it eventually did. But the commanders had decided not to subordinate their military authority to a civilian judge who knew nothing about the training requirements for antisubmarine warfare. If they couldn't make their case in a federal courtroom, the admirals assumed they'd find a more receptive hearing at the White House.

• • •

During all of the pinballing of the Southern California sonar case between the trial and appellate court levels that fall, Reynolds was enduring another, more personal trial. In September he'd taken his mother to the doctor to assess her failing memory. He was surprised when she received a diagnosis of acute anemia, which progressed to leukemia by October. She was clearly on a steep downward slope, so the family decided to move her to stay with Reynolds' sister, Ellen, in Madison, Wisconsin, where the children and grandchildren spread across both coasts could visit.

While work on the Southern California case progressed, Reynolds flew back and forth to Wisconsin to be with his mother and the extended family that had gathered there. He edited briefs in the airport, and on the plane rides, and after his mother and everyone else in the house had gone to sleep. He brought each of his children for a final visit with his mother, ferrying them between Los Angeles and Madison. He'd just returned to Los Angeles with his youngest daughter one night in early December when he learned by phone that his mother was fading fast. He caught the next flight back to Madison, but she died before he got to see her again.

DECEMBER 17, 2007
West Wing of the White House

Admiral Daly made sure that the key decision makers from all the relevant agencies were assembled for the White House strategy meeting: Navy lawyers from Environmental Readiness, the Judge Advocate General, and the Navy general counsel; the leadership and lawyers from Fisheries; and the senior staff and attorneys at the parent agencies, NOAA and the US Department of Commerce.

They had all convened on the weekend before Christmas to convince the Council on Environmental Quality, a White House advisory group with offices across the street at Jackson Place, to intervene on the Navy's behalf. Though it was rarely invoked, the Navy lawyers had identified an obscure provision in regulations enacted under the National Environmental Policy Act that might allow the CEQ to suggest "alternative arrangements" to a full Environmental Impact Statement. The roomful of government lawyers worked through the weekend to craft a credible legal rationale for the White House agency to supersede the courts' authority in deciding that the Navy had failed to comply with federal environmental law.

At the same time, another team of Navy lawyers was working with the White House general counsel on a parallel strategy: asking the president to issue an executive order exempting the Navy from compliance with other federal statutes. On Monday morning, the Secretary of Defense and the Secretary of the Navy delivered their request to the president. They asked that he sign a letter, for the first time, invoking his authority under the Coastal Zone Management Act to exempt the Navy from compliance, in the interest of national security.

President Bush signed the exemption letter the same day that the Council on Environmental Quality issued its alternative arrangements to allow the Navy to proceed with its Southern California sonar exercises regardless of the court's decision. With the stroke of two pens, the president and his White House environmental advisor elevated a dispute over a preliminary injunction to a constitutional confrontation over the separation of powers between the executive and judicial branches of government.

NRDC promptly opposed the Navy's actions, arguing that both the president's exemption and the council's alternative arrangements should be dismissed as unlawful attempts by the executive branch to trump a federal court's right of judicial review.

Two weeks later, Judge Cooper ruled for NRDC, rejecting on a litany of legal grounds the White House's attempted end run around the judiciary. The Department of Justice immediately appealed her ruling to the Ninth Circuit, telling the court of appeals that for reasons of national security and readiness, the Navy needed a decision within a week. The appeals court pushed back, telling the Justice Department and the Navy that they couldn't dictate the court's schedule.

On February 29, two days after a hearing in its Pasadena courtroom, the court of appeals issued a 110-page decision upholding Judge Cooper's preliminary injunction and rejecting both White House waivers. However, the court of appeals waited to impose the injunction to give the government the opportunity to petition the US Supreme Court.

• • •

The decision whether or not to appeal to the Supreme Court was a difficult call for the Justice Department and the Navy. If the Supreme Court ruled against them, they'd have no recourse in the courts, no leverage in any settlement negotiations, and no way to save face with the media. Despite its power and privilege at sea, on Capitol Hill, and in the courts, the Navy leadership cared deeply about public opinion. They disliked being perceived as bullies or as bad stewards of the environment. Most of all, they hated being seen as losers in face-offs against environmental activists.

Back at Woods Hole, Retired Admiral Dick Pittenger worried that appealing to the Supreme Court could prove disastrous. He thought that the Navy was in denial about its dismal track record in the courts. Every judge to date, in multiple sonar cases, had agreed with NRDC's arguments that the Navy's sonar training protocols violated federal environmental laws. Even the industrial manufacturers of naval sonar seemed intimidated by Reynolds. It hadn't escaped Pittenger's notice that not one of the sonar companies had raised a voice in defense of the Navy or of their own technology—a silence he attributed to their fear that they might become the next target of an NRDC lawsuit.

The Navy needed to wake up to the fact that every time it got knocked down in court, it gave up another piece of whatever moral high ground it still held in the public's esteem. He was as concerned as any other admiral about the need to train for combat missions in real-world conditions. But the courtroom had proven to be NRDC's winning battleground, not the Navy's. It would be much more prudent, he told his fraternity of retired admirals and anyone who would listen in the secretariat, for Secretary Winter to sit down with Reynolds and hammer out an agreement the Navy could live with.

Admiral Pittenger's view was not shared by the fleet commanders. The admirals in charge weren't interested in settling with NRDC. They believed that the conservative Supreme Court offered them their best chance to finally prevail. After all was said and done, they were warriors who planned for victory, not negotiated terms of surrender.

On the last day of February, the Department of Justice filed the Navy's request for the US Supreme Court to hear the case.

• • •

No one knew whether or not the Supreme Court would agree to hear the government's appeal. Of the more than 7,000 petitions for hearing that the US Supreme Court receives each year, it grants fewer than 100, or less than 2 percent. But Reynolds knew that when the request is made by the solicitor general—the attorney who argues for the federal government before the Supreme Court—the court's acceptance rate shoots up to 70 percent.

Even before the solicitor general's petition was filed on the Navy's behalf, Reynolds and his team had begun intensive preparation for what they saw as the inevitable battle to come in the Supreme Court. Richard Kendall added more legal talent, recruiting several of his law firm partners with extensive Supreme Court experience—specialists who would look at the case with a fresh eye, propose alternative approaches to the legal issues, and develop the arguments most likely to sway the justices in NRDC's favor. Work began on a brief opposing the solicitor general's expected petition for review, and 30 days after the petition was filed, NRDC submitted its brief.

At 6:00 a.m. on June 24, Reynolds turned on his laptop and logged on to the SCOTUS (Supreme Court of the United States) blog for the real-time announcement of the cases the court had agreed to hear in its upcoming term. He scrolled through the list of petitions pending to where he found the court's one-word decision on the petition to hear *NRDC v. Winter:* "Grant."

His heart sank. For the Supreme Court to agree to hear a case, four of the nine justices needed to vote yes. Usually, though not always, a vote to hear a case meant that the judges wanted to review the lower court's decision and might well be inclined to overturn it. So Reynolds understood that even before the arduous months of preparation to come, the solicitor general likely had at least four justices leaning his way, with only a fifth needed to overturn.

After riding a five-year wave of courtroom victories against Navy sonar, Reynolds feared that the tide was beginning to turn.

White-beaked Dolphin (*Lagenorhynchus albirostris*)

28

The Highest Court in the Land

Ever since he was a young lawyer, Joel Reynolds had a compulsion for over-preparation that revealed itself in a recurrent anxiety dream. The setting, progression, and outcome of the dream were always the same. It was his Supreme Bad Dream.

The nightmare begins en route to court. Whether or not the traffic-clogged streets resemble Washington, DC, he knows right away that it's the Supreme Court he's trying to get to—and he's running late.

When he finally arrives, he recognizes the courthouse by its neoclassical design, the 16 Corinthian columns guarding the doorway beneath the inscription: "Equal Justice Under Law." But everything's warped. The wide flight of marble steps leading to the doorway feel soft and spongy underfoot, and no matter how quickly he tries to climb them, they seem to propel him backward as if on a down escalator.

Suddenly, against all laws of gravity and physics, he's standing inside the chambers, face-to-face with the nine black-robed judges arrayed like phantoms behind the raised mahogany bench. His oral argument is about to begin.

The green light flicks on, signaling the start of his allotted time. But when Reynolds looks down to consult his notes, he realizes to his horror that they're blank. He rifles through his briefcase but finds only blank pages inside. That's when he realizes he's not dressed for court. No tie, no white shirt, and no suit!

Reynolds had, in fact, once argued a real-life nightmare in front of the Supreme Court, preparing relentlessly for weeks and in vain to find the elusive arguments—any argument—that might salvage his client's prospects in the high court. Back in the 1980s, he'd represented the community living near the Stringfellow Acid Pits, a huge toxic waste dump outside his hometown of Riverside, California. Two dozen corporations and the US Air Force had been dumping toxic waste at the site for years, ultimately contaminating the groundwater aquifer beneath the site. Reynolds first lost the case but then won a reversal from the court of appeals. When the polluters convinced the Supreme Court to review that decision, Reynolds lost 9–0.

The funny thing was, his Supreme Bad Dreams had begun years *before* the Stringfellow case and persisted for decades afterward.

When the Supreme Court agreed to hear *NRDC v. Winter*, Reynolds and Kendall both knew that having Kendall out front during oral argument would increase their chances of winning. They needed all the help they could get. They'd be appearing before the most conservative Supreme Court since the 1930s, and the most activist judicial panel anywhere in the country that had consistently favored government and corporate interests for the past five years.[1] In the prior term, the Supreme Court had reversed eight out of ten cases it had reviewed from the San Francisco–based Ninth Circuit Court of Appeals. Reynolds figured he was better off having a major-firm litigator of Kendall's caliber and reputation, and a long list of Fortune 500 clients, making the case against Navy sonar. Kendall had already argued several times in the Supreme Court, so there was no question that he was up to the task. And he was entitled to his moment at center stage. From the start, he and his firm had delivered the kind of added firepower that Reynolds needed in a case of this intensity and complexity—especially with the Navy determined to appeal all the way up to the Supreme Court.

As the court date approached, Reynolds' biggest fear wasn't simply losing but the risk of losing badly: a so-called hard landing. In a worst-case scenario, a hard landing could make bad law under a range of environmental statutes, establishing bad precedent and even reversing decades of legal gains—not just by NRDC but by other advocacy organizations as well. In overturning *NRDC v. Winter*, the court could make sweeping rulings on national security versus the environment or undermine the power of the courts to restrict agencies of the executive branch. It might also impose strict limitations on who had standing in environmental lawsuits or raise the bar for injunctive relief in future cases. To bolster their arguments, Reynolds and Kendall reached out to other groups and individuals to submit amicus, or "friend of the court," briefs arguing specific points of law.

In the meantime, the Navy Office of Information launched a public relations charm offensive, inviting reporters and politicians on overnight destroyer tours, placing articles in magazines about the Navy's green stewardship of the ocean environment, and lobbying newspaper editorial boards. NRDC mounted a counteroffensive, and Reynolds had to juggle his work on the case with meeting editorial boards, writing op-ed essays, and being interviewed on radio and television. At every opportunity, he emphasized that NRDC and its co-plaintiffs had no intention of interfering with the military's combat mission or national security. All they were asking was that the Navy observe the laws of the land and avoid harming marine mammals during training exercises.

To date, NRDC had held its own with the Navy in terms of favorable newspaper editorials—including from the *New York Times*, the *Washington Post*, and the *Los Angeles Times*—which was one meaningful measure of how his case was doing in the court of public opinion. Just as importantly, coverage by the major papers, newsweeklies, and networks had spiked now that the Supreme Court was hearing the case. Regardless of what the nine justices decided, the broader public had finally been introduced to the topic of acoustic threats to whales and what NRDC was asking the Navy to do to reduce them.

OCTOBER 7, 2008, 3:00 P.M.
Georgetown University Law Center, Washington, DC

On the day before the court was scheduled to hear *NRDC v. Winter*, Reynolds and Kendall were staging their third moot court in two weeks to polish Kendall's oral arguments. At the two previous mock sessions, or moots, as they are called, law school professors at UCLA and Harvard had played the roles of specific judges, posing questions in the style of Chief Justice John Roberts or Antonin Scalia or Anthony Kennedy. Kendall had reserved the final moot for Georgetown University Law Center, which boasted the optimal stage for a dress rehearsal moot court: a precise replica of the Supreme Court chambers. Not only were the law professors seated in the position of the justices, but the dais was raised to the exact height of the original, precisely 18 feet in front of the facing counsel's table. Behind the justices stood the same four neoclassical pillars, burgundy curtain, and hanging clock as in the actual courtroom a half mile away.

During oral arguments before the Supreme Court, each side is allotted a strict time limit of 30 minutes. But your carefully prepared 30-minute argument is likely to be interrupted by one or more justices within the first 20 seconds. Sometimes two judges will ask you questions almost simultaneously or address their remarks to each other. The challenge for the lawyer making an oral argument is to answer the justices' questions directly and courteously, while never losing sight of the main points that you want to convey.

The focus of this final moot, and of much of the previous week's preparation, was the presumed swing vote among the nine justices: Anthony Kennedy. If NRDC had a chance of preventing the high court from reversing its lower court victories, it lay in convincing Kennedy. Reynolds assumed that Chief Justice Roberts and Justices Scalia, Clarence Thomas, and Samuel Alito made up the four-justice bloc that had already voted to hear the case. The government needed to persuade only one other justice to reach the majority required to overturn. Justices Ruth Bader Ginsburg, David Souter, and Stephen Breyer were expected to be more sympathetic to NRDC's position and therefore more likely to vote to affirm, despite the wild card of the military in this particular case.

The ninth justice, and the only one who had served in the military during wartime, was the elderly John Paul Stevens, who had been a naval intelligence officer during World War II. Would that incline him, Reynolds wondered, to defer to the Navy's assessment of national security? But if Stevens was lost, the case was lost, so they focused on Kennedy, the likeliest swing vote decider in this case.

Reynolds and his team had combed through years of Kennedy opinions; even those he wrote when he was a judge on the Ninth Circuit Court of Appeals. But they found little to go on. The most encouraging decision was Kennedy's break, during the previous term, with his conservative colleagues to cast the fifth and deciding vote to overturn indefinite internment of foreign fighters at Guantanamo Bay, Cuba, based on a habeas corpus petition. His rationale, one potentially applicable in the sonar case, was the notion that even the government must comply with the law of the land.

After lunch, NRDC's entire legal team reconvened at the offices of Paul, Hastings, Janofsky & Walker, a corporate firm that had prepared one of the four amicus briefs submitted in support of NRDC and had agreed to lend one of its conference rooms for use as a war room. One last time, they peppered Kendall with questions, critiquing his responses, proposing nuances, and trying to anticipate the reactions of the nine justices and the potential traps that some of them might lay. About midafternoon, the meeting broke up, and Kendall returned to his hotel room to finish preparing his argument and get some sleep.

As Reynolds walked back to his own hotel, passing the White House and the monuments that lined the Great Mall, he tried to stop preparing and just enjoy the moment. The next morning, NRDC's most high-profile sonar case would be argued in front of the highest court in the land. Perhaps it was a fitting climax to his 12-year battle with the US Navy, but it was not where Reynolds had wanted things to end up. He understood that they faced long odds. His young associates—Jasny, Wetzler, and Horowitz—liked to place joke bets before a big court date, if only to release some of the tension: If we win this case, they'd wager, we'll all take our families to Paris for the weekend. If we lose, we'll have to watch Paris Hilton videos for a month. What Reynolds didn't know was that his associates had handicapped NRDC's odds against winning at 8–1.

Reynolds was convinced that NRDC had the better legal arguments in the case. But he knew that justice is less a meritocracy than a complex matrix of politics, personalities, and legal precedent. And Supreme Court justices, unlike lower-court judges, don't have to worry about their decisions being reversed on appeal, which gives them a lot more latitude in their rulings.

What worried Reynolds most was the high court's tradition of deferring to the military during wartime. Perhaps the most egregious historical example was the Supreme Court's 1944 decision to uphold the government's right to confine more than 100,000 American citizens of Japanese descent in internment camps following the attack on Pearl Harbor—based solely on the military's anxiety that some of them might be disloyal and give aid to the enemy. In his 6–3 majority opinion in *Korematsu v. United States*, Chief Justice Harlan F. Stone wrote: "We cannot reject as unfounded the judgment of the military authorities . . . that there were disloyal members of that [Japanese American] population, whose numbers and strength could not be quickly and precisely ascertained." While *Korematsu* would stand as an embarrassing black eye in Supreme Court case history, it illustrated to Reynolds how otherwise thoughtful judges could subordinate their judicial review to perceived national security threats during wartime.

OCTOBER 7, 2008, 11:00 P.M.
Henley Park Hotel, Washington, DC

Finally, there was nothing left to do. Reynolds lay on top of his bed and stared at the ceiling while CNN recapped the day's news. The Dow had plunged 508 points in its latest heart-stopping free fall following the Lehman Brothers meltdown. Iceland's financial system was cratering, and several European banks appeared close behind. Reynolds didn't have any money in the market, but it occurred to him that if the next day brought news of another major bank default, it might crowd out reporting on the Supreme Court arguments. It was hard enough to generate sympathetic media attention for stranded whales during wartime, much less in the midst of a global economic collapse.

Beyond the profound shift in the political landscape, so much had changed on a personal level since Reynolds had first confronted the Navy over ship shock back in 1994. Wetzler and Jasny had joined his legal team, gotten married, and started families. Just that week, Jasny's wife was expecting their second son, so Michael was back west with his family instead of pacing the hallways of the hotel. After spearheading NRDC's international sonar campaign with Jasny for four years, Wetzler had moved on to NRDC's Chicago office to work on other cases.

Reynolds' family had gone through its own life cycle during the 13-year sonar campaign. His parents were both gone now. His son and two daughters had grown from infants into adolescents. And his second marriage, which had begun with a surge of romantic optimism in the early 1990s, was finally and irretrievably finished. He'd tried to keep things afloat, hoping for a renewal or at least a stay until the kids were up and out. But his and Susan's life together had become untenable, and all that remained were the divorce negotiations. The best he could hope for now was to spare the kids some of the pain of the breakup, and to get things with his soon-to-be ex back on a civil footing so they could be decent parents, even if under separate roofs.

Many of his colleagues from his early days at the Center for Law in the Public Interest had gone on to lucrative careers in private practice. Some lived in big houses in the canyons and had box seats at the ballparks. Reynolds still lived in the 1920s-era house he'd bought near the beach in Venice 20 years earlier, and he drove a ten-year-old Ford Focus with fender dents he'd never bothered to repair. He didn't care much about the car, though he sometimes felt bad for his kids when he picked them up at school. His legacy to his children wasn't going to be financial. That much was clear. If he'd failed to give them the kind of happy home life he'd been blessed with, at least they could feel proud of the conservation work he'd done.

Reynolds pulled his dark blue suit from the closet and laid it across the bed. He'd bought the suit years earlier while in Bangkok, Thailand, for a meeting of the World Conservation Congress. It had been so inexpensive he'd bought two of them. Since then, the suits had served triple duty at weddings, funerals, and court appearances. On closer inspection, he realized that the gabardine fabric had grown shiny and a bit threadbare.

Then he noticed a hole near the right shoulder of his jacket. A small circle of white batting showed through the dark fabric, too big to sew closed. He remembered a trick he'd learned from his father—his role model since youth in the art of frugality. Once, en route to a choral concert he was conducting in Riverside, his father realized that he'd left his black bow tie at home. Stopping quickly at Kmart, the only bow tie they could find featured garish black and white checks. So his father bought a black Magic Marker and colored in the white squares. He assured Joel that no one would notice.

Three blocks from the hotel was a CVS drugstore that stayed open till midnight. Reynolds was grateful for an excuse to take a late-night walk. It was a balmy October evening, and each time he crossed an intersection, he glimpsed the illuminated obelisk of the Washington Monument on his left. He found a navy blue Sharpie pen for $1.89. Back at the hotel, it took only a minute to dot in his repair. Not an exact match for the suit color but close enough to escape notice, he hoped.

OCTOBER 8, 2008
US Supreme Court

Reynolds awoke before dawn for the 10 o'clock oral arguments. The Supreme Court distributes fewer than 100 seats to the public on a first-come, first-serve basis, and the line on the sidewalk outside the court was already full by 6:30, with the majority of visitors appearing to be uniformed naval personnel. Reynolds recognized some friendly faces from NRDC's Washington, DC, office. Naomi Rose from the Humane Society was there with her husband, dolphin researcher Chris Parsons.

Reynolds was relieved to see that his 16-year-old son, Sam, had made it to the court in time to secure a place in line. For this special occasion, Reynolds had flown Sam in from Los Angeles the evening before to hear the oral arguments.

Reynolds met Kendall inside the building, where they were ushered into the clerk's conference room for the traditional preargument greeting from the clerk. Once inside the chamber itself, Reynolds was again surprised by the small scale and intimacy of the Supreme Court chamber. To the left of the bench, raised up like box seats in an old-fashioned theater, was the press gallery, with the most senior Supreme Court reporters seated closest to the justices. Nina Totenberg of NPR and the *PBS NewsHour* had the prime perch up front.

As the public spectators filed into the rear of the gallery, Reynolds noticed that the front row of invited guests, facing the justices' dais, was filled with admirals in full dress whites. He shook hands with Admiral Daly, who had recently earned his third star and a promotion to deputy commander and chief of staff at US Fleet Forces Command.

Before Daly left Washington for Norfolk, the newly confirmed solicitor general, Gregory Garre, had asked him for a briefing on the military details of the case he'd be arguing, which Daly had been pleased to provide. Daly had wanted to be here today, both to show the flag and to see how well the solicitor general had mastered the facts of the case.

At 10 o'clock sharp, the marshal of the court instructed everyone to rise as the black-robed justices filed in and took their assigned seats, by seniority, on either side of the chief justice. For all the tension surrounding the outcome, Reynolds delighted in the high drama of the scene. Beneath the theater of the judicial garb, the solemn chambers, and immutable rituals lay the ideological battle lines among the justices. And underlying the political blood feuds was the incalculable human factor, multiplied by nine. One woman, eight men. Their only common feature was their unassailable power to uphold or rewrite the law in the world's most powerful democracy.

After six years of overlapping sonar lawsuits and more than a year of non-stop work on this one case, it was shocking how brief the oral arguments were. Not much longer than back-to-back rounds of *Jeopardy!*—and with just as strict a clock.

Gregory Garre had the first 30 minutes to argue the Navy's case. During his opening, Garre did his best to stake out his central theme of national defense.

JUSTICE KENNEDY:

I take it that you are here because you find the decision of the Ninth Circuit, and I take it of the district court, prejudicial for the government on an ongoing basis; and what are the principal reasons for that?

SOLICITOR GENERAL GARRE:

Because of its impact on national security, Justice Kennedy.

Justices Souter and Ginsburg soon began picking apart Garre's contention that a federal agency has the authority to sidestep environmental protections by declaring an emergency. Souter pressed him to acknowledge that the Navy had brought the "emergency circumstances" on itself by waiting until the exercises had begun to conduct a complete Environmental Impact Statement. Justice Scalia waded in to throw the solicitor general a lifeline.

JUSTICE SCALIA:

Look, the problem you face—and maybe you're being whipsawed—is that . . . at the time the Environmental Assessment was issued, it was a good faith completion of the Navy's responsibilities. And that's the argument being made against you. It assumes the Environmental Assessment wasn't enough. And I'm not sure that . . . assumption is valid.

SOLICITOR GENERAL GARRE:

Well, that's right. And as I indicated earlier—I want to be clear—the Navy believes that its Environmental Assessment was not only prepared in good faith, but was appropriate and reached the right conclusions.

Before his time elapsed, Garre made sure to assert, "No marine mammals will be killed as a result of these exercises . . . They hear the [sonar] sound, and they go in the opposite direction. It also has some temporary effect on their feeding patterns."

Then it was Kendall's turn to argue for NRDC. As soon as he began speaking, several justices—particularly Roberts—interrupted to make their points veiled as questions. The chief justice wondered aloud why District Judge Cooper hadn't weighed the harm of sonar to marine mammals against "the potential that a North Korean diesel-electric submarine might draw close to Pearl Harbor undetected." Alito asked skeptically if a judge could be considered an expert on antisubmarine warfare, adding, "Isn't there something incredibly odd about a single district judge making a determination on a defense question that is contrary to what the Navy has made?" When Alito and Scalia started ganging up on Kendall, Ginsburg interjected a response that allowed him to reclaim the train of his argument.

Reynolds followed carefully every word, every inflection of the justices' comments. He listened particularly intently to whatever Kennedy had to say. But the much-scrutinized "swing" justice had learned to keep his cards close to his chest, though he did remark at one point that when the president and the Defense Department "jointly made the determination that this [sonar training] was necessary for the national defense . . . they certainly must be given great weight."

Thomas, as usual, said nothing at all during the oral arguments, keeping his eyes closed most of the time. The only surprising line of questioning, to Reynolds' ear, came from Justice Breyer, who they'd presumed would be friendly to their arguments. At one point, Breyer made a statement that seemed to sum up the government's national security position more succinctly than the solicitor general had managed to:

JUSTICE BREYER:

Look, I don't know anything about this. I'm not a naval officer. But if I see an admiral come along with an affidavit that says—on its face, it's plausible—that you've got to train people when there are these layers [in the water], all right, or there will be subs hiding there with all kinds of terrible weapons, and he swears that under oath. And I see on the other side a district judge who just says, "You're wrong," I then have to look to see what the basis is, because I know that district judge doesn't know about it either. So, the basis so far I'm thinking on this one is zero.

MR. KENDALL:

There was also a prior exercise in Hawaii. You will recall from the brief that we had a prior litigation that resulted in the consent decree in [which] the Navy agreed to train with a surface ducting powerdown.* So, they had

---

* "Surface ducting" occurs when a concentration of warm water on the surface funnels and amplifies sonar sound signals, as had occurred in the Bahamas during the March 2000 mass stranding.

previously told the same judge that they were capable of training in surface ducting conditions with that powerdown, else they would not have agreed to that decree. The problem that the judge had is that the Navy cannot be judge of its own cause. Deference does have its limits . . .

JUSTICE BREYER:
Generalities. You see, of course, I agree with you as a generality. What I am missing here is the specifics, because I am nervous about it, as you can see. And what I am nervous about is that there just wasn't enough on the other side, on your side.

Near the end of Kendall's argument, Breyer interrupted to ask rhetorically, "How does the basic thing work? Because to a layperson, when I think of the armed forces preparing an Environmental Impact Statement, I think, the whole point of the armed forces is to hurt the environment [*laughter from the gallery*]. I don't understand how it's supposed to work. Of course they are going to do something that's harmful."

To which Kendall responded without missing a beat: "I think the point of the armed forces is to safeguard our freedoms while causing the least damage possible to our environment."

And then, at 11:05, the oral arguments were over, and everyone spilled out onto the courtroom steps. Nina Totenberg commandeered a corner of the stairs for her on-camera commentary and an interview with Reynolds. NRDC's entire team, joined by lawyers for the California Coastal Commission, posed for pictures, and then Reynolds posed with his son.

Afterward, the team converged once again at the Paul Hastings conference room for a debrief of the morning's argument. As seasoned court watchers, they knew it was impossible to predict from the justices' questions how they would line up on a vote. They'd just have to wait and see.

Peale's Dolphin (*Lagenorhynchus australis*)

29

Endgame

On November 4, 2008, almost a month after the Supreme Court arguments, Barack Obama defeated John McCain to become the 44th president of the United States. Reynolds was relieved that President Bush wouldn't be succeeded by McCain, a former Navy captain whose father and paternal grandfather had both been four-star Navy admirals. Obama would soon be appointing new leadership at all the agencies Reynolds had been warring with for the past decade. And in all likelihood, Obama would someday fill some vacancies in the Supreme Court. But for the time being, the outcome of the sonar case still rested with the current nine justices.

A week later, Reynolds was in Wellington, New Zealand, the first stop in a two-week energy and climate change fact-finding tour with utility executives and state regulators. At 5:05 in the morning, he was awakened by a phone call. His first thought, on reaching for the receiver in the pitch-dark hotel room, was: it's never good news at five in the morning.

"We lost the sonar case," said the voice on the other end of the line. It was Mitch Bernard, a close friend and NRDC's litigation director, calling from the New York office. Bernard gave him a rundown of the ruling the court had just released. It voted 5–4 on one issue, and 6–3 on another. The justices had broken down along predictable lines, with Chief Justice Roberts writing the majority opinion.

Reynolds went down to the front desk to retrieve the full decision that Bernard had faxed over. He took it back upstairs and sat on the edge of his bed to read.

Roberts invoked two presidential quotations to bookend his decision.[1] He opened his opinion with George Washington's statement: "To be prepared for war is one of the most effectual means of preserving peace." Twenty-four pages later, he closed with Theodore Roosevelt: "The only way in which a Navy can ever be made efficient is by practice at sea, under all the conditions which would have to be met if war existed."

In between those two calls to arms, Roberts presented his rationale for overturning Judge Cooper's and the court of appeal's injunction. His central argument was that "the lower courts failed to properly defer to senior Navy officers' specific, predictive judgments about how the preliminary injunction would reduce the effectiveness of the Navy's Southern California training exercises."

In weighing the "balance of hardships" between the Navy and the plaintiffs, he ruled: "We do not discount the importance of the plaintiffs' ecological, scientific, and recreational interests in marine mammals. Those interests, however, are plainly outweighed by the Navy's need to conduct realistic training exercises to ensure that it is able to neutralize the threat posed by enemy submarines."

The good news, for Reynolds and NRDC, was that in order to convince Justices Kennedy and Stevens to sign on to his majority opinion, Roberts had framed the decision in the narrowest possible terms. The court overturned only two of the six mitigation measures imposed by Judge Cooper's injunction: the extended safety zone around the sonar ship when marine mammals were sighted, and the "powering down" during surface ducting conditions. The court's ruling left the other four provisions of the injunction in place.

Justice Ruth Bader Ginsburg wrote an impassioned dissent, which Justice Souter joined.[2] "There is no doubt that the training exercises serve critical interests," she wrote. "But those interests do not authorize the Navy to violate statutory command." Ginsburg's dissent was faint consolation to Reynolds, since dissents have no force of law. But they can be cited in subsequent legal arguments, and they can hold sway with judges in later rulings. It didn't escape Reynolds' notice that it was four female judges—Laporte on LFA, and Cooper, Fletcher (of the Ninth Circuit Court of Appeals), and Ginsburg on midfrequency—who had shown the grit to stand up to the US Navy in the course of the sonar cases rather than defer to the "predictive powers" of the Navy's fleet commanders.

Bernard called back to tell Reynolds that NRDC was holding a telephone press conference in an hour. Bernard wanted him on the call to frame the Supreme Court decision in the most positive light and then respond to questions. There was no way to spin the decision as anything other than a setback. But on the soft-landing side, Reynolds could emphasize that the court had chosen not to rule on the broad, more damaging issues the Navy had asked it to resolve, including whether preliminary injunctions were allowable in environmental actions to protect individual animals from harm.

The court had narrowly ruled that the public interest lay in securing the strongest military defense rather than in enforcing marine mammal protections. Roberts affirmed the military's accountability to the law, while granting it an exemption in this instance: "Of course, military interests do not always trump other considerations, and we have not held that they do," he wrote. "In this case, however, the proper determination of where the public interest lies does not strike us as a close question."

All in all, Reynolds and Bernard agreed, the court's opinion was a soft landing that would do little to limit NRDC's and other groups' power to litigate against federal agencies in the future.

After the telephone press conference, Reynolds barely had time to shower and dress before boarding a bus for a day of meetings and a tour of a geothermal plant 50 miles out of town. All day long, he conducted interviews via cell phone about the Supreme Court decision with reporters in the United States, Europe, Australia, and New Zealand.[3]

At 11 o'clock that night, after he'd finished a final newspaper interview, Reynolds needed to clear his head. He set out for a walk through the hilly streets of Wellington. The colorful Victorian houses were cloaked in a soft, misting rain that reminded Reynolds of San Francisco. Or perhaps he was just homesick. He wished he could be with his kids now, doing something other than thinking about the case he'd just lost.

As he walked downhill toward the harbor, he emptied his mind of all the rationales and reassurances he'd been feeding himself, and the media, since dawn. How the odds had been stacked against them once the Supreme Court accepted the case. How he was relieved that they'd eked out a soft landing. How he was fully satisfied with the case they'd argued and wouldn't have done anything differently. How he'd always reminded his young associates that if you can't stand to lose big cases, you don't belong in advocacy law—that if you don't lose the big ones from time to time, you're not taking on tough-enough cases, not fighting the most important, most difficult battles. They were all true, in the hollow way that platitudes can describe but not inhabit the truth.

Reynolds had reached the harbor now, and he looked out across Cook Strait to the coastline of South New Zealand. For millennia, herds of humpback, right, minke, and sperm whales had passed through the strait each year on their way from their feeding grounds in Antarctica to their breeding grounds in the South Pacific. During his maiden voyage in 1770, Captain James Cook described the whales off New Zealand as too numerous to count. A hundred years later, dozens of whaling stations lined the shores on either side of the strait, until the right whales were hunted to extinction. In the twentieth century, floating factory ships extended commercial whaling to the extreme southern latitudes, and by the early 1960s, the Japanese, Russian, and New Zealand fleets finally exhausted the stocks of humpbacks and sperm whales.

Each June and July, the Cook Strait was now the site of an annual whale survey to count what was left of the migration. The numbers had been creeping upward since the end of commercial whaling in 1964. In 2007 the survey counted just 25 humpbacks and one southern right whale passing through the strait.

Reynolds wondered if saving the whales was simply a grandiose fantasy.

Having barely escaped commercial whaling, were the survivors doomed to be overrun by the ceaseless naval arms race after more and more powerful acoustic weapons? Would judges and politicians continue to defer to admirals in their "balance of hardships" calculations, until there were no more whales left to save?

Reynolds could feel the anger he'd been staving off all day finally flooding in. The phrases from Roberts' ruling hammered in his head. They seemed to him less about the law than bare-knuckled politics—like *Gore v. Bush* eight years earlier, when the court had turned a blind eye to long-established precedent in order to reach a political result. The chief justice of the Supreme Court had the unassailable power to make new law, so long as he could muster a majority. But this was the battleground where he'd had to stand and fight. So be it.

He didn't try to soothe his anger. He welcomed it, like an old and trusted ally. He knew that he needed it as fuel and as firepower for the battles that lay ahead.

A month after the Supreme Court ruling on *NRDC v. Winter*, Reynolds began negotiating with the Navy's lawyers. There was, it seemed, always another settlement to negotiate. And in Reynolds' experience, that's where he could make tangible progress, mark his position, and draw the future battle lines.

After a year and a half of nonstop litigation over *NRDC v. Winter*, the lawyers on both sides felt a bit like boxers who had gone 15 bruising rounds without landing a knockout. The Roberts decision had thrown out two of the six safety measures imposed by the lower-court judge, but little had changed in the rules of engagement, and few of the underlying legal or procedural issues had been resolved. In addition, both sides wanted to settle the pending midfrequency sonar case that NRDC had filed back in 2005, which had become mired in discovery motions. Bush was leaving office in six weeks, and no one could predict where President Obama and his new Secretary of the Navy would come down on the environment–versus–defense question.

Reynolds was willing to clear the decks of the sonar cases if he could get commitments on comprehensive Environmental Impact Statements and secure targeted funding for future research. The Navy had already codified a number of important safety measures: exclusion zones around coastlines, biologically important areas, and marine sanctuaries were now institutionalized, as was visual and audio surveillance for whales before and during trainings—although the specifics of the safeguards were still in dispute. He knew he'd have to leave some issues on the table for future negotiation. But in a few months, he'd be sitting across from the newly appointed NOAA and Fisheries administrators, who in all likelihood would be more receptive to his point of view.

By the end of the negotiations, the Navy agreed to a schedule for filing comprehensive Environmental Impact Statements for all its training ranges. The Office of Naval Research agreed to earmark $14.75 million over the course of the next three years for research in key beaked whale and other whale habitats in sonar training areas, on methods to improve whale detection, and on effects of sonar-induced stress on marine mammals.

What the Navy leadership and its lawyers wanted most—and what they felt entitled to after finally winning a case in court—was a respite from "death by injunction," as they had come to refer to NRDC's litigation tactics. They wanted NRDC to agree to talk first and sue second when disputes arose: specifically, a 120-day cooling-off period during which both sides would try to mediate disputes before going to court. Reynolds was agreeable, so long as he didn't forfeit any right to sue if mediation failed. He always preferred negotiation over litigation, but he also knew that without the threat of a lawsuit, he had no leverage to negotiate.

When he was finally finished negotiating the settlement, Reynolds felt wrung out. But his anger had receded enough for him to acknowledge what he'd accomplished. While they'd suffered a setback, litigating the sonar case in front of the Supreme Court had elevated the topic to a level of national discussion that was unimaginable even a few years earlier. He felt confident they were slowly but surely reining in the Navy's use of sonar in training exercises. They still had a ways to go to bring the Navy into full compliance with federal laws, but the issues under discussion were like night and day compared with the way the Navy operated back in the mid-1990s, under a veil of secrecy and accountable to no rules but its own. He needed to keep pushing for better safeguards, but the Navy's obligation to comply with federal environmental laws was no longer in dispute.

Still, Reynolds knew better than to become complacent. He'd learned that you never truly win a conservation battle—you just win the right to fight another day. Like an alcoholic, the environment is never saved. It always needs saving. So do the whales.

When Ken Balcomb heard about the Supreme Court decision, he was posting flyers up and down the Oregon coastline asking residents to report any killer-whale sightings to the Orca Network website. He found an internet café and logged on to the Supreme Court website to read the decision and the dissents. The last time he'd read a Supreme Court decision was in a Philosophy of Law class he took as a prelaw undergraduate at Berkeley. Reading the Roberts decision online, he was glad he'd decided against going to law school. He had to laugh at the idea of Roberts making his case by invoking Teddy Roosevelt—the ultimate warmonger with his "big-stick" gunboat diplomacy. The Supreme Court, in his view, was just another omnipotent gunboat redrawing the legal boundaries as it steamed ahead. Just like Teddy Roosevelt had.

Balcomb believed that the lawsuits had been the right medicine at the right time. It had taken that kind of 4x4 across the forehead to make the Navy see reason and put some limits on its sonar exercises. But he wasn't convinced that the problem was going to get resolved in the courts. As a Navy veteran who understood military chain of command, Balcomb considered it the responsibility of the president, as commander in chief, to set things straight. The president couldn't issue the Navy a waiver that exempted it from the law, the way Bush had tried to do. But the president sure as hell could order the fleet to *obey* the law. Back in the summer of 2000, immediately following the Bahamas stranding, he'd written President Clinton and asked him to direct Navy Secretary Danzig to permanently exclude known whale habitats from sonar training exercises. He'd written the same letter to George W. Bush in 2001. Now he would write to the new president and ask him to intervene.

Balcomb wasn't so naïve as to think that President Obama would follow his advice. But he still had to write the letter. That was his job. To write to politicians. To talk to journalists and to anyone else who would listen. To keep tabs on the whales in Puget Sound and on the Navy ships in the area. To keep beating the drum as loud and as long as he could.

EPILOGUE

First they ignore you, then they laugh at you, then they fight you, then you win.

—*Mahatma Gandhi*

FIVE YEARS LATER; AUTUMN 2013

Joel Reynolds had been willing to suspend sonar lawsuits for a while, but he was constitutionally incapable of "cooling off." He immediately threw himself into a fight to stop development of the Pebble Mine in southwest Alaska, which—if built, as proposed, at the headwaters of the Bristol Bay watershed—promised to become one of the largest open-pit copper and gold mines anywhere, generating some billion tons of contaminated mining waste and threatening the most productive wild salmon fishery left in the world.

It was a trademark, Joel Reynolds-led NRDC campaign, involving alliances with local groups on the ground, public pressure on the multinational backers from its membership, and media attention generated by NRDC trustee Robert Redford. Reynolds held face-to-face meetings with the mining interests, and confronted their lobbyists on Capitol Hill. Within four years of Reynolds and NRDC's entering the fray, all three of the major mining company partners had pulled out, leaving only a small Canadian company remaining, in search of partners. After an in-depth EPA study found that large-scale mining threatened the Bristol Bay region with "catastrophic" risks, Reynolds—recently elevated to western director of NRDC—called on that agency to use its authority under the Clean Water Act to stop the project. In February 2014, EPA initiated a formal process to do just that.

Meanwhile, Ken Balcomb had also refused to cool off. In 2009, when the Navy introduced proposals to build a mine-warfare range in its Northwest Training Range Complex, Balcomb spearheaded the local protests. The Puget Sound orca population continued to struggle following the crash of their prey species, the Chinook salmon. The pods had to venture farther and farther afield each season for food. Since underwater explosives would further disrupt their foraging patterns, Balcomb pressed Fisheries to enforce the "endangered" protections the orcas were due under the Endangered Species Act.

Dozens of local groups lodged protests with Fisheries, and NRDC submitted a 20-page legal and scientific declaration. While the suit was pending, Michael Jasny, who had recently been promoted to head of NRDC's Marine Mammal Protection Project, helped Balcomb convene a cross-border conference with Canadian conservationists and Fisheries officials to implement a coordinated plan for protecting both the Southern and Northern Communities of orcas.

In the five years since the Supreme Court decision, consensus had built inside the research community—even among Navy and Fisheries researchers—about the threat that noise pollution, including military sonar, poses to whales. Research into whale distribution and behaviors—funded largely by ONR as part of the sonar settlement—revealed that much lower sound levels than previously believed cause whales to change their migration patterns and eating and communication habits. Most importantly, chronic noise pollution depresses their reproduction. In particular, research into beaked whale populations in the waters off California—as well as a study of beaked whales in the Bahamas published by Diane Claridge as part of her PhD thesis—documented a dramatic drop-off in reproductive health.[1]

Meanwhile, whales continued to mass-strand—sometimes in alarmingly high numbers—in the presence of sonar.

Sixty dolphins stranded along the coast of Cornwall, England, in 2008, by far the largest marine mammal mortality ever recorded in British waters. The forensic investigation involving 24 experts from five countries and multiple government agencies identified nearby exercises being conducted by the Royal Navy—in collaboration with American Navy forces—as the only possible cause of the strandings.[2]

At least ten, and possibly dozens, of Cuvier's beaked whales stranded or washed ashore dead on the Greek island of Corfu in December 2011. The stranding coincided with a major Italian navy exercise using sonar in the nearby Ionian Sea.[3]

And on May 30, 2008, a pod of more than 100 melon-headed whales stranded in a mangrove estuary on the northwest end of Madagascar. Despite intensive rescue efforts by both local authorities and experts from around the world, 75 of the whales died on the shore. An independent review panel of five scientists appointed by the International Whaling Commission spent several years examining evidence. They "systematically excluded or deemed highly unlikely" nearly every other possibility before concluding in their final report (to which Darlene Ketten appended a 26-page analysis of the specimen CT scans) that these deep-water whales had been driven ashore by an underwater mapping sonar that the ExxonMobil Corporation was using nearby to search for oil and gas deposits.[4]

Then in 2012 the Navy filed public notice of its plans for expanding exercises on its Undersea Warfare Training Ranges up and down its East and West Coast ranges. In addition to increasing its sonar exercises on both coasts and in Hawaii, the Navy proposed new mine warfare and firing ranges for torpedoes and other underwater explosive ordnance. The Navy's own Environmental Impact Statements predicted millions of marine mammal "takes," including nearly one thousand deaths and 13,000 serious injuries. For the first time, the Navy included explosives testing along with sonar trainings in its projections, which gave a more comprehensive picture of the overall impacts of the expanded activities.

Fisheries was preparing to approve permits for the Navy's expanded undersea warfare activities across its ranges by January 2014, and it was already girding for the response—not just from NRDC, which had resolved to return to court to challenge the permits, but also from a host of national, international, and grassroots organizations.*

SEPTEMBER 7, 2013
Smugglers Cove, San Juan Island, Washington

Reynolds had never visited Balcomb at his research station home on San Juan Island, but now that he was heading back into the fight against the Navy and Fisheries, he wanted to check in with Balcomb in person and ask him to re-up. With his intensive involvement in the Pebble Mine campaign, Reynolds was frequently traveling through Seattle. So a week earlier, he'd called to see if Balcomb would be around to talk. "I'm still here," said Balcomb. "So are the orcas. Come on over."

The last time Reynolds had seen him—when they were both members of a congressionally mandated advisory group meeting on ocean noise pollution some years earlier—Balcomb was undergoing treatment for his prostate cancer and looked like hell. When Reynolds pulled up behind his cedar shingle house on Smugglers Cove and Balcomb greeted him at the door, Reynolds was reassured by how ruddy and robust he looked at 73 years of age. He was wearing jeans and one of his trademark T-shirts—"Pacific Beach: A quaint little drinking town with a fishing problem"—along with his customary wide, toothy grin.

Reynolds had recently taken his two teenaged daughters to a screening of *Blackfish*, a documentary about captive orcas in which Balcomb appeared. When they heard that their father would be visiting Balcomb, they said he had to come back with a picture. So Balcomb set up a camera on a tripod and shot the two of them against a backdrop of whale skulls that lined the foyer of the house.

They updated each other on their personal lives. Balcomb was healthy

---

*In December 2013, Fisheries approved a five-year permit allowing the Navy to expand its sonar and explosives training activities on its Southern California and Hawaii ranges. Within a month, in separate lawsuits, Earthjustice and NRDC, along with half a dozen co-plaintiffs, sued the Navy and Fisheries for violations of the Marine Mammal Protection Act, the Endangered Species Act, and the Coastal Zone Management Act.

again, having had follow-up treatment for his prostate cancer. He had a couple of girlfriends who moved in and out of Smugglers Cove, seasonally, like the whales. Balcomb acknowledged, with a smile, that he wasn't sure whether the women were coming to see him or the orcas.

Now, in mid-September, the summer interns and most of the whales had departed for the season. Dave Ellifrit had moved to San Juan Island in 2008 and bought a house. Other researchers had married each other, divorced, and remarried other young colleagues on the team. Balcomb joked that it was harder to keep track of the researchers' couplings and uncouplings than those inside the resident orca pods.

Reynolds told him about his fiancée and showed him photos on his phone. Jenny was an environmental chemistry professor at UCLA whom he'd been dating for several years. They'd recently gone to city hall to get a marriage license. But the day they showed up, it was swamped by hundreds of gay and lesbian couples who'd arrived for licenses during the week after the recent Supreme Court ruling that upheld California's same-sex marriage law. The line was out the door and around the block, so they decided to go out for lunch and return another day.

Balcomb led him on a tour of the grounds, including the 1929 Ford and 1956 Chevy parked in nearby sheds. Back inside, he gave Reynolds a tutorial on some of the finer points of beaked whale hearing, using the three skulls in his living room as teaching props. Then Reynolds sat down at a white piano set incongruously among the skulls; the piano had come with the house, and Balcomb liked having it around as a reminder of his chanteuse mother. Reynolds played a country-and-western song he'd recently written about an old red pickup truck and a woman driving away at dawn with his heart in the flatbed.

When they moved onto the back deck to watch the sunset over Haro Strait, Reynolds immediately recognized the view from the video that Balcomb had shot in 2003 of the USS *Shoup* blasting high-intensity sonar while J Pod cringed along the shoreline. Reynolds had always thought of it as the Zapruder film of whale strandings. He stood there and took it all in. The splendor of the cove at sunset, with the specter of the *Shoup* still hovering in the background.

On this late afternoon, six kayakers were paddling near the shore, and a few fishing boats transited the mouth of the cove. As the sun dipped behind Vancouver Island, Balcomb shot a time-dated photograph, as he did every evening.

Reynolds had bought a bottle of scotch from the ferry station dock. They sipped their drinks as the lights of Victoria, Canada, came up across the strait. Balcomb described how the resident orcas had continued to dwindle in number, down to 80 from a peak of 100 back in 2000. In addition to the drop-off in the local salmon population due to overfishing and runoff from logging operations, Balcomb attributed the orcas' decline to man-made noise from shipping and increased sonar and explosives trainings in their homewaters. Meanwhile, his funding from Fisheries to monitor the orca pods throughout the Pacific Northwest had been cut back from $125,000 to $80,000 a year, which meant less money to hire staff and maintain and operate his research vessel. The Capitol Hill budget battle and sequestration hadn't helped things.

They talked about the upcoming court dates with the Navy and the ways the two of them might work together, particularly on the Northwestern ranges. They ticked through a roll call of all the players who had cycled out of the various federal agencies over the years, from ONR and the fleet and the Navy secretariat, from Fisheries and the Department of Justice. But Balcomb and Reynolds were still here. And so were the whales. They lifted their glasses in the direction of the cove.

Balcomb turned on the speakers connected to the underwater hydrophones, and suddenly the serene visual landscape was overlaid by a cacophony of mechanical sound. A speedboat crossed the mouth of the cove, trailing a rattling roar in its wake. They heard the lower-pitched rumble from the engine of a distant fishing trawler as it chugged past.

Just as the last amber light faded to dark gold, a bank of fog drifted in from the south and unrolled like a deep-pile carpet across the cove. The lights of Victoria went soft, and the drone of the distant engines was interrupted by the occasional bleat of a foghorn.

Just then a different sound came over the hydrophone speakers. A chirping, overlapping conversation, like a flock of shrill birds.

"You hear those chatterboxes?" said Balcomb, rising from his seat and peering into the dense fog. "Sounds like five or six of them, heading in this direction." As the sound of the pod drew closer, the two men moved to the porch railing and strained to look and listen through the fog-damped silence. Then, just below them, something moved through the water. A gentle lapping rose up through the fog.

"Wait for this . . . ," Balcomb said quietly.

And then they heard it: the unmistakable whoosh of air being forced through a half dozen blowholes. Soft yet powerful, like the rumor of a whale.

POSTSCRIPT

In the year since the hardcover edition of *War of the Whales* went to press, the battle between naval sonar and whale conservation has reignited on two fronts.

In the first week of April 2014, during joint antisubmarine exercises among the US, Israeli, and Greek navies, at least five beaked whales stranded and died on the coast of Crete. As graphic photographs of dead whales in the bloody shallows circulated on the Internet, a team of Greek veterinary pathologists rushed to the scene to retrieve fresh organ samples for analysis. The autopsies found hemorrhaging inside the whales' internal organs, bleeding from the ears, and tissue evidence of decompression-like sickness seen in other deep-diving whales following rapid ascents.

Twelve months later, on March 31, 2015—in the most significant case since the Navy prevailed in the 2008 Supreme Court decision—the federal court in Honolulu ruled on a lawsuit filed by NRDC and Earthjustice that challenged the Navy's five-year permit for sonar and other training activities on its Southern California and Hawaii ranges. In unusually strong language, US District Judge Susan Oki Mollway found both the Navy and NMFS in violation of a range of federal laws, including the Marine Mammal Protection Act, the Endangered Species Act, and the National Environmental Policy Act. The court concluded that NMFS's decision to issue the Navy a permit was "arbitrary and capricious," and that "the problems this court identifies are so fundamental that the court cannot conceive of a new Final Rule or new LOA's [Letters of Authorization] that simply tweak the earlier documents and regurgitate old language." Regarding the Environmental Impact Statement on which the permit was based, the court found that "the Navy's categorical and sweeping statements . . . allow for no compromise at all as to space, time, species, or condition."

The court will next determine a remedy for what it has ruled as an illegally issued permit. A settlement of this specific lawsuit may be negotiated, or the Navy may decide to appeal the ruling. Regardless, the legal standoff between the Navy and environmentalists seems likely to continue.

It's been 20 years since Joel Reynolds and NRDC first challenged the Navy over its planned deployment of Low Frequency Active sonar. The compliance gap has narrowed to the point where a single issue stands in the way of a comprehensive legal settlement of the various sonar cases: geographic and seasonal exclusion of sonar testing and training from biologically-important habitats. This exclusion would keep the Navy from conducting sonar trainings in certain habitats during specific times of year when whales are present.

A case in point: during the two decades when NRDC and the Navy have been locked in legal combat, climate change in the Pacific Ocean has forced the California blue whales to migrate further north in search of summer feeding grounds. The only species of blue whales known to have recovered from near-extinction levels, these 100-foot-long Leviathans now spend much of June through September near the Channel Islands, just 25 miles off the Southern California coast.

These are the same Channel Islands where the Navy proposed detonating 10,000-lb explosives during Ship Shock tests in 1995—before Reynolds and NRDC persuaded a judge to block the tests, leading to a settlement in which the Navy agreed to conduct the explosives test away from coastal areas where whales and other marine life are known to congregate.

Similarly, if the Navy would now agree to suspend sonar trainings in these waters from June through September, it could be a pivotal step toward resolution of the decades-long dispute over sonar exercises off the California coast. But the Navy—at least prior to the latest court ruling—has refused to concede the Southern blue whales' summer feeding grounds as a seasonally excluded zone.

After seven years researching and reporting this legal battle, I've come to see the conflict as a culture war between two factions of American society that care deeply about the oceans and marine mammals, but for very different reasons. The disputed issues separating the two sides have narrowed to the point where a negotiated settlement seems within grasp. But the sea of suspicion that divides the combatants is as wide and deep as ever.

While most of the progress towards legal compliance and risk reduction has been propelled by litigation, a comprehensive resolution is unlikely to emerge from the adversarial arena of a courtroom. Judges are ill equipped to impose a settlement of a long-running dispute that is only partially about the law. The Navy is a warrior culture. Many of its leaders view full compliance as "caving in" to environmentalists, who they believe are intent on continuing their legal fight, regardless of whatever concessions or compromises the Fleet might agree to. For their part, leaders on the conservation side tend to view the US Navy as a monolithic adversary, rather than as a diverse group of decision-makers with a spectrum of opinions.

I've drawn some optimism for the possibility of a negotiated global settlement from my own interactions with Navy leaders in the year since the publication of my book. The Navy has an internal tradition of rigorous after-action analysis. Recently, it's been examining the whales-and-sonar conflict as a case study in how to better manage the environmental impact of its training exercises.

The reviewer for the Navy's leading monthly magazine, *Navy Proceedings*, recommended *War of the Whales* as "of great interest to anyone concerned with the uneasy balance between the competing desires for national security and environmental protection . . . I only wonder if some of the real world actors in this drama would have behaved differently, perhaps better, if they knew their actions would be made public."

Last fall, the US Naval Academy in Annapolis, Maryland, made *War of the Whales* assigned reading for its Environmental Security class. When I was asked to speak to midshipmen and faculty at the Academy, I was impressed by how seriously this generation of future officers and their professors embraced the Navy's responsibility as environmental steward of the oceans.

More significant was the invitation I received from the US Naval War College in Newport, Rhode Island, to be a keynote speaker at its Spring Symposium on Maritime Power and International Security. In contrast to the junior officers at the Academy, the 56 men and four women attending the

War College symposium were drawn from the ranks of senior officers in the Navy, Marines, and other services, as well as highly placed military academics and policy analysts.

My takeaway from three days of candid and often self-critical conversations with Navy leaders was that many of them see the courtroom confrontation over sonar as a legal war of attrition. If allowed to continue unresolved, it poses a tactical obstacle to their primary mission of national defense. They want to fix it and move on.

After 20 years of wrangling in the courts, and in the court of public opinion, the Fleet commanders who grasp the tactical self-interest of a comprehensive resolution should take the lead in forging a settlement. If not, it's time for the Navy's civilian leadership—either the Secretary of the Navy or the Commander in Chief—to impose one.

The whales have been waiting long enough.

ACKNOWLEDGMENTS

Researching and writing this book turned into a seven-year odyssey that sent me around the world and, at times, around the bend. I am deeply thankful to the people who guided me from shore to shore and, finally, safely home.

Had I grasped at the outset the depth of my ignorance concerning whales, submarines, the Navy, the ocean, and the law, I never would have dared embark on this project. It was my great good fortune to enlist some of the world's leading experts as my tutors along the way.

Naomi Rose, formerly of the Humane Society of the United States and now at the Animal Welfare Institute, schooled me in the basics of marine mammalogy when I was an absolute beginner. She also introduced me to the world's elite whale scientists at the biennial conference of the Society for Marine Mammalogy in Cape Town, South Africa. Darlene Ketten, whom I first met in Cape Town and later visited in Woods Hole and in Washington, DC, is a gifted teacher who patiently explained to me the fine points of whale hearing, forensic marine mammal pathology, and acoustics. Peter Tyack and Chris Clark were also generous with their time, their anecdotes, and their expertise in bioacoustics. Bob Gisiner and Roger Gentry gave me an insider's perspective on the machinations of the Office of Naval Research and the National Marine Fisheries Service, respectively. Jim Mead of the Smithsonian Institution was my guide to the hidden realm below the National Museum of Natural History, as well as the unseen world of beaked whales. Michael Stocker of Ocean Conservation Research helped me grasp the fundaments of marine acoustics.

Two historians were particularly helpful when I reached out to them for guidance. D. Graham Burnette, professor of history at Princeton University, shared his extensive research into the twentieth-century science of cetology, including his deep dive into the John Lilly archives at Stanford University. Anyone in search of a riveting book about whale science and scientists would do well to read his recently published *The Sounding of the Whale*. Gary Weir, chief historian at the National Geospatial-Intelligence Agency, shared his trove of knowledge, as well as his published and unpublished research into the early days of the US Navy's sound surveillance program. His book *An Ocean in Common* remains the best history of the Navy's patronage of research oceanography.

My special thanks to Retired Admiral Dick Pittenger at Woods Hole, who not only schooled me in the rudiments of antisubmarine warfare and sonar but also vouched for me to other retired admirals who were instrumental in my naval education. Admirals Craig Dorman, Bob Natter, Bill Fallon, Pete Daly, Paul Gaffney, and Larry Baucom all were gracious enough to share their experiences and insights drawn from decades of dedicated service.

I'm also grateful to Admiral Pittenger for introducing me to the world's greatest living oceanographer, Walter Munk, who was in residence that August at Woods Hole's geofluid physics cottage. Dr. Munk subsequently invited me to visit him at his home in La Jolla, California, near the Scripps Institution of Oceanography, where he has taught and conducted research for more than 65 years. It was my singular privilege to spend several fascinating afternoons with Dr. Munk. Further south on the California coast, Sam Ridgway was kind enough to host me at the SPAWAR (Space and Naval Warfare Systems Command) headquarters of the Navy's Marine Mammal Training Program, where he has served continuously since 1961.

I'm indebted to Ken Balcomb and Joel Reynolds, who granted me unfettered access to their friends, families, and colleagues, and patiently taught me what I needed to learn about whale research and environmental law. Michael Jasny, now head of NRDC's marine mammal program, was always ready to answer my questions on an array of topics and offer suggestions for further research.

My editor and publisher, Jonathan Karp, lashed himself to the mast of this book seven years ago and never bolted for the lifeboats—despite my many delays and detours in delivering the manuscript. I will always be grateful for his steadfast encouragement and unerring course corrections, without which I would have been lost at sea.

I am also the happy beneficiary of the topflight publishing team that Jonathan has assembled at Simon & Schuster. Special thanks to art director Jackie Seow for designing such a terrific cover and to Joy O'Meara for the elegant inside pages. (Kudos to Paula Robbins at Mapping Specialists for the excellent endpaper maps and thanks to Mary Challinor for her flawless designer's eye.) Michael Szczerban, another remarkable editor, was kind enough to read the penultimate draft of the manuscript and offer me his astute notes. Production editor Jonathan Evans lavished great attention and care on my book, and Phil Bashe combed through the manuscript with the eagle eyes of a great copy editor. The publicity and marketing group of Cary Goldstein, Sarah Reidy, Richard Rorher, and Elina Vaysbeyn is a dream team whose savvy and smarts have served me well. Finally, I want to thank Nick Greene and Megan Hogan for shepherding this book through every stage of production and for saying yes to each of my many requests.

My agents and trusted friends of twenty years, Gail Ross and Howard Yoon, brought their patented blend of professionalism and passion to this project. The Ross Yoon Agency is the gold standard for excellence and integrity in literary management. Nobody does it better. Anna Sproul, Jennifer Manguera, and Dara Kaye are talented members of the Ross Yoon Agency whom I also count as friends.

I'm pleased to acknowledge the sponsorship of the Ocean Foundation, which enables people like me to dive deeply into important marine topics without going broke in the process. My thanks to its president, Mark Spalding, and board member Angel Braestrup for helping me build bridges to funders. I am grateful for the grant support I received from the Pacific Life Foundation, the Hawley Family Foundation, the Faucett Catalyst Fund, and Furthermore, a program of the J. M. Kaplan Fund.

Every author depends on his writer friends for tough-love responses to manuscript drafts, early and late. I'm particularly thankful to Elsa Walsh for giving me detailed and incisive notes when I sorely needed a fresh perspective. I'm fortunate to have a family rich in talented writers. Tony Horwitz, Elinor Horwitz, and Geraldine Brooks waited patiently until I asked them to read, and then gave me their corrective best. So did my wife, Ericka Markman, who read my first complete draft and gave me detailed notes during what was supposed to be a vacation in the South of France. Peter Glusker is like family, which is why I felt free to ask him to read my first draft. Howie Garrett made several key corrections to my final draft. And to coach and counselor David Pellegrini, thanks for all the solid swing tips along the way.

Two friends deserve special mention for their editorial contributions. Kenneth Wapner is a talented writer and editor who volunteered for the hand-to-hand combat of whipping this manuscript, and this author, into shape. His contributions were invaluable. Stephen Mills, another seasoned veteran of the writing wars, served heroically in the trenches. I trust these guys with my life, and with my darkest writer's fears.

I want to thank Tanya, Julia, and Charlotte for sharing their father with this whale of a book for so long. Encountering the gray whales of Laguna San Ignacio alongside Tanya, and then with Julia, were the best of times for this dad. Charlotte, you're next.

Finally, my heartfelt gratitude to Ericka, who believed in me enough to say, "Go write it," when I first fell hard for this story but lacked the confidence to tell it. Throughout the long and winding passage to publication, she never stinted in her support for me—or in her tireless attention to the daily needs of our daughters—despite having recently launched her own business. She's a spectacular woman who amazes and humbles me every day.

ENDNOTES

Chapter 1: The Day the Whales Came Ashore

1. Marta Azzolini, an Italian intern working with the Bahamas Marine Mammal Survey in the spring of 2000 and one of the strongest swimmers of the group, assisted Diane Claridge by swimming alongside the Cuvier's whale and guiding him out to deeper water.

Chapter 2: Castaways

1. The Atlantic Undersea Test and Evaluation Center (AUTEC) is the US Navy's premier submarine torpedo and sonar test range. Constructed in the 1960s, AUTEC lies 117 miles east of Florida and 60 miles southwest of Abaco. AUTEC's Tongue of the Ocean waterway, at the edge of the Great Bahama Bank, is a unique, flat-bottom deep-water basin approximately 110 nautical miles long and 20 nautical miles wide, and a mile deep. Its flat basin floor enabled the Navy to install extensive arrays of bottom-mounted hydrophones to make precise measurements of acoustic activity inside and surrounding the range.

Chapter 3: Taking Heads

1. Research by Chris Clark at Cornell University on blue whales—which are baleen rather than toothed whales—indicates that they emit very loud sounds at very low frequencies (180 decibels, 14 hertz), which may constitute long-distance echolocation. The idea is that they might bounce their signals off islands, seamounts, or other oceanic features, and, by listening to the returning echo, recognize the "landmark" to locate their position.

2. The co-evolution of deep-diving beaked whales and squid is described in a journal article by two evolutionary biologists at the University of California at Berkeley: David R. Lindberg and Nicholas D. Pyenson, "Things That Go Bump in the Night: Evolutionary Interactions Between Cephalopods and Cetaceans in the Tertiary," *Lethaia* 40, no. 4 (December 2007): 335–43.

3. Until recently, sperm whales and southern elephant seals had competed with Cuvier's beaked whales for record for the deepest and longest dives by an air-breathing animal. But in March of 2014, researchers tracking Cuvier's off the California using electronic tags recorded a record-smashing dive of almost 10,000 feet in depth—the equivalent of eight Empire State Buildings stacked one on top of another. A different Cuvier's dive was timed at more than two hours, breaking the record of 120 minutes by an elephant seal. Schorr GS, Falcone EA, Moretti DJ, Andrews RD (2014) "First Long-Term Behavioral Records from Cuvier's Beaked Whales (*Ziphius cavirostris*) Reveal Record-Breaking Dives." PLoS ONE 9(3): e92633. doi:10.1371/journal.pone.0092633.

4. "The bends": Under pressure, nitrogen in the lung air's oxygen-nitrogen mix is absorbed at greater than normal concentrations into the diver's blood and tissue. The longer a diver remains at depth, the more gradually he needs to ascend to normal atmospheric pressure to allow the nitrogen to reabsorb into the lungs. If he surfaces too quickly, the nitrogen expands and forms bubbles—in much the way that a can of soda forms bubbles when you open it, quickly reducing the pressure inside. The nitrogen bubbles that form in tissue during rapid ascent cause extreme pain in the joints. If a bubble in the blood travels to the brain, it can paralyze or even kill you.

5. The deepest-diving military submarines—the Soviet Alfa-class submarines, constructed at extraordinary expense out of titanium alloy during the height of the Cold War—reached crush depth at 3,700 feet. Cuvier's beaked whales have been measured to dive to almost 10,000 feet.

6. There were multiple aerial sightings of warships in Bahamian waters from March 16–18, including by neighbors of Balcomb's in Northwest Providence Channel near Grand Bahama on March 16 and by Balcomb in Tongue of the Ocean on March 18th. For a precise linear narrative of the stranding and its aftermath, see Balcomb and Claridge's peer-reviewed and published report: K. C. Balcomb and D. E. Claridge, "A Mass Stranding of Cetaceans Caused by Naval Sonar in the Bahamas," *Bahamas Journal of Science* 8, no. 2 (May 2001): 4–6.

Chapter 4: The Loneliness of the Long-Distance Beachcomber

1. John Dominis' photographs of humpback whales appeared in the August 2, 1963, issue of *Life* magazine, pp. 38–45.

2. Balcomb, and the newspaper-reading public, later found out that the Smithsonian and Army bird-banding project was a $3 million classified program funded by the Army's Chemical and Biological Warfare Division in Fort Detrick, Maryland. The Army wanted to study the birds' migratory patterns and range to determine if (1) migratory birds might

inadvertently spread biological and germ warfare agents from test sites in the Pacific to populations on the mainland, and (2) these same birds might be deployed as an "avian vector of disease" to intentionally deliver biological weapons to targets across borders. When first confronted with rumors of such a collaboration with the Army in 1969, the leadership of the Smithsonian vehemently denied any involvement. But when documentary evidence came to light in 1985, the Smithsonian vowed to never again accept contracts for classified military research. See also P. M. Boffey, "Biological Warfare: Is the Smithsonian Really a 'Cover'?" *Science* 163, no. 3869 (February 21, 1969): 791–96; Ted Gup, "Pacific Gulls Doubled as War Hawks," *Washington Post*, May 20, 1985, A1.

Chapter 5: In the Silent Service

1. Radar, developed in the 1930s at the US Naval Research Lab to target and track surface ships and aircraft, uses echolocation by bouncing radio waves, rather than sound waves, off of objects. In addition to finding submarines once they had surfaced, radar could also detect a snorkel or periscope that penetrated the surface to breathe air or scan for ships. It wasn't until WWII that the term "sonar" was coined (for sound navigation ranging) to parallel the naming of radar (radio detecting and ranging).

2. According to Norman Polmar, "The Soviet Navy: How Many Submarines?" *Proceedings* 124, no. 2 (February 1998): 1, www.usni.org/magazines/proceedings/1998-02/soviet-navy-how-many-submarines, from 1945 through 1991, the Soviet Union produced 727 submarines—492 with diesel-electric or closed-cycle propulsion and 235 with nuclear propulsion. This compares with the US total of 212 submarines—43 with diesel propulsion (22 from World War II programs) and 169 nuclear submarines (including the diminutive NR-1). Not included are Soviet midget submarines and the single US midget, the X-1 (USS *X-1*).

3. In one of the odd coincidences of scientific exploration, a Russian acoustician named Leonid Brekhovskikh made a virtually simultaneous and independent discovery of the deep sound channel during wartime explosive experiments in the Sea of Japan. But because of the secrecy of Soviet and American acoustic research, these WWII allies and Cold War adversaries wouldn't learn of each other's discoveries for many decades.

4. Ewing's pilot rescue system was ingenious. The downed pilot would drop a hollow metal sphere from his floating dinghy into the ocean. It would sink and eventually implode at the increased water pressure at 3,000 feet, sending a low-frequency sound signal through the deep sound channel to two or more bottom-mounted receivers connected by cable to coastal listening stations thousands of miles away. Once the pilot's position was triangulated, rescue aircraft could be dispatched from the nearest carrier in the Pacific.

5. For most of the Cold War, SOSUS represented the only way a woman could claim warfare experience and compete with her male counterparts on a nearly equal basis. Before the early 1980s, when women began being assigned to surface ships and were accepted into flight training, SOSUS was an opportunity for women who wanted to serve in an operational role in the US Navy. Female line officers started being assigned to the SOSUS stations in 1970 when Norah Anderson joined the listening station on Eleuthera and became the first woman to take a place on the operations floor.

   See also Gary Weir, "The American Sound Surveillance System: Using the Ocean to Hunt Soviet Submarines, 1950–1961," *International Journal of Naval History* 5, no. 2 (August 2006): 12–18. According to naval historian Weir, "Since the Navy classified SOSUS activity as a warfare specialty, the door opened for hundreds of women to a Navy career outside of medicine, education, or administration."

6. The following concise description of the two types of military submarines appears on the US Navy's website (www.navy.mil/navydata/cno/n87/faq.html): "Attack submarines (designated SSN and commonly called fast attacks) are designed to pursue and attack enemy submarines and surface ships using torpedoes. They also carry cruise missiles with conventional high-explosive warheads to attack enemy shore facilities. Fast attack submarines launched cruise missiles against targets in Iraq during Operation Desert Storm and targets in Serbia during the conflict in Kosovo. They also conduct intelligence, surveillance and reconnaissance missions, mine laying and support special operations.

   "Fleet ballistic missile submarines (designated as 'SSBNs') carry long-range nuclear warhead missiles. They roam the ocean avoiding contact with other submarines and surface ships. The ability of the fleet ballistic missile submarine to survive a nuclear attack against the United States made them the most credible nuclear deterrent during the Cold War . . . A US Navy fleet ballistic missile submarine carries 24 Trident ballistic missiles. Each missile carries several nuclear Multiple Independently-targetable Re-entry Vehicles (MIRVs)."

7. The Soviets had their own network of underwater listening stations, but theirs was much less extensive and much more primitive than SOSUS. Balcomb reports that SOSUS operators in the late 1960s were aware of a Low Frequency Active sound system that the Soviets used to mask the sounds of their submarines and create clutter in the acoustic environment.

8. *The Silent World* (*Le Monde du Silence*), co-directed by Cousteau and a young Louis Malle, won the 1956 Academy Award for Best Documentary and the Palme d'Or at the 1956 Cannes Film Festival. Shot aboard the ship *Calypso*, it was one of the first color films to use underwater photography.

9. The highly classified nature of Navy-funded acoustic research was a chronic source of friction between ONR and the top scientific talent it recruited. Like all academics, ac-

ousticians wanted to publish their research in peer-reviewed journals. If they couldn't publish—or could publish only heavily redacted versions of their research—researchers viewed Navy work as a lot less attractive, regardless of the steady funding stream. So in the 1950s, the Navy decided to create its own in-house, peer-reviewed journal. Published under the auspices of the Navy's Underwater Sound Advisory Group, the *Journal of Underwater Acoustics* became the most prestigious publication in its field. The fact that its distribution was limited to the 150 scientists with high security clearances only added to its elitism and cachet.

10. Back in 1970, Roger Payne—who would later popularize humpback whale songs—published the first scientific paper to identify the risk that ocean noise pollution posed to baleen whales. In his largely speculative article, Payne and co-author Doug Webb estimated the progressive impact of industrial shipping, oil and gas drilling, and other ambient noise on the ability of baleen whales to communicate with one another. Payne hypothesized that baleen whales depended on the deep sound channel to communicate with mates across entire ocean basins, and that industrial noise pollution was drastically reducing the range of those mating calls—a phenomenon he called masking. At the time, Payne's theory of long-distance communication among whales was roundly derided by marine acousticians as patently implausible. Almost a quarter century later, his protégé Chris Clark, using SOSUS arrays as part of Whales '93—an ONR program designed to afford select civilian bioacousticians access to SOSUS' listening technology for marine mammal research—confirmed that the deep sound channel was in fact a great whale party line. See R. Payne and D. Webb, "Orientation by Means of Long Range Acoustic Signaling in Baleen Whales," *Annals of the New York Academy of Sciences* 188 (December 1971): 110–41.

Chapter 6: The Stranding Goes Viral

1. Hal Whitehead's lab at Dalhousie University in Halifax has been studying the biology of the northern bottlenose whales in the Gully, a submarine canyon off Nova Scotia, since the 1980s.

Chapter 7: "Unusual Mortality Event"

1. M. P. Simmonds and L. F. Lopez-Jurado, "Whales and the Military," *Nature* 351 (June 6, 1991): 448.

2. A. Frantzis, "Does Acoustic Testing Strand Whales?" *Nature* 392 (March 5, 1998): 29.

3. SACLANT Undersea Research Centre, *Summary Record, La Spezia, Italy, 15–17 June 1998, SACLANTCEN Bioacoustics Panel, SACLANTCEN M-133* (La Spezia, Italy: NATO, 1998).

Chapter 8: The Lone Rangers of the Environment

1. Mothers for Peace, which had formed in the late 1960s to protest the Vietnam War, got involved in the fight against Diablo Canyon in 1974, when it learned of a nearby fault line that hadn't been accounted for in the plant design. The organization petitioned the United States Atomic Energy Commission and remained involved in the legal challenges against licensing the plant.

Chapter 10: The Whale Coroner Arrives

1. Sam Guinness, an heir to the Guinness beer fortune, was a local seaplane pilot and friend of Ken Balcomb's.

2. To view a remarkable gallery of images from Darlene Ketten's Computerized Scanning and Imaging Facility at Woods Hole Oceanographic Institution, go to: http://csi.whoi.edu/.

   The other leading researcher working with CT and other imaging technology to illuminate the morphology of toothed whales is Ted Cranford, PhD, a biologist at San Diego State University. His gallery of sperm whale head images is at www.whalescience.com.

Chapter 11: Depth Charges

1. To see what an actual ship shock explosive test looks like, watch the video clip of the 1995 mine explosive test of the USS *Osprey* at www.youtube.com/watch?v=plAAuk9VwLs.

2. At the age of 32, Maris Sidenstecker was already a seasoned veteran of the whale wars. (She shares the same first and last names with her mother, who is also a whale conservationist.) Back in 1976, Maris had become the youngest crusader in the burgeoning whale preservation movement. At the age of 14, using her $50 savings account, she designed and printed a simple T-shirt with a blue fluke emerging from the words "Save the Whales." Maris began selling the T-shirts through *Rolling Stone* magazine and at animal rights conferences, and then used the proceeds to educate the public about the plight of endangered whales. When the media picked up on her grassroots campaign, donations increased dramatically, and she established the Save the Whales foundation to educate schoolchildren about whale habitats and conservation.

3. NRDC v. U.S. Department of the Navy, 857 F. Supp. 734, 737–38 (C.D. Cal. 1994).

Chapter 13: Cease and Desist

1. Before deploying overseas, every carrier strike group must be certified battle ready in two war-game exercises: Composite Training Exercises (COMPTUEX) and Joint Task Force

Exercises (JTFEX). COMPTUEX, normally conducted for two to three weeks six months before deployment, is built around a final battle problem that brings together all the specialty groups that have trained separately up till then. JTFEX requires naval and nonnaval forces to integrate assets and accomplish missions in a multithreat, multidimensional environment.

2. Jim MacEachern was the acoustician who directed ONR's Littoral Warfare sea tests in the Bahamas.

3. Listings of national navies that currently or formerly deploy submarines are maintained by the magazine *IHS Jane's Defence Weekly*, www.janes.com/defence.

Chapter 14: Acoustic Storm

1. Project Artemis featured an enormous WWII tanker, the *Mission Capistrano*, which ONR anchored offshore from the Naval Air Station in Bermuda. A 400-ton array of transducers—1,440 individual transducers weighing 200 pounds apiece—descended five stories deep through the hull of the ship and transmitted at 400 hertz with a source level of 247 decibels. A passive array of receivers, composed of ten strings of hydrophones was mounted underwater on 200 80-foot towers. Those towers were connected by cable to an enormous oil-rig tower that was mounted on an extinct underwater volcano in 220 feet of water. The tower rose 70 feet above the ocean surface and was capped by a two-story structure that accommodated 20 technicians. Viewed from underwater, Artemis resembled nothing so much as the mammoth walls of amplifiers and loudspeakers that were to become the hallmarks of outdoor rock concerts.

The problem with Artemis—a problem inherited by LFA a decade later—was how to filter out the echo of ordinary background noise in the ocean. The primitive state of signal processing technology in the early 1960s severely limited the Navy's ability to distinguish objects hundreds of miles from the sound source. But at least the Navy established to its satisfaction that it could build a sonic sonar blaster when the need arose.

2. John Walker Jr. was a US Navy warrant officer and career submarine communications expert who, over a period of 15 years, sold countless naval messages and the keys to decipher them to the Soviets, thus revealing a vast amount of highly sensitive information about US naval operations and capabilities. Later Walker recruited another Navy communications specialist, Jerry Whitworth, his brother, Arthur, and even his own son, Michael Walker, before he was turned in by his wife. The men were arrested in 1985 and subsequently prosecuted, but by then, enormous damage to US security had occurred.

3. Predicting ocean waves and the storms that drive them has vexed military planners since the beginnings of maritime warfare. Julius Caesar's miscalculation of surf conditions dur-

ing his first failed invasion of Britain in 55 BC cost him two full fleets. As a native of the nontidal Mediterranean, he was unprepared when high tide at Dover beach swamped his warships. And in 1281, Yuan Dynasty founder Kublai Khan's invasion of Japan was doomed by a cataclysmic typhoon. The unforeseen *kami kaze*, or divine wind, as the Japanese later called it, overwhelmed and sank the Mongol armada of 4,400 ships and the 100,000 soldiers aboard.

4. Munk's mentor at the Scripps Institution of Oceanography and his partner in his wave-prediction research was oceanographer and Arctic explorer Harald Ulrik Sverdrup, who emigrated from Norway in 1936 to become the third director of Scripps. Because of their foreign birth, both Sverdrup and Munk were under constant surveillance by the FBI throughout the first half of the war. Sverdrup's security clearance was revoked for a period, and after the war, he decided to leave Scripps and return to Norway.

5. Munk's "wind-driven gyres" derived from his observations and calculations of what he called "microscale disturbances" on the surface of the ocean: the glitter of sun that outlined the slope and fetch of ripples. Without ripples, he realized, the ocean surface would be a glassy plane, impervious to atmospheric weather. Munk's epiphany was perceiving that ripples created traction between the ocean and the air above, and that the action of the wind against this rippled layer—the wind's velocity, multiplied by the slope of millions upon millions of ripples—created sufficient force to drive the circulatory system of the world's oceans. Munk's wind-driven gyres revolutionized the macroview of ocean circulation. Prior generations of marine scientists perceived the oceans as essentially static bodies of water with ebbing and flowing tides tugging at their edges. It wasn't until the Spanish explorer Ponce de León observed the Gulf Stream's northeasterly current along the coast of the New World in the early sixteenth century that anyone noticed what Ben Franklin later called "the river in the ocean." Munk was the first person to trace the interlocking "rivers" of wind-driven gyres across the hemispheres and the world's oceans.

6. After the Soviets launched Sputnik on October 4, 1957, a small group of university-based physicists set out to close the Soviet missile gap. John Wheeler, a Princeton physicist and one of the architects of the hydrogen bomb test on Enewetak, conceived a top-secret summer study group composed of academics who would consult to the military on missile detection and related security issues. The original faculty was composed of an elite corps of less than two dozen physicists from Princeton, MIT, Harvard, Berkeley, and CalTech, many of whom had worked on the Manhattan Project as graduate students. They called themselves the Jasons.

The Defense Advanced Research Projects Agency (DARPA) was only too happy to sponsor their six-week summer study sessions, which were housed in a girl's prep school in La Jolla. Each spring the Jasons would meet for a week at the Pentagon, where various generals and admirals would brief them on problems related to missile defense or submarine detection that they were grappling with. The Jasons would choose three or four topics to explore in depth during their summer study, and then would break into subgroups of four to six researchers for each project.

In 1971 Daniel Ellsberg leaked the Pentagon Papers to the *New York Times*, which published the secret Defense Department history of the Vietnam War on its front pages. The Pentagon Papers exposed the existence of the Jasons and described the weapons systems they conceived for use in Vietnam.

7. Ann K. Finkbeiner, *The Jasons: The Secret History of Science's Postwar Elite* (New York: Viking, 2006).

8. In 1961 the Jasons invited Walter Munk to become their first nonphysicist member. Beyond Munk's accomplishments in theoretical and applied oceanography, the Jasons needed him as a tutor. The Navy had quickly become the Jasons' constant client, and the atomic and astrophysicists knew next to nothing about the oceans. The "Jason Navy," as the Munk-led study groups became known, required security clearances at even higher levels than the other Jasons. The Navy also insisted that they not discuss their work with non-Navy Jasons, which put a strain on openness and collegiality.

9. Munk's collaborators on acoustic tomography were oceanographers Carl Wunsch of MIT and Peter Worcester of Scripps. Their work was published in book form after the Cold War: W. Munk, P. Worcester, and C. Wunsch, *Ocean Acoustic Tomography* (Cambridge, UK: Cambridge University Press, 1995).

10. In 1976 the Department of Energy became the first nonmilitary client of the Jasons' when it asked them to assess the connection between carbon dioxide emissions and climate change. Munk collaborated on the study with his mentor, Roger Revelle, who had been investigating climate change for two decades and would go on to be viewed as the founding father of global warming. While teaching at Harvard, Revelle ignited the passions of one student, Al Gore, who would become a tireless public educator about climate change. For his part, Munk had studied and published on the relationship between glacial melting and rising sea levels during his Navy Arctic tours. The year after completing their summer study, Munk and Revelle published one of the first papers on global warming, "Energy and Climate," which forecast future carbon dioxide loads in Africa and around the world. Both Munk and Revelle were convinced of carbon dioxide's causal relationship to climate change.

11. Ann Gibbons, "What's the Sound of One Ocean Warming?" *Science* 248, no. 4951 (April 6, 1990): 33–34.

12. Mel Briscoe, the Heard Island project manager at ONR, knew he'd been caught flat-footed when John Twiss called up at the last minute to ask about the Navy's NMFS permit. As soon as the *Cory Chouest* sailed for Freemantle, Briscoe went to work to shore up ONR's marine biology and acoustic assets. Not to be outdone in the acronym department, Briscoe launched ORCA—Observed Response of Cetaceans to Acoustics—to study the effects of low-frequency sound on marine mammals. He brought in Dan Costa, a pinniped specialist from UC Santa Cruz who had recently worked with the Navy in Hawaii, to head up ORCA. (From author interview.)

13. The head of NOAA, physical oceanographer John Knauss, had kicked in $200,000 in funding for the Heard Island experiment from a discretionary fund he controlled. Forty years earlier, when Knauss was a graduate student at Scripps, Munk had been one of his thesis advisors.

When Knauss realized that Munk had a "whale problem," he sent the Heard Island protocol down the hall to NOAA's chief science officer, Sylvia Earle, for informal review and comment. She circulated the protocol to Bill Watkins and Peter Tyack up in Woods Hole. Watkins shared it with Darlene Ketten, who was already making a name for herself in whale hearing. All four of them shared the same concerns about the potential problems for animals from injecting high-intensity, low-frequency sound into the ocean.

Watkins, who had circled the globe recording "biological" sounds for the Navy, was familiar with the various species of whales that wintered in the waters of the South Indian Ocean near Heard Island. He knew from direct contact with them that many of these whale species were acoustically sensitive, including humpbacks, sperm whales, blue whales, fin whales, and beaked whales. He and Tyack wrote to NOAA and NMFS: "As planned, the Heard Island experiment is likely to disrupt feeding behavior and to mask communication over an area of many thousands of square kilometers of prime whale feeding and social habitat, during the peak season." Watkins knew Walter Munk personally from multiple crossed paths at Woods Hole and elsewhere over the years. He also wrote to Munk to urge him to reschedule the experiment to a time of year when fewer whales were present.

NMFS concluded that ONR needed to apply for an "incidental take" permit to authorize the inevitable "harassment" of local marine mammals. When Munk heard that NMFS normally required a year or more to process such a permit, he turned to his long-time mentor, Roger Revelle, for help.

By 1990, Revelle's health had deteriorated badly in the aftermath of two major heart attacks, and he could walk only with the help of two canes. But the day Munk was due to meet with Knauss at NOAA to discuss the disposition of the Heard Island experiment, Revelle flew in from San Diego to attend. In the course of the meeting, Knauss came up with a plan for an NMFS research permit that would take only a few weeks to process, as opposed to an incidental take permit. If Munk could build a biological component into his project, he could apply for a permit to conduct research that would benefit marine mammals, even if it harassed them. The frequency of the acoustic "shots" was decreased, and a crew of biologists would observe the behavior of marine mammals from a second ship.

14. Munk raised the $35 million he needed to install and activate Acoustic Thermometry from an alphabet soup of quasimilitary agencies such as DARPA (Defense Advanced Research Projects Agency) and SERDP (Strategic Environmental Research and Development Program). Acoustic Thermometry would remain under ONR's direction, and the Navy would maintain proprietary control over the classified data from its sound transmissions. But Scripps would be the applicant for the Fisheries permit, and Munk and his Scripps-based team would direct the acoustic component.

15. In the mid-1980s, Chris Clark had conducted an acoustic census of the spring migration of bowhead whales past Point Barrow, Alaska, in order to assess whether the bowhead population could sustain a Native American hunt. Using underwater hydrophones, he'd solved the mystery of how bowheads breathed during their long migration beneath the Arctic ice pack. Clark and his team observed that the bowheads used their calls to sound out the thinnest sections of ice and then broke breathing holes in the ice using their distinctive bowheaded rostrums.

   Unbeknown to Clark's colleagues, ONR had previously recruited him to assess "biological response" to its classified Low Frequency Active sonar tests off the California coast. Working aboard the *Cory Chouest*, Clark had surveyed the surrounding waters to see if there were whales in the vicinity and, if so, to monitor their response to the sonar.

   Pittenger offered Clark an additional inducement to take the scientific lead on Acoustic Thermometry. Now that the Cold War was over and the SOSUS system was finally declassified, Pittenger worried that it might be sacrificed to peacetime budget cutting. To further enhance SOSUS' dual-use, ONR launched Whales '93.

   After decades of exerting tight control over SOSUS, the heads of naval intelligence were reluctant to open it up to civilian researchers. Bill Watkins, whose security clearance and access to SOSUS stations for his bioacoustic research went back decades, was an easy sell. Pittenger guessed that since Clark had security clearance already from his sonar work aboard the *Cory Chouest*, he could be slotted into Whales '93 alongside Watkins.

   For Clark, the SOSUS listening system was an "acoustic telescope" that pierced the dark ocean depths; a crystal-clear window into a soundscape that only cetaceans and SOSUS operators had ever explored. With advanced signal processing across ten acoustic channels, he could focus multiple hydrophones, set a mile apart with 500 sensors between them, at a single phonating whale. Over one 43-day period, Clark traced the journey of a blue whale swimming up and down the Eastern Seaboard as easily as a radar dish could track a plane's flight across the sky. Most exciting of all was being able to eavesdrop on blue whales as they called to one another through the deep sound channel across 1,000 miles of open ocean.

16. Richard Paddock, "Undersea Noise Test Could Risk Making Whales Deaf," *Los Angeles Times*, March 22, 1994, Home edition, sec. Main News: A-1.

17. Sylvia Earle was a high-profile oceanographer, the only prominent woman in her field, and a generation behind Munk. While still an undergraduate at Florida State University, she assisted Winthrop Kellogg in his pioneering dolphin echolocation experiments. After forcing her way onto all-male oceanography expeditions in the 1960s, Earle collaborated with Roger and Katy Payne and Peter Tyack on humpback whales research in Hawaii. In 1970, when ONR and NASA sponsored a Sealab spinoff called Tektite 2 and refused to let women divers join male aquanauts in the deep-submersion research station, Earle insisted that they field an all-female expedition. After leading the first female team to work at the bottom of the ocean and writing about it for *National Geographic* magazine, Earle became a bona fide oceanography celebrity on par with Jacques Cousteau. In 1979 she made a record dive to 1,250 feet in a specially designed diving suit. And in the mid-1980s, she founded Deep Ocean Engineering to manufacture the Deep Rover research vessels.

Chapter 15: The Sonar That Came In from the Cold

1. The Navy's three-part scientific research program for LFA sonar:

Phase I would transmit low-frequency sonar from the *Cory Chouest*, positioned west of the Channel Islands, to measure its effect on blue and fin whale vocalizations.

Phase II would broadcast from a sound source anchored on a sea mount off the coast of California, directly in the migration path of Pacific gray whales.

Phase III would study the effect of low-frequency sound on the songs of humpback whales off the Kona coast of Hawaii.

2. Late one night, when he was wrestling with how to respond to Gisiner's offer, Tyack called his old friend Hal Whitehead for guidance—or perhaps, his blessing. Whitehead was sympathetic to Tyack's dilemma. Unlike Canada, where Whitehead taught, US researchers had few funding sources other than the Navy. "Soft money" researchers like Clark and Tyack had to spend half their time raising money. With a budget of $16 million, the LFA research program was the best-funded bioacoustic project the Navy, or anyone else, had ever sponsored.

3. Administrative record cited in NRDC's summary judgment brief in 2003 LFA lawsuit *NRDC v. Evans*.

4. Shortly after the anti-LFA demonstrations in Hawaii, Exxon applied to Fisheries for a permit to conduct seismic surveys off the coast of Southern California in the migratory path of gray whales. When Reynolds threatened to sue, Exxon said it wanted to sit down and talk—perhaps mindful of the possibility of Ben White and his cohort descending on the scene in a flotilla of small boats with bullhorns. Reynolds negotiated a 30-point agreement that included mitigation measures to limit the time and location of the survey to avoid migrating whales.

    Reynolds knew that a single settlement wasn't going to change the way big oil did business. But it convinced him that so long as he had the law on his side, it was usually more productive to negotiate incremental improvements than to litigate against giant energy companies with entire law firms on retainer and pockets deep enough to stay in court for decades.

5. Michael Jasny et al., *Sounding the Depths II: The Rising Toll of Sonar, Shipping and Industrial Ocean Noise on Marine Life* (New York: Natural Resources Defense Council, November 2005), www.nrdc.org/wildlife/marine/sound/sound.pdf.

Chapter 17: A Mind in the Water

1. Whaling in the 1930s was rapacious, particularly by factory ships in the Antarctic. Tens of thousands of large baleen whales—blue, sei, fin, and humpbacks—as well as sperm whales, were killed each year from 1930 to 1940, and whaling continued to take a lethal toll on many species well into the 1960s. For a statistical overview of twentieth-century whaling by species and region, see: http://luna.pos.to/whale and D. G. Chapman's "The Plight of the Whales," www.cengage.com/resource_uploads/downloads/0534094929_46524.pdf.

2. Like whales, bats had long defied the efforts of scientific classifiers to perceive their true natures. In the fourth century BC, Aristotle made the first systematic effort to classify animals into three groups according to their method of locomotion: creeping, flying, and swimming. In this system, whales were grouped with fish, and bats were grouped with birds. Two thousand years later, Carolus Linnaeus classified the two kingdoms of plants and animals into groups according to their form. In the tenth edition of his *Systema Naturae*, published in 1758, Linnaeus finally moved whales and bats out of their respective fish and bird categories and into the mammalian class, alongside *Homo sapiens* and other primates who, true to "form," have mammary glands with which to suckle their young.

3. During World War II, the US military hatched a novel plan for deploying bats in combat. Working inside Harvard's psychoacoustics lab, Griffin was assigned to the Bat Bomb

Project, the brainchild of a dental surgeon and bat enthusiast named Lytle Adams. After the attack on Pearl Harbor, Adams sold the War Department on his idea of surgically implanting incendiary devices into the chests of thousands of bats, and then releasing them from planes over Japanese cities. Adams theorized that the bats would nest under the eaves of the wooden houses that dominated Japanese cities. When their time-delayed fuses expired, the bats—and the buildings—would explode into flames. The War Department built a mock Japanese village in the desert outside Carlsbad, New Mexico, to war-game the bat bomb. Once unleashed, the planeload of incendiary bats burned the wooden village to the ground, but a few errant bats managed to also incinerate a nearby military research facility. The War Department decided to abandon bat bombs in favor of the conventional incendiary bombs it dropped from B-29s over Tokyo and dozens of other Japanese cities in 1945.

Meanwhile, on the European front, the Navy was trying to enlist pigeons into its bombing campaigns. Another Harvard-educated researcher, behaviorist B. F. Skinner, conceived Project Pigeon to improve the guidance system of missiles targeting German battleships. Skinner placed operant-conditioned pigeons inside the nose cone and trained them to steer the missile to its target by pecking on a projected image of the battleship. Despite an effective demonstration, Skinner couldn't convince the Navy brass to trust pigeons to guide their missiles, and Project Pigeon was aborted in 1944.

4. For an insightful and heroically researched investigation of John Lilly's influence on the New Age and Save the Whale movements, see D. Graham Burnette's *The Sounding of the Whale: Science and Cetaceans in the Twentieth Century* (University of Chicago Press, 2012).

5. According to his own account, Lilly had brought along an enormous cache of anesthetic, enough "to anesthetize everyone at Marineland and still have some left," he would later write. He'd also fashioned a respirator to help the dolphins breathe under anesthesia. After removing a dolphin from the water and placing it on a stretcher, he injected it with 80 cubic centimeters of the barbiturate Nembutal. Over the next half hour, the investigators stood by and watched helplessly as the dolphin's respiration deteriorated. Unfamiliar with the anatomy of the dolphin's larynx and windpipe, Lilly couldn't figure out how to attach his respirator. Eventually the dolphin went into cardiac arrest and died.

They cut the dose in half for the next dolphin, but its blowhole also collapsed, followed by cardiac arrest. Despite efforts to revive him through artificial respiration, the dolphin died. Dolphin number three did slightly better under an even smaller dose, but after it lolled sideways in the pool and displayed clear signs of serious brain damage, the researchers decided to euthanize the animal—a simple task, given their prior attempts at anesthesia. They switched to another anesthetic agent, paraldehyde, but that also proved fatal to dolphins four and five.

6. Joan McIntyre Varawa, *Mind in the Waters: A Book to Celebrate the Consciousness of Whales and Dolphins* (New York: Charles Scribner's Sons, 1974). This collection of essays, poems, scientific discourses, photographs, and drawings became the "whole whale catalogue" of the 1970s, according to author, illustrator, and marine biologist Richard Ellis.

7. Harvard psychologists Timothy Leary and Richard Alpert (Ram Dass) were conducting the Harvard Psilocybin Project in collaboration with theology students, and their Concord Prison Experiment studied the effect of psilocybin on recidivism rates.

8. Lilly's "implorations" inside his deprivation tank inspired the 1980 movie *Altered States*, directed by Ken Russell and starring William Hurt as a Harvard researcher who self-experiments using hallucinogens in a flotation tank.

9. As recounted in Lilly's second book, *The Mind of the Dolphin: A Nonhuman Intelligence*, during ten weeks in 1965, a young female research associate named Margaret Howe cohabited with a male dolphin named Peter. Margaret interacted continuously with Peter, including trying to teach him basic human language. Eventually the dolphin became infatuated with his human companion and began making overt sexual advances—to which she eventually responded.

10. Lilly's liberation of his dolphins became the template for "dolphin liberation." The next volley in the battle for dolphin rights had been fired on April 22, 1970, when former Flipper trainer turned dolphin liberationist Ric O'Barry chose the first Earth Day to declare war on captive dolphin research. Shortly after midnight, O'Barry broke into the Lerner Marine Laboratory on the island of Bimini and cut through the wire mesh pen holding a dolphin named Charlie Brown. To O'Barry's dismay, Charlie Brown refused to leave his pen, and O'Barry was quickly arrested. As the *Miami Herald*'s front-page headline summed it up: "Trainer of Flipper in Flap; Can't Get Dolphin to Flee." But O'Barry had served notice that a new front had opened in the dolphin wars.

Chapter 18: The Killer Turned Tame

1. After the Puget Sound orca captures ended in 1976, SeaWorld and its director of collections, Don Goldsberry, moved on to Iceland. Between 1976 and 1989, Iceland proved the best source for SeaWorld and other marine parks wanting to capture or buy new orcas.

2. In 2009, 13 million people took whale-watching tours in 119 countries worldwide, generating ticket fees and tourism expenditures of more than $2.1 billion during 2008. More than 3,000 whale-watching operations around the world now employ an estimated 13,200 people, according to a study commissioned by the International Fund for Animal Welfare (IFAW). See A. M. Cisneros-Montemayor et al., "The Global Potential for Whale Watching," *Marine Policy* (2010), doi:10.1016/j.marpol.2010.05.005.

Meanwhile, watching whales in captive settings is also big business. SeaWorld, which owns ten amusement parks in the United States, including five in Florida, was sold to the Blackstone Group for $2.5 billion in 2009. In 2012 SeaWorld had profits of $77 million on total revenues of $1.4 billion. See Jason Garcia, "SeaWorld Entertainment's Profit Soars on Increases in Revenue, Attendance," *Orlando Sentinel*, March 26, 2013.

Chapter 20: The Dolphins That Joined the Navy

1. According to documents uncovered at the Lilly archive at Stanford University by Princeton historian D. Graham Burnette, John Lilly was consulting with his former CalTech classmate and director of China Lake, Bill McLean, about deploying dolphins as battle space assets even before Lilly published *Man and Dolphin*. McLean brought Lilly out to NOTS to brief his engineers, and he continued to maintain contact with Lilly as the Navy developed its own marine mammal research facility.

2. Since confirming dolphin echolocation in the 1950s, the Navy had been systematically studying whether other marine mammals and nonmammals possessed parallel abilities. Seals and sea lions, for instance, were suspected of echolocating until exhaustive studies revealed that they could track miniature submarines—and, presumably, fish—from 130 feet away by using their hypersensitive whiskers to follow the wakes left by objects moving through the water.

3. Journalists and authors David Helvarg and Steve Chapple have individually reported interviews with trainers and CIA operatives who claim direct knowledge of dolphin dark ops, including Michael Greenwood, a Navy and CIA dolphin specialists who gave 150 pages of closed-door testimony before the Church Committee Senate hearings into extralegal CIA operations. For more on this, see pages 68–75 of David Helvarg's *Blue Frontier: Dispatches from America's Ocean Wilderness* (Sierra Club Books, 2006).

4. Engineer Whitlow Au and experimental psychologist Paul Nachtigall led the Navy's Hawaii-based dolphin research program. Whitlow W. L. Au, *The Sonar of Dolphins* (New York: Springer-Verlag, 1993); Paul E. Nachtigall and Patrick W. B. Moore, *Animal Sonar: Processes and Performance* (New York: Plenum, 1988).

5. In fact, one of the Navy's Hawaii-based biosonar researchers, an experimental psychologist named Herb Roitblat, translated the neural networks of dolphin colonies into a new kind of internet search engine. He left the Navy, patented his invention, and built a start-up around his algorithm, which he called DolphinSearch.

6. The Soviets' militarized dolphin program, based in Sevastopol, Crimea, was quickly decommissioned at the end of the Cold War. In 2000 the BBC and other news outlets

reported that Russia sold its trained marine mammals to Iran: "In total, 27 animals, including walruses, sea lions, seals, and a white beluga whale, were loaded with the dolphins into a Russian transport aircraft for the journey from Sevastopol, on the Crimean peninsula, in the Black Sea, to the Persian Gulf." See "Iran Buys Kamikaze Dolphins," BBC News, March 8, 2000, http://news.bbc.co.uk/2/hi/world/middle_east/670551.stm.

In 2004 Doug Cartlidge, a dolphin expert with the Whale and Dolphin Conservation Society of London, visited the site of the former Soviet Dolphin Division, the care of which had been transferred to the Ukrainian navy. He reported that the Ukrainians were now in the business of capturing and training dolphins and other marine mammals for sale and export to various Middle Eastern countries. Anecdotal reports suggest that the Soviets' dolphin program paralleled that of the US Navy, and there are rumored accounts of similarly bizarre programs of kamikaze whales. See: www.militaryphotos.net/forums/showthread.php?73415-quot-warrior-dolphins-quot.

Chapter 22: The Mermaid That Got Away

1. Kenneth Norris, Balcomb's mentor at UC Santa Cruz, had a career path that was both unlikely and typical during the early days of the field. A zoologist specializing in desert reptiles, Norris was recruited in 1953 as the founding curator at Marineland of the Pacific, the country's first West Coast oceanarium. At Marineland, Norris conducted some of the earliest research confirming biosonar in dolphins. In 1964, along with three UCLA fraternity brothers, he co-founded SeaWorld on 22 acres of San Diego's Mission Bay. He then went on to become the first director of UC Santa Cruz's Center for Coastal Marine Studies in 1972, a year before Balcomb's arrival.

2. Marc Kaufman, "Navy Tests Linked to Beaching Of Whales; Ear Bleeding Consistent With Intense Noise," *Washington Post*, June 15, 2000, A03.

Chapter 23: In the Valley of the Whales

1. K. C. Balcomb and D. E. Claridge, "A Mass Stranding of Cetaceans Caused by Naval Sonar in the Bahamas," *Bahamas Journal of Science* 8, no. 2 (May 2001): 4–6.

2. US Department of Commerce and US Department of the Navy, *Joint Interim Report: Bahamas Marine Mammal Stranding Event of March 15–16, 2000* (Washington, DC: US Department of Commerce, 2001).

3. According to the Navy and NMFS Interim Report: "The necropsy on the spotted dolphin revealed the animal died with systemic debilitating disease. It was considered unrelated to the mass stranding event cluster."

4. M. P. Johnson and P. L. Tyack, "A Digital Acoustic Recording Tag for Measuring the Response of Wild Marine Mammals to Sound," *IEEE Journal of Oceanic Engineering* 28, no. 1 (January 2003): 3–12.

Chapter 24: God and Country v. the Whales

1. The Humane Society of the United States, the League for Coastal Protection, and the Ocean Futures Society.

Chapter 25: "It Is So Ordered"

1. The two Department of Justice attorneys representing the Navy in the Low Frequency Active sonar case were Ann Navarro and Kristen Gustafson.

2. Magistrate Judge Joseph Spero served as mediator in the Northern District's Alternative Dispute Resolution Program.

3. Correspondence between Marine Mammal Research Program officer, Office of Naval Research, and operations manager for Navy sonar system, Office of the Chief of Naval Operations (August 6–9, 2001); document AR24279 addendum in the administrative record filed in *NRDC v. Evans* (N.D. Cal. 2003), on file with NRDC.

   Here, with names and other identifying information omitted, is the complete dialogue:

   Operations Official (forwarding public comments that the researchers had submitted to NMFS): [ONR official], is the Navy funding any [of these scientists'] research? Did they say anything to you on this issue?

   ONR Official: Yes, I fund their research. They did mention that they would be sending in comments on LFA, but I did not get a copy of what they sent. I gather the input was not entirely positive.

   Operations Official: [ONR official], their comments were in the attachment. Yes, they were negative and, in my opinion, out of the box. If they are funded by the Navy, the proper way to bitch is via the sponsor [you], and not a letter to NMFS. All of the data cited was run by your office, we are not perfect and [Marine Acoustics, the Navy's contractor] has always tried to spin data, but I've tried to be objective. A letter from [these researchers] to NMFS is nothing more than an attempt to discredit the Navy and stop the deployment of LFA. Maybe I'm missing the big picture—what say you?

   ONR Official: I told them as much in a pretty scorching phone call. I think they had some inkling that they might be about to take our money and make themselves look good to the enviros, too, but I can't prove that. The main driver was [an environ-

mental group]. All through this process, [the researchers] had ignored the LFA issue, not responded to requests for comments, in the Federal Register, etc. Then one day [an environmentalist] calls them and asks them if they had read the EIS. [The lead researcher] said, "No," and [the environmentalist] said, "I'll mail you a copy, and please send your comments to [NMFS] right away." Scientists are like that; they'll review anything they're asked to review and give their honest, sometimes harsh critique, without knowing any of the politics or circumstances. It's the way you do things in peer review of a colleague's paper, and they just apply the process to everything they read. If we had asked them to review it earlier, we probably could have absorbed his criticism [on this particular issue] and thus defused any further criticism, but that's water under the bridge now. I also reminded [the lead researcher] that he was using data that he published after the EIS was written, and data that was not yet published; and I told him it was unfair to expect Navy to use information that he had not provided at the time the EIS was written. I got a sheepish apology for his not providing input earlier (even though we had not asked him directly for it), and for holding the EIS to his changing understanding of the problem as his research has progressed. But I don't know what good that does us.

Chapter 26: Counterattack

1. Marc Kaufman, "Whale Stranding in N.C. Followed Navy Sonar Use," *Washington Post*, January 28, 2005, A03.

2. Brian Kelly and Lukas Velush, "Report on Porpoise Deaths Splits Navy, Whale Groups," *Herald* (of Everett, Washington), February 10, 2004, www.heraldnet.com /article/20040210/NEWS01/402100704.

3. *Assessment of Acoustic Exposures on Marine Mammals in Conjunction with USS* Shoup *Active Sonar Transmissions in the Eastern Strait of Juan de Fuca and Haro Strait*, Washington, May 5, 2003 (Silver Spring, MD: National Marine Fisheries Service, January 2005).

4. Hert Levine et al., *Active Sonar Waveform* (McLean, VA: JASON, the Mitre Corporation, June 2004), 1 (JSR-03-200).

Chapter 27: The Admirals Take Charge

1. The Rim of the Pacific Exercise (RIMPAC), the world's largest international naval warfare exercise, is held biennially during June and July in Honolulu. It is hosted by the US Navy's Pacific Fleet, which invites allied military forces from the Pacific Rim nations to participate.

2. The RIMPAC lawsuit was brought by NRDC in conjunction with the International Fund for Animal Welfare, the Cetacean Society International, and the Ocean Futures Society, as well as OFS founder and director Jean-Michel Cousteau.

3. Judge Cooper heard both the California and Hawaii midfrequency cases. The first case was filed in the Central District of California. The RIMPAC case, in Hawaii, was filed as a related case, also in the Central District, and it went to Cooper as related.

Chapter 28: The Highest Court in the Land

1. Among the four other environmental cases decided by the US Supreme Court during its 2008 term, the court ruled against environmentalists in each case, including limiting corporate liability in toxic spills, making it easier to dump mining waste in Alaska, and allowing the EPA to use a cost-benefit analysis to evaluate allowable marine life kills at cooling structures at power plants. The US Supreme Court, going back to the Rehnquist court, has been particularly unfriendly to cases brought under the National Environmental Policy Act (NEPA), ruling against the environmentalists in 15 straight cases. See also Marcia Coyle, "High Court Losses Stun Environmentalists," *National Law Journal* (June 29, 2009).

Chapter 29: Endgame

1. Winter v. Natural Resources Defense Council, Inc., 129 S. Ct. 365, 378 (2008), www .supremecourt.gov/opinions/08pdf/07-1239.pdf.

2. 555 U.S. ____ (2008), 1, J. Ginsburg, dissenting, supreme.justia.com/cases/federal/us/555 /07-1239/dissent.html.

3. The *New York Times*, the *Washington Post*, and the *Los Angeles Times* all reported positive accounts that reflected NRDC's "soft-landing" analysis. However, the *Wall Street Journal*'s lead editorial on November 13, 2008, "The Greens Get Harpooned: The Supremes Save the Navy from the Whales," spared no mixed metaphor in gleefully skewering both "green activists" and "liberal judges":

> *The Supreme Court opened its fall term auspiciously yesterday by sinking the environmental Pequod known as* NRDC v. Winter . . .
>
> *If the bureaucratic distinction between an "Environmental Impact Statement" and an "Environmental Assessment" sounds like a flimsy excuse for second-guessing the judgment of admirals in wartime—well, this case was never really about the welfare of Baby Humpback. Instead, green activists and liberal judges were looking to assert their dominance in matters of war and peace . . .*

We are very close to making judges co-Secretaries of Defense—and next time they may want to do more than save the whales.

Epilogue

1. Diane E. Claridge, "Population Ecology of Blainville's Beaked Whales (Mesoplodon Densirostris)" (doctoral thesis, University of St. Andrews, May 2013), http://hdl.handle .net/10023/3741. Claridge's study compared the abundance and age composition of Blain-ville's beaked whales on and off a Navy range in the Bahamas. This was the first study to compare the population demographics of beaked whales regularly exposed to Navy sonar to ones rarely exposed. The study revealed a substantially lower abundance of beaked whales on the range where MFA sonar was used regularly than at the control site, where sonar was limited. Of particular concern, the study found a lower female-to-calf ratio—in other words, fewer baby whales per adult female—at the site with military sonar. After ruling out several other factors, the author concludes that the "apparent low reproductive rates and recruitment through births on the Navy range," together with impacts that have been observed on beaked whale foraging, present cause for concern.

2. Padraic Flanagan, "Navy Sonar 'Did Cause Mass Dolphin Deaths' Say Scientists Who Blame War Games Exercise off Cornish Coast for Strandings," *Daily Mail*, May 4, 2013, www.dailymail.co.uk/news/article-2319611/Navy-sonar-did-cause-mass-dolphin-deaths -say-scientists-blame-war-games-exercise-Cornish-coast-strandings.html.

3. "Scientific Committee of ACCOBAMS Statement of Concern About Atypical Mass Strand-ings of Beaked Whales in the Ionian Sea," Agreement on the Conservation of Cetaceans of the Black Sea, Mediterranean Sea, and Contiguous Atlantic Area, February 13, 2012, www.accobams.org/index.php?option=com_content&view=article&id=1118:atypical -mass-strandings-in-the-ionian-sea&catid=3:accobams-news&Itemid=68.

4. Leonard Bernstein, "Sea-Map Sonar Linked to Whale Stranding off Madagascar," *Guard-ian*, October 15, 2013, www.theguardian.com/environment/2013/oct/15/stranded-whales -sonar-underwater.

AUTHOR'S NOTES ON SOURCES AND INTERVIEWS

Much of the information in this book derives from interviews with more than 100 individuals, as well as from oral histories (most significantly from the Niels Bohr Library & Archives, American Institute of Physics, in College Park, Maryland), from memoirs, and unpublished articles, ship logs, and personal papers.

A list of individuals I interviewed, either by phone or in person, begins on page 390 of this section. Key sources were interviewed multiple times, and many of the interviews were tape-recorded to ensure accuracy. Every effort has been made to report group meetings accurately, based on interviews with multiple participants.

In addition, I drew information from a range of books, articles in newspapers, magazines, and peer-reviewed science and law journals; investigative reports by the US Navy and the National Marine Fisheries Service; proceedings of marine mammal science conferences, transcripts of legal proceedings, and published court decisions. Many of these sources are cited in the endnotes. Others are listed below, by chapter.

I reported many of the scenes in the book from locations in Southern California; Hawaii; the San Juan Islands of Washington State; Baja, Mexico; the Bahamas; and Woods Hole, Massachusetts; as well as from marine mammal science conferences in the United States and abroad.

SOURCES

Part One: Stranded

Chapters 1, 2, and 3

The narration of the March 15, 2000, mass stranding and subsequent specimen collection is drawn from eyewitness and newspaper accounts; from photographs and videotape recorded by members of the Bahamas Marine Mammal Survey who documented the event; from postings on the MARMAM marine mammal Listserv; from on-site reporting on Abaco Island in the Bahamas; from peer-reviewed journal articles; and from the Navy and National Marine Fisheries Service joint interim report released on December 21, 2001. The most precise linear narrative of the stranding and its aftermath is Balcomb and Claridge's peer-reviewed and published report: K. C. Balcomb and D. E. Claridge, "A mass Stranding of Cetaceans Caused by Naval Sonar in the Bahamas," *Bahamas Journal of Science* 8, no. 2 (May 2001): 4–6.

Key interview subjects included Ken Balcomb, Diane Claridge, Dave Ellifrit, and Bob Gisiner.

Information in these chapters regarding beaked whale evolution and echolocation was drawn from documents cited in the endnotes and from interviews with Jim Mead of the Smithsonian Institution and Darlene Ketten of the Woods Hole Oceanographic Institution.

Chapters 4, 5, 6, and 7

Information about Ken Balcomb's childhood, early research career, Navy tours, and work aboard the *Regina Maris* is drawn largely from interviews with Ken Balcomb, three of his four wives, including Diane Claridge, childhood friends, and his half brother Howie Garrett, as well as protégé researchers Dave Ellifrit and John Durban.

Much of the background information about the Navy's Sound Surveillance System (SOSUS) comes from interviews with naval historian Gary Weir, as well as from his book *An Ocean in Common: American Naval Officers, Scientists, and the Ocean Environment* (College Station, TX: Texas A&M University Press, 2001), and his article "The American Sound Surveillance System: Using the Ocean to Hunt Soviet Submarines, 1950–1961," *International Journal of Naval History* 5, no. 2 (August 2006).

Information about the early response to the stranding by the Office of Naval Research (ONR), the National Marine Fisheries Service (NMFS), and the Navy Office of Environmental Readiness (N-45) is drawn from interviews with multiple individuals, including: at ONR, Bob Gisiner, Jim MacEachern, and Admiral Paul Gaffney; at NMFS, Roger Gentry, Blair Mase, Bill Hogarth, Teri Rowles, Janet Whaley, and Laurie Allen; at N-45, Admiral Larry Baucom, Frank Stone, and Marc Laverdiere.

Part Two: Acoustic Storm

Chapters 8 and 9

The information about NRDC, its first response to the Bahamas stranding, and its campaign to save the whale nursery in Laguna San Ignacio in Baja, Mexico, comes primarily from interviews with individuals at NRDC, including Michael Jasny, Andrew Wetzler, John Adams, Stephen Mills, Joel Reynolds, and Jacob Scherr.

Other information about the Baja whale campaign and gray whales was drawn from various news reports and articles, and from Dick Russell, *Eye of the Whale: Epic Passage from Baja to Siberia* (New York: Simon & Schuster, 2001).

Information about Joel Reynolds' childhood and early legal career—in these chapters and in chapter 11—was drawn from interviews with Joel Reynolds, his five siblings and two former wives, and colleagues.

Chapter 10

The information in this chapter comes primarily from articles and interviews with Darlene Ketten, and interviews with Ken Balcomb, Charlie Potter, and Diane Claridge.

Chapter 11

The information in this chapter comes primarily from interviews with Steve Honigman, Joel Reynolds, Lindy Weilgart, Hal Whitehead, Sam Ridgway, and John Hall.

Chapter 12

Information in this chapter comes primarily from videotape of the beachside necropsy and interviews with Ken Balcomb, Darlene Ketten, Roger Gentry, and Larry Baucom.

Chapter 13

Information in this chapter comes primarily from interviews with Richard Danzig, Robert Pirie, Admiral Dick Pittenger, Admiral Bill Fallon, Admiral Bob Natter, Admiral Paul Gaffney, Darlene Ketten, and Jim MacEachern.

Chapter 14

Information in this chapter comes primarily from interviews with Admiral Dick Pittenger, Walter Munk, Mel Briscoe, Robert Frosch, Fred Saalfeld, Chris Clark, Lindy Weilgart, Hal Whitehead, Craig Dorman, Steven Ramberg, Dan Costa, Bob Gisiner, Sylvia Earle, John Adams, Peter Tyack, Katy Payne, Joel Reynolds, Annie Notthoff, Susan Jordan, Naomi Oreskes, and Naomi Rose.

Information about the Jasons, the military think tank of academic physicists, is drawn largely from Ann Finkbeiner's book *The Jasons: The Secret History of Science's Postwar Elite* (New York: Viking, 2006).

Chapter 15

Information in this chapter comes from articles cited in the endnotes and from interviews with Joel Reynolds, Steve Honigman, John Hall, Michael Jasny, Andrew Wetzler, Hal Whitehead, Peter Tyack, Dan Costa, and Chris Clark.

W. John Richardson et al., *Marine Mammals and Noise* (San Diego: Academic Press, 1995).

Michael Jasny et al., *Sounding the Depths II: The Rising Toll of Sonar, Shipping and Industrial Ocean Noise on Marine Life* (New York: Natural Resources Defense Council, 2005).

Chapter 16

Information in this chapter comes primarily from videotape recorded by Ken Balcomb, Darlene Ketten's notes and articles, and interviews with Darlene Ketten, Ken Balcomb, and Diane Claridge.

Part Three: The Reluctant Whistle-Blower

Chapter 17

The information in this chapter is drawn largely from multiple sources, including D. Graham Burnette's *The Sounding of the Whale: Science and Cetaceans in the Twentieth Century* (University of Chicago Press, 2012); Gregg Mitman's *Reel Nature: America's Romance with Wildlife on Film* (Cambridge, MA: Harvard University Press, 1999); and several books by John Lilly, among them *Man and Dolphin* (New York: Doubleday, 1961), *The Mind of the Dolphin: A Nonhuman Intelligence* (New York: Doubleday, 1969), *John Lilly, So Far . . .* (Los Angeles: Jeremy P. Tarcher, 1989), and *The Scientist: A Metaphysical Autobiography* (Berkeley, CA: Ronin Publishing, 1996).

Chapter 18

The information in this chapter is drawn from multiple news articles and books, as well as interviews with Ken Balcomb. In 1997 PBS' *Frontline* produced an excellent investigative documentary titled *A Whale of a Business* about SeaWorld and the history of captive orcas in the Pacific Northwest, which remains one of the best sources on the subject. Other sources for this chapter include Burnette's *Sounding of the Whale* and David Rothenberg's *Thousand Mile Song: Whale Music in a Sea of Sound* (New York: Basic Books, 2008).

Chapter 19

In addition to the books cited from chapter 18, the information in this chapter comes primarily from interviews with Ken Balcomb and articles by and about Ben White.

Chapter 20

The information in this chapter comes primarily from interviews with John Hall, and from books such as David Helvarg's *Blue Frontier: Saving America's Living Seas* (New York: W. H. Freeman, 2001), Forrest G. Wood's *Marine Mammals and Man: The Navy's Porpoises and Sea Lions* (Washington, DC: R. B. Luce, 1973), Whitlow Au's *The Sonar of Dolphins* (New York: Springer-Verlag, 1993), and Paul Nachtigall and Patrick Moore's *Animal Sonar: Processes and Performance* (New York: Plenum, 1988).

Chapter 21

The information in this chapter comes primarily from interviews with Ken Balcomb, Joel Reynolds, Jim Mead, Roger Gentry, Charlie Potter, Sam Ridgway, and Jim MacEachern.

Chapter 22

The information in this chapter comes primarily from interviews with Ken Balcomb, Mel Briscoe, Roger Gentry, and Diane Claridge, and from research by Peter Tyack and Mark Johnson of Woods Hole Oceanographic Institution into the diving and sound responses of beaked whales in the Bahamas.

Chapter 23

The information in this chapter comes primarily from interviews with Ken Balcomb, Roger Gentry, Michael Stocker, David Fromm, and several former Navy fleet commanders, as well as from the Navy and NMFS' interim report on the Bahamas stranding, released in December 2001.

Part Four: Whales v. Navy

Chapters 24 and 25

The information in this chapter comes primarily from court transcripts and interviews with Joel Reynolds, Ken Balcomb, Michael Jasny, Andrew Wetzler, and Joe Johnson.

Chapter 26

The information in this chapter comes primarily from interviews with members of the NRDC legal team.

Chapter 27

The information in this chapter comes primarily from interviews with Admiral Pete Daly, Craig Jensen, Jeff Luster, Joel Reynolds, Michael Jasny, and Dick Pittenger.

Chapter 28

The information in this chapter comes primarily from on-site reporting of the Supreme Court oral arguments, from court documents and transcripts, and from interviews with the legal teams on both sides.

Chapter 29

The information in this chapter comes primarily from law review articles and newspaper accounts, and from interviews with Joel Reynolds, Mitch Bernard, Dick Pittenger, Pete Daly, and Ken Balcomb.

INTERVIEWS

The author conducted one or more in-person or telephone interviews with the following individuals. Most have changed jobs and titles during the 20 years covered in this narrative. *The job titles below refer to each person's position at the time that he or she was an active participant in the narrative.*

National Marine Fisheries Service (NMFS/NOAA) Current or Former Officials

Roger Gentry	Head of acoustic research, Office of Protected Resources, NMFS.
Brandon Southall	Succeeded Roger Gentry as head of acoustic research, Office of Protected Resources, NMFS.
Penny Dalton	Assistant administrator for Fisheries, NOAA.
Bill Hogarth	Dalton's successor as assistant administrator for Fisheries, NOAA.
Teri Rowles	National stranding coordinator.
Janet Whaley	Coordinator, Marine Mammal Health and Stranding Response Program.
Blair Mase	Regional stranding coordinator for Southeast Fisheries Science Center.
Don Knowles	Director, Endangered Species Division, Office of Protected Resources.
Donna Wieting	Director, Office of Protected Resources, Marine Mammal Conservation Division.
Laurie Allen	Acting director, Office of Protected Resources.
Kenneth R. Hollingshead	Head of Permits and Conservation Division, Office of Protected Resources.

John Proni	Director of the Ocean Acoustics Division, NOAA.
Bob Brownell	Senior scientist, Southwest Fisheries Science Center.
Phil Clapham	Senior scientist, Northwest Fisheries Science Center.

US Navy

Fleet Command

Rear Admiral Richard Pittenger	Director of antisubmarine warfare for the Chief of Naval Operations; Oceanographer of the Navy; later vice president for marine operations, Woods Hole Oceanographic Institution.
Rear Admiral Craig Dorman	Program director, Antisubmarine Warfare; chief scientist at the Office of Naval Research; later director of Woods Hole Oceanographic Institution.
Admiral William Fallon	Commander, US Second Fleet.
Admiral Robert J. Natter	Deputy Chief of Naval Operations for Plans, Policy and Operations (OPNAV N3/N5).
Vice Admiral Peter Daly	Deputy, N3/N5 (Operations, Plans and Strategy) in the Navy staff; deputy commander and chief of staff, US Fleet Forces Command.
Captain Philip G. Renaud, USN (ret.)	Executive director of the Living Oceans Foundation.

Office of Naval Research

Vice Admiral Paul G. Gaffney II	Chief of naval research, 1996 to 2000.
Bob Gisiner	Manager, Marine Bioacoustics Program.
Mel Briscoe	Director, Applied Oceanography and Acoustics Division.
Captain Paul Stewart	Deputy director of the Ocean Battlespace Sensing Department; later commanding officer, Naval Research Laboratory.
Fred Saalfeld	Deputy chief of naval research, 1993 to 2002.
Robert Frosch	Director of research programs for Hudson Laboratories of Columbia University in Dobbs Ferry, New York, under contract to the Office of Naval Research; technical director of Project Artemis, a very large experimental active sonar system development.
Jim MacEachern	Acoustician in charge of Littoral Warfare sea tests in the Bahamas in March 2000.

Steven Ramberg	Director of science and technology.
Joe Johnson	Program manager of Low Frequency Active sonar program from 1994 to 2004.
Glenn H. Mitchell	Engineer and biologist, Environmental Planning and Biological Analysis Division, Naval Undersea Warfare Center.
David Moretti	Marine mammal science lead, engineering, Test and Evaluation Department, Naval Undersea Warfare Center.

Office of Environmental Readiness (N-45)

Rear Admiral Larry Baucom	Director of the Navy's Environmental Readiness, Energy and Safety Programs.
V. Frank Stone	Head of research and development, Navy's Environmental Readiness, Energy and Safety Programs.
Marc Laverdiere	JAG attorney assigned to N-45.

Navy Secretariat

Richard Danzig	Secretary of the Navy from 1998 to 2001.
Robert Pirie	Assistant Secretary of the Navy, Installations and Environment, from 1994 to 2000; later Undersecretary of the Navy and Acting Secretary of the Navy.
Steven S. Honigman	General counsel to the Navy, 1993 to 1998.
Craig Jensen	Assistant general counsel (Energy, Installations, and Environment).
Jeff Luster	Senior counsel, fleet and operational environmental law.

Scientists and Researchers

Oceanographers

Walter Munk	A physical oceanographer, professor of geophysics emeritus, and the Secretary of the Navy chair at the Scripps Institution of Oceanography in La Jolla, California.
Sylvia Earle	An American oceanographer, explorer, inventor, author, and lecturer; the chief scientist at NOAA from 1990 to 1992; since 1998, *National Geographic* explorer-in-residence.

Marine Mammal Scientists

Darlene Ketten	Senior scientist, Biology Department, Woods Hole Oceanographic Institution; assistant professor, Department of Otology and Laryngology, Harvard Medical School.
Peter Tyack	Senior scientist, Biology Department, Woods Hole Oceanographic Institution.
Michael Moore	Senior research specialist, biology, forensic analysis, Woods Hole Oceanographic Institution.
Chris Clark	Director, Bioacoustics Research Program, Cornell Lab of Ornithology.
Dan Costa	Professor of ecology and evolutionary biology, University of California, Santa Cruz.
Sam Ridgway	Veterinarian who later earned a PhD in neurobiology; one of the founders of the Navy Marine Mammal Program in 1961; editor of the *Handbook of Marine Mammals*.
Bill Evans	Bioacoustician and early researcher in the Navy Marine Mammal Program.
Whitlow Au	Chief scientist, Marine Mammal Research Program, Hawai'i Institute of Marine Biology; electrical engineer who has researched dolphin biosonar for the Navy Marine Mammal Program for decades.
Paul Nachtigall	Director, Marine Mammal Research Program, Hawai'i Institute of Marine Biology. Experimental psychologist with research focus on bioacoustics and echolocation of dolphins and small whales.
Patrick Moore	Senior life scientist, National Marine Mammal Foundation.
Hal Whitehead	Professor, Department of Biology, Dalhousie University, Halifax, Nova Scotia, Canada.
Lindy Weilgart	Research associate, Dalhousie University.
Ken Balcomb	Founder, executive director, and principal investigator, Center for Whale Research.
Diane Claridge	Co-founder and director, Bahamas Marine Mammal Research Organisation.
Dave Ellifrit	Field biologist, photo-identification specialist, Center for Whale Research.

John Durban	Research coordinator, Center for Whale Research; population ecologist, Southwest Fisheries Science Center, NOAA Fisheries Service.
Naomi Rose	Senior scientist, Humane Society International; currently marine mammal scientist, Animal Welfare Institute.
Roger Payne	Biologist; humpback whale researcher; founder, Ocean Alliance.
Katy Payne	Humpback whale researcher when married to Roger Payne; founder, in 1999, of Elephant Listening Project at Bioacoustics Research Program, Cornell Lab of Ornithology.
Jim Mead	Curator of marine mammals at Smithsonian Institution National Museum of Natural History, from 1972 to 2009; currently curator emeritus.
Charlie Potter	Collection manager, marine mammals, Smithsonian Institution.
Chris Parsons	Director of the research and education departments of the Hebridean Whale and Dolphin Trust from 1998 to 2003.
Robin Baird	Beaked whale researcher at Cascadia Research Collective.
John Hall	Dolphin trainer for the Navy Marine Mammal Training Program; later marine mammal biologist at SeaWorld.
Howard Garrett	Co-founder and director, Orca Network.

Acousticians

Michael Stocker	Director, Ocean Conservation Research.
Jim Cummings	Founder, Acoustic Ecology Institute.
David Fromm	Naval Research Lab, Washington, DC; acoustics and computational physics leader on acoustic modeling of Bahamas stranding.
Bill Ellison	Founder, CEO, and chief scientist of Marine Acoustics; lead ONR contractor for acoustic assessments.

NRDC

Joel Reynolds
Senior attorney and head of Los Angeles office; later western director. Founder and director, NRDC's Marine Mammal Protection Project.

Michael Jasny
Senior policy advocate; later director of NRDC's Marine Mammal Protection Project.

Mitch Bernard
NRDC's litigation director.

Jacob Scherr
Director, global strategy and advocacy.

John Adams
Founding director, executive director, and president from 1970 to 2006.

Andrew Wetzler
Senior attorney; later director of Land and Wildlife Program.

Annie Notthoff
Director, California advocacy, San Francisco.

Historians

D. Graham Burnette
Professor of history, Princeton University.

Gary Weir
Chief historian, National Geospatial-Intelligence Agency.

Owen Coté
Associate director, Security Studies Program, Center for International Studies, Massachusetts Institute of Technology.

Naomi Oreskes
Professor of history and science studies at the University of California, San Diego; adjunct professor of geosciences at the Scripps Institution of Oceanography.

RECOMMENDED READING AND RESOURCES

Whales, it turns out, are terrific subjects for books, photographs, movies, and other media. So are submarines. Below is a concise selection of books, videos, and online resources I found particularly engaging and informative during my research for this book.

BOOKS

The Sounding of the Whale: Science and Cetaceans in the Twentieth Century by D. Graham Burnette (University of Chicago Press, 2012) is a thought-provoking and fascinating chronicle of the scientific investigation of whales, by the rare scholar who's a pleasure to read.

The most wide-ranging and best-illustrated book about the complex, conflicted relationship between cetaceans and Homo sapiens is still Richard Ellis' *Men and Whales* (Alfred A. Knopf, 1991).

An Ocean in Common: American Naval Officers, Scientists, and the Ocean Environment by historian Gary E. Weir (Texas A&M University Press, 2001) is a comprehensive history of the US Navy's patronage of oceanography in the twentieth century.

For an engaging one-volume history of submersibles, read *The Navy Times Book of Submarines: A Political, Social, and Military History* by Brayton Harris, edited by Walter J. Boyne (Berkley Books, 1997).

My favorite nonfiction book ever written about the "silent service" of Cold War submariners is *Blind Man's Bluff: The Untold Story of American Submarine Espionage* by Sherry Sontag and Christopher Drew with Annette Lawrence Drew (Harper Perennial, 2000).

Ann Finkbeiner's *The Jasons: The Secret History of Science's Postwar Elite* (Viking, 2006) is the only book ever written about this shadowy military think tank, and a very good read.

Dick Russell's *Eye of the Whale: Epic Passage from Baja to Siberia* (Simon & Schuster, 2001) narrates the natural history and remarkable annual migration of the California gray whale.

Here's where the long, strange trip into interspecies communication all began: John Lilly's *Man and Dolphin: Adventures on a New Scientific Frontier* (Doubleday, 1961).

Take a trip back to the 1970s at the apex of metaphysical speculation on cetacean consciousness with *Mind in the Waters: A Book to Celebrate the Consciousness of Whales and Dolphins* (Scribner, 1974), edited by Joan McIntyre, with essays, poems, and discourses by the pantheon of Save the Whales apostles, from John Lilly to Paul Spong to Farley Mowat.

The "official story," but still the most detailed account of the US Navy's Marine Mammal Program, by its first director, Forrest G. Wood: *Marine Mammals and Man: The Navy's Porpoises and Sea Lions* (R. B. Luce, 1973).

For great reporting on worldwide ocean ecology and culture, read David Helvarg's *Blue Frontier: Dispatches from America's Ocean Wilderness* (Sierra Club Books, 2006).

The most authoritative and beautifully photographed book about orcas is *Killer Whales: The Natural History and Genealogy of Orcinus Orca in British Columbia and Washington State* by John K. B. Ford, Graeme M. Ellis, and Kenneth C. Balcomb (University of Washington Press, 2000).

Roger Payne's memoir of his forays into whale research and activism, *Among Whales* (Scribner, 1995) remains a fascinating read 20 years later.

For an informed and provocative investigation into whale songs and music across species, tune in to *Thousand Mile Song: Whale Music in a Sea of Sound* by David Rothenberg (Basic Books, 2008).

Two recently published cultural histories of whales, by authors with voice and humor, are Joe Roman's *Whale* (Reaktion Books, 2006) and *The Whale: In Search of the Giants of the Sea* by Philip Hoare (HarperCollins, 2010).

ONLINE RESOURCES

You can find range of links to online resources on my book website: warofthewhales.com, including the ones below.

Whale evolution is artfully illustrated in two short animated videos: from the Smithsonian Institution, ocean.si.edu/ocean-videos/evolution-whales-animation; and from the Museum of New Zealand Te Papa Tongarewa, collections.tepapa.govt.nz/exhibitions/whales/Segment.aspx?irn=161.

Ocean noise pollution and its threat to whales is concisely portrayed in the four-minute animation by Silent Oceans, http://vimeo.com/67804123.

Two excellent websites devoted to ocean acoustics are the Acoustic Ecology Institute, acousticecology.org; Ocean Conservation Research, ocr.org; and Discovery of Sound in the Sea, dosits.org.

A very cool online gallery of CT images of marine mammal ears and other anatomy is viewable at Woods Hole Oceanographic Institution's CSI Computerized Scanning and Imaging site: http://csi.whoi.edu.

ILLUSTRATION CREDITS

INSIDE COVER MAPS

Paula Robbins, Mapping Specialists

FACEPLATES

Parts 1, 2, and 3, depicting Globicepharus of Risso, the Hyperdoon, and Great Northern Rorqual: steel engravings by William H. Lizars from Sir William Jardine's 1937 *The Natural History of the Ordinary Cetacea of Whales.*

Part 4, of White Beluga: from William Scoresby Jr.'s 1820 book *An account of the Arctic regions with a history and description of the northern whale-fishery.*

CHAPTER HEAD ILLUSTRATIONS

F. Wenderoth Saunders, from Ivan T. Sanderson's *Follow the Whale* (New York: Bramhall House, 1956).

IN-TEXT GRAPHICS

Page 156

Pidwirny, M. (2006). "Surface and Subsurface Ocean Currents: Ocean Current Map." *Fundamentals of Physical Geography, 2nd Edition.* Public domain. U.S. government publication. http://www.physicalgeography.net/fundamentals /8q_1.html.

Page 159

From "The Heard Island Feasibility Test," Walter H. Munk, et al., *Journal of the Acoustical Society of America,* Vol. 96, No. 4, October 1994.

Page 322

Sourced from GlobalSecurity.org and US Department of the Navy

PHOTO INSERT

1, 5, 7, 10, 11, 26, 27, 37, 38: Photo by Ken Balcomb

2: Photo by Charlotte Dunn

3, 40, 41, 42: Photo by Joshua Horwitz

4: Photo by John Calambokidis, Cascadia Research

6, 8: Photo by Diane Claridge

9: Photo by Bahamas Marine Mammal Survey

12: Courtesy of Woods Hole Oceanographic Institution

13: Courtesy of WHOI Computerized Scanning and Imaging Facility, Woods Hole Oceanographic Institution

14: Photo by Chip Clark, Smithsonian Institution

15, 16, 17, 19, 20, 21, 22, 23, 24, 25, 28, 43: Courtesy of Ken Balcomb

18: Photo by Robert S. Balcomb

29, 30, 31, 32, 33, 34: Courtesy of Joel Reynolds

35: Photo by Vidal Martin of SECAC

36: Photo by permission of Prof. Antonio Fernández (Institute Animal Health), University Las Palmas, Canary Islands, Spain

39: Photo by Michael J. Elderman, provided by UC Riverside

INDEX

Note: Page numbers in *italics* refer to illustrations.

Bahamas:
  beaked whale research in, 4, 63–64, 131,
    262, 284, 313
  deep sound channel of, 47–49, 51, 52–53,
    139, 285
  evidence gathered in, 11–12, 24–25,
    29–32, 56–57, 64–65, 98, 115, 183, 190,
    220, 231, 256, 270, 290
  flight over, 25
  investigation meetings, 261–64
  media stories on whale beachings,
    130–31, 132–33, 149–51, 152, 222,
    283–85
  moving whale heads to Boston from,
    184–88, 284
  Navy exercises in, 115–16, 130–31, 138,
    140, 141, 152, 230–31, 244, 285
  separation from mainland, 26
  tourist activities in, 3–4, 21, 22
  whales beached in (2000), 3–13, 15,
    18–19, 20, 22–23, 73, 100–101, 111–12,
    130–31, 136, 151, 152, 153, 182–83,
    220, 222, 230–31, 245, 252, 283,
    285–90, 298
Bahamas Journal of Science, 270, 366
Bahamas Marine Mammal Research
    Organisation, 313
Bahamas Marine Mammal Survey, 63–64,
    187, 262, 284
Bahamian Ministry of Fisheries, 189
Bahrain, dolphins clearing mines in, 242
Baird's beaked whales, 63, 101
    (Berardius bairdii), 170
    studies of, 16, 29–32, 40, 60
Balcomb, Anne (first wife), 38–39, 41
Balcomb, Barbara (mother), 35–36
Balcomb, "Blue" (father), 34–35, 37–38,
    290–92
Balcomb, Camille (third wife), 59–60, 193,
    211, 217–19
Balcomb, Julie Byrd (second wife), 43, 55
Balcomb, Kelley (son), 39, 41, 219
Balcomb, Ken:
  beaked whale research of, 6, 7–8, 30–31,
    63–64, 77, 123, 187, 262, 289

bird-banding assignment of, 42
cancer diagnosis of, 313, 352, 353
and chain-of-custody forms, 129, 185,
    188, 192, 231
childhood and teen years of, 34–38
desire to be included in ongoing
    investigation, 129, 261, 264
and Diane, see Claridge, Diane
and Earthwatch, 3–5, 130
evidence gathered by, 11–12, 19, 24–25,
    29–32, 56–57, 98, 131, 183, 189–90,
    220, 222, 229, 231, 244–46, 256, 257,
    261, 262, 268, 289–90, 310, 353–54
and Gentry, 133–34, 192, 247, 256–57,
    263–64
and Gisiner, 14, 15–16, 18–19, 57–58, 77,
    133, 192, 256–57
and his father, 34–35, 37–38, 290–92
and initial reports of strandings, 5–6, 18,
    130–31
and interim report, 272–73, 290
and Ketten, 100–101, 103–4, 107, 126–27,
    129, 134, 274
and lawsuit against Navy, 289–92, 296–97,
    299–300
MARMAM posting by, 66–67, 81, 98, 111
"A Mass Stranding of Cetaceans Caused
    by Naval Sonar in the Bahamas" (with
    Claridge), 270
Navy assignments of, 43–44, 45, 48,
    50–55, 131–32, 289
and Navy mine-warfare range, 350
and Navy oath of secrecy, 33, 111, 132,
    230
Navy undercover work of, 33, 59, 60, 132,
    153
orca census of, 4, 16, 60, 210–11, 217–20,
    257, 308–12, 347
and Orca Network, 347
photographing whales, 41, 217–19, 229,
    262
and press conference, 56, 222, 228–31,
    246–50, 256–57, 274
reputation of, 257, 273–74
rescue attempts by, 6–13, 289–90

Secretary of the Navy (*cont.*)
  public and political fallout handled by, 136–37, 141, 267
  and settlement mediation, 305
  temporary shutdown ordered by, 150, 152
  and White House strategy meeting, 326
sei whales:
  communications of, 54
  killed by whalers, 377n1
September 11 attacks, 272, 285, 291
Shamu (orca), 215, 223
sharks:
  cookie-cutter, 7
  lemon, 11
  and stranded whales, 11
  tiger, 11
  whale defenses against, 31
  whales attacked by, 7
Sharpton, Al, 139
Shearman & Sterling, 122
shrews, echolocation by, 27
shrimp, snapping, 54
Sidenstecker, Maris, 116–17
Sikorsky Seahawks, 57
60 Minutes, 229, 231, 244–46, 270
The Six Million Dollar Man (movie), 240
Skinner, B. F., 378n3
Smith, Greg, 130, 131
Smithsonian Institution, 250–54
  and investigative team for Bahamas strandings, 74
  mammal specimens collected by, 251–52
  US Army contract of, 42, 366–67n2
Smits, Jimmy, 139
Society for Marine Mammalogy, 77, 178, 220, 252
SOFAR channel, 49
Solomon Islands, black market in dolphins, 22
sonar:
  acoustic cueing, 143
  acoustic modeling, 265, 274, 299
  and Acoustic Thermometry, 164–69, 171–72, 175–76
  and acoustic warfare, 145–46

active systems, 46–47, 143–46, 148, 153–54, 177, 277
audio evidence of, 310
and biological investigations, 268
coining of term, 367n1
documentation of threats to whales, 255, 270, 289–90, 293, 299, 314
and echolocation, 46
effects on human divers, 177
environmental laws breached by, 172
force field of sound produced by, 299
and Heard Island, 158–64, 374n13
international campaign against, 306
legal limits on, 296, 299, 302–3, 306
LFA program of, *see* Low Frequency Active (LFA) sonar program
and Magellan I and II, 169, 170–75
and marine mammal strandings (2003), 309–11
midfrequency active sonar, 143, 273, 284, 290, 310, 313–16; *see also* midfrequency sonar lawsuit
Navy investments in, 288
Navy's court record in cases of, 327
and Navy's "need to operate," 305–6, 323–24
passive, 47, 276–77
public awareness of threats from, 308
and regulation process, 145–46, 289
and settlement mediation, 303–6
sonobuoys, 52, 107, 131, 141, 150, 276
sound levels increased in warm water, 265, 274, 277–78, 290
technical problems in, 300
testing of, 113, 116, 131, 140, 168, 269, 272, 273
transmission frequency 250 hertz, 170
whale sensitivity to, 142, 162, 163, 165–66, 176, 178, 255, 270–71, 273, 283–85, 287, 288–89, 293, 299, 302, 331, 350–51, 374n13
and whale strandings, *see also specific sites*
Songs of the Humpback Whale, 225–26
SOSUS, *see* US Navy

ABOUT THE AUTHOR

Joshua Horwitz is a Senior Fellow at The Ocean Foundation and the co-founder and publisher of Living Planet Books, which specializes in works by thought leaders in science, medicine, and psychology. He lives in Washington, DC, with his wife and three daughters.

For more information go to: www.warofthewhales.com